AFTER ELLIS ISLAND

AFTER ELLIS ISLAND

Newcomers and Natives in the 1910 Census

Edited by

Susan Cotts Watkins

RUSSELL SAGE FOUNDATION   •   NEW YORK

The Russell Sage Foundation

The Russell Sage Foundation, one of the oldest of America's general purpose foundations, was established in 1907 by Mrs. Margaret Olivia Sage for "the improvement of social and living conditions in the United States." The Foundation seeks to fulfill this mandate by fostering the development and dissemination of knowledge about the country's political, social, and economic problems. While the Foundation endeavors to assure the accuracy and objectivity of each book it publishes, the conclusions and interpretations in Russell Sage Foundation publications are those of the authors and not of the Foundation, its Trustees, or its staff. Publication by Russell Sage, therefore, does not imply Foundation endorsement.

Library of Congress Cataloging-in-Publication Data

After Ellis Island : newcomers and natives in the 1910 census / edited by Susan Cotts Watkins.
    p. cm.
    Includes bibliographical references and index.
    ISBN 0-87154-910-7
    1. United States—Emigration and immigration—Statistics.
2. United States—Census, 1910. 3. United States—Publication—
Statistics. I. Watkins, Susan Cotts, 1938–
JV6461.A93 1994
304.6'0973'09041—dc20   93-191610
                                                    CIP

RUSSELL SAGE FOUNDATION
112 East 64th Street, New York, New York 10021
10 9 8 7 6 5 4 3 2 1

CONTENTS

CONTENTS

CONTRIBUTORS

Robert F. Dymowski
Westat Corporation, Rockville, MD

Douglas Ewbank
Population Studies Center, University of Pennsylvania

Margaret E. Greene
Postdoctoral Fellow, University of Chicago

Mark Hereward
Rockefeller Foundation, Beijing, China

Jerry A. Jacobs
Population Studies Center, University of Pennsylvania

Antonio McDaniel
Population Studies Center, University of Pennsylvania

Andrew T. Miller
Department of History, Union College

Ann R. Miller
Population Studies Center, University of Pennsylvania

Ewa Morawska
Department of Sociology, University of Pennsylvania

S. Philip Morgan
Population Studies Center, University of Pennyslvania

Samuel H. Preston
Population Studies Center, University of Pennsylvania

Arodys Robles
Postdoctoral Fellow, Johns Hopkins University

Shilian Wang
Department of Sociology, Brown University

Susan Cotts Watkins
Population Studies Center, University of Pennsylvania

Michael J. White
Department of Sociology, Brown University

PREFACE

A SUBTITLE of this volume might well be a reversal of *E Pluribus Unum:* instead of "One from Many" it could be "Many from One." Immigrants passed through Ellis Island or other points of entry and then dispersed in various directions; they were captured briefly by the enumerators of the Census Bureau, who asked all of them the same questions, and then they returned to live their diverse, day-to-day lives. Similarly, all the chapters in this volume are based on a single census, and, with the exception of Chapter 6, all the authors are or were associated with the Population Studies Center of the University of Pennsylvania. Yet, starting from a single data set we also go in a variety of directions. Each chapter focuses on a different aspect of the immigrant experience: mortality, fertility, families and households, neighborhoods, schooling, and industrial affiliation. Moreover, we take different analytic approaches: some authors stay close to the descriptive level, while others use multivariate statistical analyses to explore the association between demographic behavior and the social and economic circumstances in which the different groups lived. The range of approaches taken is expanded by Ewa Morawska's chapter, which speaks directly to the historians and sociologists who have delved deeply into local sources, and asks on their behalf: "Where can we who do it differently go from here?" The unity, then, is our use of a single census and our close collaboration; the variety of our approaches mirrors the variety of the experiences of immigrants in the United States in 1910.

The first step in the chain of events that led to this volume was the creation of a national random sample of the manuscript schedules of the census. This Public Use Sample (PUS) was drawn at the University of Pennsylvania under the leadership of Samuel H. Preston, and the project was funded by the National Institutes of Health and the National Science Foundation. One out of every 250 households in the manuscript census was selected, and, under the direction of Michael Strong, the information on those manuscript schedules was made machine-readable. Some of the analyses also make use of a special subsample of

Southern blacks, drawn under the direction of Douglas Ewbank with support from the National Institutes of Health.

A first round of these analyses of the Public Use Sample was presented at a workshop held at the University of Pennsylvania, February 9–11, 1990. A comprehensive review of the history of immigration legislation by the late Edward P. Hutchinson, Emeritus Professor of the University of Pennsylvania, set the stage for our discussions.

At the workshop, the discussants were:

Myron Gutmann
Department of History
University of Texas at Austin

Michael Haines
Department of Economics
Colgate University

Michael Katz
Department of History
University of Pennsylvania

Walter Licht
Department of History
University of Pennsylvania

Douglas Massey
Department of Sociology
University of Chicago

Ewa Morawska
Department of Sociology
University of Pennsylvania

Silvia Pedraza
Department of Sociology and Program in American Culture
University of Michigan

Joel Perlman
Graduate School of Education
Harvard University

Daniel Scott Smith
Department of History
University of Illinois at Chicago

Warren Sanderson
Department of Economics
SUNY-Stony Brook

Herbert Smith
Department of Sociology and Population Studies Center
University of Pennsylvania

Mark Stern
School of Social Work
University of Pennsylvania

Stuart Tolnay
Department of Sociology
SUNY-Albany

Etienne van de Walle
Department of Sociology and Population Studies Center
University of Pennsylvania

Francine van de Walle
Population Studies Center
University of Pennsylvania

In addition, the workshop was attended by graduate students from several departments at the University of Pennsylvania: Renbao Chen, Sherm Dorn, Ellen Eisenberg, Katherine Hempstead, Mary Ellen Hughes, Miriam King, and Ellen Kramarow. The comments of all these participants were extensive and contributed greatly to the revisions of these chapters.

We also benefited from the comments of others who read all or parts of the manuscript. These include Gretchen Condran, Donna Gabaccia, Allan Kraut, Nancy Landale, Suzanne Model, and John Alexander Ross. We are particularly grateful to Emmett Dye, who read each chapter searching for inconsistencies of language and logic; to Charles Tilly, whose judiciousness was very helpful; and to Ewa Morawska, who shared with the editor her deep and broad knowledge of immigrant historiography.

LIST OF TABLES

LIST OF FIGURES

1

INTRODUCTION

Susan Cotts Watkins

T HIS VOLUME portrays immigrants and their children as they passed
through the 1910 census. In 1910, 14.6 percent of the total population enumerated in the U.S. Census was foreign-born, higher
than in any subsequent census; in contrast, an estimated 8.5 percent of
the 1990 population are foreign-born (United States 1913, p. 125; Passel
and Edmonston forthcoming). If one counts the children of the foreign-
born as well, approximately one-third of the 1910 population was of foreign stock, in contrast to about one-fifth in 1990 (United States 1913, p.
126; Passel and Edmonston forthcoming). Although the numbers of foreign-born and foreign stock were smaller in 1910 than they are in 1990,
their proportion of the population was considerably higher.

Not all came through Ellis Island, of course: that only opened on
January 1, 1892. But Ellis Island symbolizes the points of entry through
which all immigrants passed, not only to another national territory but
also to another society that in many respects was quite different from
the ones they had left. Some stayed only briefly and then returned to
their home countries. But most remained. Those who had not come in
family groups sent for relatives abroad to join them or they returned to
collect relatives or to marry and then reimmigrated; others married here.
They settled, often in neighborhoods with those who had been neighbors in the old country; they sought jobs, bore children, sent the children to school. This volume presents a picture of the foreign-born as
they appeared to census enumerators in 1910, when some had only recently arrived and others were well established.[1]

---

[1]The foreign-born who appear in the census are, of course, selected in a number of
ways: in particular, they met the immigration criteria and they did not leave before the
census date. (For a discussion of historical changes in the criteria used by the United
States to determine who might immigrate, see Jasso and Rosenzweig 1990, Chapter 1).
Return migration was substantial: Passel and Edmonston (forthcoming) estimate that of
the 8,024,000 who entered between 1900 and 1910, 3,104,000 left, for a net immigration

With each successive wave of immigration—first predominantly Irish, Germans, Scandinavians, and others from Northwestern Europe, then predominantly Italians, Jews, Poles, and others from Eastern, Central, and Southern Europe—commentators debated the differences between the newcomers and the "Americans," who were often, of course, the descendants of earlier newcomers. In the two decades preceding the 1910 census there was considerable popular and official concern, as there is today, about whether the fires under the melting pot were still adequate to the task. Previous waves of immigrants from Northwestern Europe had, in the eyes of some, barely been digested: was it possible that the new immigrants from Central, Eastern, and Southern Europe would ever be "like us"? As in previous decades, the alarmists were both right and wrong. By 1980 many of those whose parents or grandparents or great-grandparents had been enumerated in the 1910 census as foreign-born were unable or unwilling to trace their ethnic ancestry, identifying themselves as "just Americans" (Lieberson and Waters 1988). For others, however, an ethnic identity remained important. In a recent survey conducted in a Northeastern city, nearly two-thirds of the respondents claimed an ethnic identity, although for many this identity was highly qualified: "I guess I would say French Canadian," or just "mutt" (Alba 1990, pp. 49–50; see also Waters 1990). Students of immigration as well as policymakers now ask about the demography, work patterns, or schooling of recent immigrants, such as those from Latin America or Asia, but few studies pay attention to differences in these areas of social life for the descendants of the immigrant groups that were so prominent around the turn of the century. It seems particularly appropriate now to provide a basis for comparing the circumstances of the foreign-born in 1910 with those of today.

We do not take on the larger question of assimilation or the maintenance of ethnic identity here: that would require tracing the ethnic groups both before and after 1910, and it would require using more sources than the 1910 census. But we do provide a launching pad for such analyses. We use a sample of the 1910 census to describe precisely ethnic differences in a number of areas of social life that are thought to be consequential for the subsequent trajectories of the ethnic groups in the United States: their mortality and fertility, their family and household structure, their residential concentration, the schooling of their children, and their industrial affiliation.

---

over the decade of 4,920,000. Some of those who left then returned: for example, Caroli (1973) estimates that about one-sixth of the Italians who entered between 1899 and 1910 had been in the United States before (p. 46).

What We Do in this Volume

The analyses in this volume are all based on a national random sample of the 1910 manuscript census. This census provides basic information on all (or nearly all) the inhabitants of the United States. The sample contains 3.66 times the number of individuals than did the previous sample of the 1900 census. It is large enough to compare the largest of the immigrant groups to one another and to the native-born of native parentage, both black and white.

The 1910 census was conducted near the end of the flood of immigration to the United States that began in the 1880s, a flood that was interrupted by World War I and slowed considerably after the restrictive immigration legislation of the early 1920s. The 1890 census was largely destroyed by fire; the 1900 census, for which a previous national sample is available, covered both a smaller population and one with a smaller proportion of foreign-born; the 1920 census has just been opened to the public, and it does not contain as much information on several important topics as does that of 1910.

The 1910 census was relatively rich for a census: for example, far more questions were asked of the entire enumerated population than were asked on the short form of the 1990 census. And because of the considerable concern at the time about the effects of large numbers of foreign-born on the nature of American identity, many of the questions were designed to delineate the characteristics of the foreign-born. The questions included country of origin and, for the first time, mother tongue. The ethnic map of Europe was quite complicated, and the inclusion of both place of birth and mother tongue permits us to identify different linguistic groups within the same country as well as groups that are better identified on the basis of mother tongue than place of birth (e.g., Yiddish-speakers and Polish-speakers).

Although this volume provides a more extensive description of the nation's immigrants and their children in 1910 than was available previously, some of the issues treated here were dealt with earlier. The Census Bureau published many tabulations from the 1910 census, but the vast majority of these compared the foreign-born as a group with the native-born, and with very few exceptions neither place of birth nor mother tongue was cross-tabulated by other social or economic characteristics. In addition, the Census Bureau published special tabulations of the 1910 census done subsequently, especially in conjunction with the 1940 census. Another valuable source of information is the report of the U.S. Immigration Commission (1911); the commission, however, relied heavily on the earlier 1900 census as well as on special investigations of local areas. Other analyses have been made by researchers working with the manuscript censuses for particular locations and focusing on particular ethnic groups.

The aim of this volume is to describe central aspects of immigrant life. In addition, we examine whether the differences among ethnic groups are modulated—or even disappear—when only individuals in the same circumstances are compared with one another. It might be, for example, that Scandinavians had unusually low infant and child mortality (which Chapter 3 shows is the case), not because they were "Scandinavian" but rather because most of them lived in the healthier rural areas. What happens when we examine the mortality of Scandinavians who lived in cities? Similarly, it might appear that Jews (Yiddish-speakers) tended to cluster together in city neighborhoods. But is this because much of what we know about the residential patterns of Jews comes from analysis of New York City? What happens when we look at Chicago? The opportunity offered by the individual-level information provided by the census to compare members of the various ethnic groups in similar circumstances and across geographical areas is, thus, a great advantage in understanding the sources of apparent ethnic differences.

Some analysts have interpreted ethnic differences as evidence of deep-rooted differences in culture, where the term "culture" encompasses a range from formalized beliefs to ways of interpreting and coping with daily life. Others have emphasized the influence of location in the material world, under the assumption that differences in jobs and in schooling underlie perceived variation among ethnic groups. Whereas some scholars have sharply distinguished between "culture" and "structure," others have insisted on their interaction. The multivariate frameworks that we use permit us to examine these interactions statistically: for example, we are able to consider whether residence in a large city has a different effect on fertility for Jews than for Italians.

Most of our analyses evaluate differences in immigrant behavior associated with what contemporaries would have called assimilation. Many at the time believed that the faster the immigrants learned English and "American values" the better, and that the longer they remained here the more they would become "like us." We have no measure of "American values." But we can examine differences between immigrants who had lived in the United States longer and recent arrivals, and between those who claimed to speak English and those who did not. Is it true that those who by 1910 had been in the United States a long time—perhaps coming as children—and who spoke English were indeed more "like us"? Or do ethnic differences persist even when we introduce statistical controls for length of time in the United States and English-speaking?

What is New in this Volume?

This volume adds to what was previously known in several ways.

First, some of the information we use was not previously published. Census enumerators asked women about the number of children they had ever borne and the number surviving. The answers were not, however, punched on the Census Bureau's data cards and thus were not tabulated for the national population at the time (Truesdell 1965). The children-ever-born data were subsequently tabulated in conjunction with the 1940 census, but the children-surviving data are available here for the first time. The chapters on both mortality and fertility make use of these children-ever-born and children-surviving data, as well as developing new techniques to exploit these data.

Second, because the census covers the entire population, we are able to provide a national picture against which more detailed studies of particular locations and individual ethnic groups can be compared.

Third, and to my mind the most valuable, this volume provides an opportunity for detailed description of a variety of ethnic groups. The Census Bureau publications present many ethnic groups, but with little detail; the work of historians and historical sociologists usually presents one or two ethnic groups, but with much detail. All the chapters in this volume present information for at least the largest of the immigrant groups defined by place of birth and/or mother tongue: the British, Irish, Germans, Scandinavians, Italians, Poles, and Jews (Yiddish-speakers). A tabular appendix to this volume (Appendix B) provides selected information for many smaller groups.

Last, because the manuscript census provides information on individuals rather than the aggregate classifications published in the tabulations of the Census Bureau, our sample permits a much wider range of cross-tabulations than those available in the census publications, as well as multivariate analysis.

Appendix A to this volume and Chapter 2 provide background for all the chapters: Appendix A by describing the process by which the sample was drawn, and Chapter 2 by discussing the main categories used in the subsequent chapters—the definitions of ethnic groups, the definitions of urban and rural residence, and so on.

Chapters 3 and 4 use demographic data to depict intimate areas of family life: whether children survived or died, and whether childbearing patterns suggest deliberate control of fertility. There are few survivors of those who bore children in the years before the 1910 census was taken; we cannot interrogate them directly about their feelings when a child died or their attitudes toward the use of contraception. But by examining the dry census records, we can show which groups experienced higher losses of their children, which fewer, and which groups bore more children, which fewer. Ethnic differences in mortality and fertility are no doubt due to some mix of the attitudes and values that the immigrants brought with them and the circumstances in which they found themselves living. Did groups who lived in the relatively salubrious rural areas see fewer of their children die than those who lived in crowded, noxious cities? Did some have fewer children because they had learned "tricks" of birth control from their low-fertility native neighbors, perhaps because they had lived in the United States longer and spoke English?

The concern of contemporaries with immigrants focused on what they saw as improper social and family practices and indecent or immoral living conditions, and the fear that these would be passed on to their children. Immigrants were believed not only to be more prolific in their reproduction but to crowd together under the same roof not only husbands, wives, and children but also a motley assortment of kin as well as boarders and lodgers. Chapter 5 asks how the households and families of the various immigrant groups differed from one another as well as from the natives of native parentage (both blacks and whites), and whether these differences persisted beyond the initial stages of immigration. Were the larger, more complex households of some immigrant groups simply the result of the recency of their immigration, or do they seem to reflect different attitudes toward family relations?

In Chapter 6 we consider residential segregation, which is taken as an indicator of the social distance among groups. It is likely that those who lived in mixed neighborhoods had more diverse contacts than those who were highly concentrated in "ethnic" neighborhoods: in mixed neighborhoods, women would meet in the neighborhood stores, children would go to school together and play together in the streets after school. If social distance replicates physical distance (or vice versa), how distant were the various ethnic groups from the natives of native parentage—both blacks and whites—and from one another?

The next two chapters follow the immigrants out of their households, to school (in Chapter 7) and to work (in Chapter 8). As the authors of Chapter 7 point out, we often tell an "immigrant morality tale," in which the "good" immigrants sought education for their children, while the "bad" immigrants were shortsighted, anti-intellectual, and exploitative of their children; it is the value placed on education by immigrants that indicates their worthiness to participate in the American dream. But is it true that the groups differed significantly from one another in the proportion of children who attended school? And even if they did, do these differences diminish when we compare those in the same circumstances—those with similar access to schooling, for example, an access that differed in rural and urban areas, or those whose teenage children could work because work was available? Where did the immigrants work? Chapter 8 examines the industrial sector in which the foreign-born worked, to evaluate the contribution of the foreign-born to the economic development of the United States, that is, to the relative decline in the numbers of persons engaged in agriculture and the increase in the numbers in manufacturing.

Underlying the diversity of topics and approaches in these chapters is the authors' shared assumption that it is valuable to have as detailed a description of immigrants in the United States in 1910 as the census materials permit. The 1910 Public Use Sample (PUS), however, although it offers unprecedented opportunities for description at the national level, is limited to the information asked by the Census Bureau (religion, for example, was not asked). Moreover, even as large a sample as the PUS was limited in the degree to which it could depict individuals in the local contexts in which they lived. In the Afterword Ewa Morawska makes explicit the limitations of national-level analysis using only census data. Reading the previous chapters from the perspective of a different theoretical position, and informed by the rich literature on specific immigrant groups in specific local contexts, she points out where our findings confirm or contradict what was previously known from local studies by historians and sociologists. In so doing, she draws from our findings a provocative set of questions for further research.

Finally, we present in Appendix B of this volume a tabular description of immigrants. In principle, the sample of the 1910 manuscript census that we use here permits an analysis of all the various subgroups of the foreign-born: there are at least fifty-eight distinguishable places of birth for the foreign-born, and fifty-five distinguishable mother tongues. In practice, however, although our sample was quite large, the numbers of many ethnic groups in our sample were still too small to support analysis, including some of the immigrant groups who play an increasing role in American society today, such as those from Asia or from Central or South America.[2] A compromise solution was reached, by which the analyses in the chapters include the largest ethnic groups, and the smaller ones are either omitted or combined into larger categories (e.g.,

---

[2]For example, although there were approximately 230,000 Bohemians in the United States in 1910, there are fewer than 1,000 in our sample. The fertility analysis focused only on women (405 Bohemian women were in our sample). It is obvious that were we to classify these women by age and by the number of children they had borne by the time of the census as well as by rural or urban residence, by occupational group, and so on, some categories would have no women, and others would have very few.

"Other Eastern Europeans"). To aid those whose interest is in these smaller groups, we present in Appendix B descriptive information for ethnic groups for which there are more than 200 members in our sample. We also specify in detail how the ethnic groups and categories were defined.

FIGURE 1.1

Number of Foreign-born Whites, by County: 1910

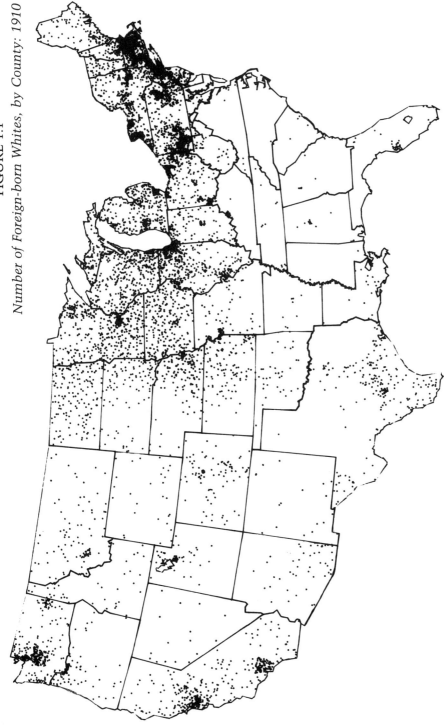

SOURCE: Data sets: U.S. Bureau of the Census. Thirteenth Decenial Census of the United States, 1910: Volumes II and III, *Report on the Population of the United States* (Washington, D. C.:1915). In Inter-University Consortium for Political and Social Research. Historical, Demographic, Economic, and Social Data: The United States, 1790–1970. Boundary files: Carville Earle and Changyong Cao, *The U.S. Historical County Boundary Files, 1850–1970* (Baton Rouge: Geoscience Publications, 1990).

FIGURE 1.2

Number of Native Whites of Foreign Parentage, by County: 1910

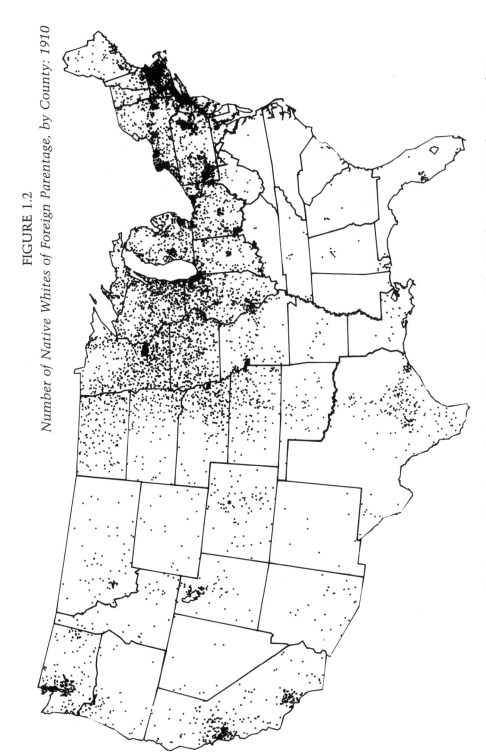

SOURCE: Data sets: U.S. Bureau of the Census. Thirteenth Decenial Census of the United States, 1910: Volumes II and III, *Report on the Population of the United States* (Washington, D. C.:1915). In Inter-University Consortium for Political and Social Research. Historical, Demographic, Economic, and Social Data: The United States, 1790–1970. Boundary files: Carville Earle and Changyong Cao, *The U.S. Historical County Boundary Files, 1850–1970* (Baton Rouge: Geoscience Publications, 1990).

2

BACKGROUND:
ABOUT THE 1910 CENSUS

Susan Cotts Watkins

T HIS CHAPTER introduces the 1910 census and the categories used frequently in this volume.[1] Much, for example, rests on how ethnic groups are defined by place of birth and/or mother tongue; it is thus important to know not only how these are defined but also what problems these definitions present. The second aim of this background chapter is to caution against reification of the categories used in the following analyses. The 1910 census was of high quality, and the 1910 Public Use Sample (PUS) is a random sample of that census. However, there are inevitable discrepancies between the "true" nature of the U.S. population and that population as it appears in the 1910 census. The published census tables, the machine-readable data tape used in these analyses, and the tables in the following chapters present a world that appears like a black-and-white photograph: just as light and dark are distinct in photographs, so also do the words *rural* and *urban*, for example, conjure up images of starkly different worlds, and tables with figures given to the second decimal place imply precise boundaries to these worlds. But the actual picture of the 1910 population should be seen as more like an impressionist painting than a photograph: although the category names and the numbers attached to them may suggest tidy divisions between one category and another, the boundaries of these categories are sometimes more blurred than they appear here.

---

[1]I am grateful to the following colleagues for useful comments on an earlier version of this chapter: Douglas Ewbank, Donna Gabaccia, Margaret Greene, Nancy Landale, A. T. Miller, Ann R. Miller, Sue Model, Ewa Morawska, Silvia Pedraza, G. Alexander Ross, and Daniel Scott Smith.

Census Questions:
The Place of 1910 among Previous Censuses

The first census of the United States was conducted in 1790; by the time the Census Bureau was established in 1902 the census was a familiar decennial routine. By 1910 considerable professional expertise had accumulated in developing census questionnaires, instructing enumerators, tabulating the results, and evaluating the quality of the census data (Anderson 1988). Nonetheless, despite the professionalism of Census Bureau officials, like all censuses and surveys, the 1910 census was a social and political document. Congress had a say in it. Moreover, census officials were men and women who, we can assume, read the newspapers and talked with their neighbors. Given the attention paid in the press to the "immigrant problem," and perhaps as a result of their own experiences with individuals who looked to them "different," or "unusual," it is likely that these officials had formed an opinion of what immigrants were like, and that these opinions informed the questions on the census schedule and the instructions to the enumerators.[2] And although the vast majority of the immigrants came from countries in which regular censuses had been established before the time of their departure, the immigrants too would have responded to the census enumerator on the basis of their own experience with civil officials, as well as on their understandings of, for example, family relationships. Thus, what appears in the manuscript schedules is the product of an interaction among the Census Bureau officials who made up the forms, the enumerators who went door-to-door questioning the populace, and the respondents who answered their questions.

The decades of the 1890s and 1900s were ones of intense concern not only about the number of immigrants but about their characteristics. As Edward Hutchinson (1981) has shown, the list of barriers to immigration became ever more lengthy and detailed (see also Jasso and Rosenzweig 1990). The concern of Congress reflected, and no doubt fueled, popular nervousness about the degree to which the changing immigrant stream threatened to alter the nature of the American population. Although the "old" immigrants from Western Europe had stimulated nativist sentiments in mid century, when the composition of the immigrant stream changed in the 1880s to predominantly those from Eastern and Central Europe, it seemed to contemporaries that in retrospect the

---

[2]For a review of the coverage of immigrants in the print media, see Simon 1985.

co-residents. The undercounting probably varied across ethnic groups. Boarding was far more common among some ethnic groups than others: over one-third of adult Italian and Polish immigrants boarded, whereas only 10.5 percent of Germans in this category did so (Miller, Morgan, and McDaniel, this volume, Table 5.2).[6]

Another category that causes difficulty is temporary migrants. It is thought that many migrants came expecting their stay to be brief (see, for example, Thomas and Znaniecki 1927; Morawska 1991). Some of them remained in the United States, others returned; of those who returned, some reemigrated. The 1910 census no doubt missed some who were temporarily absent. The extent of return migration and reemigration varied by ethnic group (U.S. Immigration Commission 1911): for example, Italians seem to have participated in a particularly high degree of back-and-forth migration. Because they typically departed from the United States between March and May and returned between October and December; they would not have been present for the census in April (Foerster 1919, p. 37).

The instructions further note that some "may not wish to answer the enumerator's questions. In case your authority is disputed, show your official badge, and also your commission . . . " (U.S. Bureau of the Census 1910, p. 12).[7] Although the instructions are optimistic that tact and persuasion would persuade the reluctant to answer, we might imagine that some were sufficiently averse to being counted that tact and persuasion might fail. This seems to be especially likely among the "new" immigrants from Eastern, Central, and Southern Europe, because many contemporaries (often reformers) emphasized their suspicion of civil authorities (Williams 1938; R. E. Park and Miller 1921; Pozetta 1971, p. 75). Contradicting this is the report of a contemporary survey of housing conditions in "Back of the Yards," a predominantly Polish and Lithuanian area in Chicago:

[6]It is difficult to identify group quarters in the PUS. Some of them consisted simply of a group of men living together, with one of them designated on the census schedules as household head; others were headed by a man and his wife, who provided some services (Hunt 1910). If we simply take the percentage of individuals who lived in (noninstitutional) households with ten or more residents, 16.2 percent of foreign-born Italians, 10.8 percent of foreign-born Poles, and 10.1 percent of foreign-born Irish lived in such households; at the other extreme are Yiddish-speakers and Germans, with under 6 percent in each group living in large households (see Miller, Morgan, and McDaniel, this volume, Table 5.1).

[7]Under "Refusals to Answer," the instructions are as follows: "In case your authority is disputed, show your official badge, and also your commission, which you should carry with you. But it is of the utmost importance that your manner should, under all circumstances, be courteous and conciliatory. In no instance should you lose your temper or indulge in disputes or threats. Much can be done by tact and persuasion. Many persons will give information after a night's reflection which they refuse to give when first visited" (U.S. Bureau of the Census 1910, pp. 12–13).

The student investigators who made the house-to-house canvass reported that their authority was rarely questioned among the less Americanized groups; the people were uniformly submissive, and apparently it never occurred to them that they had a right to ask why strangers could come in and measure their doors and windows" (Breckinridge and Abbott 1910, p. 439).

Even when the individual was enumerated and "submissive," not all the questions were answered. For each question, the number of "unknown," "blank" (or "illegible") is small, generally under 1 percent of the total; as will be shown later, however, when these responses are analyzed by ethnic group, the proportion of missing responses can become substantial for some categories of some ethnic groups.

Let us now turn to the census questionnaire itself, and examine the areas of ambiguity in the categories used most frequently in the analyses that follow. Figure 2.1 shows the manuscript census schedule, but with the information typed. The first two columns show the street address and the house numbers (in cities or towns); the next two distinguish between dwelling places and families by numbering each separately in the order of visitation. A dwelling house was defined as "a place in which one or more persons regularly sleep (including not only houses but a loft, a boat, a tent, etc.)"; a family was defined as "a group of persons living together in the same dwelling place" (U.S. Bureau of the Census 1910, p. 26). As in 1900, in defining a family, sleeping arrangements were given priority over dining: a servant who slept in the house was to be included with the family for which he or she worked, and a person who boarded in one place but roomed at another was to be returned as a member of the family where he or she roomed.[8] Those living in apartments or tenements were to be recorded as distinct families; persons living alone were also to be recorded as a separate family (U.S. Bureau of the Census 1910, p. 27).

As D. S. Smith has pointed out for the 1900 census, the questions progress from ascribed or personal characteristics (name, relationship to the head of the family, sex, color, or race, age last birthday, marital status, number of years in the present marriage, children born and children surviving, and nativity) to achieved and/or social attributes (citizenship, ability to speak English), occupation (employer/employee/self-employed, unemployment, education, ability to read or write, school attendance), and finally, characteristics of the residence (owned or rented,

[8]The *Instructions to Enumerators* uses both male and female pronouns in describing servants, but only the male pronoun in describing boarders and lodgers—perhaps because it was less common for women to live apart from their families than men (Meyerowitz 1988).

whether a farm or a house) (D. S. Smith 1991, pp. 35–36). The question on mother tongue was inserted as a result of an amendment to the Thirteenth Census Act, too late to be included on the printed enumeration forms. The enumerators were instructed to insert the answer in column 12, after the name of the country of birth.

At first glance the questions seem quite straightforward, and for most respondents they may have been. There was inevitably, however, room for genuine ambiguity and for discrepancies between what the Census Bureau had in mind as appropriate answers, what the enumerators understood or accepted, and how the respondents interpreted the questions. In some cases the Census Bureau's instructions left enumerators considerable discretion. For example, the enumerators were asked to distinguish between "negroes" and "mulattoes." As Miller, Morgan, and McDaniel note in Chapter 5 in this volume, the distinction between the two was left up to the enumerator, leaving room for preconceptions about the characteristics associated with lighter or darker skin.

The enumerators were required to exercise discretion in evaluating the "truthfulness" of the replies. "You have a right not only to an answer, but to a truthful answer. Do not accept any statement which you believe to be false. Where you know that the answer given is incorrect, enter upon the schedule the fact as nearly as you can ascertain it" (U.S. Bureau of the Census 1910, p. 13). Although some deviation from truth would have been obvious (a person who looked 60 but claimed to be 6), much would depend on the range of answers that the enumerator considered likely, and thus on the range of his or her own experience. In a clash between the culture or experience of the enumerator and the culture of the respondent, the enumerator was required to overrule the respondent.

Misunderstandings between enumerators and respondents were likely, given that 22.8 percent of foreign-born whites over 10 did not speak English (United States 1913, p. 1267, Table 2). The Bureau officials clearly recognized that language was a problem. They included provisions for paid interpreters, if necessary, but encouraged the enumerator to call on some other member of the family or a neighbor of the same nationality as an unpaid interpreter (U.S. Bureau of the Census 1910, p. 16). Even were the language similar, however, hostilities and suspicions among groups that spoke the same language (e.g., Yiddish-speaking "Uptown" and "Downtown" Jews) might have led to less than candid responses when the enumerators were from one group and the respondents from another. Consider, for example, something as basic to the analyses of mortality, fertility, and households in this volume as marital status. Would a wife who had been deserted by her husband admit or conceal this information? In some ethnic groups there was considerable concern

FIGURE 2.1
Page of the Census

State, _Iowa_

County, _Henry_

Township or other division of county, _Center township_

[Insert proper name and, also, name of class, as township, town, precinct, district, hundred, beat, etc. See instructions

Name of institution, ✕

[Insert name of institution, if any, and indicate the lines on which the entries are made. See instructions.]

[ILLUSTRATIVE EXAMPLE OF MANNE]

DEPARTMENT OF COMMERCE AN[

THIRTEENTH CENSUS OF TH[

	House no.	Dwelling	Family	NAME	RELATION	Sex	Color	Age	Marital	Yrs. marr.	No. born	No. living	Birthplace Person	Birthplace Father	Birthplace Mother
1	8	9		Callender, Bert O.	Head	M	W	55	M 1	26			Indiana	Ohio	Switz.—German
2				—, Annie	Wife	F	W	49	M 1	26	4	4	Switz.—German	Switz.—German	Switz.—German
3				—, David	Son	M	W	25	S				Nebraska	Indiana	Switz.—German
4				—, Harry E.	Son	M	W	14	S				Nebraska	Indiana	Switz.—German
5				—, Mabel	Daughter	F	W	11	S				Nebraska	Indiana	Switz.—German
6	9	10		Firth, Martha	Head	F	W	60	Wd		1	0	Eng.—English	Eng.—English	Eng.—English
7				Long, Margaret	Granddaughter	F	W	9	S				California	Ata.—English	Ata.—English
8				—, William R.	Grandson	M	W	6	S				California	Ata.—English	Ata.—English
9				Dover, Jane	Servant	F	B	24	S				Georgia	Georgia	Georgia
10	10	11		James, Peter	Head	M	W	45	M 1	20			Ohio	Can.—English	Can.—English
11				—, Lucy	Wife	F	W	43	M 1	20	0	0	Michigan	Michigan	Michigan
12				Lewis, Gertrude	Niece	F	W	29	D		1	1	Ohio	Can.—English	Can.—English
13				—, Maggie	Grandniece	F	W	11	S				Ohio	Michigan	Ohio
14	11	12		Mason, Daniel	Head	M	B	49	M 1	25			Maryland	Maryland	Maryland
15				—, Lillie M.	Wife	F	Mu	44	M 1	25	7	7	Virginia	Virginia	Virginia
16				—, William H.	Son	M	Mu	11	S				Pennsylvania	Maryland	Virginia
17				—, Annie R.	Daughter	F	Mu	8	S				Pennsylvania	Maryland	Virginia
18	12	13		Peterson, Henry	Head	M	W	67	M 2	37			Michigan	Michigan	Ohio
19				—, Susan	Wife	F	W	57	M 1	37	6	3	Indiana	Indiana	Indiana
20				—, John	Son	M	W	22	S				Michigan	Michigan	Indiana
21				Ling, Ah	Servant	M	Ch	37	S				Chi.—Chinese	Chi.—Chinese	Chi.—Chinese
22	13	14		Dick, James	Head	M	In	38	M 1	6			California	California	California
23				—, Lupena	Wife	F	In	36	M 1	6	1	1	California	California	California
24				—, Lily	Daughter	F	In	5	S				California	California	California
25	14	15		Takemata	Head	M	Jp	35	S				Jap.—Japanese	Jap.—Japanese	Jap.—Japanese
26				Had	Partner	M	Jp	18	S				Jap.—Japanese	Jap.—Japanese	Jap.—Japanese
27				Mikawa	Hired man	M	Jp	16	S				Jap.—Japanese	Jap.—Japanese	Jap.—Japanese
28	15	16		Vennello, Antonio	Head	M	W	42	M 1	19			It.—Italian	It.—Italian	It.—Italian
29				—, Mary	Wife	F	W	38	M 1	19	9	5	It.—Italian	It.—Italian	It.—Italian
30				—, Michael	Son	M	W	17	S				It.—Italian	It.—Italian	It.—Italian
31				—, Lena	Daughter	F	W	4	S				New York	It.—Italian	It.—Italian
32				Romano, John	Boarder	M	W	60	M 1	29			Aust.—German	Aust.—German	It.—German
33				—, Kate	Boarder	F	W	48	M 1	29	0	0	Russ.—Lithuanian	Russ.—Lithuanian	Ger.—Lithuanian
34	16	17		Bahar, Hyman	Head	M	W	55	M 1	26			Aust.—Bohemian	Aust.—Bohemian	Aust.—Bohemian
35				—, Deborah	Wife	F	W	52	M 2	26	4	3	Aust.—Bohemian	Aust.—Bohemian	Aust.—Polish
36				—, Wolf	Son	M	W	24	S				Aust.—Bohemian	Aust.—Bohemian	Aust.—Polish
37				—, Solomon	Son	M	W	19	S				Aust.—Bohemian	Aust.—Bohemian	Aust.—Polish
38				—, Mary	Daughter	F	W	17	S				Aust.—Bohemian	Aust.—Bohemian	Aust.—Polish
39	17	18		Rosen, Benjamin	Head	M	W	50	M 1	26			Russ.—Polish	Russ.—Polish	Russ.—Polish
40				—, Rebecca	Wife	F	W	50	M 1	26	1	1	Russ.—Polish	Ger.—Polish	Russ.—Polish
41				—, Abraham	Son	M	W	24	S				Russ.—Polish	Russ.—Polish	Russ.—Polish

Column numbers across the schedule: 1–2 (Location), 3 (Name), 4 (Relation), 5 (Sex), 6 (Color or race), 7 (Age at last birthday), 8 (Whether single, married, widowed, or divorced), 9 (Number of years of present marriage), 10 (Number born), 11 (Number now living), 12 (Place of birth of this Person), 13 (Father), 14 (Mother).

Street, avenue, road, etc.: _Burlington road._ (rows 1–21); _Fort Madison road._ (rows 22–41)

NOTE.—Entries limited to 41 persons, for want of space, although schedule provided lines for 50 entries to ·ach page.

LABOR—BUREAU OF THE CENSUS.

Supervisor's District No. _1_

Sheet No. _1_

UNITED STATES: 1910—POPULATION.

Enumeration District No. _55_

Name of incorporated place, X _____
[Insert proper name and, also, name of class, as city, village, town, or borough. See instructions.]

Ward of city, X _____

Enumerated by me on the ___16th___ day of April, 1910,

John Smith, Enumerator.

15	16	17	18	19	20	21	22	23	24	25	26	27	28	29	30	31	32	
		English	Farmer	General farm	Emp			Yes	Yes		O	F	F	1	✓			1
1861		English	None					Yes	Yes									2
		English	Sailor	Merchant vessel	W	No	0	Yes	Yes									3
		English	None					Yes	Yes	Yes								4
		English	None					Yes	Yes	Yes								5
1898		English	Farmer	Dairy farm	Emp			Yes	Yes		O	M	F	2				6
			None							Yes								7
			None							Yes								8
		English	Servant	Private family	W	No	0	Yes	No									9
		English	Dairyman	Dairy farm	W	No	0	Yes	Yes		R		H					10
		English	Dairywoman	Dairy farm	W	No	0	Yes	Yes									11
		English	Stenographer	Lawyer's office	W	No	7	Yes	Yes									12
			None															13
		English	Laborer	Odd jobs	W	Yes	6	Yes	No		R		H					14
		English	Laundress	Hotel	W	No	0	Yes	No									15
		English	None					Yes	Yes	Yes								16
			None							No							D D	17
		English	Farmer	General farm	Emp			Yes	Yes		O	F	F	3	U A			18
		English	None					Yes	Yes									19
		English	Farm laborer	Home farm	W	No	0	Yes	Yes									20
1890	Al	English	Servant	Private family	W	No	0	Yes	Yes									21
		English	Wood chopper	Lumber camp	W	No	10	Yes	Yes		R		H					22
		English	Housekeeper	School	W	No	0	Yes	Yes									23
			None							Yes								24
1905	Al	English	Farmer	Fruit farm	Emp			Yes	Yes		R		F	4				25
1907		Japanese	Artist	Landscape painter	O A			Yes	Yes	No								26
1909		Japanese	Laborer	Fruit farm	W	No	10	Yes	Yes	No								27
1902	Na	English	Miner	Coal mine	W	Yes	0	Yes	Yes		O	F	H					28
1902		Italian	None					Yes	Yes									29
1902		English	Laborer	Coal mine	W	Yes	0	Yes	Yes	Yes								30
			None													Bl		31
1890	Na	English	Herder	Stock ranch	W	No	0	Yes	Yes									32
1890		English	Farm laborer	Working out	W	No	0	Yes	Yes									33
1906	Pa	English	Foreman	Coal mine	W	No	0	Yes	Yes		R		H					34
1906		German	None					Yes	Yes									35
1906	Pa	English	Conductor	Street car	W	No	0	Yes	Yes									36
1906		English	Apprentice	Plumber	W	No	0	Yes	Yes	No								37
1906		English	Saleswoman	Grocery store	W	No	0	Yes	Yes	No								38
1908	Al	Polish	Blaster	Stone quarry	W	No	0	Yes	Yes		R		H					39
1908		Polish	None					Yes	Yes									40
1908	Al	English	Laborer	Street railway	W	No	15	Yes	Yes									41

19

at the time about the "problem" of deserted women (see, e.g., Zunser 1924; Waldman, 1913), yet we find few women recorded as married but with an absent husband (Miller, Morgan, and McDaniel, Chapter 5, Table 5.3; see also Robles and Watkins 1993). Morawska (Afterword) discusses possible reasons for this discrepancy.

Today efforts are made to match the race and ethnicity of the enumerators with the predominant race and ethnicity of a neighborhood.[9] We have found no systematic analysis of this for 1910. In 1880, 1890, and 1900 both supervisors and enumerators had been appointed by Congress; appointees were given noncompetitive examinations to determine whether or not they had the ability to fulfill their duties. In 1910, however, prospective census employees were given open competitive exams (U.S. Bureau of the Census 1979, p. 2), although it is likely that many were still patronage appointments.[10] In 1910, "a larger proportion of the Negro population was convassed by Negro enumerators . . . than in any other census year," and the Census Bureau concluded that this increased the proportion returned as mulatto (U.S. Bureau of the Census 1922, p. 17). Watkins and London (1991) estimated that slightly over 20 percent of foreign-born Italians living in urban areas and under 3 percent living in rural areas were enumerated by Italians.[11]

Who within the household was the respondent—the head of household himself? his spouse? an English-speaking child? In an evaluation of the age reporting, the Census Bureau concluded that there were over twice as many males as females of unknown age, and that this was probably due to the fact that "there were more males than females away from home at the time the enumerator called and therefore more as to whose age the person who furnished the information was ignorant" (United States 1913, p. 295). An examination of Appendix B to this volume shows more missing data on most variables for males than for females, probably for the same reason.

But even were there no differences in language or background between enumerator and respondent, there was room for justifiable ambiguity. Consider, for example, the designation "child of the head of the household." What about adopted children? These were not mentioned in the instructions to the enumerators. Would enumerators have thought of this category? At least some did: there are fifteen children in the PUS who were reported to be the adopted son or daughter of the head of the household. How would parents who had adopted a child in infancy and

[9]David Pemberton, Bureau of the Census, personal communication.
[10]David Pemberton, Bureau of the Census, personal communication.
[11]The name of the enumerator is given in the manuscript census, but it was not included in the 1910 PUS. Watkins and London (1991) assigned an ethnicity to the enumerator on the basis of his or her last name; thus, the estimates are only rough.

come to think of it as their own have answered this question? Or take boarders who were relatives. We know that immigrants often came to cities where they had relatives (Morawska 1990), and novels and memoirs describe them as staying with relatives until they could establish their own households. It is thought that kin often considered their stay in other households to be "boarding" (Hareven and Modell 1980, p. 350). Would the person answering the enumerator's questions have described a cousin who was boarding as a cousin or as a boarder? This may have varied by the degree of kinship (perhaps brothers were described as brothers, but cousins as boarders). But if the various immigrant groups differed in the significance they gave to various kin classifications, the responses may have varied by ethnic group as well. Morawska notes that it may have been impossible to explain to an enumerator the intricacies of relationships for which there was no term in American English, so a simple "boarder" or "lodger" may have been given instead (Morawska, this volume). Categorization of relationships may also have varied by gender. The larger number of nieces than nephews reported in nineteenth-century American censuses may be due to the tendency to label the former as relatives, the latter as boarders (D. S. Smith 1992, p. 443).

The methods used to detect errors while creating the data tape for the PUS consisted primarily of identifying implausible combinations (e.g., a female son) and rechecking the manuscript census (see Strong et al. 1989 for a more detailed description). An examination of these inconsistencies showed that the vast majority were the work of the original enumerators, and not of the data-entry operators. Data-entry errors were corrected; some of the enumerator errors were corrected, but others were not. The code book for the 1910 PUS states:

> Rather than present a data file that was as close as possible to the original records, we elected to correct some of the most obvious errors of enumerators and respondents. Having eliminated as many operator errors as possible through the rechecking procedure, we re-examined the remaining inconsistencies. In the end, the solution to a particular problem depended upon its frequency and importance, and the quality and quantity of the related evidence that could be used in determining the probably "correct" response. For many variables the problem was very rare and appeared to pose no threat to data analysis. In other instances, the information available did not allow us both to identify an incorrect response and to provide a correct one, so the entry was left unaltered (Strong et al. 1989, pp. 43–44).

Major Categories Used in this Volume

Ethnic Groups

All the analyses in this volume compare the foreign-born (the first generation), distinguished by place of birth or mother tongue or by a combination of both, with native whites of native parentage (those who were born in the United States and whose parents were also born in the United States). The native whites of native parentage are here called NWNP. Most of the analyses also include separate comparisons with blacks and mulattoes (sometimes separately, sometimes combined), and with U.S.-born children of the foreign-born (the second generation).

Table 2.1 lists the largest ethnic groups used in the analysis. There is considerable variety in the number of ethnic groups included in the analyses that follow: for example, the chapters on fertility (Chapter 4)

TABLE 2.1
Ethnic Groups

	Mother Tongue	Place of Birth
British		England Wales Scotland
Irish		Ireland
Scandinavians	Swedish Norwegian Danish Icelandic Finnish	Sweden Norway Denmark Iceland Finland
Germans	German	Germany
Italians	Italian	Italy
Poles	Polish	
Central European Jews	Yiddish	Germany Austria Austria-Poland Hungary Romania
Eastern European Jews	Yiddish	Russia Poland Russia-Poland

NOTE: Details of these definitions are given in Appendix B.

and household arrangements (Chapter 5) concentrate on seven major groups of foreign-born (omitting all other foreign-born), whereas the chapters on schooling (Chapter 7) and industry (Chapter 8) aim for comprehensiveness by including all the foreign-born. This diversity in approach was the consequence of decisions made by the individual authors as to the trade-off between comprehensiveness, sample size, and the purpose of the analyses. Some authors wanted to include all the foreign-born; because the sample sizes for some groups were too small for analysis, the cost of this strategy was to combine some of the smaller groups into aggregates that to specialists in ethnicity mix together groups that are quite different from one another. In contrast, the chapter on fertility concentrates on the demographic process of fertility, and its authors were satisfied with discussing this on the basis of a smaller number of ethnic groups for which the sample sizes were sufficiently large for multivariate analyses. Appendix B to this volume includes some of the basic tabulations for many smaller ethnic groups; it also discusses the justification for some of our decisions.

The major ethnic groups are usually defined as they are in Table 2.1. Individual research interests, however, led to different definitions for other than the major groups. To avoid repetition, in the chapters that follow the ethnic groups will be defined only when the definitions differ from those shown in Table 2.1. Although we use the term "ethnic group," and sometimes refer to "ethnicity," strictly speaking the term "ethnicity" as it is used here refers only to groups defined by the information on place of birth and mother tongue. Although the instructions say that a list of places of birth was provided to the enumerators, this was not printed in their instruction booklet; a list of *principal* foreign languages spoken in the United States was, however, included in the *Instructions to the Enumerators.*[12]

The Census Bureau, recognizing that the correspondence between nativity and mother tongue might be complicated, specifically instructed enumerators not to rely on language spoken to determine place of birth, but to ask place of birth separately. Examples were given: "If a person replies that he was born in Russia and that his mother tongue is Lithuanian, write in column 12 *Russ.—Lithuanian.*" Most of the examples applied to areas of the Austro-Hungarian Empire and Eastern Europe; the Census Bureau recognized that the linguistic situation there was particularly complicated, and it may also have been particularly

[12]After the amendment authorizing inquiry into mother tongue was passed, enumerators were told to replace page 30 of the *Instructions to Enumerators* with a new page 30. Here it says that the abbreviations for country of birth were on a separate "List of Foreign Countries" (U.S. Bureau of the Census, 1910, p. 30).

concerned to classify immigrants from the nationality groups in these areas.

But the instructions may sometimes have been confusing to enumerators. For example, Poland was not an independent country in 1910: the original instructions called for the listing of Poles in their respective states, with a designation of their Polish nationality in parentheses. Thus place of birth was to be listed as "Germany (Pol.)," "Austria (Pol.)," or "Russia (Pol.)." The new instructions, distributed after the mother tongue amendment was authorized, made no mention of Poland. Some enumerators classified individuals as born in Poland, whereas others classified them according to the international boundaries of 1910. "Poland" as a place of birth includes only those individuals whom enumerators listed as being from Poland, with no other country mentioned; the numbers in our sample in the categories "Poland" (as well as "Russia Poland," "Austria Poland," and "German Poland") are very small (much smaller than the number listed as speaking Polish as a mother tongue).

It is difficult to evaluate how the immigrants would have responded to the question about place of birth. Philpott (1978) writes that "seasoned workers in the Immigrant Protection League believed that some Slavs simply identified themselves as Poles to avoid confusing census takers and other social investigators" (p. 139). Especially among the "new" immigrant groups, identification seemed to be with more local places of origin than the Census Bureau would have had in mind: where compatriots gathered—for example, to form churches and mutual aid societies—the sense of common identification was, at least initially, with villages rather than countries (Golab 1977; Orsi 1985; Yancey et al. 1976). Unfortunately, the census did not ask for more local descriptions of place of origin: given the demographic diversity within the sending countries (Watkins 1991), this would have been quite useful information to have. The ethnic groups as they are defined here probably include quite diverse subcultures, often associated with smaller regions within a country. For example, Italians from northern and southern Italy (especially Sicily) are generally considered to be quite distinct from one another in many respects, in part because they spoke quite different dialects (Sartorio 1974 [1918]). There is also religious heterogeneity within some ethnic groups. Whereas virtually all Italians were at least nominally Catholic, other groups, such as the Irish and the Germans, were of mixed religions (Catholics and Protestants in the case of the Irish; Catholics, Protestants, and Jews in the case of the Germans). The information from the 1910 census does not permit us to capture either these regional or religious differences.

For mother tongue, the census enumerators were instructed to ascertain the "customary speech of the homes of the immigrants before immigration," but the Census Bureau later cautioned that in some cases enumerators returned "ethnic stock" and "ancestral language" instead of the language of customary speech (United States 1913, p. 959). For example, although the instructions to the enumerators say that enumerators were instructed to combine Serbian and Croatian, and to include with them Bosnian, Dalmatian, Herzegovinian, and Montenegran, there are individuals in our sample who are identified with a mother tongue of Serbian, others with Croatian.

At times enumerators entered a country rather than a language for mother tongue. Where linguistic homogeneity was evident—for example, Sweden—the PUS coders simply changed the country to the language—e.g., Swedish for Sweden. In other cases, the coders made use of the responses to the English-speaking question: this was asked only of those over 10, and the enumerators were supposed to write in the language spoken if the respondent did not speak English.[13] Thus, if a non-English-speaker responded to the mother tongue question with "Switzerland" but answered the language question with "French," the coders entered Switzerland for place of birth and French for mother tongue (Strong et al. 1989).

The inclusion of Yiddish as a mother tongue permitted us to identify many but not all immigrant Jews in the United States in 1910.[14] We have assumed that all of those who claimed Yiddish as a mother tongue were Jewish. It is likely that Jews from Russia—the majority of the Jews in the United States in 1910—gave Yiddish as their mother tongue; most Jews in Russia spoke Yiddish as their maternal language (Rubinow 1907, pp. 488, 566–570, 577; see also Rosenwaike 1971).[15] Although we use the term "Jews" in our analysis, strictly speaking this means only Yiddish-speakers. It is quite likely that some Jews claimed another mother tongue, so that we have not identified all the Jews. In particular, we think that some German Jews would have given their mother tongue as German (in the PUS, less than 1 percent of those born in Germany claimed Yiddish as a mother tongue). We also expect that some Jews from Hungary would have given Hungarian as a mother tongue, because many

---

[13]Because many foreign-born responded that they did speak English, the numbers speaking another language are much smaller than the numbers elicited from the mother tongue question; therefore we have used the mother tongue question to categorize ethnic groups and the language question only to clarify ambiguities.

[14]Some reported "Hebrew" as their mother tongue; the census classified these with the Yiddish-speakers (United States 1913, p. 960), as did those who coded the 1910 PUS.

[15]The Census Bureau compared returns for Yiddish-speakers with the counts of "Hebrews" in the reports of the Commission General of Immigration; for immigrants from Romania, the United Kingdom, and Germany, the percent speaking Yiddish in the 1910 census was smaller than the percentage speaking Hebrew among the immigrants (United States 1913, p. 960, Endnote 3).

late-nineteenth-century Hungarian Jews considered themselves Magyars of the Hebrew faith (Benkart 1980, p. 463).[16]

In Table 2.1 we distinguish between those Yiddish-speakers from central Europe (roughly the Austro-Hungarian Empire and Germany) and those Yiddish-speakers from Eastern Europe (primarily Russia). "Central Europe" includes not only Yiddish-speakers born in Austria, Austria-Poland, and Hungary but also a small number who gave their place of birth as Germany and a slightly larger number who gave their place of birth as Romania (although Romania had become independent in 1878, and could have been included in the "Russian" category instead of the "Austro-Hungarian Empire" category).[17] In the "Eastern Europe" ("Russia") category the vast majority are Yiddish-speakers who gave their place of birth as Russia.[18] In some analyses in the following chapters a single category of Jews (Yiddish-speakers) is used: when this is done, the category includes those born anywhere (e.g., England, Turkey).[19]

Very rarely does a foreign-born child have a different mother tongue or place of birth from that of his or her mother or father. Where these attributes differed from parent to child, it was more likely to be in place of birth than in mother tongue. For example, 1,292 immigrants in the PUS gave a mother tongue that differed from their mother's mother tongue. The largest group of these (469) were from Canada. Other large groups are from Germany (162), England (131), and Ireland (112), with smaller numbers from Russia (47), Austria (45), and Italy (25), and a few from other countries. A total of 2,725 in the PUS gave a place of birth that differed from their mother's place of birth. Again, the largest group was from Canada (1,309), with other large groups from England (461), Germany (162), Ireland (116), and Scotland (108), and smaller numbers from other countries. For both Yiddish-speakers and Polish-speakers, 99 percent reported the same mother tongue for both their parents as for themselves.

---

[16]The Hungarian Nationality Act of 1868 recognized only one political nationality and only one official language, and the government attempted to promote assimilation into the Magyar group (Benkart 1988, p. 463). The (1910) census of Hungary cross-classified religion (Israelite) by mother tongue; 75.66 percent of "Israelites" gave Hungarian as their mother tongue (Lajos 1922, p. 466). (I am grateful to Erika Czer for her translation.)

[17] In our sample there were no Yiddish-speakers who gave their place of birth as Austria-Hungary, Bohemia, Croatia, Germany-Poland, Serbia, Montenegro, or Bulgaria.

[18]In our sample there were four Yiddish-speakers who were recorded as born in Poland and eight Yiddish-speakers recorded as born in Russia-Poland.

[19]Ninety-one Yiddish-speakers were recorded as born neither in the Austro-Hungarian Empire nor in Russia (as defined here): these include sixty-six Yiddish-speakers whose place of birth was given as England, two from Sweden, two from France, and so on.

First and Second Generations

As noted above, first-generation ethnics were those who themselves were foreign-born, and second-generation ethnics were those born in the United States of foreign-born parents. Because information on place of birth and mother tongue was asked only about the individual and his or her parents, it is usually not possible to identify the grandchildren of immigrants. Exceptions would include an individual listed as the native-born child of the head of the household where the head responded that he was U.S.-born and that he had at least one foreign-born parent. But if a grandchild of an immigrant were no longer living with a native-born parent, the information on the parentage of the individual's grandparents would not be available from reports of the individual's parent. It is unlikely that there were many third-generation individuals whose ancestry was Eastern or Southern European, but this would not have been the case for groups such as the Irish and the Germans.

Assigning a generational status to the foreign-born poses little problem, for it is based simply on the place of birth of the individual. In some cases, however, a U.S.-born individual was the child of a marriage between an ethnic immigrant and either a second-generation immigrant or an NWNP. Similarly, although most couples were of the same ethnicity, in some cases the ethnicity of the parents differed. Because of the high degree of generational and ethnic endogamy (see Miller, Morgan, and McDaniel, Chapter 5; see also Pagnini and Morgan 1990), there were rather few children of generationally or ethnically mixed marriages. In these cases, most authors assigned the mother's nativity status or ethnicity to the child (where authors deviated from this practice it is noted).

Although some analyses do compare the first and second generations, these must be interpreted cautiously for two reasons. First, for the "new" immigrant groups, there are very few adults in the second generation. Over 70 percent of second-generation Italians, Poles, and Jews were age 15 or younger, compared to about 25 percent of second-generation British and Germans (Appendix B, Table B.2). Although most chapters include the second generation in at least some of their analyses, the small number of adults makes interpretations of comparisons with the first generation difficult.

Second, it is natural to look to comparisons of first- and second-generation ethnics as if these comparisons spoke to changes that occurred over time. But here the two generations are contemporaneous: both were captured by the census in 1910. Changes in the nature of the immigrant stream would lead to differences between the generations that could have little to do with the differences in their place of birth. For example, the early years of Italian immigration (i.e., before the 1880s) were dominated by Italians from the north, the later years by Italians from the south (Foerster 1919, pp. 37–38; U.S. Immigration Commission 1911), and there are similar differences in the composition of the migration stream for Slavs (Morawska 1985). Thus, generational differences cannot be interpreted easily without knowing more than the census information provides about changes in the migration stream.

Duration in the United States

All the foreign-born were asked their year of immigration; if the person had come to the United States more than once, the enumerators were to ask for the date of first arrival. To calculate duration in the United States we subtracted arrival date from 1910.

We sometimes use the terms "old" and "new" immigrants. As these terms were used at the turn of the century, the "old" immigrants included the British, Irish, Scandinavians, and Germans, while the "new" immigrants were those from Eastern, Central, and Southern Europe. This distinction implies, but is not exactly congruent with, duration in the United States. It is true that the bulk of the "new" immigrants came in the two decades that preceded the 1910 census. Between 75 and 85 percent of Italians, Poles, and Jews in the 1910 PUS immigrated between 1890 and 1910, and most of the "old" immigrants came before 1890: about three-quarters of the Germans, two-thirds of the British and Irish, and slightly over one-half of the Scandinavians. Yet nearly one-third of the British and Irish and almost half (46 percent) of the Scandinavians arrived between 1890 and 1910, the same decades that saw the great influx of Italians, Poles, and Jews (see Appendix B to this volume, Table B.1; see also Carpenter 1969 [1927]).

By use of current age and date of immigration it is possible to calculate age at immigration. Striking proportions of the immigrants arrived in the United States as children (i.e., under age 16): 29 percent of males and 37 percent of females.[20] These numbers are generally substantially higher among "old" groups that among "new," but Scandinavians ("old") resemble the "new," and the Irish ("old") are intermediates.

Although the total percentage of the sample with an unknown date of immigration is small, there are marked variations by ethnic group. Unknown immigration dates are substantially greater among the "old" immigrants than among the "new": between 10 and 12 percent of

[20]These calculations were made by Mark Keintz.

foreign-born British, Irish, Scandinavians, and Germans lack a date of immigration, but only approximately 6 percent of Italians and Poles, 4 percent of Eastern European Jews, and 3 percent of Central European Jews lack a date of immigration (A. R. Miller, this volume, Table 8.6). The higher proportions of missing immigration dates among the "old" immigrant groups may be attributable to the immigrations having occurred so long ago. Moreover, the higher proportion of missing immigration dates for children among the "old" immigrant groups suggests that there may have been some tendency for enumerators to fill in information for this question only for the family head (Philip Miller, personal communication).

Another possible source of error is in the information on date of immigration associated with back-and-forth migration. As the Census Bureau understood in asking for "first" immigration, some immigrants would have entered the United States, then left, then returned again, perhaps several times. There is clearly room for confusion here. The census taker may not have expected more than one date of immigration, and have failed to specify "first" immigration; the enumerators may have expected more back-and-forth migration for some groups than others, and have differentially specified "first" immigration for some groups. Back-and-forth migration was more common among the "new" immigrants (U.S. Immigration Commission 1911), suggesting more potential for error for these groups. Moreover, it was more common among the Italians and Poles than among the "old" immigrants for one member (usually an adult male) to precede the others (Robles and Watkins 1993). But it is possible that it was the "family" immigration date—for example, either when the husband had returned to the home country and escorted his family to the United States or when the wife and children joined their husband and father—that appeared most salient to the immigrants, and that they reported.

The duration measure no doubt also picks up changes in the characteristics of the immigrants over time. If the nature of the immigrant stream changed—for example, if earlier immigrants differed in their background or area of origin from later immigrants—then, like the differences between generations, differences by duration will represent these generational differences in the migration stream as well.

English-speaking

The census enumerator asked whether or not each foreign-born person in the household (age 10 years or older) spoke English. No criteria were given in the instructions to the enumerators as to what this might mean.[21] It is likely that the proportion speaking English was over-reported, because there was some status associated with the ability to speak English. For example, writing about Jewish men, Hutchins Hapgood says:

> He picks up only about a hundred English words and phrases. . . . Of this modest vocabulary he is very proud, for it takes him out of the category of the "greenhorn," a term of contempt to which the satirical Jew is very sensitive. The man who has been only three weeks in this country hates few things so much as to be called a "greenhorn." Under this fear he learns the small vocabulary to which in many years he adds very little (Hapgood 1902, pp. 10–11).

The desire not to appear a greenhorn may have led some respondents to tell the census enumerator that they spoke English when they spoke very little. The group of English-speakers is probably quite heterogeneous, including many who did not know enough English for it to be a medium of communication—for example, to chat with neighbors or to read English-language newspapers—as well as those whose English was fluent. On the other hand, those who are described by the census enumerator as not speaking English probably knew very little English. Thus, although we use the term "speaks English" in our analysis, caution is necessary in interpreting what this might have meant.

Urban-rural

Most chapters follow the 1910 census in defining as rural those places with a population of under 2,500. Although the distinction between urban and rural is made for analytic purposes, and our results show that it often has meaning, the categories should not be reified. There was considerable internal migration in the United States at this time (Carpenter 1969 [1927]). As a result, some who were counted in urban areas were recent arrivals, while (less likely) some in rural areas may have recently returned from the city.

It is also obvious that the term *rural*—as well as the term *urban*—is inherently heterogenous. Places of 2,500 near a large city or near a swamp might differ from one another as much as they differ from Minneapolis; similarly, Galveston and New York might differ from each other as much as they do from many rural areas. Thus, different defini-

[21]In the 1890 census, this was defined as "able to speak English so as to be understood in ordinary conversation"; in 1900 and 1910, however, enumerators were instructed to ask a yes or no question, with no interpretation given (United States 1913, p. 1265).

tions might well be appropriate for different research purposes. Most authors distinguish between rural and several size categories of urban places. In some analyses it is the distinction between rural and urban that matters (the fertility analysis by Morgan, Watkins, and Ewbank, for example), while in others there is a rather steady gradient by size of urban place (the mortality analysis by Preston, Ewbank, and Hereward, for example).

Moreover, the interpretation of the meaning of rural versus urban differs from chapter to chapter: in Chapter 3, on mortality, the distinction between rural and urban is taken to reflect differences in density relevant for the transmission of infectious diseases; Chapter 4, on fertility, takes these differences to represent either presumed differences in the costs and benefits of children or the ease of transmission of information and attitudes about fertility control; the chapter on schooling emphasizes differences in the availability of schools in urban and rural areas.

Occupation

Enumerators were instructed to enter occupations in great detail; subsequently, the occupations were classified and grouped by the Census Bureau. Occupations were coded for the PUS by both the 1910 and the 1980 classification systems.

As is the case with rural and urban residence on the census date, there is likely to be some fluidity in these occupational categories: people changed jobs or people held more than one job (perhaps in different categories). Although the instructions to the enumerators do not say that the enumerators were to ask whether there was a second occupation, there are instructions about how to enter occupations for a person who had more than one. It was left up to the enumerator to determine whether this was a problem; then, directions for solving it were provided.

As was the case in earlier censuses, far fewer women than men are recorded as working (A. R. Miller, this volume). The Census Bureau made deliberate attempts to improve the reporting of women's work in the 1910 census. The section on Occupations in the instructions to the enumerators begins by saying:

> An entry should be made in this column for *every* person enumerated. The occupation, if any, followed by a child, of any age, or by a woman is just as important for census purposes, as the occupation followed by a man. Therefore it must never be taken for granted, without inquiry,

that a woman, or a child, has no occupation (U.S. Bureau of the Census 1910, p. 32).

The instructions to the enumerators give examples of the kinds of women's and children's work that are to be recorded. They specify that women working at housework for wages should be given the occupation of housekeeper, servant, cook, or chambermaid; that if the woman in addition to doing housework in her own home regularly earns money by some other occupation, either inside her home or outside, that occupation should be listed (e.g., a laundress or washerwoman working at home); that children working for their parents on a farm were to be given the occupation "farm laborer" (U.S. Bureau of the Census 1910, p. 34).

Despite the Census Bureau's efforts to record women's and children's occupations more fully, Folbre and Abel (1989) have concluded that it was almost certainly underestimated, perhaps by as much as 25 percent. This may be in part due to lack of information by the respondent. A survey of the "Back of the Yards" area in Chicago found that

> it was not possible to find out how many married women were employed. When the woman was away from the house, the children and neighbors frequently did not know whether she was at work or not, and the returns, therefore, as to the employment of the women, were too incomplete to be valuable (Breckinridge and Abbott 1910, p. 439).

The Census Bureau's emphasis on enumerating women's occupations was probably undercut by its insistence that the woman must *regularly* earn income and that the income must be a principal source of support in order to be listed with an occupation.[22] For example, a woman who laundered clothes for others in addition to doing her own housework was to be called a laundress only if she regularly earned money as a laundress (U.S. Bureau of the Census 1910, p. 34). And those who kept boarders or lodgers were only to be given an occupation if the person relied upon it as "his or (her) principal means of support or principal source of income" (U.S. Bureau of the Census 1910, p. 35).

In an era when men and women were still expected to have "separate spheres," with men responsible for the financial support of the family and women responsible for the domestic hearth, this emphasis on the woman's contribution as the "principal" source of support almost certainly contributed to the underreporting of women's occupations, especially those of married women. The women themselves may not have

---

[22]Women (and children) doing farm work were treated differently. Those who worked regularly at outdoor farm work, including the family farm, were to be listed as farm laborers even if they did not receive cash wages for their work.

defined what they did as "work"; women who "helped out" in their husbands' businesses or who took in boarders may have chosen these ways of contributing to the family economy precisely because such jobs did not challenge current conceptions of appropriate domestic work (Spector, Watkins, and Goldstein 1991). Moreover, this may well have varied across ethnic groups; for example, Yans-McLaughlin (1977) notes the tactfulness with which immigrant Italian women chose to earn money in ways compatible with maintaining the domestic role of the wife (such as seasonal vegetable picking or keeping a few boarders).

There is also question about the accuracy of the occupations that were recorded. Alba Edwards (in charge of occupational statistics from 1910 to World War II) instructed clerks to make use of supplemental information on the census form to classify ambiguous occupational returns; if an individual stated an occupation unusual for ethnic, race, age, or sex group, the coder was to reject the stated occupation and use a different code (Conk 1980, p. 139). It was "inconsistent," he said, for "women, children, and colored persons to be working at certain occupations." Although his instructions concerned the tabulation stage, it is possible that census enumerators shared his views and modified the occupations they recorded.

Summary

This chapter has examined the major categories used in the following chapters. The Census Bureau imposed some categories through the census schedule: for example, it asked only whether the individual spoke English, leaving it up to the individual how much fluency qualified him or her to say "yes" or "no." Other categories were created by the authors in this volume; for example, duration in the United States by decade.

The creation of categories is necessary for tabulation and for analysis, yet it is important to bear in mind not only how these categories were defined but also that the classifications mask inevitable ambiguities. Perhaps most individuals fell neatly into one category or another, but some may have had several statuses that could not be encompassed by the census schedule: a nephew who was also a boarder, for example. The chapters in this volume describe and analyze the behavior of individuals in ethnic groups defined simply by place of birth and/or mother tongue, comparing one group with another. Yet how the respondents answered the questions of the enumerator and what the enumerator considered an appropriate answer surely were influenced by the culture of the enumerator and the culture of the respondents.

3

CHILD MORTALITY DIFFERENCES
BY ETHNICITY AND RACE
IN THE UNITED STATES: 1900–1910

Samuel H. Preston
Douglas Ewbank
Mark Hereward

I N THIS chapter we describe patterns of child mortality by ethnicity in the United States around the turn of the twentieth century.[1] The 1910 U.S. Census of Population asked questions of ever-married women regarding the number of children they had ever borne and the number of them who had survived to the time of the census.[2] The Public Use Sample (PUS) from this census reported 285,208 births, of whom 218,443 survived; thus, about 23 percent of these children had died by the time of the census.

No tabulations from these questions were published in conjunction with the 1910 census. The data on children-ever-born from the 1910 census were subsequently published in special reports from the 1940 census, but no use has been made of the children-surviving question. We will use responses to these two questions in the PUS to estimate levels of child mortality among various groups for a period centered around

[1]This chapter is a revised version of a paper originally prepared for the Workshop on the 1910 Census, Population Studies Center, University of Pennsylvania, February 8–10, 1990. We are grateful to Susan Watkins, Gretchen Condran, Michael Haines, Daniel Scott Smith, Ann Miller, Arodys Robles, Susan Modell, Ewa Morawska, Margaret Greene, Michael White, Miriam King, Andrew Miller, Terry Labov, and Sherman Dorn for comments and discussions that pointed us in useful directions. This research was supported by a grant from the National Institute of Child Health and Human Development, HD22099.

[2]Specifically, both questions fell under the general heading, "Mother of how many children," with separate columns under that heading for "number born" and "number now living." Enumerators were explicitly instructed not to include stillbirths (U.S. Bureau of the Census 1979).

1902. This effort is a direct descendant of an effort to study child mortality based on a similar pair of questions contained in a Public Use Sample from the 1900 census (Preston and Haines 1991). We will borrow liberally from information and interpretation contained in that study. However, the PUS for 1910 is far better suited than the PUS for 1900 for studying ethnic differences in mortality. It contains 3.66 times the number of individuals, and because of heavy immigration between 1900 and 1910, a higher fraction of them were born abroad. Furthermore, we have substantially expanded the number of births under investigation by devising a strategy for including women who were not in their first marriage with husband present.

Ethnic Influences on Health and Mortality

A good deal of attention has recently been focused on ethnic differences in child mortality. In a study of fifteen developing countries conducted at the University of Pennsylvania that used techniques similar to those employed here, very large ethnic differences in child mortality levels were revealed in many countries even after available social and economic variables were controlled (United Nations 1985). For example, women of Chinese heritage had unusually low child mortality wherever they were located. It was argued that these differences reflected variations in unobserved child care practices among the different groups, a theme that has been usefully elaborated by John Caldwell (e.g., 1990).

Among the most important child care practices, at least in an unsanitary, high-mortality context such as the United States at the turn of the century, is the length of breast-feeding. Woodbury's (1925) classic study of infant mortality among 22,967 births in eight American cities between 1911 and 1916 found that, for the first nine months of a child's life, the death rates among those not breast-fed were three to four times higher than among the breast-fed. The advantages of breast-feeding lapsed quickly after nine months.

Table 3.1 presents data compiled from the Woodbury study that describe the wide ethnic differences in the extent of breast-feeding in these cities, of which Baltimore contributed 47 percent of the observations. The babies of Jewish and Polish women spent the lowest fraction—11 percent—of their first nine months being fed exclusively artificial foods, while French Canadian children at 44 percent were a clear outlier at the other extreme. Polish and Italian children were the most likely, and French Canadian children the least likely, to be exclusively breast-fed. Jewish children were more likely than any other group to be fed a com-

TABLE 3.1
Type of Feeding, by Color and Nationality of Mother; Months Lived from Birth to End of Ninth Month by Infants in Eight Cities: Children's Bureau Study, 1911–1915.

Color and Nationality of Mother	Total Months Lived from Birth to End of Ninth Month	Percentage of Months of Exclusive Breast-feeding	Percentage of Months of Partial Breast-feeding	Percentage of Months of Artificial Feeding
Total	192,212.5	57.4	17.6	24.9
White	180,397.5	57.6	17.1	25.2
Native	102,285.5	56.2	15.4	28.3
Foreign-born	78,112.0	59.4	19.3	21.1
Italian	11,943.0	68.6	18.3	13.1
Jewish	10,688.0	61.5	27.1	11.3
French Canadian	8,666.0	42.7	13.3	44.0
German	6,514.0	56.5	22.0	21.5
Polish	10,391.5	65.9	22.7	11.1
Portuguese	5,410.5	48.8	19.3	31.9
Other	24,471.0	60.3	16.5	23.2
Not reported	18.0	27.8	33.3	38.9
Black	11,815.0	54.8	25.5	19.7

SOURCE: Woodbury (1925).

bination of breast milk and other foods. Children of native whites and blacks were not very different from children of the aggregate foreign-born group in these cities. It should be noted that Children's Bureau studies in six scattered rural areas at about the same time invariably found women to be breast-feeding their children for longer average periods than these urban women (Preston and Haines 1991, Chapter 3).

Other aspects of child care bear a less obvious relation to child survival in this era, and there is much less systematic evidence about their extent and variation among ethnic groups. For example, in a modern context, one would expect that a woman's encounters with systems of medical care would be an important factor in child survival, but this connection was far less important at the turn of the century. It is not clear that hospital births had better outcomes than births at home, or that births attended by physicians fared better than those attended by midwives. It does appear that midwives, who delivered about half of the nation's births in 1900, attended an even larger fraction of deliveries to foreign-born women (Kobrin 1966). But the assistance of a midwife is not likely to have been an important factor in mortality (Preston and Haines 1991). More important than the type of attendant was the training that midwives and physicians had received, particularly regarding proper hygiene. If their training was good, midwives could reduce infant mortality rates below those achieved by physicians, as in Providence, RI (Chapin 1919, p. 1517). However, it seems likely from accounts of the period that midwives attending the black population were poorly informed about sound hygiene (e.g., Dart 1921).

About other specific child care practices there is even less systematic information. Italian, Portuguese, and black mothers were sometimes said to feed their babies rough, hard-to-digest food at too early an age; Irish mothers, to be fatalistic about child death; and Polish mothers to be grossly ignorant of the laws of hygiene. But charges of hygienic ignorance were also leveled at college-educated women (Hollopeter 1906, p. 821). We know of no way to investigate such claims directly. As in many other studies, we are forced to assume that whatever ethnic differences in mortality are uncovered are in part a result of variations in child care practices among ethnic groups.

Although it is reasonable to suppose that specific child care practices influenced mortality, it is also the case that children shared the epidemiologic and social environment of their parents. Death rates at different ages are very highly correlated across populations, at 0.80 or higher (Coale and Demeny 1983). One specific connection between the mortality levels of adults and children is the physical health of mothers. Women whose own growth was impaired in childhood by disease and undernourishment are more likely to have low-birth-weight babies, who are at greater risk of death. Mothers can also transmit infectious diseases to their children. There is evidence from many countries that the late nineteenth and early twentieth century was a period when childhood conditions had a lasting impact on adult health (Kermack et al. 1935; Preston and van de Walle 1978). There is some evidence that these cohort effects were partially inherited by the next generation of infants (Kermack et al. 1934).

Health conditions in most of the countries from which immigrants were arriving were poorer than those in the United States, reflecting in part their lower standards of living. The United States at the turn of the century had the highest per capita income in the world (Kuznets 1966). Female life expectancies at birth in some of the major sending countries at the time are informative:[3]

	e_o
United States, Whites, Death Registration Area, 1901–1910	52.5
United States, Blacks, Death Registration Area, 1901–1910	35.7
Italy, 1901–1910	44.8
Germany, 1901–1910	48.3
Bulgaria, 1900–1905	40.3
Russia, 1896–1899	33.4
England and Wales, 1901–1910	52.4
Netherlands, 1900–1910	53.4
Belgium, 1891–1900	48.8
France, 1898–1903	49.1
Norway, 1901–1910	57.7
Sweden, 1901–1910	57.0
Denmark, 1906–1910	57.9

Clearly, the Southern and Eastern European countries from which the bulk of the new immigrants were coming had poorer health conditions than whites in the United States Death Registration Area, which itself had worse mortality than the United States as a whole (Preston and Haines 1991). Western European countries had mortality levels nearly the same as the United States, whereas the predominantly rural Scandinavian countries had markedly better mortality. Judging from data on children-ever-born and -surviving from the 1911 Irish census, Ireland almost certainly had better mortality conditions than England, an advan-

[3]Sources: Glover (1921, Table 82) except Bulgaria, Russia, and Belgium, which were taken from unpublished documentation of the empirical life tables on which the Coale and Demeny (1966) model life tables were based.

tage that is principally attributable to its rurality (Preston and Haines 1991: Chapter 5).

Once in the United States, the foreign-born population as a whole had somewhat worse mortality than native-born whites. Life expectancy at age 15 for foreign-born white women in the Death Registration Area was 46.1 in 1901 and 47.8 in 1910, compared to 49.0 and 50.0 for native white women (Glover 1921, Tables 21–26). Nativity differences in life expectancy were similar for males.

A study of adult mortality among the foreign-born in New York and Pennsylvania in 1910 showed considerable variation in levels among ethnic groups (Dublin and Baker 1920):

	Female Age-Standardized Death Rates per 1000, Ages 10+	
	Pennsylvania	New York
Native-born of Native Parentage (NWNP)	12.3	12.4
Foreign-born	16.0	16.2
Austria-Hungary	13.5	12.4
Russia	12.7	12.3
Italy	12.6	13.7
Germany	14.2	14.4
England, Wales, Scotland	15.1	15.8
Ireland	20.5	23.5

In comparison to mortality levels in the countries of origin, these figures are noteworthy for the comparatively low mortality levels of Russians and the very high mortality of the Irish. Probably most of the Russian immigrants in New York and Pennsylvania were Jews, because they represented 43.8 percent of all Russian immigrants between 1899 and 1910 and a higher fraction of those in the Northeast (Dublin and Baker 1920). Jews were widely credited at the time with exceptionally low mortality relative to their living conditions (e.g., Weber 1899).

The Irish disadvantage for young adults in the United States was largely attributable to high mortality from tuberculosis (Dublin and Baker 1920). Ireland itself was 80 percent rural, but the large bulk of Irish immigrants settled in cities in the United States, where they were sometimes exposed to this devastating disease for the first time. Of course, former residents of rural areas in other countries also settled disproportionately in American cities but did not appear to experience the same excessive mortality from tuberculosis as the Irish. Whatever the cause of excessive Irish adult mortality from tuberculosis, it was probably reflected in childhood mortality as well. Although tuberculosis was not listed as a major cause of death among children, it was undoubtedly underrecorded because its symptoms were less apparent than they were among adults. Autopsy studies in several cities around the turn of the century showed that 10 percent or more of infants who died were infected with tuberculosis (von Pirquet 1909). Woodbury (1925, p. 35) reported that offspring of tubercular mothers in Baltimore in 1915 had 2.65 times the infant mortality rate of offspring of nontubercular mothers. Eighty-two percent of their excess deaths were ascribed to some cause other than tuberculosis. We expect that ethnic differences in child mortality will reflect not only differences in economic and social conditions and specific child care practices among the groups but also differences in the health conditions of mothers.[4]

Child Mortality in the 1910 Census

We focus in this chapter on an index of child mortality that is computed for individual women below age 50 in the 1910 PUS. The index is the ratio of cumulative child deaths that a woman has experienced (i.e., the difference between her numbers of children born and surviving) to her expected number of child deaths. The expected number of deaths is calculated by multiplying her number of children-ever-born by an expected proportion dead. The expected proportion dead is based in turn on an estimate of the length of her children's exposure to the risk of mortality, combined with a "West" model life table, level 13.73 (Coale and Demeny 1983).[5] This level of mortality gives a ratio of actual to expected deaths of 1.000 for the sample as a whole. It translates into an estimate of q(5)—the cumulative probability of child death before age 5—of .178 in the model "West" life table system. This level falls between the q(5) of .182 in the Death Registration Area life table of 1900–1902 and .161 in the life table for 1909–1911 (Glover 1921).[6] By "dating"

[4]Leavitt (1986, Chapter 3) provides a useful compilation of information about the generally poor health conditions of American women that affected their maternal performance at the turn of the century.

[5]A model life table is a representation of the average life table at a particular level of mortality for populations who belong to a particular mortality "family." Members of a family have similar age patterns of mortality. As noted in Appendix 3A, a "Far Eastern" model life table is used for blacks because its age pattern of mortality appears more appropriate. This model is chosen in such a way that it has the same q(5) value as West level 13.5.

[6]Although child mortality was higher in the Death Registration Area than in the nation as a whole for both whites and blacks, most of the bias is offset in overall figures by the very low proportion of blacks in the Death Registration Area. This result is demonstrated for the 1900 census in Preston and Haines (1984), and preliminary analysis of the 1910 census shows much the same pattern.

the mortality experience of children whose mortality is reported by mothers (United Nations 1983), we estimate that the mortality levels examined in this chapter apply to calendar year 1902, on average.

We have used a variety of methods to estimate the length of exposure of children to the risk of mortality. For the large majority of women, who were in their first marriage and whose husband was present in the household, we use the woman's duration of marriage as the indicator of exposure. For women who were not in their first marriage or whose husband was absent, we use the age distribution of their surviving children in the household as the indicator of exposure. Details of the construction of the index can be found in Appendix 3A, this chapter.

Table 3.2 presents values of the index of child mortality for major social and regional groups identifiable in the 1910 census. Note that the probability of dying before age 5 for a group (q(5)) can be estimated by multiplying the index by .178, the value of q(5) used as a standard. The results contain few surprises in light of results from the 1900 census (Preston and Haines 1991). Residents of urban areas (places with 1,000 or more inhabitants) had substantially higher child mortality than rural residents, and their disadvantage increased with city size. Midwesterners enjoyed the lowest levels of child mortality, and mothers who were literate, who spoke English, who were not in the labor force, and whose husbands were in farming also had below-average child mortality.

Children of foreign-born women had mortality levels that were 23 percent (1.069/.870) higher than those of native white women born to native-born mothers (NWNP). However, second-generation women (those who were born in the United States to foreign-born mothers) had a child mortality level that was within 1 percent of that of NWNP. Negro and mulatto women (henceforth referred to as blacks) had extremely high child mortality, 71 percent above that of NWNP.

Using model life tables as a standard, native–foreign-born differences in child mortality are consistent in magnitude and direction with measured differences in adult mortality between the groups. Both the 23 percent difference in child mortality between the foreign-born and NWNP, and the differences of about 2.5 years in life expectancy at age 15 between natives and the foreign-born that we cited earlier, are equivalent to a difference of 1.5–2.0 "levels" in the Coale-Demeny West model life table system. This standard appears highly appropriate for the U.S. population at this time (Preston and Haines 1991). That is, the mortality of foreign-born adults as indicated by vital registration data is about the same "distance" (in a model life table system) from the mortality of natives as is the mortality of their children from that of natives' children. No unique disadvantage for *children* of the foreign-born is evident; they appear to share the disadvantages of their parents.

Among migrants, the child mortality rate differs substantially be-

TABLE 3.2

Index of Child Mortality for Major Social Groupings:
United States, 1910

	Child Mortality Index	Number of Women	Number of Children-Ever-Born
All Women	1.000	46,766	172,938
Race and Nativity of Woman			
White	.922	41,320	149,237
Foreign-born	1.069	9,473	39,292
Married after immigration	.954	4,797	18,313
Married before immigration	1.206	2,741	12,950
Native-born, foreign mother	.864	6,742	22,648
Native-born, native mother	.870	24,498	84,996
Black and Mulatto	1.486	5,118	22,250
Black	1.508	3,942	17,531
Mulatto	1.407	1,176	4,719
Other	1.536	328	1,451
Nativity of Husband (whites only)			
Foreign-born	1.036	9,555	39,318
Native-born, foreign mother	.829	5,530	18,944
Native-born, native mother	.867	21,731	75,808
Nativity of Husband and Wife (whites only)			
Husband Foreign			
Wife foreign	1.072	7,126	30,604
Wife native, foreign mother	.899	1,484	5,505
Wife native, native mother	.898	916	3,080
Husband Native, with Foreign Mother			
Wife foreign	.979	781	3,012
Wife native, foreign mother	.801	2,606	9,162
Wife native, native mother	.800	2,122	6,690
Husband Native, with Native Mother			
Wife foreign	.958	656	2,085
Wife native, foreign mother	.839	1,965	5,792
Wife native, native mother	.865	18,965	67,342
Region			
New England	1.049	3,200	11,030
Mid-Atlantic	1.067	9,829	33,881
East North Central	.869	9,308	31,786
West North Central	.798	5,618	20,613
South Atlantic	1.125	6,368	26,714
East South Central	1.071	4,338	17,742
West South Central	1.083	4,638	19,480
Mountain	1.121	1,312	5,012
Pacific	.807	2,154	6,679

TABLE 3.2 (*continued*)

	Child Mortality Index	Number of Women	Number of Children-Ever-Born
Rural-Urban and City-Size			
Rural	.942	22,172	91,132
Urban	1.063	24,528	81,507
10 Largest cities	1.168	6,294	21,275
Other 25,000 +	1.070	8,454	27,277
5,000–24,999	1.032	5,069	16,921
1,000–4,999	.942	4,711	16,034
Ten largest cities (by size in 1900)			
New York	1.218	2,524	8,828
Chicago	1.089	1,111	3,714
Philadelphia	1.316	795	2,754
St. Louis	1.016	357	1,117
Boston	1.125	334	1,114
Cleveland	.978	286	947
Baltimore	1.271	284	1,004
Buffalo	1.003	211	688
San Francisco	.861	199	541
Cincinnati	1.200	193	568
Marital Status			
Married 1, husband present	.950	39,233	145,439
Married 1, husband absent	1.147	1,058	2,894
Married 2 +, husband present	1.384	2,731	11,117
Married 2 +, husband absent	1.421	141	528
Divorced	1.082	412	1,110
Widowed	1.186	3,191	11,850
Woman Able to Read?			
No	1.386	3,930	19,418
Yes	.948	42,120	150,805
Husband Able to Read?			
No	1.369	3,162	15,296
Yes	.938	38,552	140,224
Husband's and Wife's Literacy			
Both able to read	.912	36,390	130,232
Only wife can read	1.170	5,730	20,573
Only husband can read	1.268	2,162	9,992
Neither can read	1.417	1,641	8,288
Woman's Ability to Speak English			
Does not speak English	1.260	3,242	13,951
Speaks English	.977	43,523	158,984

TABLE 3.2 (continued)

	Child Mortality Index	Number of Women	Number of Children-Ever-Born
Woman's Speaking English by Literacy			
Does not speak English			
Does not read	1.369	1,263	5,678
Does read	1.179	1,833	7,700
Speaks English			
Does not read	1.394	2,667	13,740
Does read	.935	40,286	143,102
Husband's Ability to Speak English			
Does not speak English	1.311	1,946	8,081
Does speak English	.963	40,015	148,464
Husband's Occupation			
Not in the labor force	1.009	514	1,897
Manager, professional specialist	.884	3,026	9,138
Technical, sales, support	.827	4,823	14,171
Service	1.158	1,420	4,680
Farming, forestry, fishing	.926	15,542	67,056
Precision labor	.998	7,452	26,987
Operator, fabricator, laborer	1.151	9,067	32,189
Military/Not specified	.832	116	424
Husband Out of Work at All in Last Year?			
No husband	1.180	4,802	16,382
No	1.032	18,981	64,942
Yes	1.176	4,161	15,975
Not in labor force	1.015	505	1,847
Woman's Occupation			
Not in labor force	.947	39,677	145,957
Working	1.311	6,535	24,781
Manager, professional specialist	1.065	296	836
Technical, sales, support	.994	392	1,113
Service	1.512	2,270	8,096
Farming, forestry, fishing	1.235	2,427	11,417
Precision labor	1.091	539	1,557
Operator, fabricator, laborer	1.404	600	1,732
Military/Not specified	.781	11	30
Farm Living by Mortgage Status[1]			
Mortgage Status: Blank			
Not farm	1.115	20,542	68,152
Farm	1.009	6,149	26,063

TABLE 3.2 (*continued*)

	Child Mortality Index	Number of Women	Number of Children-Ever-Born
Mortgage Status: Owned Outright			
Not farm	.978	6,177	21,937
Farm	.813	5,216	23,000
Mortgage Status: Mortgaged			
Not farm	.950	4,274	15,320
Farm	.790	3,105	14,007
Mortgage Status: Probably Owned Outright			
Not farm	1.119	956	3,074
Farm	.786	78	319
Farm Living by Ownership			
Ownership Status: Owned or Mortgaged			
Not farm	.967	10,675	38,411
Farm	.806	8,362	37,198
Ownership Status: Rented			
Not farm	1.115	20,484	67,958
Farm	1.009	6,148	26,030
Ownership Status: Probably Owned			
Not farm	1.142	782	2,393
Farm	.572	37	160

[1]The categories "Probably owned" and "Probably owned outright" arise because the question in the census was supposed to be answered by an "O" for ownership and "R" for rented, and "M" for mortgaged and "F" for owned free. Instead, the enumerator frequently put a check mark. This is what we term "probably owned" and "probably owned outright."

tween women who married before immigration and those who married after immigration (Table 3.2). Child mortality levels were 26 percent higher among the former group than among the latter. This difference probably reflects many factors, including different selectivity processes for younger and older migrants. Some of the children of those married abroad were undoubtedly born abroad and experienced the higher child mortality levels of Southern and Eastern Europe. They would also have faced the hazards of passage and resettlement. In the aggregate, however, the children of such women would probably have experienced most of their exposure to risk of death in the United States. Foreign-born women in our sample who married abroad were married an average of 5.87 years before immigrating to the United States. They had been married an average of 15.04 years at the time of the census, so that an average of 61 percent of their married years had been spent in the United States; an even higher fraction of their children's exposure to death occurred in the United States.

Accounting for Differences in Mortality by Nativity

A major question that we will examine is the extent to which differences in child mortality by nativity and ethnicity are explicable in terms of the social, economic, and residential distinctions measured in the census. Multivariate analysis is the most precise means of investigating this question, but a useful introduction is provided by examining how the different nativity groups are distributed on variables related to mortality differentials.

Table 3.3 presents such information for some of the major variables available in the census. It also shows the mortality index for groups of women classified by these variables and nativity. With this information, we can ask a simple question: how much of the nativity differences in child mortality would be eliminated if a particular group were distributed among categories of a variable in the same way as were NWNP? There are two basic ways to answer this question. One uses the gross "effects" of a particular variable in the full sample, shown in Table 3.2, to weight the compositional differences. In other words, all the raw differences in mortality according to literacy, for example, are ascribed to literacy per se. This is the normal procedure used in standardization. A second procedure uses the net effects of variables of mortality, once all other variables are controlled in a multivariate framework (described below), to weight the compositional differences.

More precisely, we compute for each variable

Gross effect of compositional differences $\qquad = \Sigma \ M_i(c_i^J - c_i^N)$

M_i = mortality index for category i in the full sample

c_i^J = proportion of births in nativity group J that are in category i

c_i^N = proportion of births in native-native group that are in category i

Net effect of compositional differences $\qquad = \Sigma_i \ R_i(c_i^J - c_i^N), \textbf{ where}$

R_i = regression coefficient for category i in the full sample (from Appendix Table B)

TABLE 3.3
Child Mortality Index, by Nativity and Certain Other Variables, and Distribution of Nativity Groups on those Variables: United States, 1910

	Foreign-born		Native Whites with: Foreign Mother		Native Whites with: Native Mother		Black	
	Index	% CEB	Index	% CEB	Index	% CEB	Index	% CEB
Region								
New England	1.823	14.84	.967	8.12	.862	3.67	1.852	.56
Mid-Atlantic	1.815	37.37	1.066	26.53	.869	14.37	1.844	2.95
E N Central	1.452	23.48	.771	29.60	.812	17.51	1.475	2.19
W N Central	1.428	12.50	.647	18.94	.799	12.43	1.451	1.60
S Atlantic	1.421	1.83	1.094	2.73	.912	17.49	1.443	46.02
E S Central	1.441	.41	.897	1.57	.882	13.39	1.464	25.18
W S Central	1.522	2.55	.872	3.56	.934	14.38	1.546	20.90
Mountain	2.391	2.49	.708	3.63	1.192	3.21	2.429	.40
Pacific	.662	4.53	.878	5.31	.644	3.53	—	—
Rural-Urban								
Rural	.865	24.72	.716	34.42	.857	65.19	1.363	71.99
Urban	1.136	75.28	.934	65.58	.898	34.81	1.806	28.01
10 Largest	1.186	31.00	1.080	20.91	1.056	4.16	2.052	3.01
Other 25,000+	1.130	25.09	.913	23.43	.864	10.83	1.968	10.89
5,000–24,999	1.092	12.39	.891	11.80	.914	8.99	1.688	6.38
1,000–4,999	1.010	6.80	.721	9.44	.857	10.82	1.577	7.73
Marital Status								
1st mar, H pres*	1.048	88.01	.807	86.27	.895	86.28	1.399	67.49
1st mar, H abs*	1.184	1.36	1.270	1.58	.957	1.48	1.386	2.94
2+ mar, H pres*	1.316	4.00	1.366	4.79	1.150	6.04	1.821	13.14
2+ mar, H abs*	1.128	.24	1.042	.19	1.041	.24	2.171	.76

Divorced	1.136	.35	.821	.53	.974	.64	1.288	1.25
Widowed	1.171	6.05	1.076	6.65	.939	5.32	1.596	14.43
Woman Able to Read?								
Illiterate	1.283	16.55	1.082	1.40	1.206	4.80	1.558	34.55
Literate	1.025	81.62	.860	97.48	.853	94.07	1.442	62.36
Husband Able to Read?								
No husband	1.170	8.00	1.095	8.94	.948	7.69	1.567	19.37
Illiterate	1.310	10.06	.979	1.72	1.140	5.10	1.566	27.47
Literate	1.029	81.44	.835	88.87	.848	86.71	1.412	51.88
Woman Speaks English?								
Illegible	—	—	—	—	—	—	—	—
No	1.210	27.64	.914	2.00	1.518	1.73	1.409	.96
Yes	1.015	72.36	.858	98.00	.860	98.27	1.488	99.04
Husband's Occupation								
No husband	1.170	8.00	1.095	8.94	.948	7.69	1.567	19.37
Not in labor force	.811	1.16	1.120	1.30	.902	1.10	2.225	.50
Man., prof., spec	.987	4.44	.826	7.92	.828	6.05	1.665	1.27
Tech, sales, supp	.965	9.77	.779	11.75	.758	8.58	1.551	.63
Service	1.160	3.56	1.006	3.88	.971	1.80	1.722	3.44
Farm, forest, fish	.822	16.98	.684	25.33	.835	47.63	1.351	55.82
Precision prodn.	1.081	25.07	.864	19.70	.929	13.44	1.595	3.74
Ops, fabs., labs	1.216	30.68	.982	20.96	.972	13.48	1.772	14.98
Military/N.S.	.851	.35	.595	.22	.787	.21	1.174	.23

TABLE 3.3 (continued)

| | Foreign-born | | Native Whites with: | | | | Black | |
| | | | Foreign Mother | | Native Mother | | | |
	Index	% CEB	Index	% CEB	Index	% CEB	Index	% CEB
Husband out of Work in Last Year?								
No husband	1.170	8.00	1.095	8.94	.948	7.69	1.567	19.37
Not out of work	1.107	46.73	.877	44.40	.906	33.63	1.570	29.91
Out of work	1.213	14.03	1.057	8.80	1.002	7.50	1.770	7.67
Not in labor force	.837	1.13	1.120	1.30	.908	1.08	2.357	.41
Blank/Illegible	.923	30.11	.723	36.56	.815	50.10	1.334	42.63
Woman's Labor-Force Participation								
In labor force	1.186	4.53	1.117	4.35	.987	4.90	1.571	33.69
Not in labor force	1.055	90.79	.843	91.08	.858	89.83	1.392	45.11
Blank/illegible	1.176	4.68	.833	4.34	1.036	4.29	1.553	21.21

NOTE: % CEB is the percentage of births to women in a particular nativity or racial group that occurred to women in the specified category.

*H pres and H abs refer to women with husbands present and absent, respectively.

The regression analysis is described below. Our principal interest is in the comparison between the foreign-born and NWNP and between blacks and NWNP, because the second generation has a child mortality level that is very close to that of NWNP.

Table 3.4 shows that the foreign-born had an adverse distribution on most variables. That is, their child mortality would have been reduced had they been distributed on a variable in the same proportions as native-natives. By far their most serious disadvantage was their distribution by city size: for example, 75.3 percent of births to foreign-born women occurred to those living in urban areas, compared to only 34.8 percent among NWNP. If they had the same distribution of births as NWNP in the city-size categories shown in Table 3.3, the difference of .199 in the child mortality index between the groups (1.069-.870 from Table 3.2) would have been reduced by .082 in the gross effects and .069 in the net. These effects are similar because city-size differences in mortality are robust to the introduction of other variables.

Using the more precisely measured net effects, some 35 percent of

TABLE 3.4

Estimated Change in Mortality Index
if the Distribution of Certain Variables
Was the Same as That of Native Whites of Native Parentage

| | Effects | | | |
| | Foreign-born | | Blacks | |
	Gross	Net	Gross	Net
Region	−.028	.007	.085	−.007
Rural/Urban/City-size	.082	.069	−.005	−.002
Woman's Characteristics				
Marital status	−.008	−.007*	.058	.025*
Woman's literacy	.053	.018	.134	.045
Woman's labor force participation	−.003	−.001	.158	.052
Woman's English-speaking ability	.073	.036	−.002	−.001
Husband's Characteristics				
Husband's literacy	.023	.007	.125	.038
Husband's occupation	.055	.001	.017	.021
Husband's unemployment in previous year	.040	.008	.004	.001

* Based on results of regression analysis that does not include husband's characteristics.

the excess mortality of the foreign-born (.069/.199) is attributable to the fact that they lived disproportionately in cities, especially large cities. If we treat each of the ten largest cities separately in this decomposition, we can account for 48 percent of the excess mortality among the foreign-born, in large part because of their concentration in the high-mortality cities of New York and Philadelphia. These cities had made limited progress in cleaning up water supplies by the turn of the century and had made virtually no progress in purifying milk supplies, probably a more important factor in child mortality at the time (Preston and Haines 1991: Chapter 1). Because of the congestion in cities, infectious diseases were also more likely to spread from person to person than among rural residents, who were partially protected from one another by distance.

Yet this conclusion is an oversimplification because there were interactions between city size and nativity. In fact, the excess mortality of large cities was most prominent among the foreign-born, the second generation, and blacks. Among NWNP, there was only 5 percent higher mortality in urban than in rural areas, compared to 30 percent among second-generation women, 31 percent among the foreign-born, and 33 percent among blacks (Table 3.3). In part, this reflects the fact that NWNP urban dwellers were more likely to live in smaller cities. But even within the large cities, their advantage was pronounced; in Boston, Cleveland, Buffalo, and San Francisco NWNP actually had lower child mortality than NWNP in rural areas (not shown in tables). However, their indexes were 1.07, 1.17, and 1.28 in New York, Philadelphia, and Baltimore, respectively. It appears, therefore, that NWNP in cities were able to find protection from the worst hazards of urban living. Much of that protection, as we suggest later, appears attributable to their better social standing on such variables as literacy and occupation.

Other variables are less helpful in accounting for the excess mortality of the foreign-born (Table 3.4). Only two of the remaining variables explain more than a .01 difference between the mortality of the foreign-born and NWNP in the net effects. Inability to speak English was a liability, and its greater frequency among the foreign-born explains .036, or 18 percent, of their excess mortality of .199. The greater extent of illiteracy among the foreign-born accounts for .018, or 9 percent, of their disadvantage. However, the collective effect of all variables is considerable. Adding the net effects together, we account for .138, or 69 percent, of the original difference of .199 between the foreign-born and the NWNP. Thus, most of the child mortality disadvantage of the foreign-born appears explicable in terms of variables other than nativity. These variables help demonstrate the pathways through which the foreign-born achieved excess mortality; but they do not "explain away" their excess, because foreign birth is causally prior to all the other variables.

This decomposition is much less successful among blacks. A glance at Table 3.3 is sufficient to indicate that blacks suffered extremely high mortality within every category of every variable, so their high overall mortality level could not be entirely attributable to an adverse distribution on other variables that we can measure. In some respects, they were actually advantaged relative to NWNP, most obviously in their high proportion in rural areas. In addition, 92 percent of their births occurred to women living in the South, a (mildly) favored region in the multivariate analyses.

But other variables do tell part of the story. The higher illiteracy rates among both black mothers and fathers (35 percent illiteracy in both cases) and the higher labor force participation among black women each accounts for 6–9 percent of their excess mortality of .616 (1.486–.870 from Table 3.2) relative to NWNP. The greater extent of marital disruption among blacks accounts for 4 percent of the original differences. However, by adding the net effects in Table 3.4 we can "explain" only .172, or 28 percent, of the original excess in black child mortality. The difference of .444 that is left *unexplained* is twice the size of the *original* foreign-born excess and dwarfs the unexplained difference of .048 for the foreign-born. Being black in 1910 was clearly associated with disadvantages that are manifest in child mortality levels and that are only imperfectly reflected in their distribution on other measured variables.

The Mortality Levels of Specific Ethnic Groups

To this point, we have examined the mortality of the foreign-born and second-generation Americans irrespective of nation of origin. To examine mortality among specific ethnic groups, we use an ethnic classification system that combines information on place of birth and mother tongue. Once women are divided into foreign-born and native-born, Polish and Jewish women are defined entirely on the basis of their mother tongue (Polish and Yiddish, respectively); Irish and British (England/Wales/ Scotland) women are defined entirely on the basis of their place of birth; and Italian, German, and Scandinavian women are defined by both place of birth and mother tongue. That is, all three groups were born in the appropriate country or region and listed a mother tongue of Italian, German, or one of the Scandinavian languages. The group of Eastern Europeans is defined by place of birth but excludes those whose mother tongue was Polish or Yiddish. (For more details on this group, consult Appendix B, this volume.) French Canadians and English Canadians were born in Canada and had a mother tongue of French or English, respectively. The

TABLE 3.5

Child Mortality among Major Ethnic Groups, United States: 1910

	Foreign-born		Native-born of Foreign Mother	
	Mortality Index	Number of Births	Mortality Index	Number of Births
British	1.156	3,176	.900	2,791
Irish	1.223	3,879	1.007	5,463
Scandinavian	.891	3,673	.615	1,366
Eastern European	1.081	4,820	.800	535
French Canadian	1.401	1,407	1.097	750
English Canadian	.858	1,725	.806	912
German	.911	6,757	.772	8,793
Jewish	.960	3,547	.725	90
Polish	1.260	3,312	.811	260
Italian	1.266	4,133	1.116	220
Other Non-Black	1.197	2,804	.948	3,272

classification system for women born in the United States whose mother was born abroad is identical, except that the place of birth and mother tongue criteria are applied to the woman's mother rather than to the woman herself.

Table 3.5 presents values of the index of child mortality for these ethnic groups. (Values for more detailed groups can be found in Appendix B.) Among the ten major groups of the foreign-born whom we distinguish, six had mortality indexes above 1.00 (i.e., above the national average). The large groups of Irish, Polish, and Italian women had child mortality levels that were 22–27 percent above average. French Canadians had the highest mortality, 40 percent above average. On the other hand, English Canadians had a mortality level within 2 percent of the NWNP figure of .870. Other groups with below-average mortality were Scandinavians, Germans, and Jews.

Some carryover of differences in child mortality in countries of origin is apparent in these figures. The high mortality of immigrants from Eastern Europe and Italy, and the low mortality of those from Scandinavia, correspond to the relative position of mortality in their nations of origin. Similarly, within Canada, Quebec had much higher child mortality than the remaining provinces when complete vital registration first became available in 1925–1927 (Nagnur 1986). A family reconstitution study in the Saguenay region in northern Quebec finds exceptionally high infant mortality rates of 215–222/1000 in 1900–1909 (Gauvreau 1990). Within Montreal itself, French Canadians had 50 percent higher infant mortality in 1859 than Protestants or Irish Catholics (Thornton and Olson 1990).

German and Irish experiences are at variance with national rankings. As noted above, the Irish in the United States faced circumstances radically different from those in Ireland, with a heavy concentration of Irish Americans in large cities. In Germany, there was enormous interregional variation in infant and child mortality, variation that appears closely associated with differences in breast-feeding practices (Kintner 1987). It is possible that the Germans who came to the United States in the period 1870–1910 were disproportionately drawn from lower mortality areas. Certainly there is nothing in Table 3.1 that would suggest that German American women breast-fed their babies for unusually short periods.

Some light is cast on the nature of the mortality transmission from the Old World to the New by examining ethnic differences in child mortality between women who married abroad and those who married in the United States. Table 3.6 shows that, for every group but two, child mortality was higher among women who married abroad. One of the exceptions was British women, where the disparity was only 1 percent. The only major exception is the Irish, among whom child mortality was 7 percent higher for those who married in the United States than for those who married abroad. This result is consistent with the suggestion

TABLE 3.6

Child Mortality among the Foreign-born
Relating to Marriage in the United States or Abroad,
United States: 1910

	Married in the United States		Married before Immigration	
	Mortality Index	Number of Births	Mortality Index	Number of Births
British	1.095	1,460	1.080	943
Irish	1.139	2,492	1.072	447
Scandinavian	.858	2,235	.950	789
Eastern European	1.007	2,020	1.201	1,962
French-speaking Canadian	1.431	717	1.488	464
English-speaking Canadian	.808	889	.848	417
German	.829	3,868	1.190	1,230
Jewish	.623	1,089	1.099	2,055
Polish	1.030	1,358	1.456	1,440
Italian	1.109	1,244	1.359	2,433
Other, Non-Black	.768	1,097	1.150	932

that health conditions for women and children in Ireland were less hostile than those they met in the United States.

The largest disparities between those married abroad and those married in the United States are observed among Eastern and Southern European women. These women came to the United States from what were generally more severe health environments, as shown above. It is not surprising that women who spent more time in that environment, and sometimes bore children there, had higher cumulative child mortality levels. It is also likely that some married women were left to raise children in Europe while their husbands preceded them to the United States. The difference between the marital-location groups ranged from 23 percent higher mortality for Italian women married abroad than for those married in the United States to 76 percent among Jewish women. Immigrants from Eastern and Southern Europe were also more likely than others to have been married abroad. For women whose place of residence at marriage could be established, between 49 percent and 66 percent of births among Poles, Jews, Italians, and Eastern Europeans occurred to women who married abroad. Presumably, a much smaller fraction of *births* to these groups occurred abroad, since childbearing would often start or continue in the United States among those married abroad.[7] But these women must be treated with care in any statistical analysis: some of their experience with child mortality is not simply a reflection of practices and conditions transmitted from Europe but also of their living environment and child care practice while they were still in Europe.

As indicated earlier in Table 3.2, second-generation women in the United States had child mortality levels that, on average, scarcely differed from those of NWNP. This equality was achieved despite their adverse distribution on such variables as city size. Table 3.5 shows that, for each of the ten ethnic groups, child mortality was lower among the second generation than among the first generation. The mean reduction from one generation to the next is a very substantial 23 percent. Although mortality levels improved from one generation to the next, the rates for the Irish, Italians, and French Canadians remained 16 percent–28 percent above those of NWNP. If we restrict the foreign-born comparison group to those married in the United States, the second generation still had lower mortality for all but Italians, where the difference was only .01, and Jews, for whom only ninety births were recorded in the second generation.

[7]For members of the various ethnic groups who married abroad, the mean percentage of their married lives spent abroad was 21 percent for Germans and Irish, 36 percent for the British, 39 percent for Poles, 42 percent for French Canadians, 44 percent for East Europeans, 46 percent for Italians, and 49 percent for Jews.

The results shown in Table 3.5 are likely to be more reliable than those based on vital registration. The Death Registration Area covered only 26 percent of the country at the turn of the century (Preston and Haines 1991). To create an infant mortality rate from registration data requires taking numerators from one source (death registration) and denominators from another (birth registration), and raises the possibility of differential coverage and inconsistent reporting of mother's place of birth between the two. Lieberson's (1980, p. 47) tabulation of registration figures on infant mortality rates by mother's country of birth since 1900 shows some clear anomalies. For example, Polish women have very low rates in 1900 (112/1000 versus 142/1000 for native whites), which rise to 173/1000 in 1917 and 124/1000 in 1919. The census sample has the considerable virtue of providing reports taken from one source. Registration data are consistent in showing a very large black excess in infant mortality; race reporting was likely to be quite consistent between sources. However, only 4 percent of black births occurred in areas covered by death registration at the turn of the century.

Multivariate Analysis

The most efficient and precise way of examining the extent to which the relative mortality levels of the various ethnic groups can be explained by other variables is through multivariate analysis. We choose as the dependent variable for this analysis the ratio of dead children to expected dead children for each woman, as described above and in Appendix A. The observation for each woman is weighted by her number of births, in order both to reduce problems of heteroskedasticity and to make births rather than women the fundamental units of analysis. Weighted least-squares regression is then employed. This procedure has been investigated by Trussell and Preston (1982) and found to have good statistical properties, similar in large samples to those of more elaborate schemes (e.g., Tobit) for studying limited value dependent variables.

Our analytic strategy is to introduce successive waves of independent variables and examine how ethnic mortality differences are affected by each additional stage of information. First, we introduce characteristics of the mother that were strongly affected, although not completely determined, by conditions early in her life: her literacy (i.e., whether she can read) and her ability to speak English. Then we introduce these same two early-life variables for her husband (adding a variable to indicate whether or not she has a husband). Finally, we introduce the other major variables available in the census: the woman's and her husband's labor force status and occupational category, whether they lived on a farm, whether they owned or rented their home, their region of residence, and the population size of their area of residence. The distribution of the various ethnic groups on some of these variables is presented in Table 3.7. We add one variable that is constructed from noncensus sources: the mean level of earnings in one's state of residence in 1900, controlling occupational structure in the state. This variable was constructed by Michael Haines (Preston and Haines 1991, Appendix A). Regression coefficients for the nonethnic variables can be found in Appendix 3B to this chapter.[8]

In all regressions, we introduce a time location variable that indicates the number of years before the 1910 census to which a woman's child mortality experience pertains. This variable is constructed from information on her age (see United Nations Population Division, 1983). The variable is designed to control for any time trends in mortality, and its positive (and significant) coefficient in all regressions indicates that child mortality was declining.

Results pertaining to ethnicity and race are presented in Table 3.8 and Figure 3.1. The right-most column of Table 3.8 presents the final-stage regression coefficients for ethnic groups when the sample is purged of foreign-born women who were married outside the United States (and of the 10.2 percent of foreign-born women in the sample whose date of immigration was missing). In all cases, we present the difference in the mortality index between the ethnic group and NWNP, as well as the statistical significance of that difference. We will discuss these results in combinations of ethnic groups whose members show similar patterns.

Germans, Scandinavians, and English Canadians

At no stage of the analysis do these groups have mortality that differed significantly from that of NWNP: their mortality was below the national average before any account was taken of their other characteristics, and it remained below average after such an accounting. The introduction of other variables had little effect on their relative positions,

---

[8]We created a set of variables to indicate whether foreign-born wives were married to native husbands and whether native wives were married to foreign husbands or to the large second-generation groups of British and Germans. These crossover groups did not have mortality levels that differed substantially or significantly from groups that married within their nativity category. The twenty-two detailed male occupational categories are based on the 1910 occupational classification. In Table 3.7 and for females in Appendix 3B, where greater brevity is desired, we use the 1980 classification system because its condensed categories appeared more homogeneous than those in the 1910 classification.

TABLE 3.7

Distribution of Births to Mothers in Various Ethnic Groups on Certain Variables*

	Mother Literate %	Mother Speaks English %	Live in Cities 25,000+ %	First Marriage Husband Present %	Of Women with Husband Present, Proportion Who Are	
					Farming[1] %	Laborers[2] %
British	96.06	99.46	49.28	85.11	8.04	29.15
Irish	95.88	99.64	75.66	81.52	9.96	41.99
Scandinavian	96.35	86.06	30.57	90.25	39.66	21.26
Eastern European	77.85	51.06	45.19	89.64	19.80	37.87
French Canadian	82.73	65.74	45.70	89.91	12.36	48.96
English Canadian	97.80	99.71	46.61	84.46	22.41	19.33
German	95.16	88.68	49.64	86.40	31.12	27.74
Jewish	66.53	60.94	94.35	91.25	.84	22.07
Polish	67.66	45.20	64.13	90.13	8.61	51.63
Italian	45.71	38.42	69.17	92.98	6.35	43.40
Native White with Native Mother	94.05	98.26	15.01	86.20	51.60	14.59
Native Black	62.30	99.06	13.80	67.44	69.45	18.50
Overall	87.20	91.93	28.07	84.10	42.83	20.56

*The distribution refers to the percentage of births that occurred to women in a particular category among women in the 1910 PUS mortality file. See Appendix 3A for a description of the file.

[1] Men with 1980 occupation codes 473–499: Farming, fishing, and forestry.
[2] Men with 1980 occupation codes 703–889: Operators, fabricators, and laborers.

TABLE 3.8

Regression Coefficients Expressing the Difference Between Child Mortality Index for Various Groups of Foreign-born Women and That for Native Women of Native Parentage

Variables Controlled	All Foreign-born Women				Foreign-born Women Married in the U.S.
	Time Location of Births	Plus Mother's Literacy and English	Plus Father's Literacy and English	All Variables Controlled[a]	All Variables Controlled[a]
British	.252**	.260**	.258**	.151**	.127*
Irish	.314**	.321**	.314**	.149**	.115*
Scandinavian	-.008	-.029**	-.031**	.019**	.019
Eastern European	.212**	.083*	.063	.010	.002
French Canadian	.499**	.408**	.399**	.348**	.403**
English Canadian	-.038	-.027	-.028	-.049	-.087
German	.004	-.012	-.012	-.035	-.074
Jewish	.082*	-.048	-.053	-.235**	-.425**
Polish	.388**	.227**	.202**	.115*	.017
Italian	.397**	.181**	.150**	.008	-.006
Native Women with Foreign-born Mothers					
British	.020	.031	.047	-.010	
Irish	.109**	.121**	.142**	.045	

Scandinavian	−.237**	−.225**	−.208**	−.112
East European	−.033	−.433	−.038	−.030
French Canadian	.231**	.215*	.216*	.176*
English Canadian	−.063	−.053	−.042	−.013
German	−.112**	−.103**	−.079**	−.093**
Jewish	−.118	−.119	−.114	−.243
Polish	−.009	−.029	−.036	−.042
Italian	.290	.284	.262	.147
Black Women				
Blacks	.611**	.556**	.525**	.410**

NOTES: *Significant at the 5% level.
  **Significant at the 1% level.

[a]The variable controlled in these regressions can be found in Appendix 3B to this chapter.

FIGURE 3.1
*Mortality among the Children of Foreign-born Mothers
Relative to Children of Native Whites of Native Parentage*

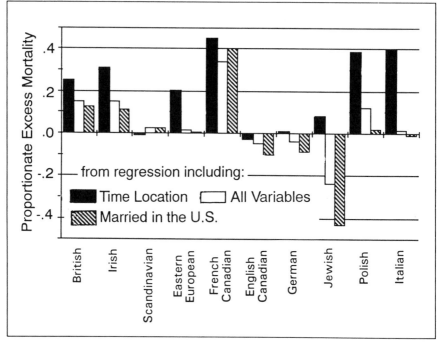

implying that their characteristics on mortality-relevant variables were about the same as those of NWNP. These are the three ethnic groups with the highest fractions of husbands in farming, for example, and they also rank near the top of foreign-born groups in literacy levels (Table 3.7). Germans, the largest ethnic group in both the first and second generations, had high levels of literacy and English-speaking ability. Only 4 percent of German-born mothers could not read, a slightly lower figure than among NWNP, and only 11 percent could not speak English. The largest occupational group among husbands of German-born women, as among NWNP, was farmers, and German-born women in this occupational group actually had lower mortality than NWNP wives of farmers.

Eastern Europeans, Poles, and Italians

Immigrants from Eastern and Southern Europe (excluding Jews, who are dealt with separately) came primarily from the countryside and settled in American cities, where they generally occupied the lower rungs of the social and economic ladder (see Table 3.7). There are vivid accounts of how difficult it was for these groups to adjust from a predominantly outdoor life to one spent largely indoors in cramped quarters (e.g., Davis 1921, Chapter VI). Their low social standing in the United States was reflected in high rates of child mortality. Before controlling other variables, these groups begin with mortality levels that are 21–40 percent above those of NWNP, differences that are highly significant. After all other variables are entered and attention is confined to women who married in the United States, none of the differences is as large as 2 percent and none is significant. Polish-born women as a whole do have 12 percent higher child mortality than NWNP, but the excess disappears when women married abroad are removed.

Thus, the large groups of Eastern and Southern European immigrants appear to have higher mortality in the United States primarily because of their adverse social and economic circumstances and not because of any unusual child care practices or other unmeasured variables associated with ethnicity. That is not to say that these groups did not have child-raising customs that affected mortality—Poles breast-fed for very long periods, for example—only that the net effect of these practices was not marked. In accounting for their high child mortality, much of the explanatory power of social, economic, and residential variables is captured by the woman's literacy and English-speaking abilities alone. When this rudimentary information is added to the regression, the coefficients for Eastern Europeans, Poles, and Italians fall by 61 percent, 41 percent, and 54 percent, respectively. Among Polish women, their husbands' occupational distribution accounts for more of their mortality disadvantage, since 52 percent of their husbands (the highest concentration of any ethnic group) were in occupational category VI: operatives, fabricators, and laborers.

Irish and British

Women born in Ireland and Britain (some of whom were undoubtedly of Irish descent) had 25–32 percent higher child mortality than NWNP, and it was still 11–13 percent higher after all other variables were controlled and attention was limited to women married in the United States. None of the reduction in their excess mortality is attributable to literacy or to the English-speaking ability of mothers or their husbands. A substantial reduction occurs when all other variables are entered, probably reflecting in large measure their predominantly urban locations.

The excess of 11–13 percent that remains after other variables are controlled is, of course, harder to account for. Before ascribing it to child care practices, we should recall that among women in New York State and Pennsylvania in 1910, Irish and British women had the highest mortality levels of any ethnic groups (see text figures above). The causes of death accounting for the excess among adults are not very informative because both groups showed substantially higher mortality than native whites from nearly all causes, although as noted earlier tuberculosis was a special problem among the Irish (Dublin and Baker 1920).

So children of the Irish and British appear to have shared in the hostile disease environment of their parents. One explanation may lie in their housing conditions, which we have measured only very crudely through our ownership/rental variables. Haines' (1989) analysis of American working-class budgets in 1889–1890 found Irish immigrants to be spending significantly less on housing (at a given income level and family composition) than native-born Americans and less than any other ethnic group. The British were also well below average, although not significantly so. Haines finds no evidence that the Irish were spending more than other ethnic groups on alcohol and tobacco, despite suggestions that alcoholism was an unusually serious health problem in the Irish community (Diner 1983, Chapter 5; Davis 1921, pp. 48–49). It is possible that the Irish were buying cheaper alcoholic products or that Haines' data were not representative of the Irish population; rates of hospitalization for alcoholism were high among the Irish in New York State (Davis 1921), and the many accounts of heavy drinking among the Irish are difficult to discount.

French Canadians

The ethnic group with the highest mortality by far were the French Canadians. Their peculiar position was not primarily a consequence of their distribution on other variables that we can measure. Even after all other variables are entered, their mortality was 40 percent higher than that of NWNP. Undoubtedly, their exceptionally short average length of breast-feeding is related to this result. Woodbury (1925) demonstrated that breast-feeding was an important part of the explanation of the very high mortality of French Canadians in eastern cities. Before differences in breast-feeding practices were controlled for in his study, French Canadians had an infant mortality rate that was 83 percent higher than that of native whites; after controlling for breast-feeding patterns, the difference was reduced to 58 percent (Woodbury 1925, pp. 104, 115). Other dimensions in Woodbury's study on which French Canadians were disadvantaged relative to the foreign-born as a whole were a high percentage of births to women outside the optimal age range of 20–34 and a high percentage of mothers who worked during pregnancy and the first year of the infant's life (27 percent and 16 percent, compared to 17 percent and 10 percent for all foreign-born women) (Woodbury 1925, pp. 118, 120). As is evident in Table 3.7 and the first two columns of Table 3.8, French Canadians were also disadvantaged by slightly above-average levels of illiteracy and a large fraction of mothers who did not speak English.

Interestingly, husbands of the French Canadian women earned substantially more than average for the foreign-born in Woodbury's study (1925, p. 122). According to the Children's Bureau study of Manchester, NH, where French Canadians were the most prevalent, they were "generally thrifty, self-respecting people, ambitious to own their homes and to accumulate property. . . . On the whole, they occupy a relatively favorable position among the foreign-born in the community as regards both economic and social status" (Beatric Sheets Danan and Emma Duke, cited in Davis 1921, pp. 62–63).

Through a happy coincidence, Tamara Hareven has explored in considerable depth social relations among Manchester French Canadians in the early part of the century. Using many documentary sources, including interviews in the 1970s with elderly survivors of the period, she paints a picture of family relations that offers some clues about sources of their high infant and child mortality. In her interviews, the thrifty and ambitious character of French Canadians noted by Danan and Duke becomes transformed into an obsession with advancing the family economy, especially by using to the fullest the paid labor of women and children (Hareven 1982; Hareven and Langenbach 1978). "The Canadian families had migrated to Manchester to find work for as many family members as possible" (Hareven 1982, p. 202). As noted above, an unusually high percentage of French Canadian mothers worked during pregnancy and in the early years of a child's life. An unusually high percentage of French Canadian teenagers were also in the labor force, and relatively fewer were in school. A direct tabulation from the 1910 census PUS of 10–19-year-old youth by ethnicity of their mothers shows that, among our ten ethnic groups, French Canadian youth had the second-lowest proportion in school (53.5 percent) and the second-highest proportion in the labor force (37.8 percent), in both cases ranking behind Italians.

One consequence of mothers' working was curtailed breast-feeding, as noted above. Another was that older girls in the family were often left with heavy responsibilities for raising younger siblings and even infants, sometimes with disastrous results (Hareven 1982, pp. 101, 207).

In other cases, children were "loaned" out for the work week and brought home on weekends (Hareven 1982, p. 207). Other families sent young children to live with relatives in Quebec (Hareven 1982, p. 115). In the words of one woman, "When the children come, then you have somebody take care of them or you board them out" (Hareven 1982, p. 202). Hareven notes a certain callousness toward children, citing the case of a girl sent to Quebec at age 4 and retrieved against her wishes at age 12 in order to care for younger siblings (Hareven 1982, p. 109).

The heavy use of children in the work force and home provided some incentive for large families and short birth intervals (Alice Lacasse Olivier, quoted in Hareven and Langenbach 1978, p. 256). Moreover, the strong hold of the Canadian Catholic church on family life also discouraged any steps that would limit the flow of marital births. "All the priests talked about was having children, having children. They used to preach that you had to do what God wanted, and that's what God wanted you to do, to have children. You could do nothing to prevent it" (Hareven and Langenbach 1978, p. 256). She notes that few rebelled against these strictures because they were a "people with a deep, simple, religious faith" (Hareven and Langenbach 1978, p. 257). Extended nursing was thought to be the only legitimate way of restraining marital fertility, but few evidently took advantage of it. The consequence was high fertility and short birth intervals. In Woodbury's study, 42.6 percent of births to French Canadians were of order five or above, by far the highest figure among his seven foreign-born groups (Woodbury 1925, p. 111). They also had the highest percentage of births (7.8 percent) in the combined category "plural births, premature births, and births to mothers who died within one year of confinement" (Woodbury 1925, p. 109).

It is likely that the high child mortality among French Canadians was related to the role of children and women in the family economy. Children were disadvantaged by their mothers' working, most concretely by truncated breast-feeding but also by the quality of care they sometimes received. They were also penalized by a reproductive regime, undergirded by both the family economy and the church, in which births were numerous and closely spaced. It is also possible that their own heavy labor force participation, sometimes involving overstatement of age so that they met the minimum age requirement of 14, exposed them to hardships that are reflected in our child mortality index.

Jews

Foreign-born Jews comprise women who were born abroad and whose mother tongue was Yiddish. Because few German Jews spoke Yiddish, they are for the most part excluded from the group. Foreign-born Jews reported child mortality that was 9 percent higher than that of NWNP before any other variables were controlled. After all other variables are controlled, and attention is limited to Jews married in the United States, their mortality is 43 percent below that of NWNP. This spectacular difference emerges primarily in the last stage of analysis; Jews' child mortality did not appear especially remarkable until account is taken of their adverse concentration in large eastern cities (and, to a lesser extent, in lower economic strata). In other words, their child mortality was unusually low *within* a particular social stratum. When we compare the mortality rate among Jews with husbands in specific occupational groups in which Jews were heavily concentrated to that of other foreign-born women with husbands in those occupations (analysis not shown), we find that children of Jewish tailors had a 13 percent advantage, children of managers in manufacturing a 26 percent advantage, and children of wholesalers and retailers a 25 percent advantage.

This exceptionally favorable mortality of Jewish offspring in the United States had been recognized through death registration data specific to Jewish wards. Weber (1899, pp. 350–351) ascribes the low mortality in New York's tenth ward to the careful observance of sanitary laws by its predominantly Jewish residents: the strict adherence to traditional laws regarding cleanliness, the cooking of food, and habits of eating and drinking. A small study of ethnic differences in Chicago found Jews to have the lowest child mortality rates and ascribed their advantage to their having been urbanized for 2,000 years and having adapted their customs to the conditions of overcrowded city life (Hamilton 1909, p. 78). Jewish children's healthiness was evident not only in mortality rates but also in an unusually small percentage of malnourished children in two surveys in eastern cities (Davis 1921, pp. 37–38).

Low Jewish child mortality was not unique to the United States. Ashby's (1922) study of infant mortality in England notes that Jewish wards in Manchester in 1911 had unusually low infant mortality. His lengthy explanation cites mothers' staying at home and breast-feeding their babies, their strong love for their children so that they would make any sacrifice for their welfare, and scrupulousness about providing wholesome and regular meals and good clothing. "The Jews are not especially clean in themselves, but they insist on having clean food" (Ashby 1922, p. 25). Above all, he suggests, lengthy breast-feeding is the basic reason why so few Jewish children die in infancy. A valuable compilation of comparative infant mortality rates of Jews and non-Jews in twenty-nine European countries or cities in the period 1819–1913 by Schmelz (1971, cited in Condran and Kramarow 1991) shows that Jews had much lower mortality than their neighbors nearly everywhere that they lived.

Their median advantage in the seventy-three region-period combinations investigated was a startling 40 percent, very close to their advantage in the United States (compiled from Condran and Kramarow 1991, Table 1).

Woodbury's study of eight eastern cities between 1911 and 1915 provides substantial quantitative information on factors that may account for low Jewish mortality. Breast-feeding practices account for about 28 percent of the advantage relative to native whites. Before controlling for length of breast-feeding, Jewish children had an infant mortality level that was 43 percent lower than that of native whites, but after controlling for breast-feeding, it was 31 percent lower (Woodbury 1925, pp. 104, 115). Other advantages of Jewish babies were a very low incidence of short preceding birth intervals (16 percent versus 26 percent for native whites); a very low proportion of Jewish mothers who worked during pregnancy (2 percent versus 7 percent for natives and 17 percent for the foreign-born as a group) or during the baby's first year of life (2 percent versus 4 percent and 10 percent). Economically, Jews and French Canadians had the lowest incidence of low-earning husbands among foreign-born women, but the incidence was substantially higher than among natives (45 percent versus 27 percent). (The impression that Jews may have been in economic circumstances similar to other foreign-born groups may reflect the fact that their housing conditions were scarcely better, at least in the Woodbury study.) But these factors combined explain less than half of the Jewish advantage.

It seems that the Jewish advantage in child survival was likely to be a reflection of unmeasured child care practices, having mostly to do with feeding practices and general hygienic standards. The importance of feeding practices is underscored by the causes of death in which Jewish infants were the most advantaged. Their biggest proportionate advantage was in "gastric and intestinal diseases," where the infant mortality rate was 58 percent lower than that of native whites (Woodbury 1925, p. 104). It is interesting to note that the French Canadians showed by far their highest excess mortality in this cause of death (Woodbury 1925, p. 104). Most observers of the time seemed to agree that the Jewish diet was unusually pure, but not all agreed that it was nutritious: "Jewish children suffer from too many pickles, too few vegetables, and too little milk" (Davis 1921, p. 261). The shortage of milk, resulting in part from a proscription against serving meat and milk together, could actually have been a major advantage in view of the enormous infant mortality associated with impure milk (Park and Holt 1903).

It is possible that the low mortality of Jewish children also reflected in part the good health of their mothers and a lower incidence of infectious disease in the home. "Russian" women aged 25–44 had the lowest mortality of any ethnic group in the combined data from New York and Pennsylvania in 1910—6.3/1,000 versus 6.9/1,000 for native women. Their low mortality from tuberculosis was exceptionally notable: 1.06/1,000 versus 1.83/1,000 for native women (Dublin and Baker 1920). This advantage was widely recognized at the time and was sometimes ascribed to natural selection over centuries of urban living (Davis 1921, p. 58). Some of the advantage of Jewish children and adults alike may have reflected an unusually high prevalence of such hygienic practices as hand-washing, as well as a clearer recognition of the interpersonal nature of infectious disease (Condran and Kramarow 1991). The extensive Jewish benefit societies may also have played a role in their successes.

It is also interesting to note that Jewish children were more likely to attend school than other groups. Among the foreign-born groups in 1910 investigated by Jacobs and Greene (Table 7.1), Jewish children were more likely to be in school than the offspring of native parents, although this advantage disappears once other variables are controlled. This result may reflect an unusually strong emphasis on investment in "child quality" that also appears in mortality levels and child-spacing practices. French Canadian children in this age group were the least likely to be in school.

In any event, it is clear that Jews and French Canadians were at opposite ends of the spectrum not only in child mortality but also in many other practices related to it. The most concrete among these is breast-feeding patterns, which account for about 29 percent of the raw difference between the groups in the Woodbury (1925) study. But breast-feeding practices cannot be divorced from other elements of family life, particularly since the health advantages of breast-feeding were widely known at the time (e.g., Meckel 1990). Reproductive patterns, women's work, and children's schooling also sharply distinguished these groups. From the valuable ethnographic accounts of the period, as well as from statistical evidence, a clear distinction in the degree of child-centeredness of French Canadian and Jewish families emerges. This feature of family life, although difficult to measure directly, is likely to be an important source of the differences in child mortality that we have described.

Interactions between Ethnicity and Other Variables in Their Effect on Mortality

One regression analysis was performed on a sample restricted to foreign-born women who were married in the United States in order to investigate whether the mortality of the foreign-born reacted differently to other variables available in the census. Results are shown in Appendix 3B of this chapter. For the most part, the pattern of regression coefficients is similar to that of the full sample. City-size effects, which appeared larger for the foreign-born in raw tabulations, did not differ appreciably from those in the full sample when other variables were introduced. Differentials by husband's occupation were also similar: in seventeen out of twenty-one occupations in Appendix 3B, the coefficient has the same sign for the foreign-born who married in the United States as for the full sample.

Perhaps the major difference relates to husband's literacy and English-speaking ability, which were less advantageous among the foreign-born married in the United States than among the full sample, and insignificant factors in their mortality variation (husband's English-speaking ability inexplicably taking the wrong sign). Having a husband who did not speak English appears to have been a disadvantage that was limited to native-born women (and perhaps to foreign-born women married abroad). It is possible that literacy mattered less because it had less influence on the job prospects of foreign-born men or because, since the literacy question referred to literacy in any language, it often denoted literacy in a language other than English. The mother's literacy coefficient is also reduced somewhat among the foreign-born but remains significant at the 5 percent level.

In order to investigate whether any specific ethnic group exhibited an unusual relationship between socioeconomic variables and child mortality we have explored the statistical interactions between various socioeconomic indicators and indicators of membership in the specific ethnic groups. The interactive variables that were added to the equation for the full sample reported in Table 3.8 and Appendix 3B were ethnicity and mother's literacy, ethnicity and mother's and father's English-speaking ability, and ethnicity and rural residence. To summarize the results (not shown), only one coefficient of the thirty interaction terms involving literacy or English-speaking ability was significant at the 1 percent level: inexplicably, Italian mothers who spoke English had exceptionally high child mortality. Perhaps such women breast-fed for shorter periods or were more likely to be employed. Two of the rural/ ethnicity interaction terms were significant at the 1 percent level: rural Scandinavians had exceptionally high child mortality (coefficient of .224) and rural Poles exceptionally low child mortality (coefficient of − .326). Since Scandinavians were the least urbanized ethnic group and Poles one of the more urbanized (see Table 3.7), it is possible that these interaction terms are primarily reflecting differential migration patterns: the Scandinavians who went to cities and the few Poles who wound up in rural areas may have been unusually privileged on some unmeasured dimensions. In most instances, however, we cannot reject the hypothesis that members of a particular ethnic group responded in the same way as others in the sample to the major variables.

Second-generation Mortality

As we noted earlier, the second generation on average had mortality levels that were markedly better than the first generation's and very similar to those of NWNP. Was this improvement a consequence of their moving up the socioeconomic ladder? Table 3.8 and Figure 3.2 suggest that this was not the entire story, or perhaps even the bulk of it.

First, most second-generation immigrants remained disadvantaged on social, economic, and residential variables in ways that raised their

FIGURE 3.2

Mortality among the Children of Second-generation Mothers Relative to Children of Native Whites of Native Parentage

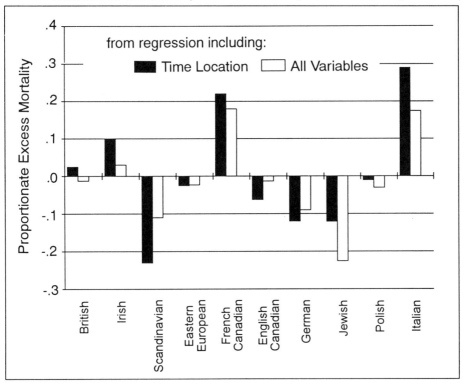

mortality relative to NWNP. This is seen in the fact that, for most ethnic groups, their mortality improves relative to NWNP when other variables are controlled. Improvements of .10 or more are observed for second-generation Jews and Italians. Second, when all other variables are controlled, the second generation had lower mortality than the first generation in eight of the ten ethnic groups (all but the Italians and English Canadians). The mean improvement from one generation to the next for these eight groups was .19.

The mortality experience of the second generation was good enough to surpass that of NWNP in seven of the ten ethnic groups. Because the number of people in the second generation was typically smaller than in the first, however, only the superior performance of Germans relative to NWNP was statistically significant. We are at a loss to explain why the second generation had generally lower levels of child mortality than NWNP once their social disadvantages were controlled. Intergenerational fertility differences are not likely to be a factor, because our analysis of marital fertility rates among Italians, Poles, and Jews (not shown) finds no significant differences between the first and second generation in any of the three groups. Since the numbers are small, we should perhaps not overemphasize the unusually low mortality of the second generation. But it is interesting to observe that a similar result emerged from the analysis of the 1900 census (Preston and Haines 1991, Chapter 4).

Despite the lower levels of second-generation than first-generation mortality, a similar interethnic pattern emerges. That is to say, there continue to be large ethnic differences in mortality among second-generation Americans, differences that echo those in the first generation. In particular, the two groups in which child care practices were specifically implicated in their anomalous child mortality levels—Jews and French Canadians—were at the top and bottom of the rankings for both the foreign-born and the second generation. One can surmise that these practices and the general family environment that supported them were transmitted from generation to generation, at least in these two extreme groups.

Black Mortality[9]

As we suggested earlier, little of the excessively high mortality among black children can be accounted for by other variables in the census. As shown in Table 3.8, blacks begin with a mortality index that

[9]This section draws heavily on Preston and Haines (1991).

is .61 higher than native-natives; once all other variables are controlled, they still have an index that is .41 higher.

What accounts for this remaining disadvantage? At least in eastern cities, the explanation seems to be primarily economic. Woodbury (1925, p. 157) tabulated infant mortality levels by father's earnings and race/nativity. In income groups where there were enough black births to form a reliable rate (which leaves out the upper five income categories), the infant mortality rates per 1,000 births were:

Father's Annual Income	Native Whites	Foreign-born Whites	Blacks
<$450	170	167	163
$450–549	121	118	164
$550–649	111	122	123
$650–845	100	120	103
All Categories	93.9	123.7	152.3

In three of the four income categories, there is no appreciable difference between the mortality of blacks and that of either foreign-born or native whites. Overall, the black disadvantage was only 9 percent relative to whites when fathers' earnings were controlled (Woodbury 1925, p. 122). In contrast, French Canadian children had 55 percent excess in infant mortality when fathers' earnings were controlled.

Most blacks did not live in northern cities, of course, but in the rural South. But their economic circumstances were degraded there as well. Most lived in families of unskilled laborers or sharecroppers. Blacks had received little or no land after the Civil War, and few had been able to acquire it in the next four decades, in part because of discrimination in credit markets. There were direct obstacles to attending school for some black children and little economic payoff to schooling in a society that denied blacks jobs of skill and responsibility (Ransom and Sutch 1977, Chapters 2 and 9; Lieberson 1980, Chapter 6). Daily conditions of life among southern blacks are vividly described in two inquiries by the U.S. Department of Agriculture in the late 1890s. In eastern Virginia, blacks lived in one-, or at most two-, room cabins of primitive construction. Few families had lamps or candles; the fireplace was the only source of illumination at night, posing a constant hazard for unattended young children. Families rented "one-mule farms," about twenty acres, and paid up to half of their annual produce in rent to the landowner, who often exploited their illiteracy by overcharging them for household provisions. Hogs and hominy were the dietary staples (Frissell and Bevier 1899). Turnover was high, and because they were renters there was little incentive to improve the property on which they resided. Conditions were no better in Alabama, where clothing was described as coarse, scanty, and ragged and where cracks in the flooring of cabins accommodated insects and snakes. The status of a black farmer was determined mainly by the number of bales of cotton he could produce in a year. One family, miserably poor, subsisted for days at a time on nothing but corn pone. Dietary protein was deficient, although caloric consumption was generally adequate (Atwater and Woods 1897).

These economic disadvantages are not reflected accurately in such census variables as occupation because blacks earned lower wages within a particular occupation (Wright 1986; Ransom and Sutch 1977). Whatever education they received generally occurred in poorer-quality schools. In cities, they were residentially segregated and fell outside the reach of most ameliorative social programs (Katz 1986). Therefore, many census variables had a different "meaning" for blacks, and the result is that only the race variable itself adequately signifies their many afflictions.

Summary

The PUS from the 1910 census provides the first opportunity to examine the child mortality of various ethnic groups in a large national sample. The foreign-born population as a whole had substantially higher child mortality than native whites of native parentage, just as foreign-born adults had higher mortality within the Death Registration Area. Most of the disadvantage of the foreign-born can be attributed to their adverse distribution on social and economic variables; their concentration in cities, especially large cities, is the single most important explanation of their high child mortality.

Only two of the ten specific ethnic groups investigated had child mortality levels that differed significantly (at 1 percent) from those of native whites of native parentage once social and economic variables are controlled. French Canadian children had exceptionally high child mortality, and Jewish mortality was remarkably low. Digestive diseases were evidently a major factor in the anomalous position of the two groups, suggesting the importance of feeding and sanitary practices. Later data for eastern cities reveal that breast-feeding was very short among French Canadians and quite prolonged among Jews. The groups also differed sharply in the labor force participation rates of mothers and children and in the frequency of school attendance among children. These differences suggest different degrees of child-centeredness that may be related to the levels of child mortality. Both groups retained their relative rankings among second-generation mothers. They also demonstrated unusual mortality levels in their countries of origin.

The very high child mortality of the black population is not primarily attributable to variables measured in the census. Judging from a study by the Children's Bureau, it seems likely to reflect very low income levels among black families.

Second-generation Americans typically had lower child mortality levels than native Americans of native parentage, particularly after social and economic conditions are controlled. Reasons for their superior performance are not obvious and are a useful subject for additional research.

Appendix 3A: 1910 Mortality File Used in This Analysis

A mortality file was created that had a record for each woman in the 1910 Public Use Sample (PUS) whose number of children-ever-born was greater than zero and whose number of children-surviving was less than or equal to the number of children-ever-born. All women had to have a valid racial identification as well. Other restrictions are described below.

Women were divided into three groups in order to generate an expected proportion of children dead, in each case consistent with mortality level 13.5 in the Coale-Demeny West model life table series (e_0 = 49.75). This expected proportion dead could then be used to create a ratio of observed to expected dead children. The groups were defined as follows:

Group I

Currently married women who are in their first marriage, whose husband is present, whose marital duration is less than thirty-five years, and who are below age 50. If the marriage-number was missing, a currently married woman whose oldest child in the household was aged no more than the number of years the woman was married was considered to be in her first marriage. If a woman is currently married but her marital duration is missing, the woman is not included in the file. For women in Group I, mortality estimates were made using marital duration estimation techniques described in the next section.

Groups II and III

Women who were not currently married, or who had been married more than once, or whose husband was not present. Standard marital duration methods could not be applied to these women because marital duration could not be used to estimate the length of exposure of their children to the risk of death. Women who did not fall into Group I were separated by age: Group II has women aged 15–34, and Group III has women aged 35–49. Women who did not fit into Group I and who fell outside these ages were not included in the mortality file.

Within each of Groups II and III there are four categories:

a. Divorced

b. Widowed

c. Women married more than once. This group also includes women whose marriage-number is missing, if they are currently married and if the age of the oldest child in the household is greater than their number of years in current marriage. The woman's husband can be missing or present. If the marriage-number was missing and there were no linked children, the woman is dropped from the mortality analysis.

d. Separated, in first marriage.

Calculation of Expected Proportion Dead

The expected proportion of children who had died was calculated in different ways for each of Groups I, II, and III. The differences revolve around the way we estimate exposure of children to a constant set of mortality risks.

Group I

For Group I women, we reversed the normal Brass/Sullivan process of converting proportions dead by marital duration into life-table values and instead converted the life-table values of our "standard" into expected proportions dead. In particular, we calculated a set of conversion factors, or multipliers, from the formula in Manual X (United Nations 1983:82, equation C.3):

$$k(i) = a(i) + b(i)(P(1)/P(2)) + c(i)(P(2)/P(3))$$

where P(1), P(2), and P(3) are average parities for all women currently in their first marriage with marital duration categories 0–4, 5–9, and 10–14, as obtained from the 1910 PUS tape. The values used were:

P(1) = 0.7974
P(2) = 2.0784
P(3) = 3.1563

These multipliers were used to convert West level 13.5 life-table values (q(1), q(2), etc.) to expected population proportions dead, by marital duration of the mother, using the following equation:

$$\text{expected proportion dead}(i) = q^S(x) / k(i),$$

where $q^S(x)$ is the appropriate life-table value in the standard life table for women aged i. For "negro" and "mulatto" women, however, we used the United Nations Far East pattern of mortality for the $q^S(x)$ values. The level of mortality in the Far East pattern was chosen so that its q(5) was equal to that in West level 13.5. The multipliers, k(i), continued to be based on the coefficients derived from the Coal-Demeny West model patterns of mortality because no coefficients by marital duration for the United Nations model life tables exist. The coefficients are all close to unity, so that any bias is likely to be negligible.

Group II

For Group II women—those aged 15–34 who were not currently in their first marriage or whose husband was not present—we used the Preston-Palloni method to estimate expected proportions surviving (Preston and Palloni 1978). This method uses information on the ages of surviving children to estimate childrens' exposure to mortality. The expected proportions surviving were calculated for the subgroups (a to d) previously mentioned, further subdivided by "racial" groups: whites, urban blacks, rural blacks, and others; and by four age groups: 15–19, 20–24, 25–29, and 30–34. That is, we applied the surviving-children method to sixty-four subgroups. For each group, we reconstructed the time distribution of births by back-projecting surviving children by the level of mortality in a model life-table system that gave the observed ratio of births to surviving children. Having reconstructed births, we then applied the standard West model life table (level 13.5) to estimate what fraction of births should have died to women in various age groups if the standard mortality level prevailed. (The Far East pattern was again used for blacks). The expected proportions surviving are as follows:

	White	Urban Black	Rural Black	Other
a. Divorced				
15–19	0.8776	—	—	—
20–24	0.8588	0.8457	0.8517	0.8462
25–29	0.8387	0.8450	0.8075	0.8241
30–34	0.8175	0.8147	0.8193	0.8332
b. Widowed				
15–19	0.8805	0.8715	0.8734	0.8494
20–24	0.8675	0.8502	0.8504	0.8617
25–29	0.8425	0.8287	0.8387	0.8286
30–34	0.8257	0.8214	0.8288	0.8203
c. Married More Than Once				
15–19	0.8798	0.8713	0.8669	0.8839
20–24	0.8692	0.8498	0.8526	0.8694
25–29	0.8504	0.8376	0.8354	0.8441
30–34	0.8323	0.8285	0.8271	0.8279
d. Separated				
15–19	0.8854	0.8731	0.8685	0.8832
20–24	0.8704	0.8533	0.8509	0.8668
25–29	0.8476	0.8302	0.8365	0.8438
30–34	0.8255	0.8257	0.8290	0.8264

NOTE: — indicates no women in this group.

Group III

Women in Group III (women aged more than 35 years who are not currently in their first marriage or who do not have their husband present) must be handled differently from Group II because many of their surviving children are no longer living with them. We have estimated their age distribution by solving the following equation for α:

$$\frac{CS}{CH} = \int_0^\infty \frac{C_H(a)}{[P_s^H(a)]^\alpha} \, , \text{ where}$$

CH is the number of children linked to women in a particular group, $C_H(a)$ is the number of children aged a linked to women, and $P_s^H(a)$ is the standard proportion of surviving children who are aged a and linked to their mother. This standard is found empirically from the PUS. In other words, we are adopting a standard age-schedule of home-leaving and then assuming that the age-schedule that prevails within a particular group is a one-parameter transformation of that standard. After solving for that parameter, α_i, we then have an estimate of the age distribution of *all* surviving children for that group, i, and can proceed to apply the procedure cited for Group II to estimate the time distribution of births.

Four sets of $P_S^H(a)$ are used: whites, urban blacks, rural blacks, and other races. They generated forty-eight values of alpha, one for each of the three age, four "race," and four marital status groups. The values of α_i are used to find $S_i(a)$, the proportion of children surviving in each of the forty-eight groups who are each at age a in the following equation:

$$S_i(a) = H_i(a) / [P_S^H(a)]^{\alpha i}$$

where $H_i(a)$ is the proportion of linked children of women in each of the forty-eight groups (i) who are aged a.

Finally, $C_i^S(a)$ can be calculated as shown below:

$$\frac{S_i(a)}{\Sigma S_i(a)} = C_i^S(a)$$

and then used in the standard Preston-Palloni formula:

$$\frac{CEB}{CS} = \int \frac{C_i^S(a)}{p^S(a)} \, da$$

It should be noted that, after this process is completed, marital status differences in child mortality are surprisingly small. In a regression that includes all women's social, economic, and residential characteristics, and marital status, the only marital status group whose child mortality level differs significantly from that of women in their first marriage with husbands present (Group I) are women in their second or higher-order marriage, whose mortality was elevated by 34 percent. Widowed, divorced, and separated women did not have mortality levels that differed by more than 5.2 percent from those of women married once with husband present.

For tabulations shown in the text, we have multiplied the ratio of actual to expected deaths given by level 13.5 by 1.0158, so that the full sample for our analysis has a ratio of actual to expected deaths of 1.000. The new level is equivalent to West level 13.73. The multiplicative properties of the q(x) functions at different mortality levels in the same model life table system that are assumed by this procedure have been demonstrated by Trussell and Preston (1982).

Appendix 3B

TABLE 3B.1

Comparison of Coefficients in Regression Equations
Predicting Ratio of Child Deaths to Expected Deaths,
Full Sample and Foreign-born Women Married in the United States

	Coefficient, Full Sample	Coefficient, Foreign-born Married in U.S.
Intercept	2.500**	−0.784
Time Location	0.020**	0.036**
No Husband	1.717**	−0.510
Nativity of Husband (reference category is native-born husband with native mother)		
Foreign-born	−.013	−0.049
Native-born with foreign mother	−.071**	0.004
City Size (reference category rural)		
New York City	0.268**	0.165*
Philadelphia	0.335**	0.105
Chicago	0.190**	0.083
Other 10 largest	0.144**	0.102
Other city > 25,000	0.077**	0.091
City 5,000 – 25,000	0.042	0.047
Town 1,000 – 5,000	−0.041	0.071
Region (reference category New England)		
Middle Atlantic	−0.072	0.109
East North Central	−0.069*	−0.032
West North Central	−0.059	−0.068
South Atlantic	−0.055	0.190
East South Central	−0.038	0.260
West South Central	0.028	0.019
Mountain	0.258**	−0.267
Pacific	−0.072	−0.304**
Log of State Earnings Level	−0.237**	0.299
Mother Is Literate	−0.126**	−0.156**
Mother Speaks English	−0.130**	−0.082
Husband Is Literate	−0.118**	−0.046
Husband Speaks English	−0.085*	0.049
Woman Unemployed in Previous Year	0.015	0.078
Husband Unemployed in Previous Year	0.081**	0.002

	Coefficient, Full Sample	Coefficient, Foreign-born Married in U.S.
Husband's Occupation (reference category is farmers)		
Farm laborers	0.022	0.064
Farm foremen	−.143	−.660
Fishermen, foresters, and lumbermen	0.122	−.017
Other agricultural pursuits	0.114	0.356*
Mine owners and foremen	0.107	0.341
Mine operatives	0.204**	0.165
Manufacturing laborers	0.070	0.021
Manufacturing semiskilled operatives	−.021	0.114
Manufacturing officials	−.058	−.146
Other manufacturing occupations	−.012	−.017
Transportation proprietors and officials	−.110	0.234
Transportation foremen	−.222*	−.427
Other transportation workers	0.046	0.086
Bankers, insurance agents, real estate agents	−.036	−.005
Sales workers	−.125*	−.131
Other tradesmen	0.030	0.056
Public service workers (police, fire)	0.015	−.042
Professionals	−.074	−.266
Domestic and personal service workers	0.130**	0.033
Bookkeepers, cashiers, accountants	−.241**	−.264
Other clerical workers	0.025	0.230
Woman's Occupation (reference category is not in the labor force).		
Managers,	0.206	0.064
Professionals	0.036	−0.660
Technical and support	−0.031	−0.017
Sales	0.054	
Service	0.284**	0.356*
Farmers	−0.827	0.341
Farm laborers	0.055	0.165
Precision production excluding miners	0.076	0.021
Miners	1.980*	0.114
Operators and fabricators	0.318**	−0.146
Laborers	0.165	−0.017
Nonspecified	−0.315	0.234
Home Is a farm	−0.102	−0.125
Ownership of Home (reference category is rented)		
Owned	−0.055**	−0.014
Probably owned	−0.028	0.061

	Coefficient, Full Sample	Coefficient, Foreign-born Married in U.S.
Mortgage Status (reference category is mortgaged)		
Owned outright	−0.008	0.034
Probably outright	−0.020	−0.080
Invalid Codes		
Place of birth	−0.021	—
Husband's place of birth	0.007	—
Woman unemployed	−0.038	−0.059
Husband unemployed	−0.027	0.015
Husband's occupation	1.419	0
Woman's occupation	0.032	0.008
Farm dwelling	0.059	0.236
Ownership	−0.019	0.408
Woman's literacy	−0.068	−0.168
Woman's ability to speak English	1.084**	—
Husband's literacy	−0.072	0.295
Husband's ability to speak English	−1.829**	—

NOTES: *Significant at 5% level.
      **Significant at 1% level.

4

GENERATING AMERICANS: ETHNIC DIFFERENCES IN FERTILITY

S. Philip Morgan
Susan Cotts Watkins
Douglas Ewbank

COMPARED TO other issues examined in this volume (mortality, family structure, and education, for instance), much was already known about differences in fertility between natives and immigrants at the turn of the century. We knew that immigrant fertility was higher than native, that there was substantial fertility variation among immigrant groups, and that second-generation ethnic groups had fertility levels between those of the natives and the first generation (see literature cited in the next section).

But many interesting and important questions remain. Among the most important: Are these differences in fertility simply the consequence of variations among these groups in the timing of marriage, with those groups that married earlier bearing more children than those who married later? Do marital fertility differences indicate deliberate fertility control? Do differences between immigrants and natives, and among the immigrant groups, persist even when we confine comparisons to women in the same circumstances, for example, those who lived in large cities and whose husbands were laborers? Are there indications that some immigrants may have imitated the fertility patterns of the natives?

These questions speak to both the concerns of those interested in ethnicity and those interested in the process of fertility decline. For the former group, a central consideration has been understanding the adaptation of immigrants to their new environments—a blend of accommodation to the socioeconomic circumstances in which they lived, the pressures to assimilate, and the attachment to distinctive ethnic patterns. For the latter group, a central consideration has been to explore the roles of structural changes, diffusion, and cultural traditions in accounting for the decline in fertility. By examining the fertility of the foreign-born in the United States in 1910 it is possible to gain more precise knowledge about the process of fertility decline, and thus, we would argue, the adaptations that immigrants made in their private lives.

The 1910 PUS offers the possibility of examining immigrant fertility in much greater detail than was previously possible. Its predecessor, the 1900 PUS, is much smaller; moreover, it could not encompass the huge amount of new migration occurring in the 1900–1910 period. The 1910 sample permits a comparison of the fertility of the foreign-born with that of the native white women, as well as one ethnic group with another, and it allows distinctions between the effect of marriage and of marital fertility. Very importantly, it permits a serious exploration of the sources of ethnic differences, of whether the influences on the fertility of the immigrants were similar to or different from the influences on the fertility of native-born white women, and of whether the various immigrant groups seem to have responded to their circumstances in similar or in idiosyncratic ways.

Previous Research

Because previous research on fertility provides the foundation for the analyses presented here, it is useful to summarize it in some detail. Most notably, this research has shown the behavior of married couples to be critical. The adoption of fertility control within marriage marks a decisive break in fertility patterns. Once fertility control within marriage is adopted among some groups in the population, the subsequent decline is usually rather rapid and pervasive; in Western Europe there was little evidence of fertility control in most countries before 1870, but by 1930 marital fertility was low almost everywhere (Coale and Treadway 1986; Watkins 1986). Moreover, both in Europe and in the Third World declines in marital fertility have typically been monotonic, at least until very low levels of fertility have been reached (Watkins 1987).

By the time of the 1910 census, fertility control was well established among married couples in the native white population. Fertility control was already evident in some small New England communities nearly a century earlier (for a review of studies of early fertility decline in the United States, see Ewbank 1991). By 1900 there was evidence of substantial fertility limitation in urban areas in most states, and in rural areas in most states outside the South and West (Tolnay, Graham, and Guest 1982; David and Sanderson 1987; Haines 1989; Ewbank 1991). It is clear that by 1910 many native white women deliberately stopped childbearing after they reached the number of children they wanted; in addition, some of them probably adjusted the spacing of their children (Anderton and Bean 1985; Ewbank 1989), and others remained voluntarily childless (Tolnay and Guest 1982; Morgan 1991). The lowest levels of fertility, and the strongest evidence of deliberate control of fertility, were in the Northeast and North-Central states, where most of the immigrants lived in 1910.

A comparison of the timing of the fertility declines in Europe and the United States leads us to expect that fertility would be higher among the foreign-born in the United States in 1910 than among the native whites of native parentage (NWNP). Many of the foreign-born came from areas or from social groups in which the long-term decline in the fertility of married couples had not yet begun at the time of their departure. Fertility decline was evident at the national level in Ireland, Poland, and Italy only after the turn of the century (Coale and Treadway 1986), and even later among groups that supplied many migrants at the turn of the century.

In addition, we expect to find that the specific ethnic groups would differ in their fertility from one another. In particular, we expect to find higher fertility among the "new" immigrants, from Eastern, Central, and Southern Europe, than among the "old" immigrants, from Britain, Germany, and Scandinavia.[1] The fertility decline occurred later in Eastern, Central, and Southern Europe, as well as in Ireland, than in Northwestern Europe. Most of the immigrants from Eastern, Central, and Southern Europe were recent arrivals, and thus would have come before the onset of fertility decline at the national level (we discuss local variations below).

The rich literature from historians and sociologists on the family patterns of the immigrants suggests differences among the immigrant groups that might influence fertility by affecting the use of contraception (including abstinence and withdrawal) and abortion. For example, female labor force participation is often associated with lower fertility, as are children's roles (Guest 1981). Italians, it is said, tried to avoid having their women work outside the home, while Irish, Polish, and French Canadian families saw outside work as more acceptable (Yans-McLaughlin 1977; Diner 1983; Hareven and Langenbach 1978). Such dif-

---

[1]In distinguishing between "new" and "old" usage we follow usage at the turn of the century, but note that some of the foreign-born in 1910 from Northwestern Europe were recent arrivals; in particular, both German and Irish were major parts of the immigrant stream between 1890 and 1910 (Carpenter 1969 [1927]). Immigrants from Eastern, Southern, and Central Europe were, however, relatively small proportions of the immigrant stream before the mid-1880s.

ferences could affect the demand or desire for additional children and thus the willingness to prevent births.

There have been some useful attempts to address such questions. The census questionnaires of 1890, 1900, and 1910 contained questions about childbearing and infant and child survival. The published census volumes contain no tabulations of this information.[2] However, the Immigration Commission used 1900 census manuscripts from three states (Rhode Island, Ohio, and Minnesota) to tabulate marital fertility rates for various immigrant groups (U.S. Immigration Commission 1911; see also Guest 1982). No other information on fertility was published from the censuses of 1890, 1900, and 1910 until a special tabulation of the 1910 questions was made by the research division of the Milbank Memorial Fund (see Notestein 1931) and by the Census Bureau in conjunction with the 1940 census (see U.S. Bureau of the Census 1945). The former focused only on natives, but the later study produced useful tabulations that contrasted natives of native parentage with the foreign-born and with natives of foreign-born parents.

From these tabulations we can conclude that (by the date of the census) foreign-born women (at most ages over 30) had borne more children than had native women and that these differences held in rural and urban areas and in various regions of the country. In one table (U.S. Bureau of the Census 1945, Table 96) the foreign-born were disaggregated by country of origin, so that it is possible to compare number of children-ever-born (to women of various ages) across ethnic groups. Although these tabulations were nationally representative, one cannot tell whether the differences arise due to different ages at marriage or to different behavior within marriage; groups with an earlier female age of marriage would, *ceteris paribus*, have higher fertility than those that married later. In addition, one cannot tell whether the higher fertility of some groups occurred before or after their arrival in the United States.

Analysis of the Immigration Commission's data for three states suggests that residence in the United States may have influenced immigrant fertility. For a broad range of groups, fertility was lower for the NWNP than for second-generation natives, and was higher still for immigrants (Guest 1982). As contemporaries would have expected, the "new" immigrant groups (e.g., Poles, Italians, and Russians) had higher fertility than the "old" immigrant groups (British, Irish, Germans, and Scandinavians). Although the characteristics of first- and second-generation

---

[2]The 1890 and 1900 questions were punched on Hollerith cards by the Census Bureau but never tabulated; the 1910 questions were neither punched nor tabulated (Truesdell 1965, pp. 82–83).

immigrants may have differed in ways that compromise the comparison (see Chapter 2), these data suggest a process of fertility change, with the second generation having fertility rates midway between the rates for the foreign-born and the NWNP.

Other evidence that residence in the United States was associated with fertility decline comes from a comparison of the fertility of foreign-born Italians in the United States with the fertility of non-immigrants still in southern Italy (the area that provided many of the foreign-born Italians resident in the United States in 1910). In 1918, the fertility of foreign-born Italians in the United States was about twice as high as that of native women, but by 1936 it was lower than native fertility (Livi Bacci 1961). An examination of the timing of the fertility decline in an area of Sicily shows that fertility did not fall among the *bracciante* (laborers) until after World War II. Although fertility was low among European immigrant groups in the United States in 1940 (Lieberson 1980), as it was in their countries of origin, these two studies taken together suggest that the fertility decline of at least some U.S. immigrant groups may have been more rapid than among comparable groups in Europe.

Most previous research permits only limited comparisons of ethnic groups, because the studies are restricted to either small geographical areas and usually concentrate on only one or two ethnic groups (e.g., Hareven and Vinovskis 1978; Haines 1980) or, when national samples are used, to all the foreign-born together, presumably for reasons of sample size (e.g., Guest and Tolnay 1983). In addition, many studies (like the published census tabulations described earlier) do not make the important distinction between the effects of marriage timing and control of fertility within marriage.

What was it about residence in the United States that might have influenced immigrant fertility? Two sources of possible influences can be identified from the extensive literature on ethnic groups in the United States: those associated with changes in the social structure (e.g., moves from rural to urban environments), and those associated with contact with another society. These roughly parallel the debate on the causes of fertility decline: are fertility declines simply due to adaptations to changed circumstances, particularly to industrialization and urbanization, or do they involve the diffusion of innovative reproductive practices?

At the turn of the century many believed that immigrants would become "American" by contact with the natives. Proponents of the development of a specialized pedagogy for Americanization programs put teaching English at the top of their list of goals, followed by lessons in hygiene and then, in sixth place, by American values (Sharlip and Owens 1928). It was not only pro-assimilationist natives who thought that contact would lead to Americanization; ethnic leaders shared this view. For example, rabbis in Russia warned that moving to America would mean the abandonment of orthodox observances (Howe 1976). The relevance of contact for fertility is suggested by an analysis of fertility by residential patterns in Detroit in 1880. When German women lived with other German women, the child-woman ratio was higher than when they lived in clusters dominated by the NWNP (Zunz 1982, p. 79).

A more impressionistic account is given in a summary of Scandinavian literature in the United States (Skårdal 1974). In one novel of the late nineteenth century, a Norwegian American father of two children wishes for more:

> But such was not the custom here. This was one of the first things his wife had found out about, how she could keep from having more than two children. . . . Most of the other families had the children they brought along from Norway and perhaps one or two more—they learned fast. It was shameful to have many children—no "fine" family had more than one or two—and it was desirable to be among the "fine";—and then one could give the children such a better education when one had only one or two (Skårdal 1974, p. 245).

If contact with the natives were relevant for fertility, previous studies of the fertility transition suggest that it would be through the diffusion of new ideas about appropriate family size, the legitimacy of fertility control, or, perhaps, new techniques. We would thus expect those who had been in the United States longer, and who had more opportunity for contact with the NWNP, to have lower fertility than recent arrivals.

Modern analysts of assimilation have placed more emphasis on the transformations expected to follow changes in the location of the immigrants in the social structure, first through the movement from rural to urban areas that often accompanied migration, and then through the incorporation of the immigrants into an industrial labor force. Correspondingly, modern analysts of fertility have generally emphasized the effects of urban residence and occupation on the costs and benefits of children in accounting for differentials in fertility.

In this chapter, our first aim is to provide a precise description of fertility in the United States in 1910, focusing particularly on differences between the NWNP and the foreign-born, and, within the foreign-born, among the largest ethnic groups. Our second aim is to examine whether these differences persist after differences in occupation and rural/urban residence are taken into account, and whether different ethnic groups seem to respond in idiosyncratic ways to these social-structural influences. Third, we consider whether there is evidence that contact with others outside the particular ethnic group—or more precisely, the opportunity for contact with natives or with English-speaking immigrants in other ethnic groups—mattered for fertility: did those who had been in the United States longer and spoke English have distinctly different patterns of fertility from members of their ethnic group who were more recent arrivals and did not speak English? Lastly, we examine whether ethnic differences in fertility disappear when we confine comparisons to women in the same circumstances; or do unmeasured aspects of ethnicity show a robust influence on fertility? We note, however, that distinguishing between "social structure" and "contact" with the variables available here is imprecise at best. Urban living, for example, may change the cost-benefit ratio of children, but the greater population density of urban areas may also foster the more rapid diffusion of new ideas. Similarly, those who spoke English had opportunities for contact with natives that were less available to those who did not, but speaking English may also have offered opportunities for earning a living that were not open to monolingual immigrants.

It is important to emphasize that although cross-sectional information (such as that provided by the 1910 census) satisfactorily allows for the precise description of fertility differentials (our first aim), inferences about fertility *change* are problematic. We only know about the population at a single point in time, and we use that information to describe a process of family formation that occurred over time. In addition, the foreign-born in the United States in 1910 are a multiply selected group: they left the country of origin, came to the United States rather than to another country, and remained in the United States (or returned but reemigrated), so that they were present when the census was conducted. The immigrants in the United States in 1910 may have differed from those who remained in the home country, or who came to the United States but then returned, in ways that are relevant for their fertility. We do not know about their lives in Europe—whether they lived in urban or rural areas, in what occupations they worked—so we cannot tell whether immigration involved a change in their socioeconomic circumstances. We can, however, examine whether immigrant couples who lived in cities, or who made their living in occupations where children were presumably not economically valuable, had lower fertility than those who lived in rural areas. We also can examine whether those who had greater opportunities for contact with NWNP (as well as other immigrant groups, some of which were clearly controlling their fertility, as we shall see) because they had been in the United States longer and spoke English were more likely to have lower fertility than those who had recently arrived and did not speak English.

Data and Methods

Measures of Fertility

We are limiting our analysis to childbearing that occurred in the United States. All measures are restricted to women between the ages of 15 and 49, living in the United States but outside the South at least some time between 1905 and the census date.[3] We are focusing on fertility of non-southern women in the United States because of our interest in comparing immigrant and NWNP women in similar circumstances: non-southern NWNP are a more appropriate comparison group than all the NWNP because fertility patterns in the South were somewhat different from those elsewhere, and few immigrants (under 10 percent) lived in the South. We are limiting the time period to the five years preceding the census because we want the characteristics of the women (e.g., urban or rural residence) to be measured close to the time that they were bearing children.

We will begin by comparing levels of fertility across the various ethnic groups, using age-specific fertility rates and total fertility rates. The total fertility rate is the sum of the age-specific fertility rates, and is thus a measure of the number of children that would be born over a woman's lifetime if she experienced the fertility rates of 1905–1909. We will then switch to measures that take marital status as well as age into account, and finally proceed to measures that take the woman's parity (the number of children she has previously borne) into account as well.

The total fertility rates provide a basic comparison of levels of childbearing. Age-specific fertility rates allow us to examine how fertility varies across stages of the family-building process. Older women (those over age 35) have lower fertility because reproductive capacity declines with age and, perhaps, because many have borne all the children they desire and they act to limit childbearing. Fertility rates for groups of women defined by age and parity allow us to identify precisely where fertility differences between groups are concentrated. This more precise description provides clues to the factors and motivations that lie behind observed differences.

To calculate age-specific fertility rates, and age-and-parity-specific fertility rates, we need to keep track of the age of each woman and the number of children she has previously borne for each year that she is at risk of a birth between 1905 and 1910. In the 1910 census each woman

---

[3]The South includes the South Atlantic (Delaware, Maryland, District of Columbia, Virginia, West Virginia, North Carolina, South Carolina, Georgia, Florida), East South Central (Kentucky, Tennessee, Alabama, Mississippi), and West South Central (Arkansas, Louisiana, Texas, Oklahoma Territory).

was asked her age in 1910, how many children she had borne, and how many of her children were still alive. To establish her parity, we examined the list of household members and linked each woman of childbearing age with her children living with her.[4] For a woman who was living with all the children she had ever borne, we can use the reported ages of the children to determine their year of birth. Because the ages of all the children are known, we can determine the birth order of each child: this, then, provides the mother's parity after that birth (see Ewbank, Morgan, and Watkins 1992 for details).

Two categories of children are missing from the household listing, causing us to underestimate fertility (and misstate parity): those who had died and those who were living elsewhere. The correction for mortality is the most important for this analysis, because mortality differed considerably across ethnic groups (see Preston, Ewbank, and Hereward, Chapter 3). The census asked for both children-ever-born and children-surviving. For women who reported more children born than surviving, we adjusted their fertility, in effect, by "resurrecting" dead children, thus raising our fertility estimates. To provide these (dead) children a place in the birth order we allocated a year of birth to each deceased child based on the woman's age or marriage duration. (The exact procedure is described in Ewbank, Morgan, and Watkins 1992). The age-specific and total fertility rates have also been adjusted for estimates of children living elsewhere. The adjustments were based on tabulations of the proportion of children under 5 who were not linked with a mother.[5]

In addition to age-specific and total fertility rates, we used the odds ratio to compare childbearing in one group with childbearing in another. For each ethnic group we tabulated the number of years with a birth and the number of years with no birth in the five years preceding the census according to the age (or the age and parity) of the woman in each year. We then calculated the odds of having a birth (number of years with a birth/number of years with no birth) for women in each age and parity category, by ethnicity.[6] We then compared the odds that women in one

[4]Because individuals were identified in the census by their relationship to the head of the household (usually a male) rather than to their mother, the children needed to be linked to their mothers. In most households with children there was only one married adult woman, so the linking was relatively easy; in households with more than one adult woman, it was necessary to use information on the ages of the children, their place of birth, and so on (the linking procedure is described in detail in Strong et al. 1989).

[5]We inflated the fertility rates by the factor: 1 + (the proportion of children not living with mothers). See Ewbank, Morgan, and Watkins 1992 for details.

[6]An equivalent expression for the odds is the fertility rate divided by (1-the fertility rate). We did not adjust these odds ratios for children living elsewhere, since Miller, Morgan, and McDaniel (Chapter 5) show that the number of children under age 5 who did not live with mothers was small and did not vary greatly among immigrant groups. Thus, although the absolute level of fertility would be affected slightly by the absence of some

group would have a birth with the odds that a woman in another group would have a birth. We asked, for example, how much more likely were foreign-born Italian women of ages 25–29 who had already borne two children to have had a birth than a NWNP woman of the same age and parity. These comparisons are expressed in terms of odds ratios: for example, women in one ethnic group might be twice as likely to have a birth than native women, whereas women in another ethnic group might be only 1.5 times more likely to have a birth than native women.

To examine how these odds varied with age and parity as well as the woman's other characteristics, we estimated a set of logistic regression models, in which the dependent variable is the odds that a woman had a birth in a given year. We began with a simple model that included only information on the woman's age (using seven age groups, from 15–19 to 45–49) and parity (using four categories of parity: childless; parity one; parities two, three, and four; and parity five or higher). We then added indicators of ethnic group and various independent variables and asked whether the new information significantly improved the fit of the statistical model to the observed data.[7] We ultimately chose a preferred model for the data based on substantive plausibility, goodness of fit, and parsimony.

Ethnic Groups

Only the largest of the immigrant groups in the United States in 1910 are considered in this analysis: British, Irish, Germans, Scandinavians, Italians, Poles, Central European Jews, and Eastern European Jews. These groups are defined on the basis of their place of birth and/or mother tongue (for definitions, see Appendix B, this volume; for caveats about

---

children from the household, whether fertility was relatively higher or lower in one ethnic group compared to others would be little changed.

[7] If f_{ijk} is the marital fertility rate for women age i, at parity j, in ethnic group k, then the model for the log odds is:

$$\text{Log } [f_{ijk}/(1 - f_{ijk})] =$$

a	[main effect for reference group]
$+ B_i \ (Age_i)$	[age main effects]
$+ C_j \ (Parity_j)$	[parity main effects]
$+ D_{ij} \ (Age_i * Parity_j)$	[age-parity interactions]
$+ E_k \ (Ethnicity_k)$	[ethnic main effects]
$+ F_{ik} \ (Ethnicity_k * Age_i)$	[age-ethnic interactions]
$+ G_{ik} \ (Ethnicity_k * Age_i^2)$	[age^2-ethnic interactions]
$+ H_{jk} \ (Ethnicity_k * Parity_j)$	[ethnicity-parity interactions]
$+ I_{jk} \ (Ethnicity_k * Parity_j^2)$	[ethnicity-parity^2 interactions]
$+ M_l \ (Other \ Covariates_l)$	
$+ N_{kl} \ (Ethnicity_k * Other \ Covariates_l).$	

the heterogeneity of these groups and problems with identifying them, see Chapter 2, this volume). As discussed in Chapter 2, although we use the terms "Jews" and "Poles," these two groups are defined only on the basis of their mother tongue: Jews are those who reported Yiddish-speaking, thus excluding those Jews who might have reported another mother tongue, and Poles are those who reported Polish-speaking.

Findings

We begin with age-specific fertility rates and the total fertility rate (TFR) shown in Table 4.1. The age-specific fertility rates show a typical pattern of higher fertility in the younger ages, and then a drop with age. In the United States, contemporary observers had much to say about the prolific foreigners (see King and Ruggles 1990). But we can see that only some ethnic groups were "prolific." In the column of total fertility rates, the high fertility of the Italians and the Poles stands out, followed by the other new immigrants, the Central European and Eastern European Jews. The Germans, Scandinavians, and British have levels of fertility that are closer to the natives, whereas the fertility of the Irish is below that of the natives.

Selected Immigrant Groups, by Generation, 1905–1909

Table 4.1 also includes age-specific fertility rates and total fertility rates for a number of smaller immigrant groups. The relatively low value reported for Magyars (3.99) reflects the fact that Hungary began its fertility decline relatively early. The high value for Slovaks (7.58) is probably more representative of Slavic groups in the United States.

In a few cases we can compare these total fertility rates with values from the European countries of origin (Haines 1990). The TFR for British-born women in the United States is 2.96, nearly identical to the 2.9 in England and Wales in 1911. The rate of 3.6 recorded for Sweden in 1908–1912 is slightly higher than the 3.3 reported here for Swedish immigrants to the United States. In contrast the TFRs for Norway in 1916–1920 and Denmark in 1906–1915 (3.4 and 3.6) are lower than the 4.3 and 4.1 reported for Norwegian and Danish immigrants. The TFR of 3.9 for German-born immigrants is substantially lower than the 4.9 recorded in 1881–1890 in eight German states. The Magyar-speakers in the United States had lower fertility (4.0) than the rate in all of Hungary in 1906–1915 (4.9). On the other hand, the French-speakers from Europe

TABLE 4.1

Age-specific Fertility Rates and Total Fertility Rates, Selected Immigrant Groups, by Generation: U.S., 1905–1909

	15–	20–	25–	30–	35–	40–	45–	TFR	s.e.
NWNP	53	165	178	154	108	46	6	3.56	.024
NWNP—Non-South	37	133	149	124	88	34	5	2.85	.024
NWNP—South	83	225	234	212	150	73	8	4.92	.043
Blacks	97	216	211	200	143	73	24	4.81	.069
Mulattoes	94	201	181	190	128	59	7	4.30	.119
Foreign-born White									
Total	54	195	228	197	133	61	9	4.38	.041
British	16	125	184	122	96	43	4	2.95	.113
English	15	123	190	124	91	40	5	2.94	.134
Scottish	14	117	168	113	101	47	0	2.79	.232
Welsh	—	(191)	(179)	(144)	(135)	(55)	(8)	3.72	.508
Irish	8	75	146	181	90	26	1	2.64	.093
Scandinavians	17	130	206	207	136	76	13	3.93	.122
Sweden	10	98	183	190	109	61	11	3.31	.159
Norway	18	145	202	208	178	90	16	4.29	.255
Denmark	(25)	158	230	194	139	82	0	4.14	.350
Finland	17	170	293	(342)	(210)	—	—	6.29	.577
Germans	49	172	198	170	124	66	9	3.94	.111
Italians	126	307	323	283	221	116	12	6.94	.168
Poles	85	267	331	330	237	122	22	6.97	.192
Russian-Poles	99	271	339	308	229	83	(40)	6.85	.315
Austrian-Poles	79	270	304	304	205	(159)	(21)	6.71	.367
German-Poles	95	250	369	389	276	132	12	7.62	.404
Yiddish-Speakers	21	207	243	242	126	41	8	4.44	.141
Central European	31	242	243	193	108	43	0	4.29	.285
Eastern European	19	199	243	259	132	40	11	4.52	.163
Non-European	51	154	158	138	118	58	6	3.41	.100

French-Speakers	(75)	138	142	90	115	68	(6)	3.17	.356
Canadian, French	63	246	206	169	170	84	11	4.74	.243
Canadian, English	20	100	123	119	73	47	3	2.42	.119
Russians	56	185	(222)	(159)	(138)	—	—	4.02	.489
Magyars	56	224	231	152	81	(55)	0	3.99	.290
Bohemians	61	208	278	198	149	53	8	4.77	.310
Slovaks	145	313	407	277	276	(54)	(44)	7.58	.425
Lithuanians, Lettish	46	273	308	210	—	—	—	5.94	.609
Second Generation									
Total	29	132	149	129	91	41	6	2.88	.036
British	38	139	136	122	77	35	3	2.75	.100
Irish	17	84	107	114	84	37	3	2.23	.063
Scandinavians	15	106	154	159	112	76	0	3.10	.162
Germans	28	138	163	131	95	44	8	3.04	.062
Italians	63	202	(292)	(234)	—	—	—	4.97	.709
Poles	42	256	261	(170)	—	—	—	6.60	1.165

NOTES: Estimates in parentheses are based on 50–99 woman year.
– indicates fewer than 50 woman years of risk. For definitions of the groups, see Appendix B, this volume.

FIGURE 4.1

Total Fertility Rates, Immigrant Groups, by Generation:
U.S., 1905–1909

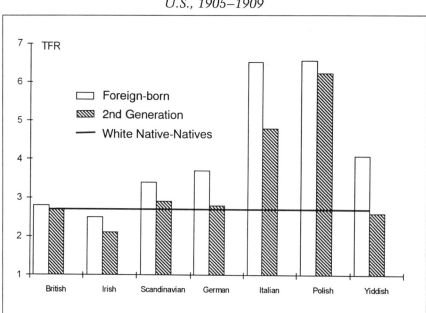

(88 percent of whom were from France and Belgium) had a higher TFR than France (3.2 compared to 2.5 in France in 1909–1913).

Figure 4.1 presents some of the information in Table 4.1 graphically, comparing the TFRs for first- and second-generation women in each ethnic group.[8] The pattern of differences among second-generation women is very similar to the pattern among the foreign-born, a conclusion very similar to that reached by Guest (1982) in his analysis of data collected by the Immigration Commission from the 1900 census. The levels, however, are much closer to the NWNP group. Note that the second-generation British, Scandinavians, Germans, and Yiddish-speakers had TFRs very close to that of the NWNP women. Although the comparison across generations does suggest an effect of U.S. residence on fertility, the first and second generations are contemporaneous, and thus the effect may reflect differences in the composition of the immigrant stream at different periods of immigration.

[8]The ethnicity of the second generation was based on the ethnicity of their parents. Because of high levels of marital endogamy, in most cases the parents were of the same ethnicity; where they were not, we used the mother's ethnicity.

There are two sources of differences in overall levels of fertility, as measured by the total fertility rates. One ethnic group might have lower fertility than another because women in that group are less likely to be married (and thus less likely to bear children) or because they are controlling fertility within marriage. How much of the variation in childbearing across ethnic groups in the United States was due to differences in nuptial patterns? This is examined in Table 4.2, where the measure of fertility difference is the odds ratio: the odds that a woman in a particular immigrant group will have a child in a given year, divided by the odds that a NWNP woman will have a child.

Column 1 may come closest to capturing what natives witnessed. It provides a gross measure of the greater tendency of foreign-born women to bear children compared to native women. An odds ratio of 1.00 would mean that there was no difference between the women in a given ethnic group and the NWNP. Again, the very high fertility of first-generation Italians and Poles is evident: they are more than three times as likely to have borne children in one of the previous five years than the NWNP. The British, Irish, Scandinavians, and Germans are more like the natives: indeed, the Irish are only 4 percent more likely to have had a birth in the previous five years than the NWNP.

When age differences are taken into account (Column 2), the difference between native and ethnic childbearing is affected very little. Taking marriage into account makes a larger difference. When only ever-married women are compared (Column 3), the differences between the "new" immigrants and the NWNP are attenuated sharply, but this attenuation is slight for the "old" immigrants (for the Irish the differential actually increases). Consider the early-marrying Italians and the late-marrying Irish, for example. When only married women are compared, the odds ratio for Italian women is 2.07 (fertility is slightly more than twice as high as that for NWNPs) rather than the odds ratio of 3.35 seen in Column 1 for all women, whereas the odds ratio for Irish women increases from 1.04 (Column 1) to 1.44 (Column 3). In other words, a substantial proportion of the variation in ethnic fertility is due to nuptial patterns. The differences between ever-married women (Column 3) and currently married women (Column 4) are small, because so few women were enumerated in the census as "married, husband absent," with little variation across ethnic groups (Robles and Watkins 1993).

Taking marriage into account, however, does not erase differences between natives and the foreign-born, or among the foreign-born. For instance, compared with NWNP fertility, Italian and Polish fertility is still roughly twice as high and Jewish fertility is about 1.5 times higher.

TABLE 4.2

Ethnic Differences in Period Fertility, Non-Southern Women Ages 15–49: 1905–1910

| | Gross Differences | | | | Differences Net of Age | | | | |
| | All Women (1) | All Women (2) | | Ever-married Women (3) | | Currently Married Women (4) | |
Ethnic Group	Effect	Effect	(N)	Effect	(N)	Effect	(N)
Native Whites of Native Parentage	—	—	(135,817)	—	(90,657)	—	(81,722)
First Generation							
British	1.16	1.24	(6,915)	1.19	(4,770)	1.15	(4,247)
Irish	1.04	1.14	(9,042)	1.44	(5,390)	1.42	(4,485)
Scandinavians	1.48	1.63	(7,048)	1.71	(4,656)	1.60	(4,250)
Germans	1.45	1.73	(10,635)	1.42	(8,357)	1.34	(7,484)
Italians	3.35	3.28	(6,481)	2.07	(4,844)	1.93	(4,605)
Polish	3.28	3.19	(5,327)	2.24	(3,679)	2.13	(3,439)
C.E. Jews	1.78	1.89	(1,563)	1.42	(1,063)	1.38	(967)
E.E. Jews	1.80	1.88	(5,248)	1.54	(3,317)	1.43	(3,082)
Second Generation							
British	1.04	1.09	(8,458)	1.00	(4,954)	.98	(4,428)
Irish	.84	.90	(17,667)	1.22	(8,733)	1.23	(7,462)
Scandinavians	1.05	1.02	(6,266)	1.28	(2,321)	1.22	(2,163)
Germans	1.13	1.19	(24,422)	1.20	(13,844)	1.15	(12,577)
Italians	1.73	2.14	(894)	1.76	(328)	1.61	(318)
Polish	1.62	1.97	(1,189)	2.07	(352)	1.89	(347)
C.E. Jews	.53	.74	(284)	.96	(72)	.87	(67)
E.E. Jews	.52	.74	(583)	1.19	(102)	1.16	(97)

Thus, it is clear that fertility behavior within marriage, and not marriage patterns, produces much of the variability in fertility across ethnic groups.

Marital Fertility, by Age and Parity

There are several sources of differences in marital fertility, the most important of which are breast-feeding practices (with longer breast-feeding associated with lower fertility) and deliberate attempts to avoid births. Although it is not possible to observe breast-feeding practices directly, Woodbury's analysis for the Children's Bureau shows longer breast-feeding among the "new" immigrants than among the "old" (Woodbury 1925); thus, the lower fertility of the "old" immigrants is more likely due to deliberate attempts to avoid births than to prolonged breast-feeding.

Fertility differences by parity have usually been considered to be the most compelling evidence of deliberate attempts to control fertility. If differences exist primarily at higher parities, then arguments about the disadvantages of large families might be appropriate. On the other hand, if differences are at young ages and parities, one needs to consider explanations for delayed or postponed parenthood or childbearing, such as more immediate economic circumstances (see Rindfuss, Morgan, and Swicegood 1988) or long-term strategies for childbearing (Anderton and Bean 1985). These different patterns also fit more general models of fertility adjustment. The traditional model identifies *number* of children as the relevant decision variable. Couples need not practice family limitation until their family-size goal is reached. This notion is codified in the well-known Coale and Trussell (1974) indices, M and m, and in the Easterlin and Crimmins (1985) conceptual scheme that operationalizes motivation for control as the difference between the number of children desired and the current number of children (when this difference reaches 0, couples will begin to control their fertility).

The second model focuses not on number, but timing. The relevant decision is whether "to have a child now or not." Thus the number of children is the outcome of a lifetime of sequential decisions. Very importantly, recent work suggests (in developed countries at least) that this "lifetime of decisions" is not based on firm plans for number of children but is strongly influenced by more immediate considerations, specifically, can we "afford to have a child now?" (see Rindfuss, Morgan, and Swicegood 1988). This perspective anticipates *spacing* or fertility delay under certain conditions. Fertility may differ not only at stopping points (higher ages and parities) but at early and intermediate stages.

Description of the extent of fertility control is easier if we use a population that takes no steps to limit the number of births as the ref-

FIGURE 4.2

Expected Odds Ratio for Native-born of Native Parentage Relative to Italian-born and Polish-born Women, Non-Southern States: 1905–1909

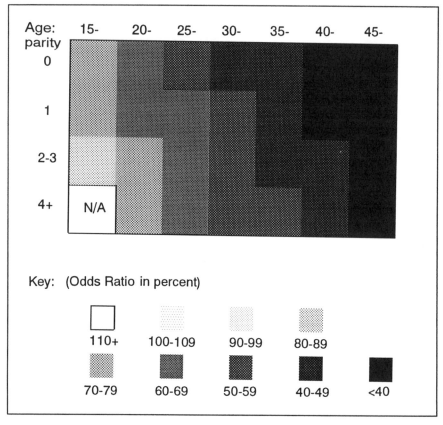

erence group. Here we compare the rates for each group to the combined rates for Italians and Poles.[9] Earlier work showed little evidence of fertility control at older ages for these groups, and little difference between the fertility patterns of Italians and Poles (Ewbank, Morgan, and Watkins 1992).

Figure 4.2 compares the marital fertility of NWNP women to that of Italians and Poles (as fitted by the preferred model for these data, see Ewbank et al. 1990). These figures are reproduced from Ewbank et al.

[9]The Hutterite fertility schedule is typically taken to represent marital fertility in the absence of deliberate attempts to regulate the number of children. We were unable to find age- and parity-specific fertility schedules for the Hutterites, and thus used the fertility of Italians and Polish-speakers instead.

(1992), but they reflect effects shown in Table A4.2 (see Ewbank et al. for details of analytic strategy). For our discussion here, note that the darker the shading of a cell defined by age and parity, the more the fertility of NWNP women deviates from that of Italians and Poles. More precisely, the darker the cell, the more fertility control practiced by NWNP women at that age-parity combination.

The figure is dominated by diagonal bands of shading, which are light at the bottom left and darken toward the upper right. These diagonal bands represent the fact that the differences between NWNP women and Italians/Poles are least among young women of high parity (for example, the fertility of NWNP women is as great as or greater than Italian/Polish women at ages 15–19 and 20–24, parity 2–4) and greatest among older, low-parity women (for example, the fertility of NWNP women is no more than 30 percent of that of Italian/Polish women at ages 45–49 and parity 0).

The key to understanding this diagonal pattern lies in understanding the heterogeneous nature of fertility control in the NWNP population. Some NWNP women are practicing no fertility control at all: these women, who predominate in the young-age, high-parity cells, are rather like young, high-parity Italian and Polish women in that they quickly have a birth, producing high fertility rates in the cells representing younger ages and lower parities. Other NWNP women are childless: they remain at parity 0. The women still childless after age 35 are those who are sterile, the subfecund, and those who are practicing birth control to avoid giving birth. In some cases, they may be women who have remarried after widowhood or divorce ended a childless union. As the fecund NWNP women who are not controlling their fertility enough to remain childless move on to higher parities, the marital fertility rates in each category of age at parity 0 rapidly become dominated by women who are effectively controlling their fertility. Because of this accumulation of successful NWNP controllers who have very low fertility, their marital fertility rates at parity 0 drop quickly with age. Among the childless Italians and Poles, however, there is a group of women who have not yet had a child who are still at risk and are not using effective contraception; they are more likely than childless NWNP women to bear a child. Thus, the gap between the fertility rates of the NWNP women at parity 0 and the Italian and Polish women at parity 0 gets larger and larger as age increases.

A similar diagonal pattern is observed in Figure 4.3 for the German-born women, but the Germans have somewhat higher fertility than the NWNP (i.e., lighter shading) at most ages and parities. British women (not shown) have a pattern indistinguishable from the NWNP group.

It is easier to understand the importance of this diagonal pattern if

FIGURE 4.3

*Expected Odds Ratio for Germans Relative to Italian-born
and Polish-born Women, Non-Southern States: 1905–1909*

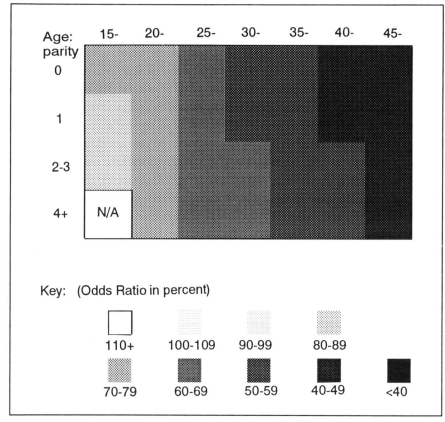

we compare it with the pattern in Figure 4.4 for Yiddish-speaking immigrants. The Yiddish had a distinct pattern of control practiced that is apparent in a comparison with the Germans. These two groups had similar total marital fertility rates (5.0 for the Yiddish, 4.8 for the Germans). The Yiddish women show a pattern that appears to involve more parity-specific control of fertility. At parities 0 and 1, the Yiddish-speaking women had higher fertility than the Germans. In fact, it was as high as or higher than the fertility of the Italians and the Poles. At parities 2 and 3, they had higher rates at the younger ages and lower rates at the older age. At parities 4 and above, the Yiddish-speakers had lower fertility than the Germans at all but the highest age group. This clearly seems to represent a different approach to the control of fertility than is apparent in the other groups.

FIGURE 4.4

Expected Odds Ratio for Yiddish-speakers Relative to Italian-born and Polish-born Women, Non-Southern States: 1905–1909

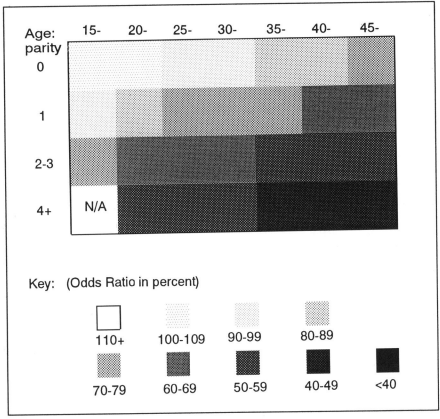

This pattern suggests several conclusions about marital fertility among Jewish immigrants in 1905–1909. First, they clearly adjusted their fertility according to parity. There is essentially no evidence of control at parity 0 and very little at parity 1. However, at parity 2 and above there was substantial control of fertility. Second, in contrast to the heterogeneous NWNP population (with some women apparently exercising little control and thus moving rapidly from one parity to another, while other women successfully stopped at one or avoided childbearing altogether), the fertility of Jewish women was much more homogeneous: virtually all had one or two children, while fertility rates of higher-parity women were quite low (thus reducing the proportion with very large families).

The pattern of fertility among the Irish is difficult to interpret. It

FIGURE 4.5

Expected Odds Ratio for Irish Women Relative to Italian-born and Polish-born Women, Non-Southern States: 1905–1909

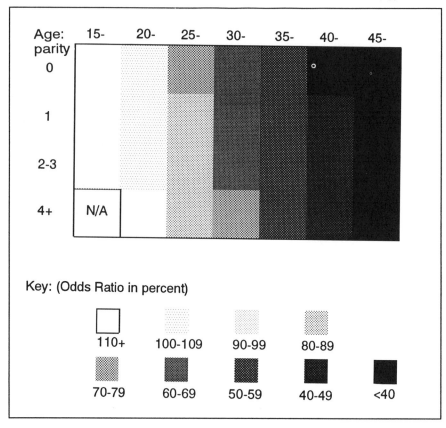

has characteristics in common with the Germans, but there is no evidence of control under age 25. The most likely explanation is that the pattern among the Irish is distorted by their late age at marriage. It may be that the married women under age 25 were selected for high fertility. It might also be due to the higher levels of spouse absence among the Irish (Chapter 5). (For other possibilities, see Morawska, this volume.)

Summary of Age-parity Results

We identify four distinct patterns of fertility. The Italian and Polish women provide the first pattern, against which the others are compared.

These Italian and Polish women married early, and in almost every age and parity category had a greater likelihood of having a birth than women in any other ethnic group. It is highly unlikely that many of them were successfully and deliberately controlling their fertility.

The second pattern is that of the white non-southern native-born women of native parentage. A moderate proportion did not marry. Among those who married, a substantial proportion remained childless or stopped childbearing at parity 1. In general, the pattern of fertility among the NWNP can be characterized by the large proportion of women at each parity who ceased childbearing. This pattern is also found to apply to the British immigrants, and, albeit to a less marked extent, German immigrants.

The third pattern is observed among the Yiddish-speakers. Their fertility was reduced only slightly by marriage patterns, because the average age of marriage was relatively early. The differences between Jews and Italians/Poles do not change much with age, but they change substantially with parity. Childless Jewish women were more likely to have a child at younger ages than Italian or Polish women, but at every other parity they have lower fertility. It appears that Jewish women had ways of effectively controlling their fertility. But either they chose not to apply, or they were not able to apply, the same control measures at the lower parities and younger ages.

The fourth distinct pattern is the Irish pattern. Like their country-women in Ireland, the Irish immigrants reduced their fertility with late marriage. However, the distinctive nature of Irish fertility extends beyond marriage patterns. The proportion of all women who married but remained childless is as great among the Irish as among the NWNP women; among married women who had any children, however, most had a relatively large number of births.

Influences on Fertility

The analyses reported above show marked differences between immigrants and natives in fertility as well as marked differences between "old" and "new" immigrant groups. It is reasonable to believe that these differences may be associated with differences in socioeconomic characteristics as well as with differences in the possibility of contacts with other groups that were controlling their fertility (e.g., the NWNP or British and Germans, whose patterns, described above, suggest considerable fertility control within marriage).

We have chosen to confine our analysis to a subset of that information in the 1910 census: residence (urban versus rural), occupation of the husband, the wife's English-speaking ability and duration in the United States, as well as the wife's generation (foreign-born versus child of foreign-born).[10] Of the information available, these best capture the important socioeconomic distinctions and the possibility of contacts with other groups discussed in the literature on immigrant adaptation and on fertility decline.

Based on previous work on the fertility transition in the United States as well as elsewhere, we expected to find lower fertility in urban than in rural areas, both for theoretical reasons (the net benefits to children are expected to be lower in urban areas, and diffusion would be more rapid in urban than in rural areas) and because Guest (1982), using evidence from the 1900 census, finds evidence of a more rapid decline among foreign-born living in urban areas. We also expected differences by husband's occupation (see Sallume and Notestein 1932; Notestein 1931; Stern 1987). We expected that fertility would be lowest among the wives of professionals. We also expected to find relatively high fertility among farmers' wives, under the assumption either that these couples would have a relatively high "demand" for children or that they were likely to be more isolated, and thus less exposed to innovations in reproductive behavior.

Immigrants were more likely to live in urban areas and less likely to work in agriculture than natives (Carpenter 1969 [1927]; A. R. Miller, Chapter 8). If fertility differences between the natives and the foreign-born were due largely to these differences in residence and occupation, we would expect the effect of ethnicity to be attenuated when we control for these other differences.

In addition to social class differences between migrants and natives (as measured by husband's occupation) and different residence patterns, some of the differences between the NWNP and the foreign-born may be due to differences in the degree of social interaction between the two groups. Based on previous research, we expected to find some diffusion from natives to immigrants. There may have been some dissemination of information and attitudes through officials (e.g., nurses and social workers), and through newspapers, although it is likely that informal, person-to-person contacts were more important (Watkins and Danzi 1992). If contact with natives was important, however, it should be apparent in lower fertility among those who had been in the United States the longest, and among those who spoke English. It is likely that English served as a lingua franca among immigrants from different ethnic groups; thus, the English-speaking variable should capture the possibility of these contacts as well.

---

[10]Too few women were recorded as having an occupation to include women's occupations in the analysis. For further discussion, see Chapter 2, this volume.

The analyses presented here are based on three occupational categories for the husbands: (1) farm, fishery, and forest workers, (2) laborers, and (3) professionals, including administrative and service workers.[11] We have also used three categories of type of place of residence: (1) rural (under 1,000 and unincorporated areas), (2) small cities and towns, and (3) cities (25,000 or more).[12] Duration in the United States is a dichotomy: in the United States more than ten years or less than ten years.[13] English-speaking is also a simple dichotomy (yes/no). In our analysis we used information on whether the wife, not the husband, spoke English; this reflects our view that informal conversations about fertility control were more likely among women than among men.

All of these variables are rather crude. For example, to examine in detail the influence of occupational position on fertility one would certainly want finer classifications of occupation. Here, however, our pur-

---

[11]We began by defining five occupational categories: (1) farm, fishery, and forest laborers, (2) craftsmen, (3) administrative and service, (4) manager and professional, and (5) no occupation reported. Statistical analysis revealed no significant differences between the administrative and professional groups or between the agricultural group and those who stated no occupation. Although more precise occupational categories would be appropriate for attempts to probe more deeply into the routes by which occupation and fertility are related, for the purposes of this chapter the larger categories are acceptable.

[12]Alternative analyses using other residence categories (including the census definition of rural as < 2,500) produced very similar results.

[13]There is a clear relation between duration in the United States and ability to speak English. Using the entire 1910 PUS sample, Cheney showed a nearly linear increase in the proportion speaking English over a ten-year period beginning with arrival, as well as large differences among ethnic groups. By the end of ten years in the United States, the foreign-born Scandinavians and Germans had the highest proportions recorded as speaking English (about 95 percent and 85 percent, respectively), while the Italians and the Poles had the least (about 50 percent and 40 percent, respectively); those whose mother tongue was Yiddish were intermediate (about 60 percent) (Cheney 1988). Differences between rural and urban areas were relatively small, but there were marked differences between men and women, with men reporting higher levels of English-speaking than women (Cheney 1988). Cross-tabulations of English-speaking by duration in our sample gave results similar to Cheney's. In each ethnic group, the majority of married foreign-born women who had been in the United States ten years or more at the time of the census reported speaking English, again with the Italians and Poles speaking the least English, and Scandinavians and Germans the most. Ethnic differences were even greater among those who had been in the United States less than ten years; although the majority of Scandinavians, Germans, and Central European Jews in this category reported speaking English in 1910, the majority of Italians, Poles, and Eastern European Jews were non-English-speaking.

It is possible to examine the association between duration in the United States and English-speaking, but we cannot examine the association between English and religion, which may have been strong. There is reason to believe that, at least for some, maintenance of the mother tongue was associated with preservation of a religion: anti-Catholics demanded English teaching in the schools (Wiebe 1967, p. 58), and it is reasonable to think that the two were associated in the minds of the immigrants as well. Thus, those who did not speak English may have been among the more devout elements of the immigrant population. A study of a German community in Texas covering a slightly earlier period shows independent effects of denomination and English-speaking, with English-speakers and Protestants having lower fertility than non-English-speakers and Catholics (although English-speaking was not statistically significant) (Gutmann and Fliess 1988).

pose is simply to see overall whether differences between natives and immigrants are due to very different overall occupational distributions among farming, laboring, and the professions, and to see whether the association of fertility with occupation is independent of other effects, for example, living in cities. For this purpose crude occupational categories are sufficient: indeed, they may be preferable, because by relying on gross distinctions (e.g., between farmers and laborers) we avoid problems produced by errors in recording. Duration in the United States and English-speaking are rough indicators too: for example, the category of English-speakers undoubtedly includes those who knew very little English (see Chapter 2, this volume, for a more extended discussion of these variables). Because the variables are measured rather crudely, we consider our findings to be suggestive rather than conclusive.

Table 4.3 summarizes the influence of these variables on marital fertility. The previous descriptive analysis and work not described here (but, see Table 4A.2) show the British patterns to be nearly identical to those of the NWNP, Italian and Polish patterns to be insignificantly different from each other, and Central European Jews and Eastern European Jews to be insignificantly different from each other. Thus the effective number of groups to be examined are not nine but six (Appendix A of this chapter gives a more detailed discussion of the model-selection procedure).

We show here three models. In each the dependent variable is the

TABLE 4.3

Effects of Generation, Not Speaking English, Time in the U.S., Place of Residence, and Husband's Occupation

	Selected Models		
	1	2	3
In U.S. Ten or Fewer Years	1.09*		1.05
Does Not Speak English	1.03		1.00
First Generation	1.05*	1.11*	1.09*
Husband's Occupation			
Farmer vs. laborers	—	.99	.99
Farmer vs. professional	—	1.22*	1.22*
Size of Place			
Rural vs. town/city	—	1.20*	1.20*
Rural vs. large city	—	1.28*	1.28*

*Differential is greater than twice its standard error.

odds of a birth. The coefficients shown measure the difference between the fertility of two groups (e.g., the contrast between the "omitted" and specified groups). These coefficients are estimated in models that include controls on the woman's ethnicity and her age and parity at the start of the year (the coefficients for these are shown in Appendix A of this chapter, Table 4A.4).[14] Model 1 presents the effects of duration, English-speaking, and generation; Model 2 considers the effects of generation, occupation, and the size of the place of residence; and Model 3 considers both sets of influences.

Consider first Model 3, which includes all of these contrasts. It is clear that English-speaking does not matter: the fertility of those who do not speak English is exactly the same as the fertility of the NWNP reference group (effect = 1.00). But foreign birth, occupation, size of place of residence, and duration in the United States are all associated with fertility. The fertility of farmers is 22 percent higher than that of professionals (increased by a factor of 1.22), although there is virtually no difference between farmers and laborers. Fertility is highest in the rural areas and lowest in the largest cities: women who live in rural areas have fertility 20 percent higher than those who live in towns or medium-sized cities, but 28 percent higher than those who live in large cities. In our model the effects are multiplicative (additive in their logs): for example, a woman who was in the United States less than ten years would have fertility 5 percent higher than one who was in the United States more than ten years, but if she were married to a farmer her fertility would be further increased by 22 percent compared to a woman who was married to a professional. The generational effect is modest— fertility is 10 percent higher for immigrants than for those born in the United States. The generation effects noted earlier (Figure 4.1 and Table 4.1) are weakened somewhat by controls on age, parity, and the other variables in the models.[15]

A comparison of the three models shows that the effects of duration in the United States, city residence, and husband's occupation are largely independent of one another. For example, although it seemed likely that a longer duration in the United States would be associated with social mobility, the effect of duration is hardly changed when the occupation of the woman's husband is taken into account. Similarly, the effects of

[14]To present the coefficients from the unconstrained model, where the coefficients are allowed to vary across ethnic groups, would encourage interpretation of small differences.

[15]These models control on the woman's initial parity as well as on age. The results in Table 4.1 and Figure 4.1 control only on age. The parity distributions of first-generation immigrant groups are higher than the second generation. Coupled with higher fertility at higher parities for both generations, controlling for parity reduces the generation effect on current fertility.

occupation or urban residence are unchanged when the other variables are included.

Table 4.3 shows effects that are constrained to be the same for all groups, including the natives. It is possible, however, that these overall effects mask differences across groups: city size might matter for some groups but not for others. In particular, we thought it likely that the high degree to which the new immigrants were residentially segregated (White, Dymowski, and Wang, Chapter 6) would limit contacts with the natives and members of the "old" groups (even for those who spoke English and had been in the United States more than ten years). This segregation might make city residence effects weaker for some immigrant groups than for others, or weaker compared to NWNP.

We tested for interactions between each of the variables and each ethnic group. We could not reject the hypothesis that some variables' effects were identical across all ethnic groups: generation, occupation, and residence are associated with fertility in similar ways for each of the ethnic groups and the NWNP. Despite the possibility, for example, that the category "laborers" includes one type of laborer for Germans and another for Italians, the effect of being a laborer is similar for both groups. And although Italians and Poles in the aggregate show little evidence of fertility control, those who lived in large cities had lower fertility than those who lived in rural areas. Because much emphasis has been given to the effects of specific city contexts in the literature on immigrants of this period, we further examined data for ten of the largest cities: New York, Chicago, Philadelphia, St. Louis, Boston, Cleveland, Pittsburgh, Detroit, Buffalo, and San Francisco. We found essentially no variation in fertility across cities and no evidence at all that the ethnic differentials documented here varied across cities (Morgan and Watkins 1992).[16]

However, the effects of English-speaking and duration do vary by ethnic group, as seen in Table 4.4. Net of all other covariates, there is no effect for the "new" immigrant groups of English-speaking or duration in the United States. But for the "old" immigrants, women who were recent arrivals or women who did not speak English had higher fertility (compared to those who could speak English and were in the United States longer, respectively). Because in this analysis the effects are multiplicative, members of the "old" immigrant groups who did not speak English and were recent arrivals had fertility about 1.27 times higher (1.10×1.15) than those who had been in the United States longer and spoke English. Taken together, these effects are as powerful as the

---

[16]The only exception was San Francisco, where fertility was somewhat lower for all groups.

TABLE 4.4

Effects of Not Speaking English and Time in the U.S.,
by Ethnic Group, Factor Change in Odds of a Birth

	Does Not Speak English	In U.S. 10 or Fewer Years
Ethnic Group		
Old		
British	—a	1.15
Irish	—a	1.15
Scandinavians	1.10	1.15
Germans	1.10	1.15
New		
Italians	1.0	1.0
Polish	1.0	1.0
CE Jews	1.0	1.0
EE Jews	1.0	1.0

NOTES: Estimate effects are net of the other variables in the model: generation, occupation and residence, and age and parity.

—a indicates that all British and Irish could speak English. As a result, effects cannot be estimated for these groups.

place of residence and occupation effects. It is the lack of an effect for the "new" immigrants that accounts for the weaker effects of English-speaking and duration estimated for all groups together (see Table 4.3).

Lastly, we consider the effect of the covariates in our models on the ethnic/native fertility differences described earlier. We compare immigrant women to NWNP women in the same category: ages 30–34, with two children, who have been in the United States more than ten years. Table 4.5 shows gross ethnic effects, and then the effects of membership in a particular ethnic group net of the effects of the covariates (see Appendix 4A, Table 4A.4: gross effects are calculated from Model 1 in this table, and net effects from Model 5). The gross effects seen here are similar to those seen earlier in Table 4.2 for currently married women: the differences in Table 4.5 are due to the inclusion of parity in this model. Although the covariates in our models have clear effects, they do not account for ethnic differences. For the British, the Scandinavians, and the Italians and Poles, including the controls lowers ethnic fertility relative to that of the NWNPs, but not by much. In the first column we see, for example, that Scandinavian fertility is 38 percent higher than the fertility of the NWNP; with controls, it is 21 percent higher. For the Irish, the Germans, and the Jews, relative fertility is slightly higher when controls are included. The most important conclusion from this table is

TABLE 4.5

Gross and Net Effects of Ethnicity on the Odds of a Birth in the Previous Year: Women Aged 30–34 with Two Children

	Gross	Net*
Natives	1.00	1.00
British	1.15	1.08
Irish	1.26	1.37
Scandinavians	1.38	1.21
Germans	1.11	1.13
Italians	1.98	1.91
Polish	1.98	1.91
CE Jews	1.20	1.31
EE Jews	1.20	1.31

*Estimated effects are net of husband's occupation and place of residence, effects are for those in generation 1, in the U.S. eleven or more years and who speak English. Effects are from Model V, Table A4.4. Net ethnic effects are much the same if the interactive effects of duration in the U.S. and speaking English (described in Table 4.4) are added to the model.

that ethnic effects are robust, persisting despite controls. Moreover, the ethnic effects in Table 4.5 (for those aged 30–34 at parity 2) are substantial in size. For Italians and Poles they are substantially greater in magnitude compared to the socioeconomic and contact variables shown in Table 4.3. Other ethnic effects are comparable in size to the socioeconomic and contact variables.

Discussion

Previous work on the fertility of immigrants at the turn of the century had demonstrated higher fertility among the foreign-born than the NWNP, and considerable variation across ethnic groups, with substantially higher fertility for the "new" immigrants (particularly the Poles and Italians) than the "old" immigrants. We have found, for a national sample, that these differences are attenuated but do not disappear when differences between immigrants and natives in age and marital status are taken into account. Although some of the higher fertility of the immigrants, and particularly the "new" immigrants, was due to their being younger and more likely to be married than the natives, most of the contrast remained when marital, age-specific fertility was examined.

In addition to ethnic heterogeneity in levels of fertility, we also find heterogeneity in *patterns* of childbearing by age and parity. The differences in the patterns of childbearing by age and parity are even more striking than the differences in level, for it is these patterns that are the most reliable indicator of whether or not a group is practicing deliberate fertility control. At the two extremes are the NWNP women, and Italian and Polish women. There is no doubt that the native women were deliberately controlling fertility. Although this is not a new finding, our analysis shows that, although some young NWNP women were apparently not practicing control (proceeding quickly from marriage to high parities), for others control among young women began early in their childbearing career. In contrast, Italian and Polish women had higher fertility in every age and parity combination than the other ethnic groups (except low-parity Jews), demonstrating in the aggregate little evidence of control.

The patterns of childbearing of British, German, and Scandinavian women are so similar to the native white women as to suggest that they too were deliberately controlling fertility, and early in their childbearing career.

The fertility pattern of the Yiddish-speakers was sharply different from that of the other "new" immigrant groups. At the start of childbearing (young ages and low parities) the Jews and the Italians and Poles were rather similar. But when comparisons were made at successively older ages and higher parities the gap between them widened. The influence of parity on Jewish fertility was far more pronounced than that of age: in every age group, Jewish women who had already had at least one child were less likely to have another than were the Italian and Polish women of the same age, but the differences between the two groups were greater at higher parities than at lower.

We interpret this as indicating considerably more deliberate fertility control among the Jews. The relatively low fertility of Jews in the United States has been observed previously (see, e.g., Goldscheider 1965). The distinctive parity-specific pattern of the Jews shown here clearly deserves more attention than is possible in this chapter, but a brief discussion, drawing on sources outside the 1910 census sample, is in order. Although religious leaders opposed contraception, at least in the United States this may not have been a major obstacle. Reform rabbis preferred to ignore the issue, exempting the question of contraception from the area of the sacred, and Conservative rabbis followed; Orthodox leaders preferred to concentrate on other issues (Sklare 1971, pp. 79–80; see also Feldman 1974).

There is some reason to believe that these patterns of parity-specific fertility control were learned in the United States. A "satirist" writes in the *American Israelite* (1887–1888) that the circumcisers complain bitterly of hard times: "They say the Jewesses have learned American tricks and that the injunction of [be fruitful and multiply] is totally ignored" (Glanz 1976, p. 187, footnote 60). Other evidence suggests that fertility control may have been established before the immigrants arrived: Jews were among the forerunners of the fertility transition in Western Europe (Livi Bacci, 1977; Goldstein 1981).

The results of our analysis lead us to conclude that fertility control may have been brought from Europe. There are three reasons for reaching this conclusion. First, our analysis of age-and-parity-specific patterns suggests that fertility control was not used in precisely the same way by Jews and natives. Jews effectively limited family size, but they did not limit/delay births early in marriage as natives did. Thus, while perhaps using the same birth control techniques, natives and Jews used them to somewhat different ends. Second, the multivariate analysis showed that duration in the United States and the ability to speak English did not influence Jewish fertility. If fertility control were adopted from natives, we would expect those Jews in the United States longer and those most likely to interact with natives (those who speak English) to be more likely to adopt these "fertility control innovations" from the NWNP. Finally, Jews were largely segregated from natives (White et al., Chapter 6), making a scenario of diffusion less plausible. Once in the United States, however, Jewish institutions may have further disseminated information about fertility control, or the advantages of small families. For example, an article on June 11, 1919, in the Jewish newspaper the *Daily Forward* titled "Better to Be Childless Than to Have Bad Children" reminded women that if they wanted children they must then worry about the children's future, bear the blame if they turned out badly, and risk being neglected or even abandoned by them in old age (Seller 1985). In summary, our analysis suggests that further research into the age-and-parity patterns of Jewish fertility in their countries of origin would be likely to show similar patterns of fertility control there.

Perhaps the most important finding from the multivariate analysis is that although residence and occupations influenced the fertility of all the ethnic groups, and English-speaking and duration in the United States influenced fertility for the "old" immigrant groups, the ethnic effects, in 1910, remained substantial. The analysis of infant and child mortality (Preston et al., Chapter 3) showed that when controls for economic and social circumstances were taken into account the immigrants looked much like the natives: the French Canadians (not considered in this chapter) and the Jews were the exceptions. In this analysis of fertility the conclusions are quite different.

We can, however, detect some influences of these social and economic circumstances on fertility. Despite the heterogeneity in age-and-parity-specific patterns of fertility that we described, occupation and city residence lowered fertility for all immigrant groups, with effects that were independent of one another (that is, while occupations in urban areas differed from those in rural, urban life evidently has other effects). These differentials, which hold across a broad range of groups, suggest structural factors to which all groups responded similarly. The higher costs of children for urban and higher-status parents might be such structural factors. Unfortunately, our cross-sectional data do not provide any leverage on whether the lower fertility of urban residents and of wives of professionals were stable differentials, or whether these were simply the first subgroups within each population to reduce their fertility. Although it is possible that different cultural traditions were associated with ethnically specific responses to residence and occupation, on the basis of our analysis we are inclined to reject such a conclusion; the burden of proof, it would seem, would lie on those who claim otherwise. These findings are particularly relevant for the Italians and Poles, who had by far the highest fertility. Clearly, large segments of these populations made no attempt (or tried in vain) to limit their number of children. But it appears that some Italians and Poles (those women who lived in large cities and whose husbands were professionals) had lower fertility and had apparently already, in 1910, adopted fertility-reducing practices.

Ethnic groups did, however, respond in idiosyncratic ways to the variables, which we have interpreted as representing the possibility of contact with natives. Here the distinction was between the "old" and the "new" ethnic groups. Longer residence in the United States and English-speaking were associated with lower fertility for women in the "old" immigrant groups (the Germans and the Scandinavians) but not the "new." Again, these effects were independent of one another: it is not simply that those who had lived in the United States longer were more likely to speak English.

Why did duration and English-speaking not have the pervasive effects on fertility in all groups that occupation and residence were shown to have? The absence of an effect of these variables on the fertility of the "new" immigrants is probably due to their recent arrival and relatively high degree of residential segregation; we suspect that were it possible to perform this analysis with data from 1930 after the "new" immigrants had had a chance to adjust to their new home, the "new" immigrants who spoke English would have lower fertility than those who did not.

Although the effects of residence and occupation were more pervasive than the influences of duration and English-speaking, we find the latter particularly interesting because they are better indicators of the influence of social interactions on fertility than are usually available to analysts of fertility differentials. Typically, analyses of fertility include information only on the social class and economic characteristics of the woman, and sometimes those of her husband. Here we have included two variables, duration in the United States and English-speaking, that represent the possibility of contact with others, both native whites of native parentage and other immigrant groups. Through these contacts, immigrants may have learned about the availability and legitimacy of techniques of fertility control, or about the desirability of smaller family sizes. As Morawska notes in her Afterword, the interaction with those in other ethnic groups may have been even more important than interaction with natives. Poles and Italians, for example, may have learned something about reproductive practices from the native women they met, but they may also have learned from Jewish or German neighbors, schoolmates, or workmates.

Our findings with respect to the importance of duration and English-speaking for the "old" immigrant groups deserve more attention than can be given here, but a few speculations follow. It is possible that English-speaking and duration are proxies for other influences on fertility that are unmeasured or unanalyzed here. These influences are unlikely to be through occupational differentials, since the effect of English-speaking and duration are independent of gross differences across professionals, farmers, and laborers. However, English-speaking may be to some degree a proxy for literacy, as those who spoke English were more literate, and thus may have had more exposure through the press or advertisements to ideas concerning the appropriate family size or to techniques of contraception.

Speaking English would also increase the possibility of informal personal contacts. We think these would be particularly important in the diffusion of what contemporaries would have called "American values," or the diffusion across ethnic groups—for example, from the Jews or the Germans to Poles or Italians—of what fertility analysts would call "innovative practices of reproduction." Not surprisingly, there is little evidence of these ephemeral channels of communication. That women of different ethnic groups might have shared the same tenement does not mean that they talked with one another. Similarly, that women had been in the United States longer and spoke English does not mean they actually had more contact with natives or members of other ethnic groups, or that this contact would have included discussions relevant for fertility.

The literature by historians and historical sociologists on immigrant groups at the turn of the century concentrates largely on a single ethnic group, or comparisons of ethnic groups, within the same context (e.g., the same city); little attention is paid to interethnic interactions. But this literature, as well as novels and memoirs, is replete with descriptions of occasions on which these conversations may have taken place. Although residential concentration was marked, ethnic residential boundaries were not impenetrable: in the Little Italies and Little Irelands of Chicago in 1893, blocks and even buildings were often ethnically mixed (Philpott 1978). Thus the main areas of female sociability—the front stoops and the neighborhood stores—may have brought together women of different ethnicities.[17] Women also met at work, and workroom life was organized around shared interests. Writing of her days working in a Chicago shoe factory at the turn of the century, Mary Anderson said:

> You talk to the person at the machine on each side of you, sometimes about your work, sometimes about your people and your life at home, sometimes about parties and boyfriends . . . (quoted in Tentler 1979, p. 68).

More direct evidence of conversations relevant for fertility behavior comes from interviews with elderly Italian and Jewish women in the United States. These interviews show that in a slightly later period (the 1920s and the 1930s) women talked with others about topics relevant to fertility control: most of these conversations were within the same ethnic groups, but sometimes they crossed ethnic boundaries (Spector, Watkins, and Goldstein 1991; see also Watkins and Danzi 1992). Talking with other women may have assisted the women in mediating mixed messages from priests, grandmothers, friends, husbands. And the views of other women were presumably particularly important to immigrants who had left mothers or grandmothers behind.

Based on the analyses presented here, we conclude that residence and occupation were associated with fertility in expected ways. However, it seems likely that a full story of the fertility behavior of ethnic groups in the United States will need to take the possibilities of the influence of a new social environment—living in the United States and speaking English—into account. The exploration of these possible channels ranks high on our future research agenda.

---

[17]The main arenas for male sociability, saloons, were largely ethnically homogeneous, although it is noteworthy that in Chicago and Boston at the turn of the century Irish and German saloons were more likely than Polish or Italian bars to be located outside ethnic neighborhoods and to serve an ethnically mixed clientele (Duis 1983, p. 145).

Appendix 4A:
Supplementary Tables and Description of Analyses

The results in Tables 4.3, 4.4, and 4.5 and Figures 4.2, 4.3, 4.4, 4.5, and 4.6 come from an analysis of the odds of a birth by the woman's age, parity, and ethnicity. Nine ethnic contrasts are allowed: natives of native mothers and eight categories of first-generation immigrants. Table 4A.1 shows the fit of selected models. Our baseline model (Model 1) allows for age and parity effects on fertility. Roughly 90 percent of the variability in fertility is accounted for by age-parity. Our interest focuses on the remaining variability. Model 2 allows for the set of ethnic con-

TABLE 4A.1

*Models Fit to Cross-tabulation of Fertility,
by Women's Age, Parity, and Ethnicity*

(Key: Fertility [birth in a given year, yes/no] = F; wife's age = A; wife's parity = P; wife's ethnicity = E). L subscript indicates that variable contrasts are scored linearly.

Model Description	X^2	d.f.
1. EAP FAP E	1,095	214
2. EAP FAP FE	501	206
3. EAP FAP FEA$_L$	454	198
4. EAP FAP FEP$_L$	440	198
5.a EAP FAP FEA$_L$ FEP$_L$	387	190
5.b EAP FAP FEA$_L$ FEP$_L$ (Preferred model, some coefficients in 5a constrained)	398	198
6. EAP FAP FEA$_L$ FE(A$_L$) FEP$_L^2$ FE(P$_L^2$)	296	171

Comparisons of Selected Models			
Models	X^2 Difference	d.f. Difference	BICM[a]
1 –2	594	−8	501
2 –5a	117	−16	−69
5a–5b	11	−8	−81
2 –5b	103	−8	10
5a–6	102	−16	−58

[a]BICM = (X² difference) − [d.f. difference. * ln (N)]. Sample size (N) = 114,281.

trasts. The improvement in fit is X^2 of 594 with 8 degrees of freedom—a clearly significant effect (even by the stringent BICM criteria). If BICM for the X^2 difference is positive (>0), then the less parsimonious model fits the data significantly better than the more parsimonious one.

Models 3, 4, and 5 add ethnic-age, ethnic-parity, and then both sets of terms to the model. These interactions are constrained to be "linear"—that is, the effects of ethnicity are allowed consistently to increase or decrease with age and/or parity. Relaxation of this linearity constraint (as in Model 6, which allows the interaction to take a nonlinear form) did not significantly improve the fit of the model or alter the substantive description of the data. Model 5b places some additional constraints on the interaction terms that will be described below. It is this model (5b) that is chosen as the preferred model. It provides a significant improvement in fit over Models 1 and 2.

Table 4A.2 shows ethnic parameters from Models 5a and 5b. Model 5b constrains some effects to be 1.00 (e.g., no effect, see "a") and constrains some other effects to be equal (see "b" through "g"). Substantively, these constraints force English-speaking and native fertility to be different by a constant amount at all ages and parities. Italian and Polish fertility levels *and* age-parity patterns are constrained to be equal, as are the two groups of Jews. See text for substantive discussion of this model.

To assess differences in first- and second-generation groups, we analyzed data for seventeen ethnic/generation contrasts (e.g., data and contrasts for the second generation were included). Table 4A.3 shows generation effects added to two models from Table 4A.2, Models 5a and 5b. The two columns on the left allow for an additive effect of generation; the two columns on the right allow for separate generation effects for each ethnic group. Regardless of model (5a or 5b) the substantive results are clear. Over all groups, being in the first generation (as opposed to the second) increases fertility by about 11 percent (i.e., by a factor of 1.12 or 1.11 depending on whether one examines effects from Model 5a or 5b). This effect is statistically significant (X^2 of Model $5 - X^2$ of Model $6 = 21$ with 1 degree of freedom).

The models that allow generation to have different effects for each ethnic group do not provide a significant improvement in fit (over the additive representation). However, the parameters clearly suggest that generation is least important for the Italians and Poles. The effects for the Jewish groups appear large, but these effects are based on relatively few observations.

Models in Table 4A.4 are fit to a new tabulation of birthrates by age, parity, ethnicity, generation, time in the United States, ability to speak English (for immigrants), husband's occupation, and place of residence. See text for description of variables. In addition to age, parity,

TABLE 4A.2
The Effects of Ethnicity, by Age and Parity: Preferred Model

	Model 5a* Unconstrained Model	Model 5b* Preferred Model
Ethnic Effects		
Natives	—	—
English	1.26	1.12
Irish	2.08	2.08
Scandinavians	1.40	1.39
Germans	1.28	1.28
Italians	1.60	1.64[b]
Polish	1.75	1.64[b]
CE Jews	2.18	1.80[c]
EE Jews	1.72	1.80[c]
Age-ethnic Interactions		
English	1.01	1.00[a]
Irish	.92	.92
Scandinavians	1.15	1.15
Germans	1.05	1.05
Italians	1.13	1.16[d]
Polish	1.21	1.16[d]
CE Jews	1.04	1.09[e]
EE Jews	1.12	1.09[e]
Parity-ethnic Interactions		
English	.92	1.00[a]
Irish	.91	.91
Scandinavians	.84	.84
Germans	.90	.90
Italians	.91	.87[f]
Polish	.84	.87[f]
CE Jews	.70	.73[g]
EE Jews	.73	.73[g]

$$X^2 = 387; \text{ d.f.} = 190 \quad X^2 = 398; \text{ d.f.} = 198$$

*Additive and interactive effects of age and parity are fit in both models but these effects are now shown here. Effects above have been transformed into multiplicative changes in the odds on a birth.

[a] Effects constrained = 1.00
[b,c,d,e,f,g] These pairs of coefficients are constrained to be equal.

and age-parity effects, Model I includes ethnic effects. Model 5 allows for the additive effects of all other covariates. A major finding is that the ethnic effects are little changed by controls on generation, time in the United States, ability to speak English, occupation, and size of place

TABLE 4A.3

The Effects of Generation on Ethnic Fertility [a]

Ethnic Group	Selected Models[a]			
	Model 3	Model 6	Model 4	Model 7
English	1.12	1.11	1.12	1.12
Irish	1.12	1.11	1.10	1.10
Scandinavians	1.12	1.11	1.20	1.20
Germans	1.12	1.11	1.11	1.11
Italians	1.12	1.11	.99	.99
Polish	1.12	1.11	1.02	.99
CE Jews	1.12	1.11	1.51	1.50
EE Jews	1.12	1.11	1.50	1.50

Fit of Selected Models[a]	X^2	d.f.
(1) Independence[b]	16,381	426
(2) Model 5a + no generation effect	652	375
(3) Model 5a + additive generation effect	629	374
(4) Model 5a + interactive generation effect	619	367
(5) Model 5b + no generation effect	672	383
(6) Model 5b + additive generation effect	651	382
(7) Model 5b + interactive generation effect	644	377

[a]With the exception of Model 1, all models adopt the structure of Models 5a or 5b described in Table A4.2.
[b]Model asserting no effects of age, parity, and other covariates on fertility.

of residence. However, several of these factors have substantial independent effects on fertility (especially husband's occupation and size of place of residence). Additive effects of generation, in United States < ten years, not speaking English, husband's occupation, and place of residence are reproduced in Table 4A.3. See Table 4A.5 for net effects of ethnicity (calculated from effects estimated in Model 5).

We now ask the question: are the effects of these covariates the same for each ethnic group? Tables 4A.3–4A.5 provide the answer for two covariates, ability to speak English and time in the United States. The preferred characterization of these effects is a "constrained interactive effects" model (see effects at far right of page, Model 4). This model allows for effects of both variables *but* only for the "old" immigrants. Comparison with Model 2 (unconstrained interactive effects) shows this to be an acceptable characterization of the effects. Table 4A.4 reproduces parameters from the preferred model.

TABLE 4A.4

Net Effects[a] of Generation, Duration in the U.S., Not Speaking English, Occupation, and Rural-Urban Residence on the Odds of a Birth: Years of Risk Within Marriage

Effects	Selected Models[b]				
	1	2	3	4	5
Ethnicity Main Effects					
Natives	—	—	—	—	—
British	1.15	1.07	1.05	1.15	1.14
Irish	1.43	1.42	1.40	1.60	1.59
Scandinavians	1.22	1.20	1.17	1.18	1.16
Germans	1.23	1.22	1.21	1.29	1.29
Italians	1.63	1.54	1.43	1.63	1.57
Polish	1.63	1.54	1.43	1.63	1.57
CE Jews	1.65	1.54	1.45	1.82	1.76
EE Jews	1.65	1.54	1.45	1.82	1.76
Age-ethnic Interactions					
English	1.00[c]	1.00[c]	1.00[c]	1.00[c]	1.00[c]
Irish	1.03	1.03	1.03	1.03	1.01
Scandinavians	1.16	1.17	1.16	1.16	1.16
Germans	1.06	1.06	1.06	1.06	1.06
Italians	1.17	1.17	1.18	1.15	1.15
Polish	1.17	1.17	1.18	1.15	1.15
CE Jews	1.07	1.07	1.08	1.06	1.07
EE Jews	1.07	1.07	1.08	1.06	1.07
Parity-ethnic Interactions					
English	1.00[c]	1.00[c]	1.00[c]	1.00[c]	1.00[c]
Irish	.90	.90	.90	.94	.94
Scandinavians	.84	.84	.84	.84	.84
Germans	.87	.87	.87	.88	.88
Italians	.87	.88	.88	.91	.92
Polish	.87	.88	.88	.91	.92
CE Jews	.77	.77	.77	.80	.80
EE Jews	.77	.77	.77	.80	.80
First generation	—	1.07	1.05	1.10	1.09
in U.S. <10 yrs	—	—	1.09	—	1.06
not speak English	—	—	1.03	—	1.01
Occupation					
Laborer vs. farmer	—	—	—	1.01	1.01
Professional vs. farmer	—	—	—	.78	.78
Size of Place of Residence					
Town/city vs. (<1,000)	—	—	—	.80	.80
Large city vs. (<1,000)	—	—	—	.72	.72
X^2	5,102	5,094	5,085	4,492	4,489
d.f.	3,637	3,636	3,634	3,632	3,630

[a]All effects are multiplicative changes in the odds of a birth. All effects shown are net of age, parity, and (age × parity) effects.
[b]All models shown here adopt the structure of the "preferred model" (Model 5b) in Table 4A.2
[c]All coefficients that equal 1.00 have been constrained to have "no effect."

TABLE 4A.5

Effects[a] of Not Speaking English and Time in the U.S. on Ethnic Fertility

Ethnic Group	Model 1 Additive Effects[b]		Model 2 Interactive Effects[c]		Model 3 Constrained Interactive Effects[d]		Model 4 Constrained Interactive Effects[e]	
	Not Speak English	In U.S. <10 Years	Not Speak English	In U.S. <10 Years	Not Speak English	In U.S. <10 Years	Not Speak English	In U.S. <10 Years
British	—	1.06	—	1.00	—	1.00	—	1.00
Irish	—	1.06	—	1.19	—	1.15	—	1.15
Scandinavians	1.01	1.06	1.13	1.21	1.10	1.15	1.10	1.15
Germans	1.01	1.06	1.06	1.11	1.10	1.15	1.10	1.15
Italians	1.01	1.06	.97	.98	.99	.99	1.00	1.00
Polish	1.01	1.06	.97	.98	.99	.99	1.00	1.00
CE Jews	1.01	1.06	1.01	1.01	.99	.99	1.00	1.00
EE Jews	1.01	1.06	1.01	1.01	.99	.99	1.00	1.00

[a]Effects are multiplicative changes in the odds of a birth in the observed year of marriage.

[b]Additive effects are from Model 5, Table 4A.4 ($X^2 = 4489$; d.f. = 3630).

[c]These effects are estimated in a model that includes all effects in Model 5, Table 4A.4, plus the interactive effects of ethnicity and "not speak English" and ethnicity and "time in the U.S." This model has $X^2 = 4483$; d.f. = 3623. The improvement in fit provided by the interactive terms is $X^2 = 6$; d.f. = 7.

[d]This model constrains some of the interactive terms. Specifically, "language" and "time in U.S." effects are estimated separately for "old" and "new" immigrants. This model has $X^2 = 4483$; d.f. = 3628.

[e]This model further constrains the interaction terms. One effect of "language" and "time in U.S." is estimated for the "old" immigrant groups. These variables are constrained to have no effect for the "new" immigrant groups. This model has $X^2 = 4484$; d.f. = 3630.

We addressed the same question with respect to the powerful effects of occupation and residence. We found no significant interactions and thus cannot reject the hypothesis that these factors affected all groups similarly (results not shown here).

5

UNDER THE SAME ROOF:
FAMILY AND HOUSEHOLD STRUCTURE

Andrew T. Miller
S. Philip Morgan
Antonio McDaniel

SINCE THE HIGH tide of immigration around 1910, scholars of ethnic history have provided a good deal of information on how immigrants structured their families in households and how various immigrant groups were distributed within or across households.[1] The same household information has been examined for groups within the native population as well, particularly with regard to African Americans. From the 1910 Census Bureau tabulations for the foreign-born to the reports of the U.S. Immigration Commission (1911), subsequent studies using census data in the years 1910–1920 were concerned with immigrants and their households mainly in regard to housing conditions and health and overcrowding.[2] In this chapter we make use of the data on place of birth and mother tongue, race, and relationship to household head to describe the household structure and family living arrangements of several ethnic groups including immigrants, their offspring, and native-born populations of whites and African Americans.

Our purpose is not simply to replicate the studies already done, though in some cases our results confirm on a national level what had previously been studied only locally. In this chapter we seek to examine

[1]This research was supported by a grant from the National Institute of Child Health and Human Development (NICHD 1RO1-HD-25856). We thank Mark Hereward and Michael Little for programming assistance and Donna Gabaccia, Margaret Greene, Ann Miller, Ewa Morawska, Michael White, and Susan Watkins for their helpful comments and suggestions.
[2]These include the major works of the U.S. Immigration Commission (1911), Edward Ross (1913), Jenks and Lauck (1913), and the Americanization Studies published by Harpers in the early 1920s under the auspices of the Carnegie Corporation.

closely and compare household structure and family structure across both immigrant and native-born groups in a given census year. By household structure we mean whether households are nuclear, extended, or augmented, particularly by the boarders and household employees typically supplied by immigration. By family structure we mean whether husbands live with wives and mothers with their children. We find that immigrants look different from both African American and white native-born of native parentage groups in household structure, whereas in family structure, it is African Americans who look different from both immigrant and native-born whites. In conjunction with other studies, it appears that the differences in household structure diminish rapidly, and thus may be mainly a function of migration itself. Family differences seem to persist, and thus may not be as much a part of immediate social circumstances as they are of deeper cultural histories.

At the beginning of this century, the extraordinarily high level of immigration to the United States was a source of pride as well as concern to social observers of the day. Although it was taken as a vote of confidence in a democratic and opportunity-rich America, there was concern that the large number of immigrants would change the character of the country. Of course, the dominant white Protestant group that articulated this concern had a very limited notion of the character of the country, and ignored large portions of the population including the native-born of African descent. The pride of ownership these people felt about America demanded that others live up to certain standards in order to participate in properly and be "worthy" of the benefits many felt America offered a bit too freely.

Their concern with rapid immigration arose from the foreign languages, religions, ideas, and customs that the immigrants brought with them, which many found obviously inferior to native-born white Protestant practices. High fertility and mortality, poor health, inadequate housing, and low social status were attributed as much to deficient cultural practices as to structural factors. The rising concern with immigrants focused on improper social and family practices and indecent or immoral living conditions, and the fear that these and their effects would be passed on to the immigrants' children. Particular concern was directed at those families and households where overcrowding, non-family units, unhealthy hygiene and housekeeping, foreign languages, and "immoral" contacts were thought to flourish and perhaps persist owing to "ignorance of habit." One of the most vocal groups attacking immigrant lifestyles during this time period was the Immigration Restriction League, for whom Henry Pratt Fairchild was a prominent voice.[3] Less hostile

---

[3]Fairchild wrote prominent articles in *The Yale Review* (1907), *The American Journal of Sociology* (1911), and *The American Economic Review* (1912), and a book, *The*

progressive and reformist groups sought to intervene in the process of possible generational transmission through the public schools for children, and settlement houses and other "services" for the adults. Faith in education as the tool of incorporation and assimilation for immigrants as well as African Americans to find their place at this time reflected the common feeling that the native white way of living was the most rational and advanced. The assumption was that if people were shown the error of their ways, they would naturally desire to emulate the native white example.[4]

The implication of such arguments for family and household structure was that immigrant family patterns would more closely resemble native patterns as these groups became "educated" and assimilated. To the contrary, our results suggest, as have others' based on local studies, that many of the differences in household structure between native whites of native parentage (NWNP) and European immigrants were short-run responses to, and consequences of, immigration (M. Gordon 1964, 1973). These differences were concentrated among the first generation and, within this group, among the more recent arrivals. Furthermore, if these adjustments were part of a pattern of cultural assimilation, it would be odd to find immigrants of such varied cultural backgrounds following such similar paths to a mainstream. As African Americans were a native-born group that in 1910 had not yet migrated extensively within the country, the persistent differences in their families and households from those of native whites must be explained by other factors.

The common and continuing efforts to compare two such vastly different groups, ethnic immigrants and African Americans, may have more to do with the fact that they are both not native whites rather than with any possible shared paths to assimilation between the two groups. These comparisons, particularly in the popular culture, have become a source of division, resentment, and misunderstanding since racial integration became more widely accepted in recent decades. In this chapter we are therefore led to address the differences between race and ethnicity at a time when the distinction was not so clear. We will present information for eight European ethnic immigrant groups separately

---

Melting Pot Mistake (1926), after his organization had lobbied successfully for restrictive legislation in the early 1920s. He pointed to high rates of crime, insanity, and pauperism among new immigrants as justification for his arguments.

[4]There are numerous examples of work reflecting these attitudes, including much of that done by the Chicago School of Civics and Philanthropy. See, for example, "Chicago's Housing Problem: Families in Furnished Rooms," by Sophonisba Breckinridge and Edith Abbott, in *The American Journal of Sociology* (November 1910). Most of the concern with the foreign-born and their "Americanization" did not include any consideration at all of the position of African Americans. However, the work and ideas of Booker T. Washington and the ways in which these were interpreted by whites were also standard at the time, and placed faith in education, of a certain type, as well.

for the first and second generations, for African Americans, separated into blacks and mulattoes as they were by the census, and for native whites of native parentage.

We start with household size and the relationships of household me.nbers to the head of the household in which they were enumerated. We then pursue factors that would influence these relationships, such as sex ratios, marital status, and age structure within various groups. There is a focus on boarding and household employment because these are distinctive features of recent immigrant household arrangements. We examine household segregation by these factors in order to test the validity of studying these phenomena in group categorizations. Then, we look at overall household structure and the position of children within households, which leads us to considerations of family structures within households. Although much of this analysis confirms the findings of previous scholars, its organization and comparison here on a national level allow clearer identification and consideration of general migration phenomena and more group-specific cultural phenomena.

Data

Our description has important advantages because it uses nationally representative data for a large set of groups. We employ standard measures as well as some new measures of family and household structure. Along with the 1910 Public Use Sample (PUS), we use additional samples of African Americans drawn from the 1910 census manuscripts (see Hereward et al. 1990). These oversamples were drawn to allow sufficient numbers for state estimates of African American mortality (Ewbank 1987).[5] While covering only selected counties in some southern and border states, the supplementary sample's features make it valuable for a range of research projects. Specifically, southern states with the largest numbers of African Americans, including much of Georgia, and all of South Carolina, Mississippi, and Alabama, were not sampled because the 1/250 PUS itself includes substantial numbers of African Americans from these states. The oversample does add more urban African Americans by sampling Atlanta and by disproportionate sampling of Maryland and Kentucky, states where larger proportions of African Americans lived

[5]These data were collected under a grant to Douglas Ewbank (NICHD #1-RO1-HD18651). The linking of household members was funded by the Research Foundation of the University of Pennsylvania in a grant to S. Philip Morgan. The oversample, including the intrahousehold links, has been prepáred as a Public Use Tape under a grant to S. Philip Morgan (NICHD #1-RO1-HD25856) and is available through ICPSR.

in urban areas.[6] The supplementary sample adds observations where they are most needed, outside the states that have the most dense concentrations of rural African Americans. (For more details on this public use data set see Hereward et al. 1990).

Ethnicity

We focus on the eight largest European immigrant groups, the British, Irish, Scandinavians, Germans, Italians, Poles, Central European Jews, and Eastern European Jews as defined in Chapter 2 and Appendix B. For the second generation, their heritage was determined by the mother's ethnicity as indicated by the same criteria.[7] Finally, we show some measures separately for southern and non-southern whites, blacks, and mulattoes. Because immigrant groups lived predominantly outside the South, and blacks and mulattoes predominantly in the South, this presentation allows for some assessment of whether some differences are due to region of residence. We omit from our analyses those who do not fall within the groups delineated above.

Although in our general national survey we do not separate rural and urban figures, we should point out that, because this is a national sample, our figures include substantial numbers of first- and second-generation ethnics living in rural areas. Much of the literature describes immigrants living in cities, which can give the impression that our national figures are comparative to urban figures. This is not the case. For example, 31 percent of first-generation Italian male immigrants lived in communities with populations under 5,000, and 42 percent of first-generation Italian male boarders lived in such communities. Yet very little literature on Italian male immigrants examines rural situations, and, to our knowledge, none of the literature on boarding does so. It is only Jews whose numbers do not include many rurally based immigrants in

---

[6]Urban areas are defined as incorporated entities with populations over 2,500. There were a number of cities in which the sections where the African American population mainly lived were unincorporated. These areas are mixed into the largely rural character of other unincorporated areas, and are thus difficult to identify on an individual basis.

[7]Computations (not shown) reveal that substantive conclusions did not depend on whether the father's or mother's ethnicity was used as an indicator of heritage. Thus, some people of mixed parentage are coded as being of a single ethnicity, but the number is quite small, especially for the newer immigrant groups.

In all cases in this chapter the ethnicity of the household is determined by that of the household head, who presumably would be the person most responsible for living arrangements within the household. This way of designating household ethnicity differs from some of the other chapters in this volume. In 1910, slightly over 3 percent of households contained members of different races, and the bulk of these involved the co-residency of blacks and mulattoes.

the United States, although much of the scholarly literature might lead one to think that nearly all immigrants of most ethnicities were urban residents.[8]

Our decision to keep blacks and mulattoes separate requires some justification: although this is how the population was enumerated, the published tables mainly combine these two groups as "Negroes." In the modern census and in the past, individuals define their race with very ambiguous results (Alonso 1987; Denton and Massey 1988). In 1910, race was not self-identified, but was observed and recorded by the enumerators, which only further complicates the issue.[9] Changing the designations from those that were gathered by the enumerators, even by collapsing categories, only adds to the ambiguity.[10] In addition, the continuing distinction between race and ethnicity also challenges us to ask questions about such distinctions and their origins in cultural or "bio-

[8]This is not true of valuable work on Scandinavians, who largely migrated to rural areas and on whom valuable work has been done by scholars like Gjerde (1985) and Ostergren (1988). However, it is not surprising that ethnic historians and scholars who seek to study a group concentrate on the areas or experiences typical of the majority of that group. A national sample allows the inclusion of the potentially significant number in any group that did not have such a "typical" experience and permits us to confirm or qualify our group impressions.

[9]In 1910 the census employed "Negro" enumerators in 2,055 census districts, mainly in areas with high African American populations. One effect of this was a significant increase in the number of individuals returned as mulatto (see Miller 1991).

[10]In the 1910 census, the responsibility for defining a respondent's race was placed in the interviewer's hands. The terms "white," "Chinese," "Japanese," "black," and "mulatto" were used, with white, Chinese, and Japanese assumed by the Bureau of the Census to be clear (United States 1910). No instructions were given to the enumerators on how to make these three distinctions; however, when referring to the "Negro" population, ambiguity was acknowledged. According to the enumerators' instructions, the term "black" includes all persons who are "evidently full-blooded negroes," and the term "mulatto" includes all other persons having some "proportion or perceptible trace of negro blood." The distinction between these terms stems from the historical experiences of the African population in the United States both internally and in interaction with the white population. On the one hand, the African American population of the United States in 1910 was composed of a mixing of various African ethnicities along with the mixing of African and European Americans. On the other hand, there has always been a great deal of color-consciousness both within and outside the African American community, along with distinctions between free and slave, house and field, and rural and urban. These status distinctions, both real and imagined, have as much to do with geographical location, personal property, and social position as they do with past intermarriage and biological heritage. The issue is not one of genotype, but one of social definitions.

Because the respondent's race was determined by the interviewer, the biases of the interviewers are those most significantly present in the data. The interviewers' prejudices could have determined what they saw as a "perceptible trace of negro blood," who they felt was "a full-blooded negro," and those to whom no such attempt at discernment was directed. We keep the categories black and mulatto as they were collected as an analysis of the socially defined status of certain individuals of African descent. In a recent paper (Miller 1991), we elaborate on the mulatto/black differences and their consequences in the census and in society.

logical" definitions. At the turn of the century, there were many who called what we now regard as ethnic groups like Italians "races," and there was keen interest in the pseudoscience of biological eugenics. In this way of thinking, a number of physical and genetic features were believed to determine behavior, and culture was a matter of hierarchy and development rather than difference. This ugly intellectual heritage still often denies culture to those categorized by race, while giving a Eurocentric cultural privilege to the categorization of ethnicities as primarily "cultural" groups. There are, of course, as the data presented in this chapter demonstrate, significant differences between the experiences of groups designated as races and those designated as ethnicities. We must be careful in the ways in which we analyze and naturalize these differences, because they largely have to do with the social history of the designation (Bennett et al. 1981).

Household Structure

The measurement of household structure rests on two procedures followed by census enumerators. First, census enumerators listed individuals by household, generally distinguished by address, beginning with the head of household, and second, they recorded each individual's relationship to the head of household. Thus, households can be described rather straightforwardly since the census enumerates individuals in households. There were some complications, as the instructions to the enumerators make clear. A "dwelling house" was defined as a place where one or more persons regularly sleep, and households were "a group of persons living together in the same dwelling place." As the instructions go on:

> It should be noted, however, that two or more families may occupy the same dwelling house without living together. If they occupy separate portions of the dwelling house and their housekeeping is entirely separate, they should be returned as separate families. All the occupants and employees of a hotel boarding house, or lodging house, if that is their usual place of abode, make up, for census purposes, a single family. But in an apartment or tenement house, there will usually be as many families as there are separate occupied apartments or tenements (U.S. Bureau of the Census 1910, p. 27).

Of course, families and households are conceptually very different social configurations, which have come to be linked through this manner of recording the census. The only members of any individual's family that we can find and link to that person are those that live in the same household—a significant limitation. In the modern West, families are primarily determined by biological or nuptial kin relations rather than by the roles they fill, while households are determined by co-residency. Because many of the traditional social functions of families can be fulfilled only in conditions of co-residency, it is often assumed that those of closest family relation, members of the nuclear family, live in the same household. Although not as common, it is also often assumed that non-relatives or more distant relatives that are co-resident in the same household are likely to take on some degree of familial role.[11] For these reasons, along with the manner in which the data were collected, we examine the interconnected attributes of family and household structure. We are assisted in examining family structure because the 1910 PUS provides links of children to their mothers and spouses to each other, as described in the users' guide (see Strong et al. 1989).

Size of Households

The first feature of households we will consider is their size and the number of family members related to the household head in them. Non-family members are those not related to the household head by blood or marriage. The left-hand column of Table 5.1 shows the number of family households in our sample for each ethnic group. In the left panel of this table we have omitted institutional households and households composed of only one person. The small sample sizes for the second-generation heads in the newer immigrant groups mean that estimates for these groups should be treated with great caution.

Table 5.1 shows substantial variability across groups in the size and composition of households. Italians and Poles, in addition to having large families, also have an average of nearly one non-family member per household, respectively.[12] The high number of family members in the households of Italians and Poles, which is exceeded only by Jews, no doubt reflects their high fertility (see Chapter 4). The impact of these

[11]Modell and Hareven (1973) maintain that boarding was a familial institution for individuals who were away from their homes, cushioning the shock of urban life and "decidedly humane." They maintain that in this way "the family was not fragile, but malleable" (p. 478). Others, like Joanne Meyerowitz (1988), disagree with this analysis and maintain that many found boarding an intrusion on privacy and a controlling institution. Some reports of the time (e.g., Junius Boyd Wood, *The Negro in Chicago*, 1916) noted objections to lodgers within certain communities, as reported by Meyerowitz.

[12]Boarders and relatives were perhaps not always systematically distinguished, so that at times some non-family members identified as boarders might actually have been more distant relatives. They would definitely be at least non-nuclear family members.

TABLE 5.1

Mean Number of Family Members (of head) and Mean Number of Individuals per Household, by Ethnicity

Ethnicity	(N)	Family Households			All Persons*	
		Family Members	Total Residents	Non-family Members	% Alone	% in HHs of 10+
First Generation+						
British	(2,046)	3.92	4.12	.30	2.3	6.4
Irish	(2,051)	4.08	4.27	.35	4.4	10.1
Scandinavian	(1,922)	4.13	4.36	.33	3.0	7.3
German	(4,027)	4.24	4.41	.22	2.1	5.6
Italian	(1,492)	4.38	4.98	.78	3.3	16.2
Polish	(1,063)	4.68	5.46	.85	1.1	10.8
C. E. Jews	(194)	4.94	5.28	.40	0.6	4.6
E. E. Jews	(919)	4.95	5.29	.35	0.4	5.1
Second Generation						
British	(1,449)	3.87	4.15	.36	1.4	5.1
Irish	(2,541)	4.01	4.26	.36	2.3	7.6
Scandinavian	(491)	3.69	3.88	.33	1.1	6.7
German	(1,146)	3.55	3.63	.25	0.9	5.4
Italian	(54)	3.24	3.25	.26	0.8	11.6
Polish	(68)	3.22	3.22	.32	1.0	11.1
C. E. Jews	(7)	3.09	2.36	.14	0.8	2.8
E. E. Jews	(28)	2.73	2.38	.11	0.6	2.9

TABLE 5.1 (continued)

		Family Households			All Persons*	
Ethnicity	(N)	Family Members	Total Residents	Non-family Members	% Alone	% in HHs of 10+
Native-Native						
White						
Non-South	(26,604)	3.63	3.82	.28	1.2	4.7
South	(14,580)	4.58	4.75	.21	0.5	5.5
Black						
Non-South	(1,256)	3.16	3.56	.59	2.9	8.4
South	(10,353)	4.16	4.34	.21	0.5	7.4
Mulatto						
Non-South	(436)	3.24	3.66	.50	1.1	7.4
South	(2,137)	4.12	4.35	.26	0.5	7.5

*These proportions are calculated from all persons in each group in order to show the impact of the smallest and largest households in these groups. "Alone" is a household of one, and large households have over ten members. If these proportions were calculated from all households, the effect of "alones" would be exaggerated, while the impact of large households would be reduced. If they were calculated from family households, most of such cases would not show up, since they are often not family situations.

+The "generation" of a household is determined by that of the household head. This complicates the right-hand columns of the table on persons, since the children of a first-generation household are second-generation individuals.

particular types of family households on all the members of any particular group is shown by the figures for all individuals in the right-hand
panels of the table.

Here one can see that there is much greater variability in the percentage of large households across ethnic groups than in the number of
family or non-family members. In the first generation, a much higher
proportion of Irish, Italian, and Polish individuals live in households with
over ten members, while large German and Jewish households affect
only about 5 percent of their populations overall. Jewish, first-generation
German, and southern households, both white and African American,
were the least likely to include non-family members. Outside the South,
African American households are much smaller than in the South, but
also much more likely to contain non-family members. These various
differences might be due to differences in the number of family members as affected by fertility and mortality discussed earlier in this volume. The numbers would also be affected by the availability of kin due
to migration or by the desirability of living with kin. Finally, there may
be differences in the non-family members present in households.

Relationship of Individuals to the Household Head

We have just shown differences between the various ethnic groups
in the size of their households and in the prevalence of non-family co-
residents. Table 5.2 shows the relationships to the head of the household of adult (over age 18) males and females within each household.
This tabulation allows us to see which type of co-resident relationships
might produce the differences observed in Table 5.1. If there were no
differences across groups in Table 5.2, then we could conclude that different levels of fertility and the living arrangements of children produced the Table 5.1 differences. Instead, Table 5.2 shows large differences across groups. What is perhaps most striking are the great differences
in the likelihood of heading a household for adult males, which was
directly related to the rates at which such individuals were found as
boarders or employees within households.[13] The exceptionally large
numbers of first-generation Italian and Polish boarders, 36 percent and

---

[13]In the manuscript census, those we call boarders appear as boarders, lodgers, room-
ers, renters, and their relatives. We must acknowledge that there is a difference between
boarders, who normally receive both rooms and meals, and the other categories. What is
important for our purposes is that all of these designations are included within a single
household and do not indicate a new, separate one. Employees are listed as servants,
housekeepers, maids, drivers, cooks, gardeners, employees, nurses, laborers, farmhands,
assistants, helpers, hired hands, and their families.

TABLE 5.2
Adult (over 18 years) Relationships to Head of Household, by Sex and Ethnicity

	Males							
Ethnicity	(N)	Head	Child	Kin	Brdr.	Emp.	No Rel.	
First Generation								
British	(2,572)	68.9	6.0	4.6	16.0	2.7	1.9	100%
Irish	(2,373)	64.4	2.2	5.3	21.3	2.2	4.7	100%
Scandinavians	(2,637)	66.1	3.4	3.7	18.2	5.4	3.3	100%
German	(4,346)	78.4	3.9	2.6	10.5	1.9	2.6	100%
Italian	(3,058)	47.0	5.1	6.1	35.6	1.9	4.3	100%
Polish	(1,971)	50.5	3.5	4.7	39.0	1.3	1.0	100%
C.E. Jews	(281)	65.1	11.7	3.9	17.4	0.7	1.1	100%
E.E. Jews	(1,279)	67.0	11.7	7.7	12.7	0.5	0.4	100%
Second Generation								
British	(2,036)	62.6	19.3	5.3	9.3	1.5	2.1	100%
Irish	(3,898)	53.4	23.0	7.8	10.8	1.8	3.3	100%
Scandinavians	(1,109)	40.5	36.2	6.3	10.3	4.5	2.3	100%
German	(5,643)	62.3	22.2	4.9	7.5	1.7	1.3	100%
Italian	(163)	29.5	48.5	6.8	12.3	0.6	2.5	100%
Polish	(212)	29.7	50.9	5.2	8.0	2.4	3.8	100%
C.E. Jews	(36)	19.4	63.9	8.3	5.6	0.0	2.8	100%
E.E. Jews	(95)	28.4	55.8	11.6	2.1	0.0	2.1	100%
Native-Native								
White	(56,785)	64.5	17.8	5.1	8.8	2.0	1.8	100%
Black	(13,521)	69.7	9.2	4.5	10.9	2.6	3.0	100%
Mulatto	(3,074)	64.8	12.8	6.4	11.9	1.6	2.5	100%

39 percent of all Italian and Polish men, respectively, is a condition noted at the time and remarked on by numerous scholars of immigration since. Only about half of the adult male immigrants in these ethnic groups head their own households in the United States. Although the number of households headed by second-generation Italian or Polish men is quite small, boarding drops dramatically in the second generation. Thus, while the second generation of these groups is composed largely of adult children of heads of households, these children are not in boarding situations.

Boarding and employment in households are most notably not found among Jewish females in the second generation, and these statuses were rare for Jewish males, too. Of course, this was indicated in Table 5.1, which showed very few non-family members in households headed by Jews. In this case, the data also confirm that Jews did not board or work

TABLE 5.2 (*continued*)

(N)	Wife	Head	Child	Kin	Brdr.	Emp.	No Rel.	
(2,073)	63.5	14.0	8.3	4.4	4.1	4.4	1.3	100%
(2,927)	49.3	20.3	1.9	4.8	4.7	15.9	3.1	100%
(1,946)	69.3	9.4	3.7	4.7	2.6	10.0	1.7	100%
(3,929)	70.1	17.3	3.1	2.2	2.3	3.6	1.3	100%
(1,468)	83.2	3.6	4.7	5.3	2.1	0.6	0.6	100%
(1,175)	77.8	5.6	2.6	2.0	7.3	4.0	0.7	100%
(268)	77.4	4.3	6.6	3.4	5.1	2.3	0.4	100%
(1,128)	70.3	5.7	13.6	5.5	4.0	0.6	0.6	100%
(2,007)	60.8	8.8	17.2	5.9	4.3	2.3	0.7	100%
(4,182)	46.9	10.9	21.9	10.6	5.2	3.5	1.1	100%
(1,124)	48.3	3.4	30.6	6.2	4.5	6.3	0.8	100%
(5,619)	61.9	7.3	19.4	5.8	2.5	2.6	0.5	100%
(145)	52.8	4.2	35.4	4.9	2.1	0.7	0.0	100%
(186)	54.4	1.6	31.5	7.1	1.1	3.3	1.1	100%
(34)	50.0	0.0	44.2	2.9	0.0	0.0	2.9	100%
(86)	34.9	1.2	61.6	1.2	1.2	0.0	0.0	100%
(56,092)	62.9	8.1	16.7	5.9	3.9	1.8	0.7	100%
(13,220)	59.3	15.8	9.8	5.1	5.4	4.0	0.6	100%
(3,749)	57.7	15.2	12.3	5.6	5.4	3.2	0.6	100%

in the households of others. As others have also shown, nearly all groups show significant declines in boarding and household employment in the second generation, though the declines may not be as drastic as among the Jews.

For adult females who are neither wives nor children, there are interesting differences across groups. These women are predominantly household heads or employees of household heads, depending on ethnicity. The Irish, Poles, and Scandinavians seem to be equally likely to reside in these two situations, while the other groups appear overwhelmingly as female household heads. The ethnic differences between heading households or being employees within them for unattached adult women may reflect different status levels and sex roles for women in different ethnic groups. They may also reflect different conceptions of the household within ethnic groups and notions of its openness, safety, or privacy. Other explanations focus on the distinct histories of the different ethnic groups as Stephen Steinberg does, for example, when he looks at why Irish women became domestics and Jews and Italians did not (1988, Chapter 6). His answer lies in the nature of the Irish immigrant flow, which included a large proportion of unmarried women who had poor prospects of marriage or employment in Europe. Migration was encouraged by companies and organizations that arranged live-in domestic work. Italian and Jewish women, by contrast, almost always came with or followed husbands who had migrated earlier.

> Culture and family morality have little or nothing to do with explaining why Irish became domestics and Italians and Jews did not. . . . It was not that as a group Irish had less aversion to working in other people's homes, but that their choices were far more limited. For these courageous women who migrated alone to the new world, domestic work was merely a temporary expedient to allow them to forge new lives (Steinberg 1988, p. 166).

Boarding was not an attractive option for women at this time, as is partially explained by literature of the period, which gives dire warnings of the moral perils of household boarding (Modell and Hareven 1973; Meyerowitz 1988). With marriage to a household head the "ideal" residential situation for adult women at the time, alternatives might be accounted for by a broad range of cultural, historical, economic, and social factors that we will not pursue further here.

In the native-born population, the black and mulatto rates of boarding and employment in households, though higher than for native whites, do not begin to approach the rates for immigrants. The most striking difference among the native-born of different races is the much lower percentage of adult African Americans who were listed as children of the head of household. This difference could be due to higher African American mortality, which reduces the availability of parents with whom to co-reside (see Chapter 3). Children could also have been encouraged to leave the household if their economic contribution was modest, or, if their earning power was adequate, these young persons would have been able to set up independent households.[14] Whatever the combination of factors, the apparent result is higher rates of headship for African American men and women, and only slightly higher rates of boarding and household employment.

---

[14]In the rural South, the structure of tenancy may have encouraged early family formation and independent households because the expense of providing a household was supplied by the landowner (see Tolnay 1984).

Marital Status

The variation in the proportion of women in each ethnicity who are listed as wives deserves closer scrutiny. Table 5.3 shows the marital status of adult men and women, and for the married, the proportion whose spouse was present in the household. The proportion of each group, single or married, varies substantially across groups, reflecting the sex ratio, as shown here, as well as different ages at marriage and, as shown later, different age structures.

Although in the contemporary United States African American women are less likely to marry than whites (Cherlin 1981), this was not the case historically (see Farley and Hermalin 1971). Table 5.3 shows that African Americans were actually less likely to have been single than native whites, though they did experience notably higher levels of widowhood and separation. Recent studies by Preston, Lim, and Morgan (1992) suggest that widowhood among blacks was overestimated in reports to the census. The black and white rates of marriage and spouse presence are generally comparable, as are their sex ratios. The mulatto sex ratio shows more women than men, which may be an effect of status issues such as living in urban areas and being employed in domestic service.

One striking figure in Table 5.3 is the high number of Irish men and women who are identified as widowed, a number that may reflect their longer presence as immigrants in the United States and consequent older age distribution, as would similar figures for the Germans. The extra spike in Irish widowhood above other older immigrant groups might also reflect the famine conditions in Ireland, which drove much Irish immigration throughout the nineteenth and early twentieth centuries. Their older ages of marriage, along with the difficulty of maintaining farms in Ireland after the death of a spouse or other family members, contributed to this phenomenon (see Diner 1983).

The differences in spousal separation between male and female Italians and Poles, and to a lesser extent for Jews, may also reflect special circumstances. A married Italian or Polish woman was much more likely to be living with a spouse than was a married Italian or Polish man. This helps explain males' high rate of boarding, since married men were living in places where their wives were not present. In fact, as the sex ratios indicate in the right-most column of Table 5.3, their wives were probably left behind in Europe (see Bodnar 1985; Morawska 1985; Hareven and Modell 1977).

Figure 5.1 makes this point clearer, showing the age and marital statuses of the Italian and Irish immigrants. In the top panel, the Italian

TABLE 5.3
Marital Status (for those over age 18), by Ethnicity and Sex

	Males						
			Married Spouse				
Ethnicity	(N)	Single	Present	Absent	Divorced	Widowed	
First Generation							
British	(2,572)	24.3	61.8	4.8	.9	8.4	100%
Irish	(2,373)	29.1	53.5	3.7	.2	13.4	100%
Scandinavian	(2,637)	32.8	56.6	3.6	.4	6.1	100%
German	(4,346)	18.4	69.9	2.5	.5	8.6	100%
Italian	(3,058)	36.5	44.8	15.5	.0	2.5	100%
Polish	(1,971)	33.4	50.0	14.0	.2	2.1	100%
C.E. Jews	(281)	30.6	64.4	3.5	.0	1.1	100%
E.E. Jews	(1,279)	27.5	66.4	4.3	.0	1.6	100%
Second Generation							
British	(2,036)	31.8	60.3	2.5	.4	5.0	100%
Irish	(3,898)	43.8	47.7	3.1	.4	5.0	100%
Scandinavian	(1,109)	62.6	34.4	1.1	.1	.7	100%
German	(5,643)	36.0	59.4	1.4	.5	2.6	100%
Italian	(163)	69.9	26.4	1.8	.6	1.2	100%
Polish	(212)	68.4	29.7	.0	.0	.0	100%
C.E. Jews	(36)	77.8	19.4	.0	.0	.0	100%
E.E. Jews	(95)	66.3	33.7	.0	.0	.0	100%
Native-Native							
White	(56,785)	30.8	61.0	2.2	.6	5.1	100%
Black	13,521)	24.8	62.6	4.5	.8	6.9	100%
Mulatto	(3,074)	27.9	60.6	4.6	.6	6.0	100%

NOTE: The proportion of men and women who have no reported marital status is very small (less than .005 in all cases).

data show an unbalanced structure, which indicates the male surplus. At the younger ages, all the male surplus is single, while at older ages there are more married men than women. Because we know from other studies that Italians were very unlikely to marry either people from other ethnic groups or natives, this imbalance must be explained by the many wives still living in Italy.

The sex-age-marital status distribution for the Irish, shown in the lower panel of Figure 5.1, is quite different. The Irish had a high rate of single-female immigration, as reflected in marital statuses and the sex ratio at ages 20–24. This "feminine" structure is quite different from

TABLE 5.3 (*continued*)

		Females					
		Married Spouse					Sex
(N)	Single	Present	Absent	Divorced	Widowed		Ratio
(2,073)	15.2	61.8	3.6	.4	19.0	100%	1.28
(2,927)	24.3	46.6	2.8	.3	25.8	100%	.82
(1,946)	17.8	67.4	2.5	.5	11.7	100%	1.39
(3,929)	8.5	65.3	2.3	.6	23.3	100%	1.15
(1,468)	7.1	84.1	1.8	.0	6.9	100%	2.11
(1,175)	11.7	78.8	2.2	.3	6.6	100%	1.69
(268)	12.3	76.1	3.4	.4	7.8	100%	1.06
(1,128)	20.0	70.7	1.1	.4	7.9	100%	1.15
(2,007)	24.2	62.3	2.1	1.0	10.3	100%	1.02
(4,182)	38.2	48.2	2.4	.5	10.7	100%	.94
(1,124)	44.9	51.0	1.0	.3	2.6	100%	.99
(5,619)	26.4	63.5	1.7	.6	7.7	100%	1.01
(145)	35.9	57.2	4.8	.0	2.1	100%	1.12
(186)	39.3	57.5	1.6	.0	1.1	100%	1.14
(34)	44.1	55.9	.0	.0	.0	100%	1.06
(86)	60.5	37.2	.0	1.2	1.2	100%	1.11
(56,092)	21.8	63.6	2.4	.8	11.3	100%	1.03
(13,220)	16.0	59.1	5.1	1.3	18.3	100%	1.03
(3,749)	16.2	58.8	5.7	1.5	17.6	100%	.83

that of other groups and was noted at the time (U.S. Immigration Commission 1911, p. 22).

When the marital status of boarders and employees is examined, as in Table 5.4, further elaborations of the ethnic differences noted above are evident. While the first-generation Italian and Polish males are the most likely to be married as boarders or employees, they are also the least likely to have their spouses with them.[15] The percentages of Italian and Polish male boarders who are married are 33 and 34 respectively,

[15]In the 1910 PUS, children have been linked to mothers, and spouses have been linked. For details of the linking process, see Strong et al. (1989).

FIGURE 5.1A

Population Pyramid for Single and Married Men and Women,
Immigrants to the U.S. from Italy

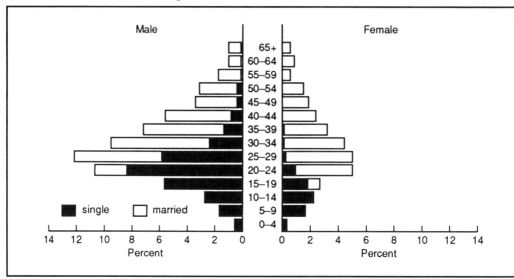

FIGURE 5.1B

Population Pyramid for Single and Married Men and Women,
Immigrants to the U.S. from Ireland

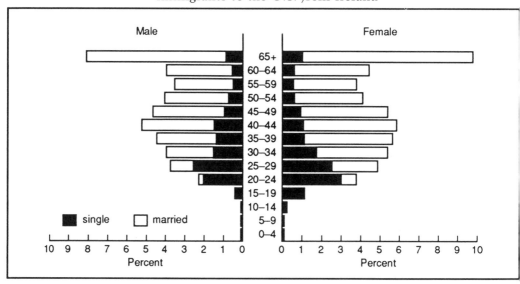

while the percentages of married men living with their wives are only 6 and 9. Thus, as confirmed by passenger lists and by the U.S. Immigration Commission itself (1911), husbands came to the United States alone, as workers, wage-earners, or "scouts," with their wives and family either awaiting their return or preparing to follow. The literature is full of such stories, and some statistical analysis of this phenomenon can be found in Robles and Watkins (forthcoming), who looked at the variations in arrival dates for family members within immigrant households. For all immigrants, those who are single, widowed, or divorced are much more likely to be found in boarding situations than individuals who are married.

Age Distribution and Recency of Immigration

As noted above, migration patterns affect sex ratios, which, in turn, affect marital status and household composition. In addition, migration patterns determine immigrant-age structures, which can be significant factors in family and household structure. Table 5.5 shows age distributions for various ethnicities. Because migration is strongly age-selective of young adults, recency of migration is a powerful determinant of ethnic age structures in the United States in 1910. Fertility is of secondary importance: although higher fertility produces "younger" age structures, we have already noted that children were less likely to migrate, but were mainly born in the United States as part of a second generation.

The age distributions show the absence of the middle-aged and elderly for some groups. In many cases these older persons, who are the most likely constituents of extended families, were still living in Europe. We will examine the prevalence of extended families in a subsequent section of this chapter, but it is clear that boarding with non-relatives is more likely when one has fewer relatives available in the United States. The first-generation Jews, Italians, Poles, and Scandinavians are clearly missing an older generation when compared with the British, Germans, and Irish as well as the native-born populations. Fewer than 10 percent of Jews, Italians, and Poles were over age 55, while the same figure for Scandinavians was less than 20 percent, and over 33 percent for German immigrants. This variability in age distributions is obvious in the second generation too, where the British, Germans, and Irish all show between 15 percent and 20 percent of their populations above the age of 45, and Scandinavians have only 2 percent, and the other groups less than 1 percent in these age groups.

This variation in the availability of older, same-ethnicity persons

TABLE 5.4

Marital Status and (for those married) Presence of Spouse for Adult Boarders and Employees

| | Boarders | | | | | |
| | Male | | | Female | | |
Ethnicity	(N)	% Married	% Spouse Present	(N)	% Married	% Spouse Present
First Generation						
British	(411)	21.7	29.2	(80)	31.3	52.0
Irish	(493)	9.5	21.3	(127)	15.8	50.0
Scandinavian	(480)	10.2	12.2	(48)	27.1	38.5
German	(456)	11.6	32.1	(83)	19.6	75.5
Italian	(1,088)	32.7	6.2	(29)	69.0	100.0
Polish	(769)	34.3	9.5	(84)	33.3	89.3
C.E. Jews	(49)	10.2	0.0	(13)	7.7	0.0
E.E. Jews	(163)	20.9	17.7	(44)	11.4	80.0
Second Generation						
British	(189)	16.4	32.3	(84)	34.4	72.4
Irish	(419)	15.0	30.2	(213)	15.0	46.9
Scandinavian	(114)	7.9	33.3	(51)	13.7	85.7
German	(423)	13.2	41.1	(135)	20.0	59.3
Italian	(20)	10.0	0.0	(3)	33.3	0.0
Polish	(17)	0.0	0.0	(2)	50.0	0.0
C.E. Jews	(2)	0.0	0.0	(0)	0.0	0.0
E.E. Jews	(2)	0.0	0.0	(1)	0.0	0.0
Native-Native						
White	(5,009)	16.4	42.0	(2,075)	27.4	59.0
Black	(1,174)	16.4	39.4	(547)	24.6	44.7
Mulatto	(291)	17.4	48.1	(154)	37.5	58.5

NOTES: Spouse presence was not recorded in the census, but is derived from the linking process. T⬛ percentage with spouse present is of those married, while the percentage married is from all individuals⬛

with whom to live can best be seen in Figure 5.2. These population pyramids show the first- and second-generation Italians (top panel) and Germans (lower panel) by sex, generation, and age. The contrast in the proportion of older, second-generation persons is striking.

The first generation is "missing" children because many young adults migrate before they marry or soon after. Their children are born in the United States, and thus comprise part of the second generation. Similarly, the second generation bears children who are third-generation

TABLE 5.4 (continued)

	Employees					
	Male				Female	
(N)	% Married	% Spouse Present	(N)		% Married	% Spouse Present
(70)	15.7	90.9	(86)		14.0	58.3
(50)	10.0	20.0	(432)		3.5	20.0
(142)	6.3	0.0	(185)		2.7	20.0
(82)	6.1	40.0	(129)		7.8	40.0
(58)	25.9	0.0	(8)		0.0	0.0
(25)	24.0	16.7	(46)		10.9	20.0
(2)	0.0	0.0	(6)		0.0	0.0
(6)	66.7	0.0	(6)		0.0	0.0
(30)	10.0	66.7	(44)		11.4	0.0
(69)	10.1	42.9	(143)		6.3	22.2
(50)	4.0	50.0	(71)		1.4	0.0
(97)	4.1	50.0	(145)		5.5	0.0
(1)	0.0	0.0	(1)		0.0	0.0
(5)	0.0	0.0	(6)		0.0	0.0
(0)	0.0	0.0	(0)		0.0	0.0
(0)	0.0	0.0	(0)		0.0	0.0
(1,121)	8.2	30.4	(966)		11.5	23.4
(284)	17.4	43.2	(399)		22.2	29.5
(38)	19.9	26.4	(91)		16.5	6.7

Americans, and thus cannot be identified as belonging to an ethnic group. The native groups all show much more similar age structures, since they are unaffected by immigration, with only slight variations produced by the higher fertility and mortality of African Americans compared to whites.

For members of each immigrant group, Table 5.6 shows recency of immigration, the factor primarily responsible for the age distributions described above. For the "old" immigrant groups, the Irish, Germans, and British, the majority came to the United States before 1890. This is in contrast to the "new" immigrants, the Italians, Jews, and Poles, the

TABLE 5.5
Age Profiles of Ethnic Groups: 1910

Ethnicity	(N)	Child 0–14	Youth 15–18	Young Adult 19–25
First Generation				
British	(5,122)	5.6	2.2	8.8
Irish	(5,433)		.8	1.0
Scandinavian	(4,887)	3.1	1.9	11.8
German	(8,702)	1.7	1.4	5.9
Italian	(5,428)	9.9	6.0	22.2
Polish	(3,596)	7.0	5.0	23.5
C.E. Jews	(645)	7.9	6.5	23.4
E.E. Jews	(3,107)	13.8	8.3	23.7
Second Generation				
British	(6,216)	25.9	8.8	13.8
Irish	(11,035)	20.0	6.5	12.5
Scandinavian	(5,181)	43.5	13.4	19.8
German	(16,823)	23.8	9.1	15.6
Italian	(2,828)	80.5	8.6	7.1
Polish	(2,639)	74.3	10.7	9.7
C.E. Jews	(498)	72.1	13.9	8.4
E.E. Jews	(1,605)	77.5	11.2	8.2
Native-Native				
White	(207,653)	36.6	8.7	13.3
Black	(50,038)	37.8	8.5	14.2
Mulatto	(12,847)	37.5	9.1	15.5

majority of whom arrived in the ten years after 1900. The Scandinavians are between these two groups, with the bulk of their immigration in the 1880s and 1890s.

When one looks only at boarders by recency of immigration and sex, as in Table 5.7, it becomes clear that boarding is predominantly a residential status of new arrivals. This has long been known, but there has been a tendency to ascribe boarding to a preference of particular ethnicities. The same is true of those who lived in a household headed by their employer. Perhaps, then, the higher rates of boarding that characterize some new groups like Italians and Poles (see Table 5.2) could be attributed to their recency of migration. Table 5.8 presents standardized boarding rates for all groups. In this table, we have computed by "duration of residency" specific rates of boarding using data in Table 5.6 and Table 5.7 and have applied them to the Italian "recency of migra-

TABLE 5.5 (*continued*)

Adult 26–35	Adult 36–45	Middle Age 46–55	Older Over 55	
19.9	21.5	17.7	24.4	100%
8.1	19.3.	21.7	17.4	100%
22.2	23.5	19.1	18.4	100%
16.2	20.4	20.5	33.9	100%
30.7	16.9	8.8	5.5	100%
33.0	17.8	8.3	5.5	100%
27.0	18.6	10.2	6.4	100%
24.6	16.6	8.7	4.3	100%
17.0	15.4	10.9	8.2	100%
19.6	20.5	14.2	6.7	100%
14.3	6.7	2.0	.3	100%
18.8	16.4	11.8	4.5	100%
2.7	.9	.2	.1	100%
4.4	.7	.2	.0	100%
3.6	1.2	.8	.0	100%
2.2	.8	.2	.0	100%
14.5	10.7	7.5	8.8	100%
15.7	10.5	6.8	6.6	100%
15.4	10.4	6.6	5.6	100%

tion" distribution in Table 5.6. Table 5.8 shows these standardized rates, which give the proportion of each group that would be boarding if they had the recency of immigration of Italians. The sharp differences in the unstandardized (observed) proportions between Italians and Poles and the "old" immigrant groups is diminished sharply by this simple control on recency of immigration.

Clearly then, one of the most striking differences among immigrant groups and between immigrant and native households can be accounted for by the migration process itself. The number of non-family members present in households, primarily boarders and employees, can be accounted for largely by more recent immigration. Effects of other migration patterns, such as sex ratios, would have a similar impact, since we have already shown that women are less likely to board.

FIGURE 5.2A

Population Pyramid for First- and Second-generation Men and Women,
Immigrants to the U.S. from Italy

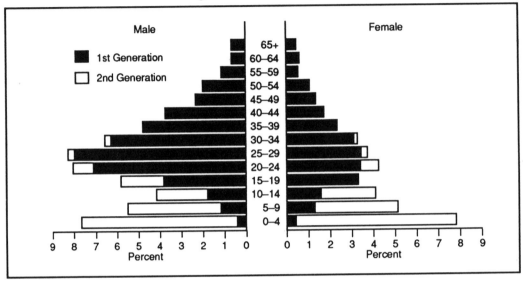

FIGURE 5.2B

Population Pyramid for First- and Second-generation Men and Women,
Immigrants to the U.S. from Germany

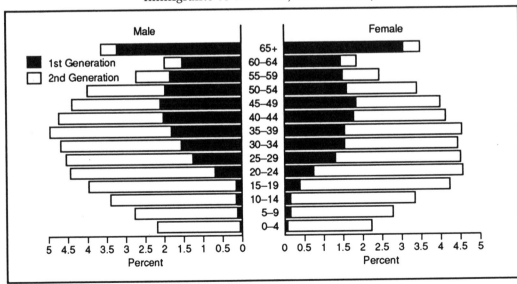

Ethnic and Racial Household Segregation

The degree of ethnic or racial homogeneity within households is an important consideration because it helps document the extent to which ethnic groups were isolated from one another. Isolation can help maintain distinct patterns of behavior, such as high fertility (see Morgan, Watkins, and Ewbank, Chapter 4). Other investigators have characterized the degree of residential segregation among ethnic groups (see Chapter 6) and the degree of endogamy (keeping to one's own group for marriage partners) among ethnic groups (see Pagnini and Morgan 1990). This section adds new information regarding the isolation of ethnic and racial groups in other areas of potential household contact. If the main reason that ethnics become more like the native-born in the second generation is that the structural distortions of age, sex ratio, and marital status caused by migration are relieved, then assimilation is not simply a cultural process. On the other hand, if there were substantial household interaction between groups, then behavioral practices could have been easily emulated by immigrants.

There are three main mechanisms that could produce households with multiple ethnicities or races. These include intermarriage, boarding, and household employment.[16] Pagnini and Morgan (1990) show extreme endogamy among the "new" immigrants, Italians, Poles, and Jews, who married in the United States. Other scholars also find that very few of the "new" immigrants married immigrants of other ethnicities or the native-born of native mothers. Table 5.9, in the left panel, shows some simple measures of endogamy and exogamy. Column 1 shows the number of marriages.[17] Column 2 shows the odds of endogamy versus marriage with any other group. The endogamy odds are roughly three times higher for "new" immigrant ethnicities than for "old"; and they are again three times higher for first-generation immigrants than for the second generation for all ethnic groups. Because we have no way of identifying ethnicity beyond the second generation, and, after their own ethnic group, European immigrants are most likely to marry native whites, the degree of endogamy can be even higher. This would be true especially for the "old" immigrant groups like the British and Germans, as the native white

[16]Although boarding and employment account for about 90 percent of the households headed by whites in which blacks or mulattoes live, for households headed by non-whites in which whites live, only 23 percent are situations of boarding or employment. The others are listed as relatives of the household head, but these are small numbers, as shown below.

[17]These are the number of marriages between men of specific ethnicities and races who married wives of any of the races and ethnicities shown. Only those marrying someone of "other" ethnicity or race are excluded. This number of excluded marriages is 6,017.

TABLE 5.6

Recency of Immigration for First-generation Immigrants

Ethnicity	(N)	Year Missing	1905–1910	1900–1904
First Generation				
British	(5,130)	12.3	15.4	7.6
Irish	(5,453)	10.8	7.9	7.8
Scandinavian	(4,897)	10.4	12.8	12.1
German	(8,706)	12.3	5.6	5.2
Italian	(5,452)	5.9	41.0	25.7
Polish	(3,603)	6.2	41.0	20.7
C.E. Jews	(645)	2.8	23.1	24.2
E.E. Jews	(3,107)	3.8	38.7	25.9

population of the United States since the seventeenth century was largely of British and German heritage. African American men are ninety-nine times more likely to marry African American women than to marry a woman of any other ethnicity.

Column 4 shows the odds that men marry native whites of native mothers, a specific type of exogamy that is the most common form for all immigrant groups except, of course, for the native whites, where this is endogamy and thus equal to the value in Column 1. These odds are close to the inverse of the endogamy odds but are not exact inverses because there is some small intermarriage with other groups. The two Jewish groups and the two groups of African Americans marry each other rather frequently but exclusively, and so have been treated as single entities in these calculations. As Pagnini and Morgan (1990) show, the small number of immigrants from "old" groups who marry outside their ethnicity are much more likely to marry into other "old" immigrant groups than to marry into "new" immigrant groups.

Interestingly, there is a very similar pattern to boarding. Columns 4–6 in Table 5.9 show calculations that parallel those just described for marriage. Although it was known that "new" immigrant boarders are much more likely to reside in households headed by immigrants of the same ethnicity than are "old" immigrants, as in marriage, the ethnic exclusivity of boarders and household heads is weaker in the second generation. As Lieberson and others have shown, it is greater for African Americans than for any other group. While it is not shown here, there is a moderate amount of interethnic boarding among the "old" immigrants, which parallels the greater intermarriage among these groups as compared to the extreme rarity of marriages across the "old"-"new" boundary.

Similar tabulations compare the ethnicity of co-resident employees of household heads (see Columns 7–9 in Table 5.9). There is greater

TABLE 5.6 (continued)

1895–1899	1890–1894	1880–1889	1870–1879	Pre–1870
5.1	10.3	25.3	10.5	13.5
6.2	10.5	23.3	11.5	22.0
5.5	12.9	28.6	10.1	7.6
3.8	11.0	30.0	13.1	18.9
10.0	8.1	7.5	1.4	.5
7.4	9.6	11.8	2.5	.8
15.0	18.5	14.4	.6	1.4
8.9	12.7	8.9	.8	.4

ethnic and racial mixing of household employees and household heads than in the cases of marriage and boarding. The odds that the employee and household head are the same ethnicity are below 1.0 in roughly half of the cases, indicating that for these groups, mixing is more common than homogeneity when it comes to household employment. The most striking contrast between boarders and employees is for African Americans, both blacks and mulattoes, for whom the odds of same-race boarding (= 53) are over 100 times greater than the odds of homogeneous employee-head co-residence (= .45). There is perhaps some indication here of the familial household interaction of boarding when compared with the more unequal arrangements of household employment. The distance between household head and servant, between employer and employee, is more easily maintained when the two have less in common.

Of the three possible mechanisms producing mixed ethnic households, only households including employees contained any large proportion of mixed households. Thus, contact is greatest where social distance is highest, which would tend to limit interaction even in those households that contained persons of different ethnicities. Moreover, households that included employees were a small proportion of all households, with only 5.2 percent of all households having a member described as an employee of the head.

For explanations of ethnic convergence that emphasize the diffusion of ideas, such as the arguments regarding fertility presented by Morgan et al. in Chapter 4, these results, along with those of White et al. in Chapter 6, and of Pagnini and Morgan (1990), suggest where household contact was greatest and where ideas may have passed most easily. The "old" immigrants were clearly less isolated from natives than were the "new" immigrants. This isolation may help account for the new immigrants' persistent and distinct fertility patterns (see Chapter 4). The isolation of African Americans appears to be at a distinctly higher level.

TABLE 5.7

Recency of Immigration for Boarders and Household Employees
(over age 18), by Sex

Ethnicity	(N)	Adult Males							
		Year Missing	1905–1910	1900–1904	1895–1899	1890–1894	1880–1889	1870–1879	Pre-1870
Boarders									
British	(411)	8.0	31.6	13.9	5.6	11.0	18.7	6.1	5.1
Irish	(493)	7.9	22.5	14.6	7.5	9.5	19.3	10.3	8.3
Scandinavian	(480)	9.8	27.9	22.9	5.4	10.8	18.1	4.0	1.0
German	(456)	10.5	20.8	11.4	8.1	12.0	23.3	7.0	6.8
Italian	(1,088)	2.8	65.8	22.2	4.4	2.7	1.8	.4	.1
Polish	(769)	1.8	76.5	14.7	2.3	2.9	1.3	.3	.3
C.E. Jews	(49)	0	63.3	24.5	6.1	4.1	2.0	0	0
E.E. Jews	(163)	2.5	62.0	19.6	3.7	9.2	2.5	.6	0
Employees									
British	(70)	17.1	38.6	12.9	7.1	5.7	5.7	5.7	7.1
Irish	(50)	12.0	26.0	18.0	4.0	2.0	24.0	6.0	8.0
Scandinavian	(142)	12.0	38.0	13.4	3.5	10.6	14.8	3.5	4.2
German	(82)	14.6	23.2	14.6	2.4	15.9	19.5	7.3	2.4
Italian	(58)	5.2	67.2	13.8	3.5	5.2	1.7	3.5	0
Polish	(25)	16.0	48.0	20.0	16.0	0	0	0	0
C.E. Jews	(2)	0	50.0	50.0	0	0	0	0	0
E.E. Jews	(6)	0	100.0	0	0	0	0	0	0
All Ethnicities									
All boarders	(14,793)	57.6	23.5	7.9	2.3	2.8	3.8	1.3	.9
Boarders reporting immigration date	(6,276)	0	55.4	18.6	5.4	6.5	8.9	3.0	2.2
All household employees	(2,605)	73.8	12.3	4.7	1.6	2.1	3.5	1.1	1.0
Household employees reporting immigration date	(683)	0	46.9	17.9	6.0	8.1	13.2	4.2	3.8

Quantitatively, it seems that the "social distance" between "new" and "old" immigrants was striking, but only one-half as great as the chasm that separated all whites from African Americans. This finding of social and physical distance within households fits with findings of Stanley Lieberson, who used ward-level statistics from the censuses of 1890 to 1930 to measure residential segregation for immigrant groups and African Americans, and with White et. al's (Chapter 6) analysis of segregation using the 1910 PUS.[18]

[18]Lieberson 1980, pp. 253–290.

TABLE 5.7 (*continued*)

	Adult Females							
(N)	Year Missing	1905–1910	1900–1904	1895–1899	1890–1894	1880–1889	1870–1879	Pre–1870
(80)	18.8	26.3	13.8	6.3	11.3	7.5	8.8	7.5
(127)	21.3	9.5	14.2	7.9	8.7	17.3	8.7	12.6
(48)	25.0	20.8	10.4	14.6	10.4	12.5	4.2	2.0
(83)	18.4	12.0	13.2	6.0	12.0	16.8	6.0	15.6
(29)	0	62.1	24.1	3.5	10.3	0	0	0
(84)	2.4	71.4	19.1	2.4	1.2	3.6	0	0
(13)	0	53.9	38.5	0	7.7	0	0	0
(44)	2.3	70.5	18.2	6.9	2.3	0	0	0
(86)	12.8	36.1	12.8	9.3	9.3	10.5	7.0	2.3
(432)	10.4	22.9	19.4	13.0	11.3	16.0	2.6	4.4
(185)	11.4	45.4	18.9	4.3	8.7	9.2	1.6	.5
(129)	17.8	30.2	12.4	5.4	16.3	7.8	4.7	5.4
(8)	25.0	37.5	25.0	12.5	0	0	0	0
(46)	4.4	67.4	8.7	6.5	6.5	6.5	0	0
(6)	0	83.3	16.7	0	0	0	0	0
(6)	16.7	50.0	33.3	0	0	0	0	0
(4,271)	83.1	7.1	3.4	1.3	1.6	1.9	.7	1.0
(722)	0	41.8	19.9	7.4	9.5	11.5	3.9	6.1
(3,157)	65.8	14.1	7.0	3.3	3.6	4.0	1.1	1.1
(1,079)	0	41.3	20.4	9.7	10.6	11.6	3.2	3.2

Extendedness, Headship, and the Presence of Children

Much of the previous analysis of household structure has focused on non-family members, especially boarders and employees. We now turn our attention to whether the families within households are nuclear or extended and whether or not the households are headed by a married couple. We examine household structure using three variables that categorize who lives in the household relationally, who heads the household, and whether or not there are children present. Looking at the relationship variable, we sort households into those that are:

a. nuclear   composed of nuclear family members only
b. extended   some non-nuclear kin but no non-relatives
c. augmented   some non-relatives but no non-nuclear kin
d. extended/augmented   both non-nuclear kin and non-relatives

We sort headship into those households headed by a male only, those headed by a female only, and those headed by a couple defined as a male head with a spouse present. Finally, we have also indicated whether or not there is present at least one child of the household head under the age of 18.

Table 5.10 shows the composition of family households by ethnic group. The third column shows the percentage of all households that are family households, which are those in which at least one household member is a relative of the head. This excludes those households that contain a single person or only individuals unrelated to the head. Although family households predominate for all groups in 1910, there is a fair amount of variability. First-generation Irish, Scandinavian, and Italian households have lower rates of being family households than other first-generation ethnicities. Rates drop for all ethnicities except the British and Irish in the second generation,[19] though the sample sizes are small for new immigrants in the second generation. Jewish households are almost exclusively family households, as indicated in earlier analyses of household size, relationships, and boarding. It is interesting that

TABLE 5.8

Proportion Boarding Standardized on Time in the U.S., by Ethnicity

Ethnicity	Observed	Standardized
First Generation		
British	.10	.16
Irish	.11	.21
Scandinavian	.11	.18
German	.06	.15
Italian	.21	.21
Polish	.25	.25
Central European Jews	.10	.15
Eastern European Jews	.07	.07

Categories used for standardization and data come from Tables 5.6 and 5.7.

[19]Jews from Central Europe also do not show a drop; however, with only eleven households represented in the second generation, this is not a finding in which there is much significance.

there is no clear pattern for the ethnic groups either between "new" and "old" immigrants or between first and second generations, while there are clear patterns for the native groups. Native white households are considerably more likely to be family households than are black or mulatto households, and households in the South are much more likely to be family households than those in the North for all groups.

The right-hand panel of Table 5.10 shows the proportions of family households that are nuclear, extended, augmented, and extended/augmented. Previous studies of Western societies have failed to find a society where the predominant form of household was not nuclear.[20] Even in non-Western societies that have strong extended families and a "preferred" extended pattern, most households are nuclear (Hsu 1943). Indeed, the modal pattern for all groups here is the nuclear household, although it is slightly lower for "new" immigrant groups in the first generation. Extended families are particularly rare in the first generation for Poles, while the Irish and Germans are notably high in the second generation. For the Poles, low levels may reflect their recent immigration, while for the Irish and Germans, extendedness may be a function of the high level of widowhood (see Table 5.3) in these ethnicities. Their levels of extendedness may indicate an older generation that is being cared for in homes of their children. But again African American households, both black and mulatto, are somewhat more likely to be extended, particularly in the South, than are households headed by a native white.[21]

Cross-culturally augmented households are relatively uncommon. They tend to occur in societies where large proportions of the population have live-in servants. However, as shown in the previous sections, a significant proportion of men were boarders in this period (see Table 5.2; see also Modell and Hareven 1973). The new ethnicities show high levels of augmented households in the first generation, which indicates their high level of boarding, as shown earlier. It is significant that when the table is restricted to family households, a number of the Italian cases seem to have dropped out. This indicates that while Jews and Poles boarded with families, the Italians exhibit a significant rate of boarding in non-family households. The Italian sex ratio in Table 5.3 together

[20]The work of Peter Laslett (1970) is important here. It has been qualified by other, more recent studies that take note of family-life-course issues and interhousehold family interactions. The controversy over Laslett is outside the scope of this chapter because it focuses on whether there was a historic transition from the extended to the nuclear family long before 1910.

[21]Our discussion of extendedness is necessarily limited by the ways in which household relationships are recorded only with regard to the head of household. There is some evidence for the theory that women are the "glue" that holds kin networks together, in that those groups that show the highest levels of female headship—Irish, blacks, and mulattoes—also show the highest levels of extendedness.

TABLE 5.9
Ethnicity of Selected Pairs of Co-residents

Ethnicity	(N)	Husband—Wife	
		Odds That Husband Has Wife of Same Ethnicity	Odds That Husband Has a Native-Native Wife
First Generation			
British	(1,088)	0.68	.39
Irish	(1,036)	3.80	.13
Scandinavian	(1,237)	4.80	.11
German	(2,310)	3.60	.16
Italian	(590)	12.00	.03
Polish	(511)	17.00	.02
C.E. Jews	(134)	31.00	.00
E.E. Jews	(415)	31.00	.01
Second Generation			
British	(1,185)	0.27	1.50
Irish	(1,912)	1.00	.52
Scandinavian	(376)	1.50	.42
German	(3,490)	1.20	.54
Italian	(41)	0.86	.37
Polish	(61)	3.70	.11
C.E. Jews	(9)	2.80	.00
E.E. Jews	(28)	2.80	.12
Native-Native			
White	(33,839)	9.80	9.80
Black	(8,588)	99.00	.01
Mulatto	(1,890)	99.00	.01

with these data would indicate that there were many households made up of unrelated Italian men.[22]

Table 5.11 shows household headship for households that contain at least one child of the household head, a subset of family households. This restriction places a rough control on the life-cycle stage of the household head. Few males alone head households with children, regardless of ethnic group, but there is substantial variability in female headship. Female headship could be produced by non-marriage, separa-

---

[22]Milton Hunt notes this phenomenon in his 1910 article, "The Housing of Non-Family Groups of Men in Chicago," in the *American Journal of Sociology*, where he takes particular note of the practice among Italians, Greeks, Bulgarians, and Croatians. He notes that Poles are almost exclusively found in families (p. 157), as we also see here.

TABLE 5.9 *(continued)*

	Household Head—Boarder			Household Head—Employee	
(N)	Odds That Boarder Has Same Ethnicity as HH	Odds That Boarder Has a Native-Native HH	(N)	Odds That Employee Has Same Ethnicity as HH	Odds That Employee Has a Native-Native as HH
(468)	1.20	.27	(148)	.56	.91
(574)	2.60	.17	(470)	.39	1.30
(499)	3.20	.14	(322)	.87	.66
(506)	1.70	.20	(218)	1.20	.44
(1,203)	28.00	.02	(75)	7.30	.09
(859)	33.00	.01	(73)	.43	.40
(64)	29.00	.01	(12)	5.50	.00
(233)	29.00	.01	(14)	5.50	.00
(271)	.64	.95	(76)	1.60	1.20
(610)	1.40	.42	(210)	1.10	.91
(186)	1.50	.38	(148)	.68	.60
(541)	.87	.51	(283)	.66	.60
(35)	2.90	.17	(9)	.13	.11
(33)	3.70	.14	(15)	.88	.50
(2)	3.30	.08	(0)	.00	.00
(11)	3.30	.08	(0)	.00	.00
(7,442)	5.30	5.30	(2,445)	6.30	6.30
(2,660)	53.00	.02	(1,066)	.45	1.70
(692)	53.00	.01	(209)	.45	2.10

tion, divorce, or widowhood, coupled with the relative possibilities for particular women to maintain their own households. Because we expect most female-headed *families* to seek co-residence in other households, given the economic constraints on female workers, we expect relatively few family households with children to be female-headed.[23]

[23]Comparing the figures for females who head households in Table 5.2 with those for female-headed family households with children in Table 5.11, one can see a distinct adjustment for British, Irish, and German women. They show high rates in Table 5.2, which fall to normal rates in Table 5.11 when controls for family and children are in place. It appears that these are either older women who head households in which all of their children are over 18, or they are running boardinghouses in which none of the residents are related to them. The age distributions of these "old" immigrant groups would favor the former interpretation over the latter.

TABLE 5.10

Family and Non-family Households and Extendedness of Family Households, by Ethnicity

	All Households		Family Households				
	(N)	% Family[1]	(N)	Nuclear[2]	Extended[3]	Augmented[4]	Extended-Augmented[5]
First Generation							
British	(2,164)	.91	(1,963)	.68	.17	.11	.04
Irish	(2,286)	.86	(1,955)	.67	.18	.11	.04
Scandinavian	(2,064)	.87	(1,796)	.71	.13	.13	.03
German	(4,210)	.90	(3,807)	.74	.14	.09	.02
Italian	(1,671)	.88	(1,470)	.61	.15	.17	.06
Polish	(1,103)	.95	(1,051)	.58	.10	.26	.05
C.E. Jews	(198)	.98	(194)	.61	.15	.20	.04
E.E. Jews	(932)	.98	(909)	.62	.15	.18	.04
Second Generation							
British	(1,533)	.91	(1,394)	.68	.15	.12	.04
Irish	(2,793)	.87	(2,442)	.63	.22	.10	.05
Scandinavian	(547)	.83	(456)	.63	.14	.14	.08
German	(1,302)	.82	(1,064)	.48	.34	.14	.03
Italian	(76)	.75	(57)	.72	.14	.11	.04
Polish	(95)	.79	(75)	.73	.16	.08	.03
C.E. Jews	(11)	1.00	(11)	.82	.09	.00	.09
E.E. Jews	(37)	.86	(32)	.78	.13	.09	.00

		[1]		[2]	[3]	[4]	[5]
Native-Native							
White							
Non-South	(28,188)	.90	(25,367)	.68	.17	.11	.04
South	(14,947)	.95	(14,193)	.70	.18	.08	.03
Black							
Non-South	(1,400)	.80	(1,119)	.59	.18	.18	.05
South	(10,576)	.88	(9,356)	.66	.23	.07	.03
Mulatto							
Non-South	(456)	.82	(373)	.61	.20	.09	.09
South	(2,193)	.89	(1,953)	.62	.25	.08	.04

[1]Households that include at least one person related to the household head.
[2]Only nuclear family members (husband, wife, son, daughter, or stepson or stepdaughter) in household.
[3]At least some non-nuclear kin, but no non-relatives in household.
[4]At least some non-nuclear relatives in household.
[5]Both non-nuclear kin and non-relatives in household.

TABLE 5.11

Percentage of Family Households with Children and Headship, by Ethnicity

	All Family Households		Headship of Family Households with Children			
	(N)	% with Children[1]	(N)	Couple[2]	Man[3]	Woman[4]
First Generation						
British	(1,963)	.52	(1,022)	.90	.03	.07
Irish	(1,955)	.47	(926)	.83	.05	.12
Scandinavian	(1,796)	.65	(1,164)	.91	.04	.05
German	(3,807)	.55	(2,094)	.90	.02	.07
Italian	(1,470)	.73	(1,079)	.95	.02	.03
Polish	(1,051)	.78	(820)	.93	.02	.05
C.E. Jews	(194)	.76	(147)	.97	.00	.03
E.E. Jews	(908)	.81	(738)	.94	.01	.05
Second Generation						
British	(1,394)	.62	(856)	.93	.02	.06
Irish	(2,442)	.58	(1,424)	.86	.04	.10
Scandinavian	(456)	.66	(299)	.93	.01	.06
German	(1,066)	.49	(526)	.93	.02	.05
Italian	(57)	.67	(38)	.84	.05	.11
Polish	(75)	.60	(45)	.98	.00	.02
C.E. Jews	(11)	.36	(4)	1.00	.00	.00
E.E. Jews	(32)	.38	(12)	1.00	.00	.00

Native-Native							
White							
Non-South	(25,367)	.55	(14,053)	.92	.02	.05
South	(14,193)	.70	(9,915)	.92	.03	.05
Black							
Non-South	(1,119)	.43	(480)	.86	.04	.09
South	(9,356)	.62	(5,823)	.82	.04	.14
Mulatto							
Non-South	(373)	.43	(160)	.81	.03	.15
South	(1,953)	.61	(1,195)	.81	.04	.16

[1] Someone in household is less than age 18 and someone has relation to head of household of (step)son or (step)daughter.
[2] The household head and his/her spouse is also present in the household.
[3] The household head is male and his spouse is not present in the household.
[4] The household head is female and her spouse is not present in the household.

As expected, the great majority of households are headed by couples, defined as married males with co-resident spouses. This is true for black and mulatto households as well, but these are also much more likely to be female-headed than are native white households. Among the first-generation immigrants only the Irish have distinctively high levels of female headship, and a similarly high level can be observed for second-generation Irish. The high observed value for second-generation Italians can be attributed to sampling variability. In any case, although the rates for the Irish are directly attributable to some extent to the Irish sex ratio shown in Table 5.3, the significantly higher rates of female headship among blacks and mulattoes are not so obviously explained.

We noted earlier that one reason we expected few female-headed households is that female employment in 1910 was much less likely to be able to support a household. For African Americans, insufficient household wages were a reality for men as well, so that there was little advantage to be gained in a traditional "male-breadwinner" household (Espenshade 1985). Whereas for white groups there was a major economic incentive for women to find male partners, many have claimed that employment prospects for African American women, particularly in urban areas at this time, were better than those for African American men.[24] African American women were thus less affected by subservient female dependence within the home, because the reality of insufficient wages required that they work for wages whether in a domestic partnership or not. This same economic effect of the male/female wage differential has been observed in white groups, most notably for the Irish, who also exhibit high rates of female headship. Other factors may also play a role: African American male mortality was no doubt important, and, as we noted earlier in Table 5.3, so was the mulatto sex ratio. In addition, several anthropologists and sociologists identify an African cultural heritage that has a generational rather than a conjugal family focus.[25] There is evidence of the perpetuation of family practices that reflect this emphasis in patterns of extendedness and child fosterage both in the United States and in Africa. Such an emphasis could increase female headship, especially in the face of unfavorable marriage opportunities.

Overall, then, although some differences exist, the strongest impression from Table 5.10 is of rough similarity in the proportion of "family households" and in the proportion of nuclear households for

[24]Sanderson (1979) makes this argument most explicitly. Also see Becker (1981) on the importance of male/female wage inequality for decisions to marry and for marital stability.
[25]Sudarkasa 1981; Radcliffe-Brown 1950; Herskovits 1941; Stack 1974; Shimkin et al. 1978; Page 1989.

whites and African Americans. In Table 5.11, black, mulatto, and, to a lesser extent, Irish households are more likely to be female-headed, even while couples predominate for all groups. The main predominance of couples is a point Herbert Gutman made repeatedly in his studies of the African American family (1976, 1987). We would add the observation that heading a household is an economic role, and is not necessarily the same as heading a family, which is a cultural role not measured by the census. The attempts to discuss female household headship as evidence of a "breakdown" in *family* life also miss the kinds of inter-household relationships found by modern ethnographers like Carol Stack (1974) in Illinois or Dimitri Shimkin (1978) in Mississippi (see also Billingsley 1968; Hill 1971; Berkner 1975).

Family Structure

As pointed out earlier, constructing "families" from census information is problematic. To begin with, only co-resident persons can be considered part of the family, and then one must decide how to divide co-residents into families. Furthermore, relationships are given only in reference to the household head, so that many family relationships within a household that do not involve the head go unrecorded. The "rules" on which decisions are based about who may be members of which families are culturally and temporally specific. Given these limitations, kinship and co-residence are still strong indicators of family membership.

Without attempting to divide households into mutually exclusive sets of families, we focus on two important norms of Western family structure. These include the living arrangements of children and the living arrangements of mothers (Laslett 1972; Hareven 1976). Rules commonly accepted in ideal Western family models expect that children live with their natural mothers, and mothers live with their husbands. Mothers are thus situated to provide care, nurturance, and socialization, and fathers to be breadwinners and disciplinarians.

To measure adherence to Western nuclear family norms, we construct three variables using the intrafamily links constructed from the manuscript records. First we identified children not living with mothers as those in households in which they cannot be linked to a mother.[26] An independent measure of child-mother co-residence is constructed for mothers, testing whether those with only young children have all of

---

[26]See Strong et al. 1989 for details of the linking process. In Morgan et al. (1993) the authors constructed a similar second measure using relationship variables for each child to see if they live with a mother or father.

their surviving children living with them. Using the same procedures, we next identify women who have more children living with them than they claim to have surviving. To ensure that these women's children should be living with them given Western nuclear residence rules, these measures are defined only for women once-married, married fewer than thirteen years, and in the age range from 15 to 35 years old.

The third variable measures husband-wife co-residence by selecting women with co-resident children and then searching the household roster to see if any person listed is likely to be her spouse. The resultant variable indicates whether or not there is a spouse present. Our question is whether racial or ethnic groups vary in the extent to which they follow the residence rule that children should live with their biological mothers. Table 5.12 shows the odds of a child's not living with the natural mother, those of "being unlinked to mother" by race or ethnicity and age.

The odds in Table 5.12 show that older children are more likely not to be living with mothers. Maternal mortality and marital disruption are certainly some of the reasons for this tendency, but we expect there to be a range of normatively acceptable reasons for older children's residing elsewhere. The biggest differences are by age and between blacks and mulattoes and all other groups.[27] Significantly, blacks and mulattoes are *very* similar despite any status and economic differences that might distinguish them. All immigrant groups have low levels similar to native whites.

We now turn to a related measure—the odds that a young mother has some of her surviving children living elsewhere. Table 5.13 shows the odds of having fewer children living with the mother than she reports surviving, indicated as odds of fewer versus same in the table. These odds range from 0 to .05 for the whites, while the odds are substantially higher, from .05 to .10, for blacks and mulattoes.[28] The estimate for the black southerners indicates that for every ten black women who lived

[27]Black and mulatto children, regardless of whether their residence is in the South or non-South, are almost 2.5 times more likely to be unlinked, that is, not living with their mothers, than natives. "New" immigrant groups were very unlikely to be unlinked—the odds of being unlinked decline by roughly 40 percent for Jews and 30 percent for both Italians and Poles relative to the natives.

Although age effects are substantial and pervasive, the effect of age is somewhat weaker for both groups of African Americans than for the other groups. These statements are based on formal analysis of these data using minimum logit chi-square regression (Theil 1970).

[28]Allowing for an age contrast has little effect on these odds, though older women are slightly more likely to have too few or too many children linked to them. The contrast of African American and white natives is sharp. Black and mulatto women are more likely by roughly a factor of 3 to have too few and too many children linked to them.

TABLE 5.12

Odds of a Child Not Living with Mother, by Age and Ethnicity

	Age							
	0–4		5–9		10–14		0–14	
	(N)	Odds	(N)	Odds	(N)	Odds	(N)	Odds
First Generation								
British	(49)	.067	(124)	.061	(115)	.162	(288)	.102
Irish	(6)	.016	(16)	.149	(21)	.110	(43)	.111
Scandinavian	(15)	.078	(70)	.016	(64)	.086	(149)	.052
German	(17)	.006	(58)	.096	(68)	.032	(143)	.055
Italian	(63)	.034	(199)	.059	(276)	.113	(538)	.084
Polish	(43)	.002	(106)	.020	(102)	.031	(251)	.022
C.E. Jews	(5)	.017	(23)	.004	(23)	.004	(51)	.006
E.E. Jews	(26)	.004	(188)	.039	(216)	.102	(430)	.069
Second Generation								
British	(507)	.024	(512)	.047	(591)	.128	(1,610)	.070
Irish	(629)	.030	(727)	.072	(854)	.142	(2,210)	.087
Scandinavian	(682)	.008	(709)	.058	(826)	.105	(2,253)	.061
German	(1,069)	.020	(1,327)	.047	(1,614)	.077	(4,010)	.052
Italian	(1,214)	.022	(665)	.033	(397)	.097	(2,276)	.038
Polish	(951)	.010	(577)	.049	(432)	.111	(1,960)	.044
C.E. Jews	(141)	.001	(116)	.010	(102)	.021	(359)	.009
E.E. Jews	(593)	.017	(352)	.042	(299)	.076	(1,244)	.038
Native-Native								
White								
Non-South	(16,746)	.029	(15,434)	.072	(14,387)	.130	(46,568)	.074
South	(10,825)	.026	(9,877)	.081	(8,616)	.142	(29,318)	.079
Black								
Non-South	(404)	.093	(389)	.174	(879)	.289	(1,173)	.183
South	(6,151)	.098	(6,184)	.184	(5,412)	.287	(17,747)	.186
Mulatto								
Non-South	(141)	.072	(152)	.146	(140)	.270	(433)	.162
South	(1,608)	.078	(1,493)	.193	(1,285)	.275	(4,386)	.175

TABLE 5.13

Odds That a Woman Has Fewer or More Children Linked to Her Than Reported as Ever Born (same): Woman less than 34 Years of Age, Married Once for Less than Ten Years

Ethnicity	Fewer vs. Same		More vs. Same	
	Odds	(N)	Odds	(N)
First Generation				
British	.040	(323)	.007	(311)
Irish	.031	(311)	.000	(302)
Scandinavian	.023	(324)	.004	(318)
German	.028	(490)	.009	(481)
Italian	.052	(586)	.000	(557)
Polish	.037	(454)	.005	(440)
C.E. Jews	.014	(91)	.000	(90)
E.E. Jews	.022	(376)	.003	(369)
Second Generation				
British	.031	(435)	.005	(424)
Irish	.027	(571)	.009	(561)
Scandinavian	.011	(302)	.004	(300)
German	.019	(1,240)	.007	(1,225)
Italian	.030	(75)	.000	(73)
Polish	.000	(84)	.000	(84)
C.E. Jews	.000	(13)	.000	(13)
E.E. Jews	.000	(21)	.000	(21)
Native-Native				
White				
Non-South	.026	(8,066)	.005	(7,901)
South	.025	(5,061)	.008	(4,976)
Black				
Non-South	.067	(347)	.011	(329)
South	.100	(2,730)	.023	(2,540)
Mulatto				
Non-South	.054	(169)	.002	(155)
South	.082	(853)	.012	(798)

with all of their children there was one who had at least one child living elsewhere.

Table 5.13 also shows the odds that more children have been linked to the mother than she claims to have surviving. This could imply an error in the data, in that the mother's surviving children could be underreported or other information was incorrectly reported so that it looked as if this child "belonged" to the woman in question. Another possibility is that these children have been adopted and are treated "as own children." The most likely cause is misreporting by mothers with infants as well as by those with particularly large families, because these two features are common to those mothers who appear to have excess children linked to them. Having too many children linked to a woman is much less likely than having too few linked.

First-generation Italian and Polish women are more likely than native whites to have too few children linked, but they are *less* likely to have too many linked. This might result if some children were left behind in Italy or Eastern Europe, but those brought to the United States followed strict residence rules. There is scattered evidence of mothers leaving one child behind when migrating to the United States, which was seen as a guarantee that the other family members would return. This may explain why in other studies the majority of women who return to Europe from the United States are married women who are normally considered less mobile (see Gabaccia 1984).

There are two possible interpretations for these findings on children's living arrangements, one that attributes these to the discrepancies of bad data, the other a more substantive interpretation. The bad-data argument assumes that people who are poor or illiterate or who are especially "different" to the census enumerator, such as African Americans, are either inaccurate in reporting or are carelessly recorded. The inaccurate data produce children who cannot be linked to mothers and to false links of children to mothers who did not really bear them, making it appear that the family structure of these disadvantaged groups is different. To state our argument briefly, however, if data were collected accurately from poor, illiterate immigrants who did not speak English, then they should be accurate for African Americans as well. Furthermore, the social prejudices against such groups, which at the time were often referred to as different and inferior races, were strong, as they have always been for African Americans. As for census enumerators, there were some efforts in 1910 to recruit local enumerators of similar ethnicity to the respondents, as shown by the use of African American enumerators for the first time in 1910. Bad data for such reasons should turn up as uniformly bad for all groups that share such characteristics, but it does not.[29] Again, note also the similar results for blacks and mulattoes, the latter group having significantly higher social and economic standing.

Rather, our findings suggest that residence rules for children vary across racial groups. The boundaries between African American nuclear families are less restrictive and rigid than for Western groups. Bound-

---

[29]For further evaluation of data quality, see Morgan et al. (1993), where several other tests were run that convincingly demonstrate the weaknesses of the "bad-data" argument.

aries for whites, and especially for European Jews, are very clearly delineated. This interpretation is consistent with much current scholarship on families in contemporary Africa, as well as with observations of the time from scholars like W. E. B. DuBois and Carter Woodson.[30]

Turning to the issue of female family headship, Table 5.14 shows the odds that a woman living with her child or children does not have a spouse in the household. Female headship is twice as likely among older mothers than it is for younger mothers. Black and mulatto women are almost four times more likely to be mothers who head families than native whites. At ages 15–24, only blacks and mulattoes surpass 10 percent as female heads of families, and female headship appears to be greatest among African Americans outside the South. However, caution is warranted because there are relatively few non-southern blacks and mulattoes.

"New" immigrants, and especially Italians and Poles, are unlikely to have female-headed households, being 30 percent less likely than native whites of native parentage. The Irish are nearly 70 percent more likely to have female-headed households than native whites and other "old" immigrant groups.

The final column shows these same odds for all age groups together. Blacks and mulattoes remain the most distinct group, but the racial differential narrows somewhat.[31] Among the immigrant groups, the Irish of both the first and second generations have higher rates of female headship than native whites or other immigrant groups. For the Irish and the "new" immigrants, these rates may have much to do with their respective patterns of immigration. As we have noted, Irish immigration at this time was disproportionately female, while the "new" immigrant groups were predominantly male.[32]

Comparing black and white patterns across native and immigrant groups provides some clues to the causes of racial differences. Demographic factors, and mortality specifically, account for some portion of the differences. African American mortality is much higher than for the other groups (see Preston et al., Chapter 3, this volume). Children cannot live with mothers who have died, and likewise women cannot live

---

[30]Page (1989); Bledsoe (1989); Isiugo-Abanihe (1985); DuBois (1908); Woodson (1936); Goody (1982); Onyango (1985). Although the contemporary works deal with populations in Africa, the earlier works point to the non-Western heritage of African Americans. This relation is explored further in current work by the authors.

[31]The racial difference is greatest at the younger ages. Black and mulatto women are over five times more likely to be living without a spouse at the youngest ages. This difference is reduced by a factor of .59 (roughly 40 percent) for the oldest (ages 35–39) category.

[32]Guttentag and Secord (1983) develop very interesting arguments and analyses concerning the social effects of sex ratio imbalances.

TABLE 5.14
Odds That a Woman with a Child Is Not Living with a Husband, by Ethnicity and Age of Woman

	Age							
	15–24		25–34		35–44		Total	
	(N)	Odds	(N)	Odds	(N)	Odds	(N)	Odds
First Generation								
British	(31)	.072	(263)	.057	(486)	.128	(780)	.102
Irish	(27)	.042	(229)	.046	(593)	.196	(849)	.150
Scandinavian	(38)	.030	(248)	.029	(524)	.103	(810)	.077
German	(61)	.018	(442)	.031	(997)	.138	(1,500)	.102
Italian	(183)	.012	(421)	.017	(352)	.073	(956)	.037
Polish	(144)	.015	(335)	.028	(264)	.124	(743)	.059
C.E. Jews	(25)	.047	(66)	.017	(75)	.121	(166)	.069
E.E. Jews	(88)	.001	(294)	.025	(282)	.106	(664)	.056
Second Generation								
British	(91)	.059	(313)	.044	(452)	.111	(856)	.081
Irish	(87)	.037	(425)	.093	(941)	.202	(1,453)	.160
Scandinavian	(73)	.015	(214)	.020	(170)	.119	(457)	.056
German	(261)	.024	(914)	.051	(1,401)	.115	(2,576)	.083
Italian	(35)	.032	(28)	.004	(14)	.406	(77)	.090
Polish	(38)	.030	(40)	.028	(15)	.078	(93)	.037
C.E. Jews	(3)	.032	(5)	.020	(4)	.024	(12)	.024
E.E. Jews	(5)	.020	(10)	.260	(6)	.016	(21)	.133
Native-Native								
White								
Non-South	(1,943)	.057	(5,585)	.051	(7,033)	.119	(14,561)	.085
South	(1,875)	.047	(3,765)	.058	(4,004)	.135	(9,645)	.088
Black								
Non-South	(66)	.381	(221)	.184	(239)	.365	(524)	.291
South	(1,229)	.252	(2,128)	.232	(2,168)	.389	(5,525)	.298
Mulatto								
Non-South	(29)	.131	(82)	.319	(84)	.410	(195)	.333
South	(357)	.203	(533)	.214	(580)	.349	(1,469)	.264

with husbands who have died, but there are several reasons to assume that mortality does not provide a complete explanation for these differences. First, the racial differences in family headship and in the proportion of children not living with mothers are greatest at the youngest ages of both mothers and children, respectively. If mortality were the full story, then the greatest differences would lie at the older ages because the force of mortality would have had longer to operate. Second, some known mortality differences are not visible in family differences. For instance, Jewish mortality is greatly below Italian and Polish mortality, but there are virtually no differences in the proportion of children not living with mothers between these groups. Third, some measures, like the proportion of surviving mothers who have children living elsewhere, are unaffected by mortality differences but still show substantial racial differences. And finally, calculating the proportion of children who have no mothers surviving (see Morgan et al. 1990) shows that mortality can account for only some of the racial difference in children's living arrangements.[33]

The sharp racial and immigrant differences we observe for household headship and family living arrangements do not fit well with economic interpretations, except when it comes to wage differentials for sexes within marriage. African Americans and immigrant groups were together at the bottom of the socioeconomic ladder at the turn of the century. Although their histories and potential for advancement in American society were quite different, some material conditions were similar. The immigrants were certainly not similar to native-born whites of native parents along economic lines, and so their alignment with these whites on certain measures most likely does not have an economic basis. Furthermore, the conditions that drove immigration streams in various groups were rather different in each case, producing groups in the United States of varying economic backgrounds in their home countries.

Perhaps, as Lieberson (1980) argues, the African Americans' position may have been markedly inferior in the South to that of immigrants in northern cities. The types of prejudice, discrimination, and violence various groups experienced were certainly quite different, yet all of these groups were regarded generally as inferior races. However, there is little North-South difference in African American behavior and a stark contrast between African Americans and all immigrant groups. Furthermore, the black-mulatto distinction, a distinction that we maintain is largely socioeconomic, has little effect on family structure variables. Be-

---

[33]A current research project focuses on widowhood reports to determine if they mask a substantial amount of non-marriage, separation, or divorce. We suspect that taking these widowhood reports at face value would overestimate the effects of mortality on African American white family differences.

cause the black-mulatto difference does show a significant difference in sex ratio, it may be, as we proposed above, that the earnings differential between African American men and women is small compared to that of whites. This may be mainly in relative terms to the large female disadvantage found for other groups, but it could contribute significantly to the higher rates of household headship found for African American women (see Sweet and Bumpass 1987).

Finally, some differentials are consistent with a cultural interpretation. The differences in living arrangements of mothers and children between African Americans and whites, both immigrant and native, could be accounted for by historical continuity in family patterns. Although the immigrant groups differ on a broad range of factors, the most notable contrast in family patterns is African American versus all other groups. Furthermore, these differences are consistent with observed patterns of family behavior in Africa, implying that there is a factor of a surviving non-Western heritage within African American family patterns (Sudarkasa 1981; McDaniel 1990; A. T. Miller 1991; Allen 1978). The extensive practice of child fosterage accompanied by patterns of extendedness throughout a large majority of African ethnicities has long been noted by the demographers of Africa. Given the extreme nature of separation between the races in the United States, and the privacy accorded the family realm within American society, it is not inconceivable that there could be such a cultural survival.[34] Our initial research points toward the further investigation of such a connection for African Americans, while finding European immigrant group differences largely structural matters associated with recent immigration.

Conclusion

The most striking household differences between immigrant groups and natives are in the number of non-family members present. Native households outside the South averaged almost .4 non-family members per household. They were even more common in Italian and Polish households at .78 and .85 per household, respectively, and much less common in southern native households of all races, which averaged only

[34]Esther Goody (1982), although not dealing with the United States, does some very interesting comparative studies of child-fosterage practices in various parts of sub-Saharan Africa, of African immigrants in London, and of West Indians of African heritage. DuBois (1908) and Herskovits (1941) pointed to an African heritage present in African American family practices, and these ideas have been developed in different ways by contemporary scholars like Gutman (1987); McDaniel (1990); and A. T. Miller (1991).

.2 per household. The distinguishing features of Italian and Polish households seem to be due primarily to the disruptions caused by immigration that led to high rates of boarding and household employment. Low household headship for males and large proportions of married men living apart from their wives are two features that stand out. These features are most visible among Italian and Polish immigrants who had very recently migrated to the United States. When we consider each group's relative recency of immigration to the United States and the distributions of the different ethnic groups, the differences decline substantially. Therefore, with these European ethnic groups, it appears that we are not observing a gradual process of cultural assimilation so much as effects of recent migration, which are relatively quickly overcome.

Differences in these areas of household structure among native groups are quite small in comparison to the household structure differences found among immigrants. It would appear that such differences have a great deal to do with the processes of migration and its attendant opportunity structures for housing, employment, and social interaction. The sharpest racial differences are found in family structure, specifically in the living arrangements of mothers and children. By and large, European ethnic groups are very similar to native whites on these dimensions of family structure. Therefore, these racial differences must arise from a different level of group experience. Certainly, African American heritage and social experience are quite different from those of recent immigrants and native whites. Even though patterns of discrimination were quite strong for some of these ethnic groups in the United States in 1910, discrimination was clearly much stronger for African Americans (DuBois 1899, 1908; Lieberson 1980). Recent immigrants and native whites may not have shared common economic status, job opportunities, religion, or ethnic heritage, and did not display similar demographic behavior, but they did share a common European, Western background, in a modernizing context.

There exists a fundamental difference between the two levels of measurement, that of the household and that of the family, and differences in one area are not comparable to differences in the other. We would argue that differences on the family level are deeper and more culturally rooted than those on the household level. Unfortunately, the way in which our data were collected precludes clearer definition of families and households, because family data are available only in terms of households. Households are primarily economic units of analysis, while families are more culturally based units. The private Western family was a structure familiar to European immigrants, and was contained within the households structured by the immigration experience. Once that experience was in the past, succeeding generations came to resemble the dominant European Americans of earlier immigration. Thus, even at the time of the most dramatic contrast and conflict between ethnic immigrants and native whites in 1910, similarities are obvious, especially when seen in contrast to other significant native-born groups like African Americans.

The expectation that African American families will or should come to resemble European models is more suspect, for even when households are similarly structured, they contain within them the living heritage of profoundly different cultural groups. There are certainly aspects of their household and family differences that are attributable to structural factors, and, indeed, such factors might explain a large part of the higher rates of female family headship among African Americans as opposed to whites. Several striking features of African American families, such as the living arrangements of children, are not so easily attributable to such structural factors. Many scholars have pointed to the unique history of African Americans, and most often to the slave experience, as a possible source of explanation.

It is true that African Americans do have a unique history, but that history did not begin or end with the slave experience. Rather, it is tied to a surviving African heritage that became a part of the American experiences of slavery, emancipation, migration, and industrialization, and is still evident in music, religious practices, language, foodways, and other cultural areas that, we would assert, include family practices. The interconnected history of Europeans and Africans in the United States has shaped both groups, but has rarely, if ever, been common or shared. Rigid segregation, particularly within the private realm of the family, has helped to preserve family practices that aided the survival of African Americans through a harsh and hostile experience in the United States (see McDaniel 1990; Nobles 1974; A. T. Miller 1991; Allen 1978). The questions of assimilation or education often avoid rather than address these profound differences that can only be bridged by acknowledging and understanding them. Our investigation thus points to a larger project of looking to include the heritage of Africa in the ongoing experience and development of African American families in the United States. Such an inclusion, as only suggested here, could round out the important structural elements and factors of social practice and prejudice that provide important parts of any explanation. This inclusion might illuminate the family practices that support children and create a wider "safety net" in the African American community and that remain quite different from those used by Americans of European heritage.

6

ETHNIC NEIGHBORS AND ETHNIC MYTHS: AN EXAMINATION OF RESIDENTIAL SEGREGATION IN 1910

Michael J. White
Robert F. Dymowski
Shilian Wang

A N ENDURING aspect of the mythology of America is its capacity to absorb immigrants.[1] Part of the mythology holds that newcomers arrive in relative hardship, but find a better life, and eventually they or their descendants journey into the mainstream. In many accounts cities operate as the melting pots of this process, blending together different groups and facilitating economic advancement and social assimilation. Debate continues on the degree to which the dominant experience of immigrant groups is described by that melting pot model. An alternative school of thought emphasizes the persistence of social, economic, and cultural differences among groups, arguing for a model of cultural pluralism.[2] To try to shed some light on this debate, we turn to one dimension of assimilation, the residential, and take a snapshot of who lives where in 1910. Residential patterns are of particular interest, because they are manifestations of the social distance between groups

[1]An earlier version of this paper was presented at the University of Pennsylvania Conference on Ethnicity in the United States, 1910. Support for this research was provided, in part, by a grant from the Weingart Foundation to the Urban Institute. Roger Avery, Calvin Goldscheider, Allan Kraut, Douglas Massey, Ann Miller, Susan Modell, Ewa Morawska, Herb Smith, Susan Watkins, and other conference participants provided helpful comments. We thank Joan Picard, Carol Walker, and Sandra Yeghian for their assistance in the preparation of this manuscript.
    [2]This is an extensive literature. For discussions see the reviews by Abramson (1980), Alba (1985), Hirschman (1983), and Morawska (1991). More contemporary writing clearly recognizes the contributions of both streams of thought. The central concept of assimilation itself has been variously defined, and many writers elect not to define it at all (e.g., Lieberson and Waters 1988).

(R. E. Park 1952). Lieberson, for instance, argues for the "significance of segregation as an aspect of assimilation in itself" (Lieberson 1963, p. 44). Where exactly residential intermingling fits into the process and casual ordering of assimilation is more difficult to determine. Undoubtedly it plays some role in other aspects of assimilation: language acquisition, acculturation, and sociostructural achievement. Generally, we share the view that residential integration may be viewed as an intermediate step in a general process of assimilation (Massey and Mullan 1984). In any case, one may interpret residential patterns as a key indicator of the degree of assimilation.

As a point of reference for our discussion, it is useful to identify a stylized residential assimilation model, a model that is consistent with the "melting pot" point of view.[3] To the degree that the experience of groups does not conform, we have evidence for the more pluralistic point of view.

The stylized model assumes that new immigrants arrive in relative disadvantage vis-à-vis the host society. They are culturally distant and often lack language and labor force skills. The model holds that new immigrant groups are initially clustered near the core of the city, segregated from one another as well as from members of the host society (Taeuber and Taeuber 1964). The residential isolation of the immigrants signals their lack of assimilation into American society. Such segregation may not have been all bad. Ethnic residential concentrations may also have provided social supports vis-à-vis the host society (Ward 1989) or provided a critical mass for an "enclave" economy (Portes and Rumbaut 1990).[4]

In the stylized model the passage of time brings a decline in residential segregation. This is presumed to occur concomitantly with the withering of ethnic differences along other dimensions. To the degree that one sees residential assimilation as an intermediate phase, socioeconomic advancement translates into residential mobility and propinquity with the majority. Residential assimilation is also associated with movement toward the urban periphery and eventual suburbanization.

The model hearkens back to the early Chicago School of Sociology (Burgess 1967; Park 1967), and it has since been applied and criticized by historians and sociologists (see Burstein 1981; Morawska 1991). Bur-

---

[3]I use the term "stylized" to make it clear that this model is a point of reference, overly simplified but still powerful. Even the adherents to the melting pot or the Chicago School models would argue that exceptions existed.

[4]The concept of an enclave economy has been advanced to describe the positive economic effects of certain kinds of segregation, although there is some dispute about whether intraurban residential proximity is necessary for enclaves to operate (Portes and Jensen 1989).

gess's (1925) ecological model of the city is particularly demonstrative, with its inner city immigrant enclaves, its area of "second settlement" farther out, and its peripheral middle-class areas.

If the model applies, individuals and groups with more years of residential experience in the United States should be less segregated. Subsequent generations should be even less isolated. Moreover, individual and group socioeconomic advancement should translate into a decline in residential segregation.

Subsequent sociological and historical research began to fill in this picture and challenge its universality. A basic challenge to the notion of highly clustered ethnic neighborhoods comes from Philpott (1978). He documents the intermingling of many groups in Chicago's neighborhoods of European stock in the early part of the century. He argues that although many neighborhoods had a distinct ethnic identity, a label accepted internally and externally, many groups besides the specific ethnicity were often represented; in short, neighborhoods were a patchwork of national origins (Philpott 1978). The identity derives more from institutions and custom than from demographic reality.

Data from the period 1930–1950 do support some aspects of the residential assimilation model. "Old" groups (German, British, and Irish) are found to be on the order of half as segregated as "new" groups (Poles, Italians, Russians, Greeks, and other Southern and Central Europeans) in Chicago, Philadelphia, and Cleveland (Duncan and Lieberson 1959; Lieberson 1963; Hershberg et al. 1981). Furthermore, Lieberson (1963) and Duncan and Lieberson (1959) found that residential integration was correlated with other indicators of assimilation, such as ability to speak English, naturalization, and education. Interestingly, however, income, housing expenditure, and occupational differences did not seem to correlate well with group "age."

Blacks have certainly faced more severe and entrenched obstacles than other groups (Farley 1985; Neidert and Farley 1985; National Academy of Sciences 1988). The residential picture is one of increasing segregation. In Philadelphia, the index of dissimilarity (blacks versus native whites) stood at 47 in 1880, increased to 61 in 1930, and reached 75 by 1970 (Hershberg et al. 1981).[5] For Chicago, Philpott (1978) finds segregation for blacks to be extremely high in 1900, and yet increasing to 1930. Clearly, mere group presence does not automatically translate into residential integration. For blacks, segregation increased in many cities

---

[5]The index of dissimilarity has been the most widely used segregation statistic. It varies from zero to 100 percent and indicates the percentage of one population (e.g. Irish) that would have to relocate in order for every neighborhood in the city to have the same proportion (Irish), the condition of no segregation.

throughout the mid-twentieth century, only beginning to fall from an extremely high level in the 1970s.[6]

A particularly salient issue for us is the degree to which segregation is determined by ethnicity itself. It is possible that other characteristics related to immigration and ethnicity, such as English-speaking ability, naturalization, generation, and years of residence in the United States, may matter the most. Often in general discussions of immigration and ethnic group adaptation, many of these different aspects are not kept distinct. With our data we can separate the effect of ethnic group per se from these other traits. Historical work on aggregated data does suggest that the second generation is slightly less segregated than the first, as are groups with higher proportions of naturalized persons, and English-speakers (Hershberg et al. 1981; Lieberson 1963). It appears to be the case that ethnicity dominates immigrant status in determining contemporary segregation patterns.[7]

The timing of the development of the urban ecological pattern of the industrial metropolis has also been questioned. Zunz (1982) made an extensive examination of the patterns of ethnic residential settlement in Detroit at the turn of the century. His spatial analysis reveals distinct clustering of groups along ethnic lines, with identifiable Irish, German, Polish, English (including Canadian), and American (native-born of native parentage) neighborhoods. Zunz goes on to argue that with industrialization, class-based social divisions gained in importance relative to ethnically based divisions.[8] The classic concentric zone pattern of metropolitan settlement, consistent with the ecological theory of the city and the spatial assimilation model, did not develop in Detroit until 1920 (Zunz 1982, p. 327). A factorial ecological study of nineteenth-century Milwaukee showed ethnicity to rank behind family structure and status in determining residential differentiation (Conzen 1975).

Utilizing manuscript census data, members of the Philadelphia Social History Project linked residence to the location of other social and economic activities. The ecological pattern is one in which workers lived very close to their places of employment. There is evidence that occupational mobility leads to socioeconomic sorting, and industrial affilia-

[6]Results from more contemporary data indicate that blacks are less able than Hispanics to translate socioeconomic gains into residential integration (Massey and Mullan 1984).

[7]Contemporary data indicate that recent immigrants are much more residentially proximate to members of their own ethnic group than they are to other immigrants who arrived at the same time (White 1989). Results from the 1980 U.S. census show that among Asians, country of origin dominates immigration status in determining residence (White, Biddlecom, and Guo 1993).

[8]While Zunz does present detailed analysis of spatial clustering and segregation, he does not present statistical measures that are directly comparable to our own values or to other conventional studies.

tion supersedes ethnicity in determining residential segregation (Burstein 1981; Greenberg 1981).

Scholarship has also questioned the degree to which initial conditions really were equivalent across groups. Steinberg notes, for instance, that among 1899–1910 immigrants, Jews were 67 percent skilled, while only 6 percent of Poles held skilled occupations (Steinberg 1989). Portes and Rumbaut (1990) argue that important differences exist across groups upon arrival, and that these differences were present historically and still operate in contemporary immigrant flows. Other chapters in this volume document that household structure (Miller, Morgan, and McDaniel, Chapter 5), infant mortality (Preston, Ewbank, and Hereward, Chapter 3), and fertility (Morgan, Watkins, and Ewbank, Chapter 4) differed, sometimes dramatically, across groups.[9] These basic demographic differentials can work to constrain opportunities for socioeconomic advancement and residential mobility. Again, an advantage of our multivariate analysis is that we can examine how the influence of certain socioeconomic and demographic characteristics compares with the effects of ethnic group membership.

Arguments about the structure of the residential assimilation model itself and about the experience of historical groups are quite relevant for contemporary discussions of ethnic group adaptation. Various versions of assimilation models make their way into policy discussions about the assimilability of groups, and about the conditions abetting or obstructing economic and social advancement. In particular, reference is made to the inferred experience of "older" groups. The degree to which the mythology matches the reality is critical.

Our objective in this chapter is to use data from the 1910 census to open a window on social assimilation at that time. We examine the residential segregation experience of several European-stock groups, as well as native-born blacks and mulattoes. The definition of European groups is generally consistent with that used elsewhere in this volume, and is based on the nativity and mother tongue of the enumerated individual and his or her parents. In our analysis both the first and second generations are assigned to one of the ethnic groups.

It is important to note that "ethnic group" really defines a subpopulation. Membership is a demographic attribute of an individual, based on race, nativity, and language. Our assignment of individuals in this way and our use of the phrase "ethnic group" speak to one aspect of life. To be sure, the texture of urban life goes beyond such measurable attributes. We cannot of course infer that individuals defined as members of

[9]Jacobs and Greene's examination of schooling points to further differences across groups. Although not exactly seen as initial conditions, group-specific differences in this realm could have long-standing consequences.

an ethnic group participated fully in the respective ethnic community with its churches, social clubs, and family and friendship groups. Nevertheless, this demographic identifier tells us of an attribute that is likely to go hand in hand with such behavior. For our sacrifice of detailed local texture, the census gives us a large representative sample based on a consistent classification of persons.

Although our census-based approach will necessarily be demographic and statistical, we are still concerned with the conduct of life in the local community. In much writing about city life, then and now, the "neighborhood" holds a special place. It is the locus of much day-to-day social interaction, political organization, childhood socialization, and the like. Of course, neighborhoods were often the basis for ethnic solidarity, or so the story goes. Rather than analyze neighborhood life per se, we will be looking at neighbors, individuals who are known to reside near one another. We will use the neighboring pattern to make inferences about the degree of residential intermingling among ethnic groups.

Not only do residential patterns provide a statistical indicator of assimilation; they also tell us about neighborhood context. Discussions of immigrant opportunity and ethnic group adaptation increasingly make reference to the context into which immigrants arrived. One facet of this context, of course, is the residential neighborhood. It is useful to know whether newly arriving groups tended to cluster (as is supposed) and the degree to which this clustering persisted. Such knowledge can help inform discussions about the exigencies of daily life for the new arrivals. Even in the face of such clustering one must caution that other institutions and activities—school, church, work—all competed for immigrants' attention, and hence the ethnic neighborhood may not have been as all-encompassing as it seemed (Bodnar 1985).

The availability of microdata gives us several advantages over previous analyses, and it also calls upon us to develop a new method for measuring segregation. As we will describe below, we can look directly at "neighbors" in space; we need not rely on the tabulation of persons by local geographic areas, whose boundaries may vary across the city and may not even necessarily conform to local concepts of neighborhoods.

Particularly important is the possibility of engaging in multivariate analysis. In this chapter we will estimate a statistical model of residential assimilation (neighboring with native whites of native parentage) that allows us to quantify the impact of ethnic group membership on neighboring while *controlling* for other demographic and socioeconomic characteristics *of the individual*. Previous research in this area has always had to work from aggregated data, correlating a group's segregation with a group's naturalization rate, and so on. By working with the 1910 Public Use Sample (PUS) we can move directly to the analysis of individual outcomes from individual characteristics. As we will describe shortly, we can also avoid having the presence of other household members confound the results. Moreover, multivariate analyses of the determinants of individual segregation are not generally possible with *contemporary* data, for which this sort of detail is disallowed owing to confidentiality restrictions. Other historical studies have done some of this individual-level linking (e.g., Zunz 1982), but these have been limited usually to very small samples of a particular city.

The next section of this chapter elaborates a model of segregation. We then discuss the novel data and the techniques we use to analyze them. The fourth section presents results on the segregation of groups in ten cities. These measures will include indexes of overall segregation in the city, group isolation, and group residential assimilation. The fifth section presents multivariate results for the entire sample and for the two largest cities. The final section of the chapter compares our results to historical and contemporary patterns of residential differentiation and draws some implications for models of residential assimilation. What we find about the past is important, for in handling the subject of assimilation so much of our present policy is based on perceptions of that past.

Ethnicity, Immigration, and Segregation

The degree to which members of one identifiable group share neighborhoods with the majority group or another minority is taken as a major indicator of social assimilation. Residential segregation may be self-imposed or, more likely, imposed by others in the host society, but in either case it serves as an indicator of social distance.

Immigration and ethnicity intersect in an important way here. Ethnicity itself is a rather malleable concept, but most definitions incorporate the notion of a common heritage by birth or descent (Glazer 1983), with language, religion, and customs indicative of ethnic group membership. In actual practice ethnic group membership has been indicated by nationality, mother tongue, and race. Nationality is measured by place of birth of the individual or of that individual's ancestors. In U.S. census data prior to 1980, nationality was identifiable only for the first generation (immigrants) and the second. The national origin of third or higher-order generations has been lost. (These persons are "administratively" assimilated.) Mother tongue is variously defined; in the 1910 census it is "the customary speech in the homes of the immigrants before immigration" (Strong et al. Appendix A, this volume). Mother tongue was measured only for immigrants and their children. Of course, the U.S. Census scheme separately identifies race, which does not have a generational component.

It is immigration, whether historically forced as in the case of slave movements, or voluntary labor movement, as in the case of much of twentieth-century immigration, that introduces ethnic diversity via race, language, and nationality. Although immigrant status (including recency of arrival) and ethnic background are closely tied, each may exert a distinct influence on the degree of residential integration of a person or group. In prior analyses the aggregation of published data made it difficult to separate them. The present analysis of urban segregation allows for their independent influence.

It is common practice to focus on the distance of each group from a culturally "core" or dominant group in the society. The U.S. experience would hold that white Anglo-Saxon Protestants of several generations' residence constitute the reference group. We cannot identify that group here; instead we make use of Native Whites of Native Parentage (NWNP). Social distance from this core group should be manifest in physical distance, Park's basic proposition (1952). In the present analysis we have no direct measure of cultural similarity or tolerance, but theory suggests that English-origin immigrants in 1910 should be the least segregated, followed by Other Northwest European groups, English-speaking Catholics (many of them Irish), and Germans.

A second aspect of group membership is relevant. Group experience in the United States is expected to condition the residential experience of the individual immigrant or descendant. Thus, a recent immigrant from Italy is expected to benefit or suffer from the accumulated experience of the population of Italian heritage in the United States at the time of the newcomer's arrival. To draw on Lieberson's (1963) terminology, a recent arrival from an "old" group (e.g., the German) is expected to be less segregated than a recent arrival from a "new" group (e.g., the Polish), who had the same socioeconomic attributes.[10]

The first generation, by virtue of having experienced much or all of its socialization in the country of origin, is expected to be more segregated than the native-born, even members of the second generation. Still, progress in language acquisition, job market skills, and other aspects of acculturation could be expected to proceed even within a generation.

[10]The "age" of a group is not easy to define. At a particular point in time, we may think of it as how long ago the median person arrived from the origin. Lieberson (1963) acknowledges that the old vs. new dichotomy identifies region of origin as much or more than time of arrival.

Therefore, length of time in the receiving country should reduce the segregation observed.

The particular urban environment will also condition an individual's residential experience. Larger urban areas are expected to exhibit not only greater social and economic differentiation but also greater ethnic segregation (Hawley 1950).[11] The population composition of the city will place constraints on the opportunity structure of neighboring, that is, how many members of one group will be available as potential neighbors for another.[12] Finally, unique aspects of history, topography, political and institutional structure, and city planning distinguish urban contexts. Because there are so many ways in which urban context can influence segregation patterns, we repeat our analysis for each city individually. It is beyond the present effort, however, to try to incorporate statistical measures of all relevant aspects of the urban environment.

The manner in which Americans of African descent should be treated in models of segregation and residential assimilation has always been open to discussion. The dating of the onset of the process of urban residential settlement is most problematic. In the case of blacks it has been argued that the timing of movement out of the rural South to the urban North constitutes a parallel to date of immigration (Taeuber and Taeuber 1964).

Economic advancement is intertwined with residential patterns. Wage or income comparison with the majority group measures one dimension of assimilation.[13] Economic progress removes only one obstacle to segregation, that of differential purchasing power for a dwelling, but it is only part of the story.[14] Our multivariate analysis will allow for independent effects of socioeconomic status (occupation and homeownership in 1910) in the determination of residential assimilations.

Our analysis of 1910 census data is designed to help us understand

[11]Most characteristics (social as well as ethnic) exhibit greater levels of spatial differentiation in larger urban areas in 1980 (White 1987).

[12]This is essentially an argument about "standardizing" for composition or removing its effect. Lieberson and Carter (1982) have argued for the use of composition-affected measures, and some subsequent research has made use of these interaction or exposure indices (Farley 1989; Massey and Denton 1987). I have argued that from the point of view of statistical association and for measuring unevenness in residential distribution as segregation composition-free measures are to be preferred (White 1986).

[13]Contemporary data indicate that immigrants appear to make appreciable economic progress in the marketplace within and across generations, but the debate about the rate of change is a lively one (Chiswick 1978; Borjas 1985; Morawska 1991).

[14]In more recent data, direct and indirect controls for socioeconomic status (SES) have shown that it plays a modest role in explaining the segregation of blacks from whites (Taeuber and Taeuber 1964; Farley 1975), but for Hispanics and Asians increasing SES is associated with declining segregation from Anglos (Denton and Massey 1988). The casual effect may be reserved as well, if segregation reduces the mobility of an individual in the labor market. The ethnic enclave economy models argue just the opposite.

FIGURE 6.1

A Model of Ethnic Segregation in 1910

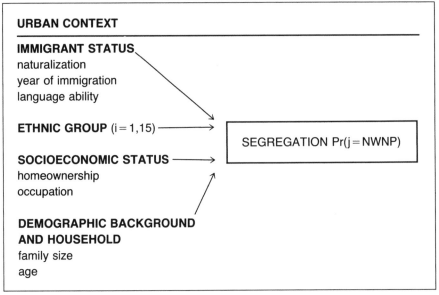

the residential realm, which groups were most segregated, and what seems to predict the level of residential segregation. We summarize our model in Figure 6.1. The outcome we wish to examine is the segregation of a particular ethnic group, with the exact measurement of that phenomenon to be specified below. In addition to calculating the overall level of segregation for each ethnic group, we wish to predict residential proximity to the reference group from characteristics of the individual. These characteristics include socioeconomic status, ethnic group membership, and immigrant status. Nationality picks up not only any group cultural distance from the majority, but also group recency. As we discussed, the degree of residential separation may differ by urban context, and so we estimate the level of segregation and its determinants separately by city.

Data and Methods

The data used for this chapter are derived from the 1910 PUS. From the sample we selected one person per housing unit, the first listed member of the household or group quarters. The availability of microdata allows us to take only one representative per household, and thereby not reduce calculated segregation merely on the basis of household co-residence. Differential family size across ethnic groups would alter measured group segregation were we to look at all members of each household. Our approach differs from that in standard segregation analyses from tabulated data, where all household members are part of the tabulation. For instance, in analyses based on aggregated tract or ward data (e.g., Lieberson 1963), parents and children are tabulated together, hence the co-residence of the second generation with the third (native of native parentage) artifactually reduces segregation.

We limit our analysis to 11,615 persons in the ten cities (municipalities) with the largest number of households in 1910. Panel A of Table 6.1 presents the sample distribution by city. Over half of the sample observations are located within the two largest cities, New York and Chicago. Because we limit our sample to one person per household from these urban locations, our sample sizes for these groups are smaller than the values reported in Appendix B, this volume.

Defining Neighbors

This analysis exploits a unique aspect of the 1910 census microdata sample. The sampling scheme for data entry moved sequentially through the files of manuscript censuses, taking approximately every 250th person and his or her household (see Appendix A, this volume). Thus, machine-readable records that are near on the data file tend to be relatively "near" in geographic space as well. This sampling propinquity contrasts sharply with contemporary census microdata files, which are randomly arranged within major geographic areas.

We make use of this feature by analyzing "neighbors" (adjacent records) on the data file as neighbors in the city. For each sampled (eligible) person, the next sampled person becomes the neighbor. We developed a series of decision rules, trying to preserve the basic inference that our selected neighbors will be reasonably close residents. To be sure, such a definition of neighbor falls short of a sociological ideal and ignores the local context in the meaning of "neighbor," but it does capture aspects of neighboring that are comparable across cities. Analogous problems exist in the use of census tracts as neighborhoods on subsequent censuses.

To return to first principles of segregation measurement, there is actually some preference for the kind of structure we find in the 1910 sample. Intuitively one may consider "segregation" to be indicated by who one's neighbors are. It can be argued, in fact, that this sort of indi-

TABLE 6.1

Sample Description

A. Distribution of Observations by City	N
New York	4,468
Chicago	1,977
Philadelphia	1,430
St. Louis	663
Boston	658
San Francisco	521
Cleveland	489
Baltimore	492
Pittsburgh	470
Detroit	447
Total	11,615

B. Distribution of Observations by Ethnic Group	N
British	834
Irish	1,753
Scandinavian	256
German	2,210
Italian	693
Polish	431
Jewish	920
French Canadian	46
English Canadian	321
Other NW European	221
Other C&E European	668
Russian	64
Black	283
Mulatto	80
Native White, Native Parentage	2,361
Other	474
Total	11,615

vidual-level measure—free from imposed boundaries and ordinal in nature—has many features that are superior to conventional measurement strategies. It is useful to note how our approach contrasts with the measurement of segregation from published or tabulated data files. In the conventional approach the number of persons in each category is tabulated for small geographic areas such as city blocks or census tracts, say, into a two-dimensional table of K ethnic groups by N geographic areas. In such geographically aggregated data, administrative boundaries—for example, census tracts—may have some meaning, but all individuals from the same household are tabulated together, and it is impossible to examine detailed socioeconomic characteristics or alternative ethnic classifications. We argue that even though the lack of geographic specificity in the 1910 data has its disadvantages, the disaggregation and the availability of detailed social and economic information compensate.

Consider Figure 6.2. Each dot or letter represents a resident household in a subsection of the city. Locations with a letter are sampled (assume in alphabetical order), and those with only a dot are unsampled. In the conventional arrangement a tabulation of all persons (or, conceivably, all household heads) is made, cross-classifying census tract by ethnicity or some other characteristic. This tabulation is used as the raw

FIGURE 6.2

Determining Neighbors from the Sampling Scheme

REEL 101, Seq 1

A . . . . . B . . . . . C . . . . . D . . . . E . . . . F . . . . . G . .

N . . . . M . . . . L . . . . K . . . . J . . . . I . . . . H

O . . P . . . Q . . . R . . . S . . . T . . U . . . V . . . . . W

REEL 101, Seq 2

A . . . . . B . . . . . C . . . . . D . . . . E . . . . F . . . . . G . .

N . . . . M . . . . L . . . . K . . . . J . . . . I . . . . H

O . . P . . . Q . . R . . . S . . . T . . U . . . V . . . . . W

REEL 102, Seq 1

A . . . . . B . . . . . C . . . . . D . . . . E . . . . F . . . . . G . .

N . . . . M . . . . L . . . . K . . . . J . . . . I . . . . H

O . . P . . . Q . . . R . . . S . . . T . . U . . . V . . . . . W

.

.

etc.

material of the segregation statistic. By contrast, our approach will look directly at neighbors, comparing the ethnicity of A and B; B and C; C and D; and so on.

As long as we can assert that those who are nearer on the data file are nearer in the original urban pattern, our approach can yield a measure of neighboring by ethnicity. Evidence suggests that this is so. Enumerators tended to work a defined geographic area at a time. The work of others who have examined the routes of enumerators suggests that the sequential ordering of the manuscript censuses will represent spatial proximity (Davenport 1985; Simon 1978). Further, our preliminary tests of the data file showed that similarity between individuals tended to decline with each remove. Immediate neighbors were more alike than second-order neighbors, and so on.

The microfilm reel numbers and sequence numbers within each reel were used to determine whether or not two individuals could be neighbors. Because the microfilm was keyed so that normally each sequence on a reel corresponded to a small to medium-sized county, we defined an individual's neighbor as the next household head (or equivalent) in the data file who had the identical reel number and sequence number within that particular reel.

Because changes of reel and sequence number indicate breaks in the processing of the 1910 census, we can be less sure that individuals located across the breaks on the data file are really proximate in space. Common knowledge about enumeration, the manuscript census work of others, and our own preliminary tabulations suggest that this strategy is valid. If, however, enumerators followed very different procedures in different cities, which themselves have different ethnic compositions, then our results are subject to inconsistency. There is, to our knowledge, no detailed historical information on this issue.

Classifying Individuals by Ethnicity

We follow the classification scheme adopted by other contributors to this volume to categorize our sample. The white population born in the United States with both parents born in the United States was classified as Native Whites of Native Parentage (NWNP). We used the census variable for race to identify the black and mulatto population, irrespective of nativity (almost none are of foreign stock). Twelve European-stock groups are classified on the basis of place of birth and mother tongue, mostly consistent with Appendix B. We include the seven major groups: British, Irish, Scandinavian, German, Italian, Polish, and Jewish. For Poles and Jews identification is solely on the basis of mother tongue.

For those whose place of birth was Canada, we differentiate between those whose mother tongue was French or English.[15] In contrast to some chapters we include distinct categories for Other Northwest Europeans, Other Central and Eastern Europeans, and Russians (not Yiddish-speakers). We include an "Other" category for all those individuals who do not fall into any of the other fifteen categories mentioned here.

We classify into these ethnic groups both the foreign-born and those native-born who have at least one foreign-born parent. We refer to these two generations as "foreign stock." For native-born individuals with one foreign-born parent, we classify them according to the nativity and language scheme of that parent. For native persons with both parents foreign-born, we used the father's classification, on the ground that father's ethnic origin would be likely to dominate in residential location.[16] Cases of potentially different classification by reference to mother's and father's nativity and language were relatively uncommon. We employ both generations in order to generate sufficient sample sizes for our segregation measures. (In the regression analysis we include a variable that indicates generational status.)

Panel B of Table 6.1 presents the frequency distribution of usable observations by ethnic group. The numbers of the foreign-stock population are smaller here than in some other chapters, because we have limited ourselves to urban populations and take only one person per housing unit. We observe that in the ten largest cities about three-fourths of the population (of household representatives) in the sample are classified as foreign stock. The largest European-stock groups are Germans, Irish, and Jewish. As of 1910 blacks and mulattoes together constituted about 3 percent of the sampled population of the large, mostly northern cities.

Sample-size considerations are important here. For modest-sized groups in modest-sized cities where there is often a sparse distribution on which to base inferences, tests of hypothesis about specific relationships are often not statistically significant at conventional levels. It should be remembered that this occurrence is partly attributable to the lack of statistical power and may not reflect an underlying lack of segregation.

---

[15]For those of a particular ethnic group who do not report mother tongue, we "misclassify" them. Of course this is just one of a host of classification problems.

[16]These definitions of the second generation differ from those in Appendix B in two ways: (1) here the second generation is those native-born with at least one foreign-born parent, while in the Appendix the second generation are the native-born with mother foreign-born; (2) where mother's and father's ethnicity differs, it is the father's ethnicity that is used. We give precedence to father's ethnicity for substantive reasons, since we believe that this will dominate in the choice of residential location.

Measures of Segregation

Having an individual-level file in a meaningful sequential order provides us with a unique opportunity to measure segregation. As described earlier, we take neighbors in the data file to stand for neighbors in urban space. The cross-classification of one person, the index individual, by his or her neighbor with respect to ethnicity provides a way to measure segregation. To provide a basic segregation statistic for each group, we proceed as follows: For each person we can assign an ethnicity (E_i; $i = 1,...16$). We can do likewise for the person's neighbor (the next household head record in the file). This yields a 16×16 matrix of neighboring patterns for each city. The matrix can be analyzed with standard contingency table methods. We also collapse portions of the table to provide analyses of particular interest.

We carry out three different cross-tabulations of ethnicity (index individual versus neighbor), each of which gives us some insight into an aspect of segregation: (1) a measure of the *overall segregation* of each city, (2) a measure of *isolation* of the group from all other groups, and (3) a measure of *residential assimilation* of the group by virtue of its proximity to the NWNP. Each of these taps a different aspect of ethnic residential differentiation in the ten cities.

The *overall segregation* measure is calculated by the full cross-tabulation of the ethnic classification for nine major groups: the seven basic European groups, blacks, and the NWNP. (We omit the others because they are too infrequently represented across all cities.) This measure gives us a picture of how segregation varies across *cities*. The statistic Cramer's V, a normed measure of association taking values in the interval [0,1], is used to compare the degree of segregation across the cities. The measure V will be larger the greater the degree to which *all* ethnic groups are separated from one another in physical space; in this sense it is a summary measure of segregation for the city, across all ethnic groups.

Second, we develop a measure of *group isolation*, which tells us how segregated one ethnic group is from *all* fifteen other groups. It tells us whether a group tends to live in its own cluster(s) or is intermingled with others. The others may be any of the other fifteen groups. We calculate the isolation measure by considering each group (British, Irish, Scandinavian, etc.) individually and tabulating a 2×2 table for membership in that group versus any other ethnic group for the index individual and the neighbor. For example, in the tabulation for Italians, we count in the upper-left cell (cell a) the number of index individuals who are of Italian stock whose neighbors are also of Italian stock. In the lower-right cell (cell d) we record the cases where neither the index individual nor the neighbor is of Italian stock. In the off diagonal cells (cells b and c), one neighbor is of Italian stock while one is not. In this example, the degree to which Italians neighbor with other Italians, and non-Italians neighbor with non-Italians, is indicated by the relative preponderance of cases along the main diagonal.

We summarize group isolation by the measure of association Yule's Q, which is calculated as $(ad - bc)/(ad + bc)$. Positive values are indicative of the isolation of the group, neighboring mostly with others of the same group. Negative values would indicate that members of the group neighbor with non-group members. (This unlikely circumstance of "negative segregation" occurs only when numbers are very small in our sample.) A value close to zero indicates the absence of any clustering. We calculate these measures for each of the sixteen groups, and separately for each of the ten cities as well as pooled for the entire sample. Since sample sizes in individual cities are sometimes small, the chi-square statistic is used to test formally for the presence of association in the table.

Third, we present a measure of *residential assimilation*, which responds to the questions of whether some groups are more likely to have NWNP neighbors than others, and whether this propensity differs by city. We take the NWNP to be the reference group for assimilation. Here we form the 2×2 table for the group membership, for example [Italian, non-Italian], for the index individual by [NWNP, non-NWNP] for the neighbor. Then we proceed as above, calculating Q and chi-square. Positive values of Q indicate residential proximity of the members of the ethnic group to the NWNP population; zero values indicate no association or segregation; and negative values point to segregation of the ethnic group from the NWNP population. A value of -1 will occur if no person from the ethnic group has an NWNP neighbor.

These three statistics, although they are all measures of segregation, are not equivalent. It might appear that the isolation and assimilation measures are just complements of one another, but they tap slightly different facets of urban residence. If a European-stock group lives intermingled with other Europeans but far from native whites (NWNP), it will tend to exhibit relatively low isolation, but also low assimilation. On the other hand, if a group frequently neighbors with NWNP but with no other groups, the isolation index would be high and the residential assimilation index would be high. Because NWNP are the single largest group in our sample (and because the third generation is NWNP), it would be unlikely for a group to have no NWNP neighbors.

Both the isolation and assimilation measures employ the entire sample for the city. The *isolation* index tabulates whether both the index person and his or her neighbor are in *that ethnic group*. The *assimilation* measure tabulates the index person as a member of the ethnic group with respect to whether the neighbor is NWNP or not.

In each case we must be concerned for whether the observed pattern could have arisen by random fluctuation. The chi-square statistic can be calculated to test precisely this.[17] In a modest-sized sample, for instance, it might be just happenstance that one group, say Scandinavians, has no NWNP neighbors. The larger the value of the chi-square, the more the table deviates from a random (unsegregated) distribution, and the smaller is the probability that that degree of residential unevenness arose solely by chance. The more statistically significant the association, the smaller the probability. We mark the probability of this deviation by asterisks.

Thus, the composition of the city and the relative segregation of each group from all others influence the statistics. It is possible for the members of an ethnic group never to share neighborhoods with the NWNP, but to be very intermingled with other foreign stock. In this case the assimilation measure would tend to be negative and of larger absolute value, and the isolation measure would be closer to zero. Moreover, this differential would be magnified the smaller the fraction of all urban residents in the NWNP category, a composition effect. To the extent that the isolation indexes for all groups are large, the overall segregation measure V will be large as well. For these reasons we make use of all three statistics in our analysis.

These tests will not be numerically equivalent to other contemporary measures of segregation—the dissimilarity index, exposure measures, and the like—because of our sample design. Still, the rank order of the groups, the comparisons across cities, and the characteristics that predict segregation will be of value for comparisons across time.

Multivariate Analysis

Our final analysis develops a logistic regression model to give some insight into the factors that predict residential proximity to the NWNP population. We go beyond the basic segregation statistics described above and determine whether these ethnic differentials will remain in the face of controls for demographic and socioeconomic characteristics. Suppose

---

[17]Herb Smith has pointed out to me that, strictly speaking, our individual observations in the table are not all independently sampled as would be required for standard inferential statistics. This arises because a neighbor becomes the next reference person as we move through the file. Given the small sample size we felt that this compromise was worth the additional information.

differences in isolation and residential assimilation among groups are merely the results of their different socioeconomic and demographic characteristics; then including these characteristics in the statistical model will vitiate the effects of ethnic group. Moreover, the multivariate model gives us general information about the determinants of residential assimilation; we can quantify how the proximity to the NWNP varies with all of these ethnic and socioeconomic characteristics. We focus on proximity to native whites (versus other ethnic groups) precisely because there has been more interest in this pattern, for it is seen to reflect the residential component of assimilation.

We estimate this model for a subsample of the entire set of observations across all cities, and for the two most populous cities, New York and Chicago. For each index individual we predict whether he or she has a NWNP neighbor (1 = yes, 0 = no) as a function of the reference person's ethnic group membership, immigrant status, and selected socioeconomic characteristics of the household. The model, suppressing subscripts for the individual, may be written:

$$\log[p/(1\text{-}p)] = b_0 + b_1 X_1 + b_2 X_2 + ... + e$$

where p indicates the probability of a NWNP neighbor; the X's are regressors with coefficients b, and e is an error term. We include among the regressors fifteen variables, which indicate the person's membership in one of the identified ethnic groups. (We include the residual category "other," and omit a variable for the NWNP population, letting it serve as the reference group.)

For the regression analysis we wanted to be able to control for socioeconomic and demographic background as well as ethnicity. The 1910 census is not strong on these measures, but we are able to identify several relevant characteristics. In an effort to get at socioeconomic status we measure whether the housing unit was owned.[18] We also take into account the sampled individual's occupational status (professional, support, domestic, service, and craft) from reference to the occupational classification codes for 1910.[19]

Several variables that tap what we term "immigrant status" are measured in the 1910 census. In the regression equations we separate the first and second generation by nativity. We expect immigrants to be less assimilated. For the immigrants we measure the number of years they have resided in the United States and whether they have been nat-

[18]Ownership is item H21 in the data file. We include both those who were explicitly listed as owners (code 1), and those for which a check mark was placed (code 3).

[19]Preliminary tests indicated that other occupational measures added no explanatory power to the model. Occupational codes were taken from item P25 as follows: Professional 740-780; Domestic 800-870; Servant 873-877; Craft 470-485; Clerical 955-999.

uralized. Both length of residence and naturalization are expected to be positively associated with residential assimilation.

We include family size (in the dwelling unit), with larger family size anticipated to restrict opportunities for residential assimilation by reducing per capita resources.[20] Age of the sampled household head (net of years in the United States for immigrants) is expected to be negatively related to residential assimilation. We expect this because residential mobility declines with age, and we are controlling for duration of residence in the United States.

Levels of Segregation by Ethnic Group and City

Overall segregation by city. Table 6.2 contains the Cramer's V statistic for the overall level of segregation in each of the ten cities. We have limited the comparison to nine major groups (British, Irish, Scandinavian, German, Italian, Polish, Jewish, Black, and NWNP) for whom adequate data exist in all cities. Cramer's V shows the degree of association in the 9×9 matrix of the index person's ethnicity by the neighbor's ethnicity. Large values of V point to segregation, that is, the absence of randomness in the residential pattern. In other words, the higher the value of V, the greater the degree to which all of these groups are clustered.

TABLE 6.2

*Overall Segregation of Nine Major Groups,
by City*

City	Cramer's V
New York	0.246 ***
Chicago	0.287 ***
Philadelphia	0.216 ***
St. Louis	0.171 ***
Boston	0.210 ***
San Francisco	0.202 ***
Cleveland	0.336 ***
Baltimore	0.230 ***
Pittsburgh	0.188 ***
Detroit	0.353 ***
Total	0.272 ***

NOTES: Significance for associated chi-square statistic: * $p < 0.10$. ** $p < 0.05$. *** $p < 0.001$.

[20]Family size is item H19.

In every city there is statistically significant ethnic clustering. Three Midwestern cities, Detroit, Cleveland, and Chicago, show the most differentiation along ethnic lines, while San Francisco, St. Louis, and Pittsburgh show the least. Such a finding is contrary to the hypothesis that residential differentiation increases with city size. There does not appear to be any clear regional ordering to the values of V, either. The timing of the arrival of the immigrants and the ethnic composition of the individual cities may play a role, but it is not evident in these results.

Isolation. Panel A of Table 6.3 presents measures of group isolation, the segregation of the specific group from all other groups. In the pooled sample (all cities aggregated, final column) all groups except the British and Other Northwest Europeans are found to be significantly isolated. Other "older" immigrant groups, the Irish and Germans, show moderate levels of isolation in the pooled results. English Canadians, presumably more like an "older" group, also fall into this moderately isolated category. (For some of the less populous groups, e.g., Scandinavians, the statistic for most of the individual cities is not statistically significant, yet the pooled data show a statistically significant and more substantial level of isolation; again, the relative size of each group in each city is making itself felt here.)

The pooled results reveal very high levels of isolation $(Q \geq .80)$ for Italians, Poles, Jews, French Canadians, blacks, and mulattoes. Members of these groups rarely have neighbors of any other group. These results indicate that in 1910 language and nationality could produce as much residential isolation as race. Although the numbers for French Canadians are small (most numerous in Chicago), we observe here that a lengthy residential experience in North America and Western European heritage are not enough to offset the other (here unmeasured) attributes of French Canadians that result in a high level of residential isolation.

Results for the cities individually tend to parallel the overall statistics, where statistically significant. In the table, cities are arrayed from largest to smallest sample sizes, left to right. In many cases, however, the presence of specific ethnic groups in specific cities is quite sparse, and the results for Q are not statistically significant.[21] Across all cities, Poles, Jews, and Italians are almost always the most isolated of the European-stock groups. In cities where there is a substantial representation of blacks and mulattoes, isolation of the former is less than of the latter. This result is inconsistent with the usual presumption of higher socio-

---

[21]In several instances the calculated value of Q is -1.0, usually an indication that only one individual in the group was present and had a neighbor of some other category. We have deleted these very low frequency entries from the table.

TABLE 6.3

Measures of Isolation and Residential Assimilation, Q,
by City and Ethnic Group

A. Isolation: Segregation vs. All Others

	New York	Chicago	Phila.	St. Louis	Boston
British	0.14	−0.23	−0.17	−1.00	0.28
Irish	0.21***	0.29***	0.15*	−0.09	0.16
Scandinavian	0.47	0.51***	−1.00	−1.00	0.62
German	0.42***	0.38***	0.34***	0.25***	0.64***
Italian	0.80***	0.90***	0.87***	−1.00	0.73***
Polish	0.75***	0.90***	0.61*	0.88	−1.00
Jewish	0.90***	0.92***	0.90***	0.92***	0.86***
Fr. Canadian	−1.00	0.79	—	—	−1.00
Eng. Canadian	−1.00	0.41	−1.00	−1.00	0.05
NW Europe	0.15	0.23	−1.00	0.27	−1.00
SC Europe	0.60***	0.80***	0.67***	−0.20	−1.00
Russian	0.65	−1.00	−1.00	—	−1.00
Black	0.79***	0.83***	0.67***	0.55**	−1.00
Mulatto	0.99***	0.88	0.66	0.86***	−1.00
Natives	0.39***	0.42***	0.24***	0.21**	0.30***

B. Residential Assimilation: Segregation vs. Native Whites of Native Parentage (NWNP)

	New York	Chicago	Phila.	St. Louis	Boston
British	0.06	0.36***	0.14	0.24	−0.03
Irish	0.16***	0.07	0.15*	−0.15	−0.25**
Scandinavian	−0.18	0.01	0.06	−1.00	−0.06
German	−0.02	−0.10	−0.17*	−0.14	0.10
Italian	−0.25***	−0.19	−0.35**	0.08	−0.24
Polish	−0.13	−0.65***	−0.35	−0.35	0.41
Jewish	−0.72***	−0.66***	−0.49***	−0.01	−0.20
Fr. Canadian	0.05	0.41	—	—	0.17
Eng. Canadian	0.08	0.23	−0.51	0.04	0.19
NW Europe	0.15	−0.20	−0.03	0.23	0.38
SC Europe	−0.05	−0.57***	−0.57***	−0.29	−1.00
Russian	−0.08	−1.00	0.64	—	1.00
Black	−0.17	−0.19	0.01	0.16	−1.00
Mulatto	−0.48	0.02	−0.56	−0.01	−1.00

NOTES: Q statistic: Q→1 indicates a high level of assimilation; Q→ −1 indicates a low level of assimilation. Significance for associated chi-square statistic: * p<0.10. ** p<0.05. *** p<0.001.

economic status (and hence presumably more residential mobility) among mulattoes. The greater segregation of mulattoes may be due to their residential location farther from blacks, who may be private household workers for the NWNP population. (We removed secondary household members, including live-in servants, from the tabulations, but other

TABLE 6.3 (continued)

S.F.	Cleveland	Baltimore	Pittsburgh	Detroit	Pooled
−1.00*	−0.11	−1.00	0.47***	0.10	0.06
0.28*	0.45**	0.15	−0.08	−0.26	0.25***
0.28	−1.00	—	—	−1.00	0.69***
−0.01	0.02	0.34***	0.16	0.49***	0.40***
0.81***	0.95***	0.82	0.67**	0.94***	0.86***
−1.00	0.96***	0.92***	0.83***	0.94***	0.91***
0.97***	0.90***	0.56	0.80***	0.93*	0.92***
−1.00	−1.00	—	—	0.93***	0.93***
−1.00	−1.00	−1.00	−1.00	−0.21	0.44***
0.34	0.65	−1.00	−1.00	0.61	0.33
−1.00	0.63***	0.88***	−0.15	0.88***	0.75***
−1.00	−1.00	−1.00	—	—	0.71***
—	−1.00	0.57***	0.67*	−1.00	0.80***
−1.00	−1.00	0.84***	−1.00	—	0.94***
0.23**	0.38***	0.14	−0.03	0.06	0.35***

S.F.	Cleveland	Baltimore	Pittsburgh	Detroit	Pooled
0.16	0.39*	0.31	−0.03	0.22	0.15***
−0.05	−0.05	0.09	0.24	0.46**	0.09***
−0.36	−1.00	—	—	−1.00	−0.19**
0.06	0.22	0.11	−0.04	−0.41**	0.06**
−0.34	−1.00	−0.53	−0.16	−1.00	−0.29***
−0.08	−0.31	−0.80**	−0.37	−0.63**	−0.46***
−0.08	−0.59	−0.46	−1.00	0.03	−0.64***
−1.00	−1.00	—	—	0.63**	0.26
−0.16	−0.33	−0.23	1.00	0.32**	0.12*
−0.18	0.05	0.65*	0.11	0.24	0.09
0.12	−0.76***	−0.33	−0.04	0.19	−0.36***
0.12	−1.00	−1.00	—	—	−0.05
—	0.43	−0.37**	0.16	−1.00	0.05
−1.00	−1.00	−0.33	−1.00	—	−0.23

domestic workers may still live in relatively close residential proximity to NWNP residents than other workers.)

Panel A of Table 6.3 does reveal some variation in ethnic isolation across cities. In cities where they are numerically well represented, the Irish, for instance, are less isolated in the Northeast (NY .21; Phil. 15; Boston .16) than in the rapidly industrializing cities of the Midwest (Chicago .29; Cleveland .45). There is some suggestion of this pattern for Italians, but not for those of German stock. Jews are very highly isolated in almost every city, and there is no indication that the level varies with city size or region.

The level of isolation for blacks is statistically significant in six cities, and does vary across these cities. Isolation is near .80 in New York and Chicago, and below .60 in St. Louis and Baltimore. Whether this variation is due to smaller sample sizes (St. Louis is still the fourth-largest city) or to a different residence pattern in these two most southern of the ten cities, it is difficult to say.

The isolation statistic for the NWNP population is instructive. It is larger than the mean in both Chicago and New York. Much more modest levels are recorded in the four smallest cities, and are not significant in three. This suggests that the size of the city (and its NWNP population) may be a factor. Still, the scale argument can be questioned, especially because the overall measure of group segregation as measured in Table 6.2 did not correlate with city size.

Residential Assimilation. In Panel B of Table 6.3 we examine the intermingling of each of the groups with the NWNP population using the residential assimilation statistic. Recall that this is a measure of the residential proximity of the particular ethnic group and the NWNP population, ignoring all other ethnic groups. As a companion to the isolation index above, it may tell the same story, but the particular pattern of intermingling with NWNP and the relative sizes of these two groups in the city can produce a different picture. Positive values indicate that members of the ethnic group often have NWNP neighbors. Negative values, by contrast, indicate residential distance between the ethnic group and the NWNP.

For the pooled data we observe statistically significant positive association between the NWNP and the British, Irish, German, and English Canadians. This finding is consistent with results from nineteenth-century Philadelphia (Hershberg et al. 1981). Pooled results for French Canadians, Other Northwest Europeans, Russians, Blacks, and Mulattoes are not statistically significant, meaning that they are neither particularly likely nor unlikely to have NWNP neighbors.

We obtain negative values on the residential assimilation measure for Scandinavians, Italians, Jews, Poles, and Other Central and Eastern Europeans. All of these groups, and especially the last four, also exhibit high levels of isolation. The negative value of the assimilation statistic reinforces that finding, and indicates that members of these groups are particularly unlikely to have either an NWNP or other foreign-stock neighbor.

For the most part Panel A and Panel B of Table 6.3 tell the same story. Simply stated, ethnic groups that are segregated from the NWNP population (lack of residential assimilation) tend to be segregated from all other groups (isolated) as well. This is consistent with the stylized model of residential assimilation we presented earlier, in which the arriving group is highly segregated from all other groups, and over time begins to intermingle with other foreign stock as well as the native population.

Still, the results are not perfectly consistent. In the pooled results, consider Jews and Italians. Both show high levels of isolation ($Q = .92$ and .86 in Panel A, respectively). Yet, residential assimilation with the NWNP is much less for Jews ($-.64$) than for Italians ($-.29$).[22] Also, in the pooled results blacks have very high levels of isolation (Panel A, final column), while the segregation from NWNP (Panel B) is close to zero and not statistically significant. The results indicate that in 1910 black Americans were much more residentially separated from the foreign-stock population than from the native white population, even after removing co-resident domestic workers from the analysis.

The Determinants of Neighboring

Table 6.4 presents our multivariate results for the probability (actually the log-odds) of having a neighbor who is native white of native parentage. We follow convention by using the NWNP group as the reference. We have estimated these equations for New York and Chicago, and for all cities pooled together. These regressions enable us to disentangle the effect of ethnic group identity itself from characteristics associated with ethnicity, such as immigrant status and socioeconomic status.

Estimated coefficients in Table 6.4 measure the impact of a unit change of the independent variable on the log-odds of living next to a NWNP person. Even though this is a transformation, larger coefficients generally indicate larger effects in the indicated direction. Below we sometimes interpret effects of the variable in terms of the probabilities themselves. The table also presents chi-square tests of significance for each of the coefficients.[23] The Gamma statistic is a measure of the overall predictive power of the equation analogous to R^2 in conventional

---

[22]The assimilation statistic is lower (in absolute value) than the isolation statistic, because many persons in the tabulation are neither Jewish nor NWNP.

[23]These chi-square values are the square of the ratio of the coefficient to its standard error, approximately the square of the more familiar t-value. We mark the associated level of significance in the conventional way.

TABLE 6.4

Logit Regression Results Predicting Native White, Native Parentage Neighbor

	New York	Chicago	All Cities
Intercept	−1.445**	−1.426**	−1.342**
	(34.38)	(13.48)	(44.36)
Homeowner	0.174	−0.017	0.138
	(1.72)	(0.01)	(2.65)
Family Size	−0.042*	−0.014	−0.007
	(3.81)	(0.19)	(0.19)
Age	−0.000	−0.000*	−0.000
	(0.02)	(0.00)	(0.00)
Immigrant	−0.276*	−0.288	−0.016
	(3.47)	(1.15)	(0.01)
Years in U.S.	−0.003	−0.008	−0.003*
	(0.45)	(1.51)	(0.60)
Naturalized	−0.325*	0.018	−0.080
	(4.92)	(0.01)	(0.46)
Speaks English	0.466**	0.479	0.472**
	(6.14)	(2.52)	(8.86)
Professional	0.379**	0.215	0.187
	(4.70)	(0.56)	(1.51)
Support	0.145	0.379	0.038*
	(0.61)	(2.68)	(0.07)
Domestic	0.129	0.148	−0.038
	(0.51)	(0.36)	(0.08)
Service	0.412	1.119**	0.377*
	(2.46)	(5.03)	(2.96)
Craft	−0.079	−0.119	0.038
	(0.52)	(0.52)	(0.21)
British	−0.433**	0.151	−0.168
	(5.61)	(0.36)	(1.56)
Irish	−0.292**	−0.443*	−0.246**
	(4.49)	(3.73)	(5.17)
Scandinavian	−0.828**	−0.422	−0.594**
	(4.42)	(1.95)	(5.52)
German	−0.557*	−0.680**	−0.582**
	(3.63)	(11.2)	(29.00)
Italian	−0.638**	−0.648	−0.924**
	(11.75)	(1.69)	(20.90)

TABLE 6.4 (*continued*)

	New York	Chicago	All Cities
Polish	−0.547	−1.671**	−1.110**
	(2.63)	(14.06)	(20.08)
Jewish	−1.900**	−1.957**	−1.859**
	(52.05)	(9.98)	(62.02)
Fr. Canadian	−0.242	0.829	0.393
	(0.05)	(1.85)	(0.76)
Eng. Canadian	−0.164	0.243	0.086
	(0.17)	(0.35)	(0.12)
NW European	−0.005	−0.463	0.101
	(0.00)	(0.60)	(0.13)
CE European	−0.161	−1.135**	−0.616**
	(0.32)	(7.18)	(6.72)
Russian	−0.166	−6.364	−0.455
	(0.11)	(0.07)	(0.64)
Black	−0.988**	−1.183*	−0.297
	(5.61)	(3.42)	(1.87)
Mulatto	−0.779	−0.510	−0.683
	(0.49)	(0.26)	(1.70)
Other	0.293	−0.384	−0.389**
	(1.49)	(1.51)	(4.61)
Gamma	0.324	0.382	0.278
N	4,468	1,977	5,889

NOTE: Chi-square values given in parentheses.

*significant at .10
**significant at 05

regression; larger values, therefore, are indicative of a better fit of the model to the data.

Results from Table 6.4 in the pooled equation (a 50 percent subsample taken because of computing constraints) indicate very few statistically significant effects of the demographic and socioeconomic characteristics. That is, knowing these characteristics does not help one to predict residential patterns. Family size and age of the household head offer little predictive power, save that there is some indication (significant in New York) that larger families are less likely to reside near the NWNP.

Homeownership, one indicator of socioeconomic status, points to a greater likelihood of a NWNP neighbor in New York and in the pooled sample, but it is not statistically significant. In the pooled sample we find that those in support and service occupations were significantly more likely to have a NWNP neighbor. Craft and professional workers (coefficients of appreciable magnitude but not significant) were also more likely to have NWNP neighbors. In New York the coefficient on the professional category was sizable and statistically significant.

We measure immigrant status with three variables: (1) an indicator for immigrant (versus native-born), (2) number of years in the United States (for immigrants), and (3) an indicator for naturalization (for immigrants). Overall the indicators do not perform strongly or in accordance with expectation. In the pooled sample immigrants are less likely than the second generation to have an NWNP neighbor, as expected, but the effect is not statistically significant. Contrary to expectation (but not statistically significant) being naturalized and having more residential experience in the United States both reduce the predicted probability of an NWNP neighbor. Only the latter coefficient is statistically significant, and the size of its effect is quite modest. The effect of being an immigrant is of greater magnitude in the expected direction in New York (results statistically significant) than in Chicago (not significant). The effect of naturalization is also strongly negative and significant in New York.

Language ability should also be associated with assimilation along many dimensions, including the residential.[24] We included an indicator for those who could speak English. English-speaking ability emerges as a statistically significant predictor of residential assimilation in the pooled sample and in New York. The effect is large enough in all three samples to raise the predicted probability of having an NWNP neighbor from 20 percent to 40 percent.

Many of the ethnic group variables, in contrast to the demographic and socioeconomic characteristics, are strong and significant predictors of NWNP neighboring. In these equations a negative coefficient indicates that the member of a group is less likely to live with the NWNP. Thus, the magnitude of the coefficients across ethnic groups provides a window on the degree of residential assimilation, controlling for other personal and household characteristics.

We find very strong segregation effects for several ethnic groups in the pooled sample and in results for New York and Chicago. The persistence of these ethnic effects indicates that the other characteristics do

[24]Causality is an issue here, since those who reside near the native population may improve their English-language ability as a result. Similar arguments can be made for other characteristics, such as naturalization and the reporting of mother tongue.

not "explain away" ethnicity. More important, though, is the degree to which there remains differentiation among the several ethnic groups. Italians, Poles, and Jews, all highly segregated in cross-tabulation results, continue to be the least residentially assimilated (large negative coefficients) in the pooled sample. Net of other personal and household characteristics, Jews are appreciably more segregated than all other groups in all three samples. A Yiddish-speaker would be less likely to live near an NWNP person than an Italian, Pole, or Scandinavian who possessed the same demographic background and socioeconomic status.

The segregation differential for Scandinavians, Germans, and Other Central and Eastern Europeans is more moderate, but still corresponds to about a 50 percent reduction in the probability of having an NWNP neighbor. (Results for New York and Chicago are generally consistent, although effects for Poles, Russians, and Other Central and Eastern Europeans are weaker in New York.) Segregation of the Irish is still less in the pooled sample in New York.

For the remaining groups in the pooled sample, the coefficient is not statistically significant, although for Russians, blacks, and mulattoes it is of comparable magnitude to the moderately segregated groups. (For the two Canadian groups and for the Other Northwest Europeans, the coefficient is actually positive.) The same is generally true of New York and Chicago, although we do find that New York exhibits significant segregation effects for the British population. The segregation differential (magnitude of the coefficient) for blacks in New York is second only to that for Jews.

Poles, Russians, and Other Central and Eastern Europeans are more segregated in Chicago than in New York. These city differences reflect, in part, the relative sizes of the various ethnic populations in the two cities. The fact that we observe strong segregation effects for blacks in New York and Chicago but not in the pooled sample indicates that in the other eight cities blacks are much less segregated (once background factors are controlled) than in the two largest urban areas.

We also tested the pooled sample for interactions between European ethnicity and selected characteristics. First, we examined the interaction between ethnicity and English-speaking ability; second, between ethnicity and alien status (i.e., generation and years in the United States); and third, between ethnicity and homeownership. Each of these interactions allows the effect of a variable to differ for the various European-stock groups. In no case did we find that the addition of these clusters of variables made a statistically significant improvement (for $p < 0.05$) in prediction. There is some suggestion that in the interaction with alien status, first-generation Irish and Other Northwest Europeans are slightly more integrated than would be predicted on the basis of their ethnicity and generation alone. The upshot of these tests is that the model presented in Table 6.4 captures almost all the variation across ethnic groups in the effects of these traits.

The overall multivariate results are noteworthy, particularly when we consider the Q values for isolation and residential assimilation presented earlier. The Q measures are summary values with no controls for background characteristics of the individual. Thus, two Q values that differ could reflect the effects of socioeconomic or demographic differentials as well as the effect of ethnic identity itself. The multivariate analysis attempts to remove those confounding effects, thereby estimating the remaining ethnic group effect.

A few illustrations may help bring out the value of this approach. First, consider Germans, whom Steinberg (1989) reports arrived with 30 percent skilled workers, versus 20 percent for all immigrants. The assimilation statistic of Table 6.3 (Panel B) takes on a value of +0.06 ($p < 0.05$), indicating that Germans are somewhat more likely to have an NWNP neighbor than others. The logit regression results, by contrast, give a value of -0.582 ($p < 0.05$) for Germans, pointing to lack of residential assimilation. This contrast indicates that the German-stock population possesses socioeconomic and demographic characteristics that are favorable to assimilation, but upon controlling for these, Germans are still segregated from NWNP.

Second, consider a comparison of Jews, Poles, and Italians. The isolation values (Table 6.3, Panel A) for these three groups are very high and are similar to one another. The groups also show markedly low levels of assimilation (Table 6.3, Panel B), with the Jews being the least assimilated residentially. The multivariate results indicate that this lack of assimilation of the Jews is *not* an artifact of less favorable socioeconomic status or immigrant characteristics. The coefficient is negative, and larger than that for any other ethnic group. Thus, the lack of residential proximity results from characteristics associated with group membership. Both discrimination and self-segregation are possible mechanisms.

For the most part the results of Table 6.4 conform (in rank order) to those of Table 6.3, Panel B; highly assimilated groups on the Q measure tend to exhibit smaller (i.e., closer to zero) coefficients, and vice versa. This gives some confidence that the comparison of residential assimilation statistics across groups is not merely a reflection of the influence of differential background characteristics, such as age, family size, socioeconomic status, and experience in the United States.

Discussion

These results shed light on the conditions of the foreign stock living in American cities at the turn of the century. Although our numerical results are not strictly comparable to studies of residential segregation and ethnic assimilation for subsequent decades, the general *pattern* of segregation across groups can be compared. In this way our results also help evaluate competing models about the determinants of residential segregation, both by drawing on data from an earlier point in the process and by including tests of the effects of different individual characteristics on residential patterns.

Models of segregation and residential assimilation alternately emphasize group identity, cohesiveness, and discrimination on the one hand, and a seemingly inexorable process of mutual accommodation, socioeconomic mobility, and residential intermingling on the other (Hirschman 1983). The stylized residential assimilation model, outlined earlier, emphasizes the increasing residential proximity of ethnic minorities to the mainstream group over time. Time promotes both accommodation (in Park's sense) and socioeconomic achievement, both of which enhance the prospects for residential assimilation. This model is developed mostly at the aggregate level, and so the group's average socioeconomic status and duration of residence in the receiving society would also play a role. Contrasting, more pluralistic, views take issue with the ineluctability of socioeconomic advancement and acculturation. They emphasize the role of cultural factors, including language differences, religion, national background, and the context of labor market "insertion" for the new arrivals. The interplay of these factors with patterns of prejudice in the host society determines the degree of residential proximity of the individual to members of the reference (mainstream) group.

Socioeconomic achievement does play a part in both of these models, of course. In the stylized residential assimilation model, income and status accumulate as groups (and individuals) climb the proverbial ladder of success, allowing them individually and collectively to purchase mainstream residential environments. For the contrasting view, socioeconomic advancement does not necessarily translate into residential propinquity, as patterns of residential discrimination are maintained by legal or other means; moreover, labor market discrimination serves to prevent or retard upward social mobility, and hence residential integration.

Cross-sectional data cannot provide a definitive test of these competing models. Our results do show, however, aspects that are consistent with each. The relatively low segregation experienced by the British and Irish and the moderate segregation of Germans (shown in both in the indexes of isolation and assimilation, as well as in the multivariate results) suggest the power of the assimilation model; the "older" immigrant groups are indeed more residentially integrated. By contrast the "new" immigrant groups, Italians, Other Central and Eastern Europeans, Jews, and Poles, are highly segregated. Socioeconomic status matters, but it does not dominate. The fact that Jews and Poles exhibit near-maximum levels of isolation and of residential segregation from the NWNP population (not attributed to differences in other characteristics), coupled with the fact that black isolation is quite high in the North several decades after emancipation, suggests that cultural differences and discrimination operate strongly.

Urban context also clearly matters. Although our results are not based on large samples, the data are robust enough to point to the different levels of segregation experienced by groups across the several cities we have analyzed with segregation indexes and in multivariate results. For example, the multivariate results show much less residential integration in Chicago for several groups (Germans, Irish, Jews, and blacks), compared to New York and the pooled sample. Lieberson's notion that a group's absolute size and timing of arrival matter much in the assimilation process is relevant here (Lieberson 1980), and it can be extended to the specific urban context. It may be the case that in cities where group migration took place early on (in terms of economic development) and then ceased, group advancement was abetted, but a test of this hypothesis is beyond our reach at this time. Elaboration and specification of these city-specific results would be a topic for further research.

It is instructive to recall the levels of residential segregation we discussed from other studies and to compare them with the present results. The Philadelphia data showed that blacks were considerably more segregated than the Irish or Germans in 1880, but that little difference existed across generations for these two European heritage groups (Hershberg et al. 1981). Half a century later, in 1930, black segregation had increased, and the new immigrant groups, Italians, Russians, and Poles, were slightly less segregated than the blacks. German-, Irish-, and British-stock segregation had declined slightly from 1880 levels. The 1930 snapshot for Philadelphia is reproduced in Cleveland (Lieberson 1963) and Chicago (Duncan and Lieberson 1959). The "older" immigrant groups exhibited modest levels of segregation at mid-century, on the order of half the levels of the "new" immigrant groups from Eastern and Southern Europe. Still, the foreign-born from Poland, Russia (many of whom were presumably Jews), Czechoslovakia, Lithuania, and Italy exhibit segregation levels only about three-fourths as large as those for blacks.

Our result that blacks are less segregated than several "new" groups in 1910 is also seen selectively in Lieberson's calculations for the early twentieth century (Lieberson 1963). He finds that in several large cities residential segregation (on the basis of ward data) shows foreign-born groups (most often from Italy, Romania, Hungary, and Russia) to be sometimes more segregated than blacks.

By 1980 the disparity between blacks and European-stock groups, old and new, had grown. The 1980 census identified persons by ancestry as well as race, and hence classified individuals of all generations. Persons of German, Irish, and English ancestry exhibit a level of segregation (each versus all other groups) less than one-third as large as the level for blacks (White 1987).[25] Persons of French, Italian, and Polish ancestry are more segregated than the old-stock groups, but still show less than half the level for blacks. American Indians and the new "new" groups (Asians and white Hispanics) exhibit 1980 segregation levels only slightly higher than those of the Poles and Italians. Notably, black Hispanics are nearly as segregated as black non-Hispanics.

These historical and contemporary results taken together suggest a selective applicability of the stylized residential assimilation model we described at the outset. For that model to apply, segregation should steadily decline from census to census; at any given census members of older groups should be less segregated than newer. Moreover, socioeconomic status should weigh heavily in determining the degree of residential assimilation.

For persons of European stock, group residential experience in the United States has a strong bearing on the degree of residential segregation; however, religion and language (and national culture, perhaps) play an important part. Witness the relatively low level of segregation among the Irish, the contrast between French and English Canadians, and the extremely high levels of segregation among Jews.

Socioeconomic advancement probably does translate into residential intermingling, but our results for homeownership and occupation provide only modest support. Still, it is likely that discrimination and minority group status, manifest in either externally imposed or self-imposed segregation, clearly overlay any basic process of residential assimilation.

The importance of group membership and experience is also evidenced. Although others' analyses have shown that groups with more

---

[25]The actual values of the index of dissimilarity (averages for 21 metropolitan areas) were: Black (.68), Polish (.34), Italian (.32), French (.28), German (.22), Irish (.21), British (.20). The index of dissimilarity measures the proportion of the group's population that would have to change neighborhoods to produce an even distribution across the metropolitan area (White 1987).

residential time in the United States exhibit less segregation, the effects of individuals' length of residence and citizenship status of residential assimilation did not conform to the conventional hypothesis.

The relative condition of the black population with regard to segregation appears to have deteriorated appreciably during the twentieth century. In 1910 blacks in the ten cities are less segregated than the newly arrived Italians, Poles, French Canadians, and Jews. By 1980, however, no other ethnic or racial group had nearly the same level of segregation as blacks. Social and institutional factors no doubt served to further segregate black Americans, at least until the arrival of the civil rights era. Only in the 1970s did black-white segregation begin to diminish in many metropolitan areas of the United States (White 1987; Farley 1989; Massey and Denton 1987).

The case of the Jews contrasts sharply. Clearly, Jews met with sharp prejudice in the United States, and they were highly segregated soon after their arrival. It is not possible to discern the degree to which that residential isolation was self-imposed or the result of discrimination. Equally unclear is whether residential clustering served as a positive force (e.g., an enclave economy) or whether other factors were influential, leading to subsequent adaptation, economic advancement, and presumably declines in residential segregation.

Our results point to a sharp differentiation across ethnic groups in the degree of measured segregation. There is support for the stylized residential assimilation model, particularly in that the newer groups from Eastern and Southern Europe tend to be the most segregated. In the multivariate results the effect of ethnic group clearly persists in the face of demographic and socioeconomic controls, with mother tongue, national origin, and race providing the basis for further differentiation. Other than the ability to speak English, most indicators of immigrant status offer little predictive power. For some observers these findings will stand as a challenge to the stylized residential assimilation model.

Such results have some implications for the present-day study of ethnic groups. Although the residential assimilation model is broadly applicable to the experience of many groups, clearly there are important deviations for particular groups and points in time, as this work and an accumulation of historical and contemporary evidence have shown. Group identity matters greatly, and social norms regarding group status, prejudice, and other patterns of intergroup activity can be decisive.

7

RACE AND ETHNICITY, SOCIAL CLASS, AND SCHOOLING

Jerry A. Jacobs
Margaret E. Greene

T HE IMMIGRANT has been a lightning rod for America's passions
since the beginning of the republic, yet the polarity of that attraction gradually has reversed.[1] At the turn of the twentieth century,
the waves of "new" immigrants arriving from Eastern and Southern Europe were resented, feared, and loathed by contemporary native whites.
The political tide of nativism ebbed after the recession of 1893–1897
and did not crest again until World War I, yet xenophobia remained a
powerful current in American culture in the interim (Higham 1988). Although we now refer to immigrants as representing a variety of ethnic
groups (reserving the term "race" to distinguish among whites, blacks,
Asians, and American Indians), contemporaries often viewed them as
separate races that were intellectually, physically, and morally inferior
to native whites. The most sophisticated scientific research of the day
concurred. The newly developed Binet Intelligence Test "proved" that
the great majority of the Jewish, Hungarian, Italian, and Russian immigrants (among others) were "feeble minded" (Blum 1978, p. 61; see also
Gould 1981).

By the 1980s, passions regarding American "ethnics," the descendants of the immigrants, still ran high, but now the ethnics were the
heroes and heroines of an American tale of liberty and opportunity. The
1986 centennial festivities for the Statue of Liberty served as a national
celebration of the success of immigrants in the United States. By this
time the statue stood as a symbol of welcome to immigrants, a view

[1]We wish to thank Michael Katz, Walter Licht, Andrew Miller, Ann Miller, S. Philip
Morgan, Joel Perlmann, Judith Porter, Mark Stern, Susan Watkins, and Michael White for
their comments and suggestions. An earlier draft of this chapter was presented at the
Population Association of America Meetings, Toronto, May 1990.

Higham notes was largely absent during the statue's first fifty years (Higham 1988). The Statue of Liberty had become so intertwined with the mythology of the immigrant that President Ronald Reagan could remind his audience that "Miss Liberty, like the many millions she has welcomed to these shores, is originally of foreign birth" (*New York Times*, July 4, 1986, Section 2, p. 3). In his 1988 presidential campaign, Michael Dukakis sought to portray himself as the all-American ethnic, the son of hardworking immigrant stock committed to the American ideals of initiative and opportunity, drawing on well-established vocabulary in contemporary political discourse. This was one of the few successful themes in his otherwise lackluster campaign.

The glorification of the ethnics' success surely represents progress when compared with the virulent hostility aimed at their immigrant parents, yet it is a story often put to less-than-benign ends. Today ethnic success is employed in invidious comparisons with the continued poverty of blacks and Hispanics. "Our parents came with nothing, faced terrible discrimination, yet prospered nonetheless through hard work, self-reliance, and a recognition of the value of education. Why can't the blacks do the same?" This refrain, embroidered with poignant tales of personal hardship and sacrifice from family histories, stands as a principal point of contention between ethnic whites and blacks. The political moral of this tale is that blacks deserve no more help than the immigrants received, no special treatment, no affirmative action policies. And the glorification of previous waves of immigrants has not dispelled suspicion and resentment toward the newest immigrants arriving from the Caribbean and Central America (Simon 1985).

In his award-winning book, Lieberson (1980) challenged the validity of the ethnic versus black comparison. After scrutinizing the historical record for evidence regarding the economic and social trajectories experienced by the different groups, Lieberson concluded that the arriving immigrants were better off than blacks, and faced fewer barriers to advancement. Most blacks resided in the rural South, where public provision for schooling for blacks was meager compared to that for whites, and where schooling even for whites lagged far behind the rest of the country. Thus, he argued, blacks and European immigrants did not start out on equal footing, and blacks were continually relegated to the back of the line in the competition for decent schools, housing, and jobs.

Another version of the immigrant morality tale plays the "good" immigrants off against the "bad" immigrants. The good immigrants, namely those who sought education for their children and prospered by it, are often distinguished from the bad immigrants, whose lack of appreciation of the value of education could be seen as shortsighted, anti-intellectual, and exploitative of their own children. The value placed on education by immigrants is taken as indicative of their worthiness to participate in the American dream. In short, the American dream is there for all who would but urge their children to study.

The most visible articulation of this viewpoint is Sowell's *Ethnic America* (1981). Sowell argues that the immigrant experience is most remarkable in its diversity. All immigrants arrived poor and faced discrimination, but some groups far outdistanced others in pursuing the American dream. Sowell sees the cultural orientation of the different groups as necessary to account for these divergent outcomes.

This cultural explanation of the differences between good and bad immigrants has been vigorously criticized by Steinberg (1988). In a series of case studies, Steinberg maintains that the role of culture has been vastly overstated in accounting for the success of some immigrant groups. Immigrant groups differed dramatically in the education, skills, and resources they brought with them and in the opportunities they faced after arriving. Much of the differences between groups, Steinberg insists, is attributable to these factors. If some groups obtained relatively little education for their children, it was a reflection of limited resources, limited exposure to educational institutions in their country of origin, and inadequate provision of schools. The value placed on education for Steinberg is not a primordial aspect of culture but rather a matter of adaptation to circumstances.

Cultural explanations are often offered without due consideration of other possible explanations. Kessner's (1977) comparison of Italian and Jewish immigrants in New York City exemplifies the uncircumspect use of cultural explanations. Kessner repeats the familiar view that Jews recognized the value of education for social mobility, whereas Italians did not. Kessner quotes Jacob Riis approvingly when he said that even "The poorest Hebrew knows—the poorer he is the better he knows it—that knowledge is power, and power is the means for getting on in this world that has spurned him so long, is what his soul yearns for. He lets no opportunity slip to obtain it" (Kessner 1977, p. 97). That socioeconomic resources might facilitate the acquisition of schooling is explicitly denied here.

Yet others have stressed the fact that Jews largely left urban settings in Europe with skills that facilitated their economic rise in the United States, and that the educational achievements of Jewish children followed their parents' economic advancement (Goldscheider and Zuckerman 1984; Howe 1976; Steinberg 1988). Further, Kessner's portrayal of the Jews as exclusively preoccupied with economic success ignores the socialist, Zionist, and Yiddishkeit movements, which all competed with the pursuit of material advancement in the Jewish immigrant community (Howe 1976; Bodnar 1985). Thus, not only does Kessner ignore the social-structural context of the Jewish community, but he also ignores the cultural currents that would complicate his argument. Lastly, Kessner ignores the enormous cultural transformation involved in moving from traditional religious education for the few to mass secular schooling pursued for the purposes of economic advancement (Steinberg 1988).

On the other hand, Kessner sees Italians as less committed to schooling because Italian parents were said to view their children as economic resources, had few aspirations for their children, and were concerned that schools would undermine their authority over their children. The fact that the relatively low enrollment levels of Italian children reflected their parents' limited economic resources and limited social resources (such as low literacy rates) is not seriously investigated. Covello (1967), in contrast, argues that the relatively low emphasis placed by Italians on the education of their children was largely due to their low socioeconomic standing and the discrimination that they in particular faced.

The fact that ethnic groups differed in economic success is not in dispute. Rather, the argument is over whether these differences are a matter of opportunity or choice. The socioeconomic explanation stresses the fact that disadvantaged groups have fewer social and economic resources, and consequently that blaming them for their limited success is simply a case of blaming the victim (Ryan 1971). The cultural explanation sees group differences as caused by the exemplary beliefs and choices of some groups and the failure of others to take advantage of available opportunities.

These issues are fundamentally contentious ones for each ethnic group and for the morality tale of America as a land of opportunity. And there are also lessons in such arguments for contemporary political choices. At stake is a principal set of justifications for public efforts to improve opportunities for the disadvantaged. Sowell (1981) maintains that discrimination cannot explain persistent poverty, because ethnic groups that have since been successful all faced initial discrimination. Since much of the rationale for public policy efforts on behalf of particular groups rests on the grounds of redressing inequalities due to discrimination, Sowell's effort to discount the significance of discrimination is clearly designed to challenge the underpinnings for such policies.

Some of the recent historiography of education attempts to sidestep the question of structure versus culture. Bodnar (1985) attempts to turn the entire question around. He maintains that immigrants' general desire to take advantage of the opportunities offered by American society was accompanied by a deep ambivalence concerning the loss of their traditions. As a result, he maintains, public schooling beyond a basic elementary education was generally viewed with suspicion by immigrants. For each group, this ambivalence was expressed in different ways, yet it was a common theme for many immigrant groups. Thus, although the structuralists assume that socioeconomic constraints made school attendance difficult, Bodnar views such constraints as reinforcing the reluctance already felt by recent immigrants regarding the schooling of their children.

Although Bodnar's synthesis of the diverse immigrant experience is in many ways quite appealing, we are not convinced that he succeeds in escaping the uncomfortable dichotomy of structure versus culture. Bodnar de-emphasizes this issue by highlighting the common concerns immigrants expressed about their children's education. While this may hold as a generalization, once it is restricted to teenagers, it is clearly an attempt to avoid the need to explain differences in schooling rates across groups. Yet the question of why some groups were more likely to send their children to school than others remains.

Morawska (1990) summarizes some principal themes culled from recent research by sociologists and historians on the immigrant experience. She notes that the attainment perspective that emphasized the importance of education above all else in explaining the successful entry of immigrants into American society has been amended by much recent research over the last two decades that has focused on opportunity structures and collective strategies. She maintains that, before 1930, the prospects for upward mobility generated by the transformation of local economies were far more important in explaining immigrants' success than their educational levels. She notes the importance of network hiring practices and immigrant enclave businesses in incorporating new immigrants into the local economy. She compares the view of ethnicity as a rational, instrumental, collective strategy for upward mobility with the atomized, individualistic model advanced by both economic and sociological attainment perspectives.

We agree with Morawska that schooling is just one part of the American success story, and that it has received a disproportionate amount of attention compared with structural factors that influence success rates. However, schooling was important for achieving middle-class status even in 1910, as Perlmann's (1988) detailed research on Providence, Rhode Island, indicates. Further, education of second-generation immigrants was important in providing a foundation for the socioeconomic advancement of their children. Research has consistently shown that parental educational attainment is an influential predictor of children's educational attainment. As education became increasingly important later in the century, some groups superseded others in employing this route out of the working class.

We feel that Morawska has properly emphasized the importance of collective strategies that have all too often been ignored in favor of individual attainment models. But education, long viewed as the paradigmatic individualistic mobility approach, need not be viewed in this way. As Walters and O'Connell (1988) have emphasized, educational decisions need to be understood as taking place within the family economy. Further, immigrant education often involved the creation of separate parochial school systems intended to mitigate the conflict between schooling and traditional values.

Parochial schools enrolled a significant portion of children in 1910. By 1910 there were over 1.5 million children in parochial schools, compared to nearly 18 million in public schools (U.S. Bureau of the Census 1975; see also U.S. Bureau of the Census 1960).[2] The most significant churches in terms of numbers were the Catholic and Lutheran. Catholics were "more sensible of the danger to the faith of their children which lurked in the atmosphere of the public school" (Burns 1912, p. 18) because of their concerns over nativist anti-Catholicism. Germans made up a large proportion of both the Catholic and the Lutheran populations of the United States. Germans were the most likely to have own-language schools, perhaps owing to their large numbers and early arrival in the United States (see Chapter 6, this volume, for evidence regarding the Germans' relatively modest residential segregation). However, by 1912 English was used almost exclusively in German Catholic schools (Beck 1939; see also Bodnar 1985).

Full-time parochial schools never flourished among the Scandinavians as they did among the Germans, as they considered the public schools to serve their interests more than parochial schools, and in fact, "the American public school system—free, democratic, under public control—was one of the very distinct advantages of American citizenship that had attracted them to this country" (Beck 1939, p. 141). French-speakers, principally French Canadians, also tended to set up their own schools. Eighty-five percent of French Canadian school attendance was in the dense French-speaking communities in New England, which had easy access to religious teachers from nearby Canada (our calculation from the 1910 Public Use Sample).

In spite of the large numbers of Italians, few parishes had Italian-language schools. In the few such schools that existed, almost all the teaching was done in English. This was the case, for example, in all the schools for Italian children in New York City. The pattern among the Polish was quite different. Nearly all parishes had a parish school, in which the Polish language was maintained. The Poles were poor, and

[2]The parochial school data were obtained from surveys of schools, not from surveys of households.

arrived speaking no English, but their transition to English, particularly for the boys, was viewed as quite rapid by at least one observer (Burns 1912). Of the other groups, only these had a handful of schools each: Spanish, Bohemian, Lithuanian, Slovaks, Greek Orthodox (schools attended by a variety of nationalities), Hungarian, and Belgian.

This brief review of parochial schooling underscores the complexity of studying schooling at the turn of the century. Not only did children from different groups enroll in school for different amounts of time—the central focus of this chapter—but groups also differed in their reliance on public schools, in their concern for preserving their native language, in their emphasis on religious versus secular education, and in the importance of skills versus cultural values in education. By focusing on one aspect of schooling, enrollment rates, we do not seek to slight these complexities. We do not highlight these features of schooling because the data we explore are of relatively little benefit in studying these different aspects of education.

Thus parochial schooling can be incorporated within Morawska's emphasis of the importance of collective strategies in understanding the history of immigration to the United States. The same could be said of immigrants' efforts to influence policies in public schools (Ravitch 1974).

Yet, with Morawska as with Bodnar, we are not convinced that the structure versus culture dichotomy has been transcended. Morawska emphasizes the way immigrant group identity was forged on the part of people with diverse backgrounds, and points to culture as a dynamic and adaptive resource rather than as a static set of values and beliefs that held people back. Yet even the "instrumental collective rationality" of immigrants is, in the end, another way of saying that culture mattered. And because one group's instrumentalism may have had more payoff than another's, we are inexorably brought back to the question of how much these strategies influenced socioeconomic success. Consequently, this terminology does not entirely remove us from the culture versus structure debate with which we began.

We do not propose to settle the debate regarding the relative importance of structure and culture for several reasons. First, we recognize that partisans of each approach are not easily swayed by contrary evidence. Consider the varying reactions to Perlmann's careful study of schooling in Providence, Rhode Island. Perlmann, in his book *Ethnic Differences* (1988), studied the schooling patterns of Italians, Jews, Irish, blacks, and native whites, and found that many (but not all) of the differences could be attributed to differences in resources across the groups. Steinberg's review (1990) points to the strong effects of socioeconomic resources on schooling as demonstrating the importance of social structure in influencing rates of school attendance. Olneck (1990), in contrast, concludes that Perlmann's research proves the importance of culture in understanding the use of schooling, as groups continued to differ in the rates of high school entrance even after socioeconomic controls were imposed.

Second, on a more theoretical level, it is important to note that the culture versus structure debate cannot entirely be resolved by appeal to data alone. The core of the empirical debate rests on the extent to which social-structural effects on education and occupational attainment can "explain away" the effects of ethnicity. The research consequently depends on the availability of a complete set of social background variables. Thus, even if ethnic differentials persist in an elaborate multivariate analysis, "social structuralists" can plausibly hold to their position that a wider set of measures would have gone further in reducing the direct effect of ethnicity on education and career outcomes. Further, the staunch structuralist might insist that whatever residual remains after controlling for social class background was ultimately due to pre-migration social structure.

Although the structuralist would maintain that differences across groups in socioeconomic resources need to be factored out of any fair comparison of groups, a steadfast culturalist may insist that these differences are themselves the result of pre-migration cultural orientations. Given this divergence of perspectives, it seems unlikely that any empirical analysis is likely to be decisive in this debate (Jacobs 1990).

We view schooling decisions in part as reflecting family strategies and in part as reflecting group strategies. These decisions would have been influenced partly by the constraints families were laboring under and partly by the strategies that the ethnic groups employed. To the extent that these decisions appear to be due to constraints under which families operated, we attribute them to the constraints of social structure. To the extent that differences across groups remain after such factors are controlled, (1) we suspect that other variables, such as measures of employment opportunity and more precise socioeconomic measures, might reduce the ethnic residuals; and (2) we are willing to acknowledge that an ethnic strategy (culture) might be responsible.

Our goal is to identify the extent of schooling—both public and private—obtained by different groups, and to identify those factors that increased or decreased the rate of enrollment. We point out the ways in which our evidence can be interpreted as supporting the view that constraints on opportunity played an important role in influencing school enrollment.

We are not attempting to show that culture does not matter, and we recognize that others may insist on a different interpretation of our results. In short, in this chapter we revisit Lieberson's terrain. We explore the patterns of schooling of immigrant groups in 1910 and compare them to those of native whites and blacks, bringing newly available data to bear on the debate outlined above. We also explore the extent to which variation among immigrant groups can be explained. The questions we ask and the analysis strategy we employ closely parallel those used by Perlmann in his investigation of schooling in Providence.

We are in the fortunate position of being able to extend the scope of previous analyses in several ways. First, we have a large, representative national sample culled from the 1910 census. Just over 100,000 children aged 5–18 are included in this data set, including nearly 24,000 children who were foreign-born or children of immigrants. We can factor into our analysis urban versus rural differences, and differences across regions. In this way, we go beyond the geographic scope possible in studies of a particular city. Further, these data enable us to explore the experiences of a large number (sixteen) of racial and ethnic groups. Many generalizations regarding the role of race and ethnicity derive from the comparison of two or three groups. Casting a broader net enables us to avoid the pitfalls associated with such restricted comparisons. For the comparison of large groups that were located in many different areas, the nationally representative data are clearly desirable. The national data set thus offers a number of advantages over studies of particular groups in an individual city. Of course, setting the national record straight does not obviate the need for local studies, which can provide the microscopic attention to context unattainable in a national overview.

Second, we explore the schooling patterns of young as well as older children. Much of the research to date has focused on enrollment rates among teenagers or high school entrants. As we will see, the role of ethnicity in influencing schooling differs sharply by age, a finding that raises basic questions regarding the role of ethnicity per se. A cultural theory of ethnic differentials would have to account for opposite effects at different ages.

Third, the availability of individual-level data allows us to attempt to *explain* differences between race and ethnic groups in enrollment patterns. Previous research on schooling patterns employing national data has not had access to individual-level data. Thus, by employing multivariate statistical techniques, our analysis will be able to go further than previous research on national data in identifying explanations for group differences in enrollment rates.

We expect much of the differences in enrollment between immigrants and native whites to be due to recency of immigration, location, and socioeconomic resources. First, we expect foreign-born children to be underrepresented in schools compared to children born in the United States. Part of the educational disadvantage of immigrant children was probably due to the fact that their parents did not speak English. Recent immigrants, particularly members of large ethnic groups, would be more likely to live in isolated ethnic ghettos where English was less essential (Chapter 6, this volume). The familial language would have made them less likely to succeed in an English-language school, and consequently less likely to persist in pursuing an education. Further, as immigrants they would likely have been behind in school upon arrival, because many were arriving from countries with less commitment to formal education than the United States. In addition, recent immigrants were poor, and immigrant children contributed to their families' earnings when possible (Bodnar 1985; Hareven and Langenbach 1978; Yans-McLaughlin 1977). Similarly, we expect second-generation immigrant children to be underrepresented in schools owing to continuing economic hardships and some continuing language barriers, but clearly to a lesser degree than foreign-born children. This differential will remain even after socioeconomic controls are introduced. Direct socioeconomic measures such as occupation and homeownership do not completely capture the economic disadvantage of recent immigrants, because immigrant families had less time to accumulate wealth than their native counterparts. When these factors are taken into account, the immigrant (and second-generation) enrollment deficit should be reduced.

Similarly, we expect the introduction of controls for socioeconomic resources to enhance the relative enrollments of recent immigrants. We expect that children whose parents were illiterate would have been underrepresented in schools compared with those whose parents could read and write. We view parental literacy less as a cultural trait and more as a social resource facilitating access to and use of public services. We also expect that children from families of limited means would be less likely to continue their education than children from wealthier families. We anticipate that this will be particularly true for teenagers, who often worked rather than attend school in order to help their families make ends meet. Measures of those resources we will employ include homeownership, father's occupation, father's self-employment status, and family disruption (whether the father was present). Once these factors are taken into account, immigrant enrollments will appear more similar to those of native whites.

Locational considerations, in contrast, generally worked in favor of the immigrants. Few immigrants lived in the South, where education lagged behind the rest of the country. Thus, immigrants' non-southern location should have favored their enrollment prospects. Immigrants were also concentrated in cities, which had higher enrollments for children under age 14 but lower enrollments of children age 14 and above compared with rural areas (Greene and Jacobs 1992).

We have examined the question of compulsory attendance and child labor laws and find little correlation between them and school enrollment rates.[3] By 1910, forty-four states had enacted compulsory attendance laws, typically requiring schooling through age 14 or 15, yet there was minimal enforcement of these laws, especially in rural areas. Furthermore, these laws typically had many exceptions: for farm children, for poor children, for employed children, for children living more than two miles from school, and so on. Thus, the limited effectiveness of these early laws in promoting school attendance is hardly surprising. Indeed, statistical analyses have shown that, at least through 1900, there was little impact of these laws on attendance rates (Landes and Solomon 1972).

Similarly, child labor legislation at the turn of the century was relatively unimportant. By 1909, all states but Wyoming had child labor laws, but these laws were poorly enforced and had remarkably broad exceptions (National Child Labor Committee 1912; Loughran 1921). An employer merely had to receive a certificate saying that a child could read and write in English before he or she could work. Thus, the effect of the child labor and compulsory schooling laws was to emphasize the citizenship role of education rather than to develop the child's intellect. However, compulsory attendance legislation became more effective after 1916, when it was combined with national legislation restricting child labor (Osterman 1980; Stambler 1968; Tyack 1974). Thus, although compulsory attendance and child labor legislation are important in the long run, neither was decisive in explaining school enrollment in 1910.

Data and Methods

Our analysis focuses on the determinants of school attendance among the 104,038 respondents in the 1910 PUS who were between the ages of 5 and 18. For a description of these data, see Strong et al. 1989; Appendix A, this volume. Respondents to the 1910 census answered questions related to their geographical origins and mother tongue, making the data set especially interesting for that period during which so much immigration to the United States took place.

The data include information on school attendance in the last year.

---

[3]Our statistical analysis of state child labor laws indicates that they had only a small net effect on the rate of school enrollment of 14–18-year-olds (less than 1 percent). Compulsory attendance laws had a slightly larger net effect on enrollments (states with more comprehensive laws had approximately 2 percent higher enrollment than states without such laws) but did not affect the differential between race and ethnic groups.

Respondents were asked if they were attending school, and enumerators were instructed to enter "yes" if the person had attended school since September 1909. (The census was taken on April 15, 1910.) We treat this question as a measure of enrollment, not attendance, because the latter would require more detailed information on the number of days actually present in school.

Although one might want to know a great many things about schooling that are not included in the census, such as grades, daily attendance, and being over-age in a grade, these limitations are in part counterbalanced by the advantages of a large and nationally representative sample.

The contrast between the census data on school *enrollment* and the *attendance* figures compiled for the Immigration Commission reports of 1911 should be noted (U.S. Immigration Commission 1911). The Immigration Commission gathered data on the attendance of children in schools in thirty-seven large cities in December 1908. Information on twenty-eight immigrant groups was compared with native-born whites and blacks. The principal advantage of the Immigration Commission data is that one may compare the age of children with their grade level to determine the proportion who were behind their expected grade level (Olneck and Lazerson 1974). These valuable data, however, are limited in several ways. First, the data were collected for only a selected group of cities. The 1910 census data, in contrast, allow for a national overview of school enrollment. Second, because data on children not in school were not collected, an estimate of the proportion enrolled in school for each group is not possible. Further, because only data on attendance, race, sex, and ethnicity were obtained, it is not possible to determine whether other factors may have accounted for these differences in schooling rates. The 1910 census data, in contrast, allow for a multivariate analysis of the determinants of attendance.

Thus, the census data will be a useful complement to the analysis of the Immigration Commission data. However, we should not expect our results necessarily to correspond with those of the Immigration Commission. It is perfectly possible for a group to have a high enrollment rate while many children lag behind their grade level, as Perlmann finds was the case for blacks in Providence (Perlmann 1988).

Much of this chapter compares the schooling rates of immigrant children with those of the native-born population. In our data we can identify children who immigrated to the United States as well as children of immigrants, whom we refer to as second-generation immigrants. Thus, in this chapter, the term "second-generation immigrant" refers to the children's generation, not to their parents' generation.

Children were classified into sixteen race and ethnic groups using five types of data: (1) their place of birth; (2) their mother's place of birth; (3) their mother tongue; (4) their mother's mother tongue; and (5) their race.

One may use maternal, paternal, or both parents' place of birth (or mother tongue) as criteria for assigning ethnic codes to individuals. Morgan and Pagnini (1990) have shown that maternal and paternal ethnicity were the same in the overwhelming majority of cases as a result of high rates of in-marriage. Our arbitrary assignment of ethnicity based on maternal place of birth is thus of little consequence, and makes our results more closely comparable to those described in other chapters in this volume.

We have expanded on the race and ethnic categories set out in Chapter 2. Of the sixteen racial and ethnic groups we examine, the NWNP, British, Irish, Scandinavians, Germans, Italians, Poles, and Jews are defined as they are in Appendix B, this volume. We modified these definitions only by grouping Yiddish-speakers into a single Jewish category. We expanded on these eight groups in order to be more comprehensive in our treatment of both immigrant and racial groups. First, we added Russians, Other Northern Europeans, and Other Southern Europeans. These heterogeneous groupings were included in the analysis because these categories can serve as points of comparison for the more homogeneous groups, and may suggest fruitful topics for more detailed investigations. Second, we also included several other immigrant groups not included in the above list, namely, Hispanic immigrants (mostly immigrants from Mexico), English-speaking Canadian immigrants, and French-speaking Canadian immigrants. In an earlier draft, we constructed a composite Asian group, but on closer analysis we have decided that this classification is simply too small and heterogeneous to be of substantive interest.[4] Finally, we included American Indians in addition to blacks.[5] All of these groups are compared with native whites of native parentage, to whom we will refer simply as "native whites." Our list of groups is as close to comprehensive as possible and avoids arbitrary exclusion of race and ethnic groups. Because our list differs in part from those in Appendix B in this volume, the specific definition of each group is given in Table 7A.1.

---

[4]By our definition, there were only 300 Asian children in the 1910 sample. The largest group was Hawaiian (a substantial minority of whom were of Portuguese origin), a significant minority of Turkish ancestry (in 1910, Turkish ancestry was divided into Asian and European components), and only a small number had Chinese or Japanese ancestry. We decided that this group was too heterogeneous to allow us to draw substantive conclusions.

[5]While we believe that it would be more appropriate to refer to American Indians as Native Americans, we felt that the frequent comparison of native whites with immigrants would make this terminology confusing.

We constructed a dichotomous variable indicating whether the respondent was foreign-born, based on the response to the place of birth question. We also constructed a dichotomous measure of parental English ability, coded as 1 if either parent could speak English and 0 otherwise. (We did not include duration in the United States in this analysis partly because of extensive missing data—appearing in Appendix B—and partly because we feel that a parent's ability to speak English more directly assesses the mechanism by which duration in the United States operates.)

Socioeconomic information is in part derived from data regarding the respondent's household and in part from the attributes of the fathers. Parental literacy was coded as 1 if either parent could read or write (in any language), and as 0 otherwise. Homeownership was a household-level measure that was simply assigned to each child in the household. Assigning the father's occupation measure to children was more difficult. The procedure involved linking each child with his or her mother, and then finding the mother's husband in the household. Of course, there are questions of assignment only when there is more than one married male in the household. Once fathers are identified, the father's occupation is assigned to each school-age child. In this analysis, we created occupational dichotomous variables for each of the major occupational groups: professional/managerial, clerical, sales, craft, service, farm, and operatives/laborers. (We employed the 1980 census occupational classifications for which all occupational data in the 1910 PUS are coded.) Factory operatives and laborers were combined into a single group, and professionals and managers together constitute the reference category. We also constructed a dichotomous variable indicating whether the father was self-employed (versus being an employee). The self-employed category combines owners of establishments and self-employed individuals. In order to include the approximately 13 percent of cases in which the father was not present, and for substantive reasons, we include a dichotomous variable indicating the father's presence or absence.

Size of place was measured by the size of the population of the respondent's county. (It should be noted that this county-size measure differs from the "location type" measure employed in other chapters in this volume.) County population was divided into four categories: rural areas represent those counties with populations ranging from 0 to 49,999 (the omitted category in the logistic regression); small cities are defined as those counties with populations of 50,000–199,999; medium cities are those counties with populations of 200,000–499,999; and big cities are those counties with populations of 500,000 or more. A dichotomous variable was constructed for each of these categories. This allows us to see whether there are curvilinearities in the relationship between city size and educational enrollment. We also include a measure of southern residence in the analysis to tap the major differences in schooling rates between the South and the rest of the country. (Although several chapters in this volume parallel our approach of distinguishing the South from the rest of the country, others present a more detailed analysis of regional differences. See Greene and Jacobs (1992) for a more detailed discussion of regional and urban versus rural differences in schooling.)

We estimate a series of logistic regression equations that test the effect of independent variables on whether the school-age respondents were enrolled in school. Because school enrollment is a dichotomous dependent variable, logistic regression analysis is the appropriate statistical technique for estimating the effects of independent variables (Aldrich and Nelson 1984).

We employ a series of models designed to test whether the effects of race and ethnicity on school enrollment persist when recent immigration, location, and family socioeconomic attributes are controlled. The first model treats school enrollment as a simple function of the race or ethnic group. The second model adds two variables related to recent immigration: foreign-born status of the respondent and a measure of parental English-speaking ability. The third model adds locational variables: residence in the South, and in small, medium, or large cities. The final model adds socioeconomic variables: parental literacy, homeownership, father's self-employment status, father's occupation, and father's presence. Models were estimated for all children aged 5–18; and separately for children aged 5–9, 10–13, and 14–18, because of the different age patterns of enrollment discussed above.

Results

Race and Ethnic Differences in Enrollment

Table 7.1 presents the proportion of individuals aged 5–18 who reported that they attended school at any time between September 1, 1909, and April 15, 1910, by race and ethnic group. Overall, 66.4 percent of 5–18-year-olds reported some school attendance during the 1909–1910 school year. The most disadvantaged groups in terms of educational enrollment were Hispanic children, only 39.4 percent of whom attended school, followed by black children, 48.3 percent of whom attended school. By comparison, the high rates of school enrollment of most of the European and Canadian immigrant groups were remarkable. Four of the immigrant

TABLE 7.1

Proportion Enrolled in School of Individuals Ages 5–18,
by Race, Ethnicity, and Nativity

Group	Total % Enrolled (n)	Born in United States % Enrolled (n)	Foreign-born % Enrolled (n)
Native White	70.2 (66,907)	70.2 (66,907)	
Black	48.3* (13,006)	48.3* (13,006)	
American Indian	58.8* (410)	58.8* (410)	
British	68.9 (1,901)	69.8* (1,648)	63.2+ (253)
Irish	72.1 (2,398)	73.4* (2,302)	42.7+ (96)
Scandinavian	70.3 (2,508)	71.9* (2,276)	54.3+ (232)
Italian	60.6* (2,118)	66.8 (1,306)	50.7+ (812)
German	64.5* (4,734)	65.4* (4,475)	47.9+ (259)
Jewish	71.2 (2,018)	76.7* (1,163)	63.6+ (855)
Russian	64.6* (715)	67.5 (498)	58.1+ (217)
Polish	55.7* (1,711)	59.4* (1,307)	43.8+ (404)
Other N. European	68.1 (705)	68.5 (587)	66.1+ (118)
Other S. European	60.5* (2,260)	65.9 (1,593)	47.7+ (667)
English Canadian	76.0* (1,344)	77.5* (1,108)	69.1+ (236)
French Canadian	61.2* (788)	65.7* (624)	43.9+ (164)
Hispanic	39.4* (515)	43.6* (282)	34.3+ (233)
Total	66.4 (104,038)	67.0 (99,492)	53.3+ (4,546)

*Proportion enrolled differs from Native White proportion enrolled, p<.05.
+Foreign-born proportion enrolled differs from second-generation proportion enrolled, p<.05.

groups equaled or surpassed the native whites in enrollment: the Irish, Scandinavians, Jews, and English-speaking Canadians. As we will see, enrollment rates varied substantially by age and region. Nonetheless, the evidence demonstrates high enrollment rates among many immigrant groups even before adjusting for a variety of factors that account for differences in schooling.

The enrollment rates of the second-generation children were even more remarkable. All of the second-generation European children except the Germans, Poles, Other Southern Europeans, and French-speaking Canadians equaled or exceeded the national average enrollment rates. Variation between second-generation European immigrant groups was surprisingly modest. Among second-generation immigrants, only the Poles fell below the average enrollment rates by as much as 7 percent, and only the Jews exceeded the average by more than 7 percent. The enrollment rates of second-generation British, Irish, Scandinavian, Italian, German, Canadian, and Russian children varied within a relatively narrow, 8 percent range.

For each immigrant group, foreign-born children had lower enrollment rates than their native-born counterparts. The foreign-born enrollment deficit was typically substantial: for eleven of the thirteen groups, the enrollment of foreign-born children was at least 8 percent lower than for their second-generation counterparts. (The difference was statistically significant for each case.) The closest case of first- and second-generation children was the Other Northern Europeans, for whom only a 2.4 percent differential in favor of the second generation was observed.

The enrollment rates of foreign-born children exceeded that of blacks in a majority of cases, and the children of immigrants far exceeded blacks in enrollment rates for each of the immigrant groups, with the exception of the Hispanics noted above. These results are consistent with the extensive evidence regarding the inadequate provision of public education to blacks, most of whom lived in the South in this period. These results confirm Lieberson's conclusion that blacks were educationally disadvantaged compared to European immigrants at the turn of the century.

Table 7.2 displays enrollment rates by ethnic group for each of three age groups: 5–9, 10–13, and 14–18. These results indicate a clear age bifurcation. Among 5–9- and 10–13-year-olds, the enrollment rates of immigrant groups usually equaled or surpassed those of native whites, while 14–18-year-old immigrants were generally less likely to be in school than their native white counterparts. Among 5–9-year-olds, eight of the thirteen immigrant groups had higher enrollment rates than native whites, three groups were not statistically different, and only two groups—Poles and Hispanics—exhibited lower enrollment rates than native whites. The

TABLE 7.2

Enrollment, by Race and Ethnicity, by Age Group

Group	5–18 % Enrolled (n)	5–9 % Enrolled (n)	10–13 % Enrolled (n)	14–18 % Enrolled (n)
Native White	70.2 (66,907)	63.8 (25,472)	92.9 (18,477)	59.1 (22,958)
Black	48.3* (13,006)	40.4* (5,106)	70.1* (3,637)	39.3* (4,263)
American Indian	58.8* (410)	53.6* (183)	72.1* (104)	55.3 (123)
British	68.9 (1,901)	73.8* (600)	95.6* (540)	46.1* (761)
Irish	72.1 (2,398)	79.6* (744)	97.3* (691)	48.4* (963)
Scandinavian	70.3 (2,508)	70.2* (793)	95.9* (733)	51.1* (982)
Italian	60.6* (2,118)	65.8 (868)	91.5 (544)	30.5* (706)
German	64.5* (4,734)	74.2* (1,391)	94.9* (1,324)	37.8* (2,019)
Jewish	71.2 (2,018)	77.0* (726)	95.6* (549)	47.4* (743)
Russian	64.6* (715)	61.1 (324)	93.9 (181)	44.8* (210)
Polish	55.7* (1,711)	58.2* (698)	91.5 (424)	27.0* (589)
Other N. European	68.1 (705)	75.0* (252)	94.9 (197)	40.6* (256)
Other S. European	60.5* (2,260)	64.8 (864)	93.6 (579)	32.6* (817)
English Canadian	76.0* (1,344)	75.4* (443)	97.2* (290)	66.5 (611)
French Canadian	61.2* (788)	76.6* (248)	94.0* (166)	36.4* (374)
Hispanic	39.4* (515)	31.3* (195)	62.9* (143)	29.4* (177)
Total	66.4 (104,038)	62.0 (38,907)	90.2 (28,579)	52.3 (36,552)

*Proportion enrolled differs from Native White proportion enrolled, p<.05.

overwhelming majority of native white 10–13-year-olds (92.9 percent) were enrolled in school. Nonetheless, the enrollment rates of six of thirteen immigrant groups exceeded that of native whites, while those of six others were not statistically different. Among immigrant groups, only Hispanic children had a shortfall in enrollment at these ages.

The immigrants' parity or advantage among children aged 5–13 was reversed among 14–18-year-olds. Here, twelve of the thirteen immigrant groups were less likely to be enrolled in school than native white teenagers, with only English-speaking Canadian teenagers not significantly less likely to attend school than their native white counterparts.

Part of the apparent advantage of immigrants in the analysis thus far is due to the fact that they have been compared to all native whites, including those living in the South. Southern schools were much less developed than northern schools, and consequently the native white enrollment rates were depressed by the inclusion of southern states, where few immigrants lived. Yet a small immigrant advantage among younger children remains when they are compared with non-southern native whites. The age patterns of enrollments are graphically presented in Figure 7.1 for five groups: non-southern native whites, southern native whites, foreign-born children, second-generation immigrants, and blacks. From age 5 through age 13, the highest enrollment rates were found for second-generation immigrant children. After age 14, second-generation immigrant enrollment rates fell much faster than those of non-southern native whites. Blacks had the lowest enrollment rates until age 15, at

FIGURE 7.1

Immigrant and Native School Attendance, by Age

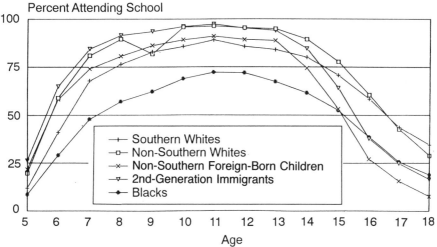

227

TABLE 7.3

Estimated Years of Schooling Completed, Ages 5–22

Group	Total		Born in United States		Foreign-born	
	Estimated Years of Schooling Completed (n)		Estimated Years of Schooling Completed (n)		Estimated Years of Schooling Completed (n)	
Native White	10.25 (83,562)		10.25 (83,562)			
Black	6.98 (16,167)		6.98 (16,167)			
American Indian	8.81 (485)		8.81 (485)			
British	10.09 (2,584)		10.24 (2,149)		9.20 (435)	
Irish	10.48 (3,302)		10.62 (3,022)		8.83 (280)	
Scandinavian	10.17 (3,426)		10.41 (2,915)		8.57 (511)	
Italian	8.57 (2,878)		9.32 (1,444)		8.06 (1,434)	
German	9.57 (6,499)		9.67 (5,977)		7.96 (522)	
Jewish	10.39 (2,670)		11.01 (1,292)		9.93 (1,378)	
Russian	9.28 (945)		10.25 (551)		8.51 (394)	

which age this distinction fell to foreign-born children. By age 16, second-generation immigrants were no more likely to be in school than blacks. A final item of note on Figure 7.1 is the relative rise in enrollment of southern native white teenagers, who by age 16 were enrolled at nearly the same rate as non-southern native whites. This delayed educational enrollment pattern reflected the relative ease of combining agricultural work and part-time schooling among southern native white teenagers.

Table 7.3 presents estimates of cumulative years of school attended,

TABLE 7.3 (continued)

Group	Total Estimated Years of Schooling Completed (n)	Born in United States Estimated Years of Schooling Completed (n)	Foreign-born Estimated Years of Schooling Completed (n)
Poles	7.96 (2,333)	8.21 (1,483)	7.39 (850)
Other N. European	9.70 (902)	9.79 (728)	9.31 (174)
Other S. European	8.72 (3,249)	9.19 (1,858)	8.01 (1,391)
English Canadian	11.00 (1,800)	11.14 (1,379)	9.37 (421)
French Canadian	9.21 (1,073)	9.37 (799)	8.55 (274)
Hispanic	5.62 (683)	6.25 (338)	5.03 (345)
Foreign-born Whites			8.39 (8,387)
Second-generation Whites		9.90 (23,930)	
Total	9.63 (132,558)	9.73 (124,149)	8.41 (8,409)

by racial and ethnic group and nativity. (Although the balance of this chapter focuses on enrollment between the ages of 5 and 18, the estimates of cumulative years of school attended are calculated on the basis of any school attendance from age 5 to age 22.) These estimates were derived by assuming that the age-specific attendance rates observed in 1910 remained constant. Although this assumption is clearly untenable, given the rapid growth of schooling during this period, it nonetheless allows us to calculate the mean number of years of schooling children would have completed given the enrollment rates at that time. These estimates can be compared with others calculated by the same method for later periods, a comparison that helps to identify the rate of change in schooling. Further, this measure transforms the age-specific enroll-ment rates into a summary measure of educational attainment that is more easily understood.

However, caution is in order in interpreting these figures. The fig-ures in Table 7.3 should be viewed as estimates of years of schooling attended, not years completed. Many teenagers attending school were enrolled in grammar school, not in high school. And many who reported that they were enrolled in school did not attend consecutively for the entire school year. Thus, these figures are probably over-estimates of years of schooling completed.

The estimated mean years of school-attended figures presented in Table 7.3 indicate that, on average, students would have attended school for 9.63 years had 1910 attendance rates endured. The two groups with the lowest attendance were Hispanics, who would have attended 5.62 years of school had 1910 rates persisted, and blacks, who would have attended 6.98 years of school. Mean attainment levels for European im-migrant groups ranged from the 7.96 years attended by Polish children to 10.48 years attended by Irish children. The attainment of second-generation immigrants was higher, and most groups fell within a narrow range around 10 years of school attended. Jews and English-speaking Ca-nadians averaged approximately 11 years of school attended, while His-panics (6.25 years) and Poles (8.21 years) remained below average, but the other immigrant groups all fell between 9 and 11 years of school attended. These results indicate that while elementary education was typical, the average student probably did not attend high school for very long.

A second generalization regarding Table 7.3 is the lower levels of schooling for foreign-born children. For each immigrant group, foreign-born children attended school less than those born in the United States, with the difference typically being on the order of 1 year. Because many of these children did not attend school full time for the full year, most foreign-born children probably received no more than a basic primary-level education at this time.

The true level of attainment of foreign-born children was probably even lower than these figures indicate. Some foreign-born children would not have been living in the United States during their entire childhood, and thus would have missed some years of potential schooling that our procedure nonetheless imputes to them. Nonetheless, the age-specific enrollment rates were higher for foreign-born children than for blacks. This is true for every group with the exception of Hispanics, noted above. Thus, blacks were educationally disadvantaged compared to newly ar-rived immigrants, and were at an even greater disadvantage compared with second-generation immigrants.

The estimates reported here are in line with Lieberson's estimates based on the 1920 census (1980, pp. 128–129). The average number of years of school attended by native whites increased slightly (from 10.25 to 10.60 years) between 1910 and 1920, while black enrollment rose from 6.98 to 8.40. Years of school attended for foreign-born whites rose from 8.39 to 8.70, while second-generation white immigrant attainment rose from 9.90 to 10.30. (We have averaged Lieberson's male and female figures for 1920.) In this period, then, the largest enrollment gains were evident for blacks, who nonetheless remained behind foreign-born whites.

Sex Differences in Enrollment

Table 7.4 presents enrollment rates by sex and age group for each of the immigrant groups. The clear conclusion evident from Table 7.4 is that differences between girls and boys within the same racial or ethnic background are small compared to differences across groups. The only statistically significant differences in Table 7.4 occur for blacks and Italians. In both cases, young women were more likely to be enrolled in school than their male counterparts, and only among blacks was this difference consistent across age groups. As far as the age-specific patterns are concerned, aside from the case of blacks, there were only a few scattered cases of statistically significant differences between boys and girls of the same age and racial or ethnic background. The similarity in enrollment rates between girls and boys is itself a puzzle, because many of the reasons that boys left school would not necessarily have applied to girls. This is one clear instance in which our results differ from those obtained by the U.S. Immigration Commission of 1911.

Table 7.5 presents the combinations of work and schooling maintained by children ages 14–18, by ethnic group and sex. The similar levels of school attendance for boys and girls in each ethnic group mask considerable differences in the tendency of each group to combine work with schooling.

For all groups, relatively few boys were neither working nor in school, while higher and widely varied proportions of girls were not in school and not working. Southern native white girls in particular were more likely to be exclusively enrolled in school than their male counterparts.

Southern boys, both white and black, were most likely to combine work with school. Relatively few teenage girls of any group managed to combine school and work, southern blacks being a notable exception at 21 percent. Majorities of 14–18-year-old boys who were British, German, Italian, Polish, Other Northern European, Other Southern European, French Canadian, Hispanic, or Southern black opted for gainful

TABLE 7.4
Enrollment, by Race and Ethnicity, by Sex and Age Group

Group	5–18		5–9	
	Males % Enrolled (n)	Females % Enrolled (n)	Males % Enrolled (n)	Females % Enrolled (n)
Native White	70.0 (33,937)	70.4 (32,970)	63.7 (12,895)	63.9 (12,577)
Black	45.8 (6,474)	50.8[+] (6,532)	38.8 (2,607)	42.1[+] (2,499)
American Indian	57.6 (210)	60.0 (200)	48.9 (90)	58.1 (93)
British	68.0 (956)	69.8 (945)	73.3 (288)	74.4 (312)
Irish	72.6 (1,134)	71.8 (1,264)	79.2 (356)	79.9 (388)
Scandinavian	68.4 (1,296)	72.3 (1,212)	68.1 (423)	72.7 (370)
German	65.6 (2,360)	63.3 (2,374)	74.8 (706)	73.6 (685)
Italian	57.9 (1,165)	63.9[+] (953)	65.2 (454)	66.4 (414)
Polish	56.0 (828)	55.4 (883)	56.9 (336)	59.4 (362)
Jewish	71.8 (1,049)	70.5 (969)	75.1 (393)	79.3 (333)
Russian	62.8 (341)	66.3 (374)	53.4 (148)	67.6[+] (176)
Other N. European	68.4 (354)	67.8 (351)	70.0 (130)	80.3 (122)
Other S. European	59.7 (1,192)	61.5 (1,068)	61.3 (442)	68.5[+] (422)
English Canadian	74.2 (674)	77.9 (670)	75.7 (222)	75.1 (221)
French Canadian	63.5 (386)	59.0 (402)	80.0 (115)	73.7 (133)
Hispanic	41.3 (254)	37.6 (261)	31.6 (98)	30.9 (97)
Total	65.9 (52,610)	66.9 (51,428)	61.4 (19,703)	62.6 (19,204)

[+]Female proportion enrolled differs from male proportion enrolled, $p < .05$.

TABLE 7.4 (*continued*)

10–13		14–18	
Males % Enrolled (n)	Females % Enrolled (n)	Males % Enrolled (n)	Females % Enrolled (n)
92.6 (9,474)	93.2 (9,003)	58.6 (11,568)	59.6 (11,390)
68.9 (1,778)	71.2[+] (1,859)	34.9 (2,089)	43.4[+] (2,174)
71.2 (52)	73.1 (52)	58.8 (68)	50.9 (55)
94.6 (278)	96.6 (262)	45.1 (390)	47.2 (371)
98.2 (339)	96.3 (352)	47.4 (439)	49.2 (524)
95.2 (376)	96.6 (357)	48.3 (497)	54.0 (485)
95.8 (665)	94.1 (659)	38.8 (989)	36.8 (1,030)
90.3 (288)	93.0 (256)	28.1 (423)	33.9 (283)
93.2 (205)	90.0 (219)	28.6 (287)	25.5 (302)
95.1 (288)	96.2 (261)	50.0 (368)	44.8 (375)
92.3 (91)	95.6 (90)	50.0 (102)	39.8 (108)
97.0 (101)	92.7 (96)	43.1 (123)	38.4 (133)
91.8 (305)	95.6 (274)	36.0 (445)	28.5[+] (372)
97.4 (155)	97.0 (135)	60.9 (297)	71.7 (314)
94.6 (92)	93.2 (74)	36.9 (179)	35.9 (195)
70.0 (70)	56.2[+] (73)	29.1 (86)	29.7 (91)
90.0 (14,557)	90.4 (14,022)	51.5 (18,350)	53.1 (18,202)

TABLE 7.5

*Economic Activity, by Race and Ethnicity and Enrollment Status,
for Boys and Girls Ages 14–18*

| Boys | N | Not Working | | Working | |
		Not in School	In School	Not in School	In School
Southern Native White	3,363	6.60	24.41	36.19	32.80
Non-South. Native White	8,203	6.88	42.12	33.90	17.10
Southern Black	1,735	6.69	9.91	60.63	22.77
Non-South. Black	354	9.04	28.25	44.92	17.80
American Indian	68	19.12	42.65	22.06	16.18
British	390	4.36	33.08	50.51	12.05
Irish	439	5.69	39.18	46.92	8.20
Scandinavian	497	7.85	34.61	43.86	13.68
German	989	6.98	27.70	54.20	11.12
Italian	423	7.57	20.57	64.30	7.57
Polish	287	6.62	22.30	64.81	6.27
Jewish	368	4.89	36.96	45.11	13.04
Russian	102	9.80	32.35	40.20	17.65
Other N. European	123	3.25	25.20	53.66	17.89
Other S. European	445	7.42	24.27	56.63	11.69
English Canadian	250	6.80	42.80	37.20	13.20
French Canadian	151	7.28	16.56	66.23	9.93
Hispanic	86	6.98	24.42	63.95	4.65

| Girls | N | Not Working | | Working | |
		Not in School	In School	Not in School	In School
Southern Native White	3,283	24.49	48.74	12.18	9.59
Non-South. Native White	8,109	23.47	56.25	16.41	3.87
Southern Black	1,814	17.92	21.61	39.25	21.22
Non-South. Black	360	25.56	32.50	28.06	13.89
American Indian	55	36.36	49.09	12.73	1.82
British	371	23.99	43.13	28.84	4.04
Irish	524	13.74	43.70	37.02	5.53
Scandinavian	485	21.24	51.75	24.74	2.27
German	1,030	25.92	32.43	37.28	4.37
Italian	283	30.39	29.33	35.69	4.59
Polish	302	19.54	20.53	54.97	4.97
Jewish	375	12.27	37.60	42.92	7.20
Russian	108	24.07	35.19	36.11	4.63
Other N. European	133	26.32	32.33	35.34	6.02
Other S. European	372	20.97	24.19	50.54	4.30
English Canadian	271	16.67	64.21	15.50	3.32
French Canadian	160	21.25	19.38	55.63	3.75
Hispanic	91	56.04	28.57	14.29	1.10

employment over continued enrollment. The highest proportions of working girls not attending school were found among the French Canadians (56 percent) and Poles (55 percent). Thus, we see that even when boys and girls had similar rates of school enrollment, they had very different levels of employment. We plan to explore these issues in greater depth in a companion paper that will try to explain why girls' enrollment rates were so similar to those of boys despite such differences in economic activity.

Race and Ethnic Differences in Social Characteristics

Much of the discussion of ethnic differences moves from the descriptive measures presented in Tables 7.1 and 7.3 to speculations about differences in the cultural attributes of these groups that would produce such outcomes. But these groups differed on many attributes that we have good reason to believe are powerful predictors of educational enrollment. In Tables 7.6 and 7.7, a number of these indicators for each race and ethnic group are summarized.

Table 7.6 indicates the proportion of children ages 5–18 from each

TABLE 7.6

Mean Values of Predictor Variables, by Race and Ethnicity, for Children Ages 5–18

Group (n)	Foreign-born %	Parental[+] Literacy %	Parental English Ability[+] %	South %	Rural[++] %
Native White (66,923)	.0	98.1	99.2	29.5	63.9
Black (13,010)	.0	74.4	99.7	83.9	78.9
American Indian (410)	.0	63.0	69.4	5.9	90.2
British (1,904)	13.3	99.0	99.7	3.7	23.0
Irish (2,398)	4.0	99.0	100.0	2.0	9.9
Scandinavian (2,510)	9.2	99.6	96.6	.5	58.4
German (4,734)	5.5	98.7	93.0	3.0	37.1
Italian (2,118)	38.3	73.4	66.6	6.0	10.4
Polish (1,711)	23.6	85.1	69.2	2.6	15.7
Jewish (2,018)	42.4	87.3	78.9	2.7	.6
Russian (715)	30.3	90.1	73.3	2.6	45.7
Other N. European (705)	16.7	98.5	92.6	2.0	39.6
Other S. European (2,260)	29.5	92.0	74.7	2.5	22.0
English Canadian (1,344)	17.6	99.3	99.6	1.7	35.6
French Canadian (788)	20.81	89.5	83.3	0.4	25.5
Hispanic (515)	45.2	63.6	21.9	7.2	64.1

[+]One or more parents were literate (or reported being able to speak English).
[++]Counties with less than 50,000 population.

race and ethnic group that was foreign-born, had one or more parent who was literate, had one or more parent able to speak English, or who lived in the South or in rural areas. There is substantial variation between groups in the proportion foreign-born, owing to historical patterns of immigration to the United States. Substantial minorities of Hispanic, Jewish, Italian, Russian, Polish, and Other Southern European children were foreign-born, whereas British, Irish, Scandinavian, German, Other Northern European, and Canadian children were more likely to be children of immigrants.

Parental literacy rates also varied substantially across ethnic groups. Although some may suggest that low parental literacy rates reflect a low cultural emphasis on education, we view limited opportunities for education in the origin countries as more likely to be responsible. Because parental literacy is a reliable predictor of children's enrollment, we expect that variation in schooling rates between groups will be due in part to variation in parental literacy.

Parental literacy differs sharply between native whites and other northern European groups, on the one hand, and all other groups on the other. Native whites and immigrant groups in which the children were overwhelmingly second-generation immigrants (the British, Irish, Scandinavians, Germans, Other Northern Europeans, and English-speaking Canadians) all had parental literacy rates of over 95 percent. (These literacy rates are no doubt exaggerated, but are nonetheless useful as approximations of the differentials across groups.) Among more recent immigrants, the Hispanics (with 63.6 percent parental literacy) and the Italians (73.4 percent) had the lowest incidence of parental literacy. Moderate parental literacy rates were also observed among the French Canadians (89.5 percent), the Jews (87.3 percent), and the Poles (85.1 percent). Among non-white American groups, both blacks and American Indians also reported relatively low rates of parental literacy (74.4 and 63.0 percent, respectively).

The majority of parents in all groups (except the Hispanics) reported being able to speak English, but here again variation across groups is notable. (As we noted above in the case of literacy, the proportion claiming to speak English is probably exaggerated.) The groups in which less than 90 percent of parents reported being able to speak English were French-speaking Canadians (83.3 percent), Jews (78.9 percent), Other Southern Europeans (74.7 percent), Russians (73.3 percent), Poles (69.2 percent), Italians (66.6 percent), American Indians (69.4 percent), and Hispanics (21.9 percent).

Relatively few immigrants lived in the South, where most blacks (83.9 percent) and a substantial minority of native whites (29.5 percent) were located. Southern schooling rates were lower than those in the rest of the country, and consequently this factor needs to be incorporated in our analysis. Similarly, the proportion living in urban areas varies widely across groups. Most native whites, blacks, American Indians, Scandinavians, and Hispanics lived in rural areas, whereas the Irish, Italians, Jews, and Poles were overwhelmingly concentrated in urban areas. This locational difference tended to work in the immigrants' favor, at least for young children, since urban areas tended to have higher enrollment rates for younger children. Among teenagers, the greater extent of job opportunities in cities tended to reduce high school attendance rates (Greene and Jacobs 1992).

Table 7.7 presents group averages for several measures of parental economic resources: the proportion with fathers employed in white-collar occupations and farming, who were self-employed (non-farm), and who owned their own home (separated by farm versus non-farm). In Table 7.7 we present two measures of father's occupation: the proportion of fathers employed in white-collar (nonmanual) occupations, and the proportion engaged in farming. In the multivariate analysis, we include a slightly more detailed series of occupational measures.

Seventeen percent of the fathers of native white children were employed in white-collar jobs in 1910, a figure substantially exceeded only by Jews (42.0 percent). The high proportion of Jewish fathers reported as white-collar reflects the definition of proprietor or manager as a white-collar occupation. Many Jewish men were self-employed proprietors of small shops or worked as vendors, another occupation classified as a nonmanual occupation.

This pattern is reflected in the proportion of fathers who were reported as self-employed. In discussing self-employment data, one must keep in mind that farmers were more likely to be self-employed than those engaged in nonagricultural pursuits. Consequently, we have divided self-employed individuals into farm owners and others.[6]

Jews were the group most likely to be employers or self-employed in non-farm settings (20.5 percent), and their rate far exceeded that of native whites (5.6 percent). Two groups were the most underrepresented among the self-employed in non-farm settings: blacks (0.7 percent) and American Indians (0.0 percent in this sample). Blacks were likely to report being self-employed farmers (46.3 percent, a figure that undoubtedly included many sharecroppers), as did one-quarter of American Indians.

The groups most likely to be engaged in farming were blacks (73.5 percent), American Indians (66.3 percent), Hispanics (52.0 percent), na-

[6]In the multivariate analysis, we included both farm and non-farm self-employed fathers in one group, because the farm category is also included in the analysis.

TABLE 7.7

*Mean Values of Father's Characteristics, by Race and Ethnic Group,
for Children Ages 5–18*

Group (n)	White- collar %	Farm Total %	Farm Owner %	Non-farm Self-employed %	Home- owner[+] %
Native White (53,521)	17.4	48.4	25.8	5.6	53.2
Black (8,189)	2.0	73.5	46.3	.7	25.3
American Indian (267)	7.5	66.3	25.1	.0	68.0
British (1,533)	17.0	10.4	4.6	5.9	36.1
Irish (1,788)	13.2	10.3	3.4	5.1	35.4
Scandinavian (2,004)	8.7	42.9	28.0	4.6	66.3
German (3,838)	11.8	33.9	20.4	6.4	57.2
Italian (1,724)	18.2	7.1	2.7	7.4	28.0
Polish (1,367)	9.7	10.5	4.2	4.1	42.4
Jewish (1,720)	42.0	1.0	.2	20.5	16.8
Russian (606)	15.3	40.6	20.3	5.9	53.8
Other N. European (586)	14.3	39.2	17.7	3.9	51.9
Other S. European (1,798)	11.3	17.5	9.2	7.0	42.0
English Canadian (1,344)	18.8	19.6	9.8	15.4	47.0
French Canadian (788)	5.8	11.0	3.9	6.4	33.6
Hispanic	6.0 (367)	52.0 (367)	7.4 (367)	2.5 (367)	28.9 (515)

[+] The number of cases for homeownership matches that reported in Table 7.6.

tive whites (48.4 percent), and Scandinavians (42.9 percent). In contrast, the Irish, Italians, Jews, Poles, and recent British immigrants were rarely found working in the agricultural sector. (See A. R. Miller, Chapter 8, this volume, for more detail on the industrial distribution of immigrants.) Again, schooling patterns of farm children differ substantially from those of non-farm children.

Homeownership is a final indicator of parental resources that tend to increase the chances of children's school enrollment. Not surprisingly, homeownership varied substantially across groups: 53.2 percent of native whites with children aged 5–18 reported owning their own homes. Several groups reported higher ownership rates than native whites, including American Indians (68.0 percent), Scandinavians (66.3 percent), and Germans (57.2 percent). The high homeownership rates among these groups are probably related to the high proportions living on the family farm. Undoubtedly, the quality of homes varied substantially across groups, and homeownership by itself should not be taken to mean middle-class status. Jews, who were more advantaged occupationally, were the least likely to report owning their own dwelling (16.8 percent), presumably because of their concentration in apartments in urban settings.

These results indicate that our sixteen race and ethnic groups varied a great deal on a variety of factors that were likely to be related to schooling. We now turn to a multivariate analysis in order to assess what impact these variables had on schooling rates.

Table 7.8 presents four logistic regression equations. Initially, a series of race and ethnic dichotomous variables alone are used to predict enrollment. We gradually add groups of other variables, which we expect to attenuate the gross ethnic effects estimated in Equation 1. Model 2 adds measures of foreign-born status, and parental English-speaking ability; Model 3 adds measures of urban and southern residence; and Model 4 includes homeownership and father's presence, occupation, and self-employment status.

The gross differentials across ethnic groups found in Model 1 have already been discussed. They are presented here to allow us to ascertain what fraction of these differentials are due to the variables added to the model. The negative coefficients indicate that the group in question had lower odds of enrollment than native whites, which is the reference, or comparison, group in this and subsequent analyses. In Model 2, we see (as expected) that foreign-born children were less likely to attend school than native-born children; and children whose parents were able to speak English were more likely to be enrolled in school than those whose parents spoke only a foreign language. As discussed above, we view each of these attributes as measures of social resources associated with recent immigration that would influence the likelihood of enrollment.

How does the introduction of these variables alter the effects of race and ethnicity on enrollment? Our principal focus will be on the extent to which the independent variables explain (reduce) the race and ethnic differentials. By comparing the size of the ethnic coefficient across models, we can see how much of the gross differential is due to the effects of recent immigration, locational factors, or socioeconomic resources. The results in Model 2 indicate that controlling for nativity and parental

TABLE 7.8

Logistic Regression Models of Enrollment for Children Ages 5–18

Variables	Model 1 Log Odds Ratio (Std. Error)	Model 2 Log Odds Ratio (Std. Error)	Model 3 Log Odds Ratio (Std. Error)	Model 4 Log Odds Ratio (Std. Error)
Intercept	.860* (.012)	−.285* (.059)	−.149* (.060)	−.943* (.073)
Black	−.927* (.021)	−.930* (.021)	−.709* (.024)	−.427* (.030)
American Indian	−.505* (.101)	−.316* (.104)	−.428* (.104)	−.275* (.107)
British	−.064 (.051)	−.007 (.051)	−.112* (.052)	−.118* (.055)
Irish	.091 (.047)	.103* (.047)	.010 (.049)	.060 (.052)
Scandinavian	−.001 (.045)	.051 (.046)	−.079 (.046)	−.126* (.049)
German	−.264* (.033)	−.225* (.033)	−.325* (.034)	−.374* (.037)
Italian	−.429* (.046)	−.108 (.050)	−.179* (.052)	−.138* (.056)
Polish	−.631* (.050)	−.412* (.052)	−.503* (.053)	−.463* (.057)
Jewish	.043 (.051)	.301* (.054)	.252* (.058)	.202* (.062)
Russian	−.258* (.079)	−.007 (.082)	−.110 (.082)	−.163* (.085)
Other N. European	−.102 (.082)	−.007 (.082)	−.108 (.083)	−.160* (.085)
Other S. European	−.423* (.044)	−.190* (.047)	−.288* (.048)	−.275* (.051)
English Canadian	.299* (.065)	.371* (.066)	.263* (.067)	.223* (.069)
French Canadian	−.406* (.074)	−.193* (.076)	−.345* (.077)	−.269* (.080)
Hispanic	−1.296* (.091)	−.491* (.100)	−.586* (.100)	−.426* (.103)
Foreign-born		−.444* (.038)	−.446* (.038)	−.305* (.039)

TABLE 7.8 (continued)

Variables	Model 1 Log Odds Ratio (Std. Error)	Model 2 Log Odds Ratio (Std. Error)	Model 3 Log Odds Ratio (Std. Error)	Model 4 Log Odds Ratio (Std. Error)
Parental English Ability		1.154* (.058)	1.157* (.059)	1.025* (.062)
South			−.426* (.022)	−.371* (.028)
Small Cities			−.022 (.022)	−.066 (.027)
Medium Cities			.070* (.031)	.128* (.037)
Big Cities			−.103* (.027)	−.052 (.033)
Parental Literacy				.288* (.025)
Owns Home				.293* (.021)
Salesman				−.007 (.064)
Clerical				.210* (.102)
Service				.099 (.077)
Farm				−.359* (.051)
Craft				−.117* (.051)
Operative				−.132* (.051)
Self-employed				.195* (.031)
Father Present				.718* (.049)
Proportion Reduction in Chi-Squared	.027	.035	.039	.049

*p < .05.

241

English-speaking ability tends to enhance the relative enrollment of recent immigrant groups. Indeed, the entire Italian enrollment deficit can be attributed to these two factors. (As we will see, the age-specific analyses for the Italians tell a more complicated story.)

Model 3 adds region and measures of small, medium, and large cities to the analysis. Enrollment was lower in the South than in other regions of the country, and was lower in small and big cities (we will see that this final result varies by age group). The locational variables lower the enrollment rates of all immigrant groups compared to native whites, because few lived in the relatively low-enrollment South. The only group in the analysis whose relative enrollment increases after locational controls are introduced is blacks, whose concentration in the South contributed to their low schooling rates (see Greene and Jacobs 1992).

In additional analyses not shown, we tested for interaction effects of location of residence and race and ethnicity. We found that rural blacks, Hispanics, and American Indians were especially disadvantaged in terms of school enrollments compared to their urban counterparts, while other groups living in rural areas had similar enrollments to those living in urban areas. We also tested for interaction effects associated with living in New York City. We explored this issue because so much has been written about immigrants in New York, and many have wondered how the immigrant experience may have differed in other locations. Our results provide little evidence for the proposition that New York was different, although we may not have had enough cases for each group to provide a very strong test of this conclusion.[7]

In Model 4, socioeconomic variables are added to the analysis. The results indicate that parental literacy increased enrollment. We tested for interactions of parental literacy and race and ethnicity, and found that parental literacy had a positive effect on enrollment for virtually all groups and that there was little evidence of variation in the size of the literacy effect across groups.[8] Homeownership also increased enrollment rates. This finding is consistent with the results of Perlmann's study of Providence and Thernstrom's research on Boston (1973), but clashes with Thernstrom's study of Newburyport, Massachusetts (1964), and Hogan's study of Chicago (1985). In analyses not reported here, we found that homeownership had a positive effect on enrollment for each race and ethnic group. We reason that homeownership indicated a certain eco-

---

[7]The only cases to have significant interaction effects for New York City were Poles and Italians: for both groups enrollments were higher in New York than elsewhere.

[8]In only two cases did the evidence suggest no positive effect of literacy: Scandinavians and Other Southern Europeans. We suspect these results may not be stable, and further evidence is needed before conclusions should be drawn in these cases.

242

nomic freedom and resources enabling children, especially teenagers, to attend school. Thus, our results do not support the view that some groups chose a social mobility strategy of homeownership at the expense of their children's schooling prospects.

The measures of father's occupation behave as expected. The children of fathers employed in white-collar jobs had enrollment rates that were not statistically different from professional and managerial children, while the children of farmers, craftsmen, factory operatives, and laborers all had lower enrollment rates. Children of self-employed fathers had higher enrollment rates than those who worked for others, while children whose fathers were present had appreciably higher enrollment rates than those whose fathers were absent.

Another important result is that the introduction of socioeconomic controls reduces the direct effect of being foreign-born. Some of the effect of recent immigration, then, was in fact due not to immigration per se but simply to the socioeconomic disadvantage associated with recent immigration.

In the initial model, five of the fifteen groups did not significantly differ in schooling rates from native whites: British, Irish, Scandinavians, Other Northern Europeans, and Jews. English-speaking Canadian children were more likely to be enrolled in school than native whites. The most substantial schooling deficit was observed among Hispanics, followed by blacks, Poles, American Indians, Italians, Other Southern Europeans, French-speaking Canadians, Germans, and Russians.

In the final model, only the Irish did not significantly differ in their enrollment rates from those of native whites with similar locational and socioeconomic resources. The Jews exceeded native-born whites in their enrollment rates once relevant controls were imposed. In four cases of "old" immigrant groups, the British, Scandinavian, German, and Other Northern Europeans, the relative enrollment rate declined once nativity, location, and socioeconomic status were taken into account. (The enrollment advantage of English-speaking Canadian children was attenuated by these controls but remains statistically significant.) In contrast, for the (mostly) "new" immigrant groups, the Italians, Russians, Poles, Other Southern Europeans, French-speaking Canadians, and Hispanics, the enrollment deficit was cut by one-third to one-half by the introduction of various controls (for the Hispanics, the reduction was two-thirds). The two native non-white groups, blacks and American Indians, both had lower enrollment rates than native whites, but in both instances the size of the deficit is cut by about half by the introduction of location and socioeconomic controls. Although the imposition of control variables does not eliminate ethnic differences, the gap between "old" and "new" immigrants does diminish substantially.

While the results of Table 7.8 may be viewed as a summary of the overall relationship between race, ethnicity, and schooling, taking recent immigration, location, and socioeconomic factors into account, we know that schooling patterns varied substantially by age. As we saw in Table 7.3, race and ethnic effects themselves varied substantially by age. Consequently, we should not rush to interpret the effects in Table 7.8 before we have considered the age-specific analyses presented in Tables 7.9, 7.10, and 7.11.

Table 7.9 presents each of the logistic regression models for children aged 5–9. The immigrant groups largely had enrollment rates higher than or similar to those of native whites for this age group. Eight cases were higher: the British, Irish, Scandinavians, Germans, Other Northern Europeans, Jews, and both Canadian groups; three other cases were not statistically different: Russians, Italians, and Other Southern Europeans; whereas among immigrants only the Poles and the Hispanics had lower enrollment rates than native whites. Both non-white native groups—the blacks and American Indians—also had lower enrollment rates than native whites.

The introduction of controls for recent immigration improves the relative position of the Poles and Hispanics. The introduction of locational variables, however, lowers the relative position of all immigrant groups except Hispanics, while it substantially improves the relative position of blacks. The socioeconomic controls have only a modest impact on these relationships for these young children.

Parental ability to speak English, southern location, parental literacy, homeownership, father's self-employment, and having a farmer as a father all have the same effects for this age group as for all children under age 18. However, being foreign-born appears to have no direct negative effect for this group (above and beyond membership in one of the groups of recent immigrants). All cities have higher enrollment rates than rural areas, a pattern that is not evident among teenagers. Aside from farming, other occupational variables do not have a consistent, ordered effect on enrollment found for older children. This apparently surprising result is not so baffling on reflection, because it is when children have competing economic choices that socioeconomic considerations have their greatest impact on schooling chances.

After all controls are introduced in Model 4, seven immigrant groups have enrollment advantages among children aged 5–9: the British, Irish, Germans, Jews, Other Northern Europeans, and both groups of Canadians; four other groups do not differ significantly from native whites: the Scandinavians, Russians, Italians, and Other Southern Europeans. Among immigrants only the Poles and Hispanics were educationally disadvantaged at this age level. Both blacks and American Indians were also educationally disadvantaged, and for both groups part of the disadvantage was due to locational and socioeconomic disadvantage.

A similar pattern is observed among 10–13-year-olds (see Table 7.10). Before controls are introduced, only Hispanics among immigrant groups have significantly lower enrollment rates than native whites. Once controls are imposed, Poles join Hispanics, blacks, and American Indians among those with lower chances of enrollment than native whites. (Locational considerations are responsible for much of the change for the Poles.) Because education was close to universal at this age level, few substantial group differences were evident.

Among teenagers aged 14–18, most immigrant groups had lower enrollment rates than did native whites (see Table 7.11). Indeed, all groups except English-speaking Canadians and American Indians had significantly lower enrollment rates in this age group, and the latter case may simply be due to the small sample. Much (but far from all) of the disadvantage of teenagers is accounted for by the control variables. Once controls are imposed, the teenage enrollment deficit disappears for the Irish, the Jews, and the Hispanics, who join the American Indians in having no statistically significant net difference in enrollment. The British, Scandinavians, Germans, Poles, Russians, Other Northern Europeans, Italians, Other Southern Europeans, French-speaking Canadians, and blacks had lower net enrollment chances than native white teenagers, while English-speaking Canadians had a net advantage. For seven of the groups, the controls reduce the size of the group differential by about half: British, Poles, Russians, Italians, Other Southern Europeans, French-speaking Canadians, and blacks. For four groups the net effect was similar to the gross effect: British, Scandinavians, Germans, and Other Northern Europeans. The imposition of control variables thus attenuated differences between "old" and "new" immigrant groups.

It should be noted that the proportion of the variance explained in these analyses is quite small. The proportion of chi-squared explained by these models is generally less than 10 percent, except in the case of 10–13-year-olds, where it ranges from 11 to 19 percent. (The proportion reduction in chi-squared in logistic regression analysis is analogous to the more familiar r-squared in ordinary least squares regression.) This is due not only to the fact that we are analyzing individual-level data, but also to the nature of the dependent variable. Models that predict enrollment rates explain less of the variance than those that predict years of schooling completed. We have focused not on the issue of variance explained but rather on the contribution of the independent variables to explaining the ethnic differentials.

TABLE 7.9
Logistic Regression Models of Enrollment for Children Ages 5–9

Variables	Model 1 Log Odds Ratio (Std. Error)	Model 2 Log Odds Ratio (Std. Error)	Model 3 Log Odds Ratio (Std. Error)	Model 4 Log Odds Ratio (Std. Error)
Intercept	.565* (.013)	−.516* (.107)	−.439* (.108)	−.826* (.116)
Black	−.953* (.031)	−.955* (.031)	−.668* (.034)	−.491* (.036)
American Indian	−.423* (.149)	−.295* (.151)	−.346* (.152)	−.310* (.154)
British	.472* (.094)	.459* (.094)	.199* (.095)	.218* (.096)
Irish	.794* (.092)	.788* (.092)	.450* (.094)	.482* (.094)
Scandinavian	.293* (.079)	.290* (.079)	.122 (.080)	.074 (.080)
German	.490* (.063)	.505* (.063)	.279* (.064)	.255* (.064)
Italian	.088 (.073)	.137 (.075)	.169 (.077)	−.028 (.080)
Polish	−.236* (.078)	−.165* (.080)	−.471* (.082)	−.350* (.083)
Jewish	.643* (.089)	.644* (.092)	.262* (.096)	.330* (.098)
Russian	−.113 (.115)	−.072 (.117)	−.285* (.118)	−.254 (.118)
Other N. European	.533* (.146)	.556* (.147)	.356* (.148)	.349* (.148)
Other S. European	.060 (.072)	.088 (.074)	−.186* (.075)	−.106 (.076)
English Canadian	.577* (.113)	.566* (.113)	.330* (.114)	.309* (.114)
French Canadian	.621* (.151)	.685* (.152)	.391* (.154)	.532* (.155)
Hispanic	−1.367* (.155)	−1.046* (.163)	−1.158* (.163)	−.923* (.166)
Foreign-born		.054 (.070)	.044 (.070)	.139* (.071)

*p < .05

TABLE 7.9 (continued)

Variables	Model 1 Log Odds Ratio (Std. Error)	Model 2 Log Odds Ratio (Std. Error)	Model 3 Log Odds Ratio (Std. Error)	Model 4 Log Odds Ratio (Std. Error)
Parental English Ability		1.086* (.106)	1.067* (.107)	1.022* (.107)
South			−.467* (.027)	−.411* (.027)
Small Cities			.175* (.029)	.164* (.031)
Medium Cities			.395* (.043)	.382* (.045)
Big Cities			.352* (.039)	.357* (.041)
Parental Literacy				.322* (.032)
Owns Home				.303* (.023)
Salesman				−.040 (.065)
Clerical				.004 (.092)
Service				.125 (.087)
Farm				−.285* (.052)
Craft				−.060 (.054)
Operative				−.052 (.054)
Self-employed				.166* (.034)
Father Present				.039 (.055)
Proportion Reduction in Chi-Squared	.030	.032	.044	.053

*p < .05.

TABLE 7.10
Logistic Regression Models of Enrollment for Children Ages 10–13

Variables	Model 1 Log Odds Ratio (Std. Error)	Model 2 Log Odds Ratio (Std. Error)	Model 3 Log Odds Ratio (Std. Error)	Model 4 Log Odds Ratio (Std. Error)
Intercept	2.560* (.028)	.796* (.117)	1.166* (.123)	.073* (.139)
Black	−1.709* (.046)	−1.733* (.046)	−1.147* (.051)	−.751* (.056)
American Indian	−1.610* (.221)	−1.192* (.238)	−1.521* (.240)	−1.192* (.245)
British	.508* (.211)	.529* (.212)	−.033 (.215)	−.046 (.216)
Irish	1.006* (.234)	.980* (.234)	.323 (.239)	.366 (.240)
Scandinavian	.594* (.189)	.615* (.190)	.119 (.192)	.014 (.193)
German	.372* (.129)	.421* (.130)	−.102 (.134)	−.206 (.134)
Italian	−.178 (.157)	.260 (.177)	−.264 (.188)	−.093 (.193)
Polish	−.183 (.177)	.045 (.184)	−.575* (.190)	−.470* (.193)
Jewish	.525* (.211)	.787* (.224)	.147 (.236)	.283 (.242)
Russian	−.178 (.312)	.638* (.327)	.170 (.330)	.114 (.330)
Other N. European	.369 (.326)	.436 (.329)	−.114 (.331)	−.187 (.331)
Other S. European	.121 (.170)	.312 (.178)	−.277 (.182)	−.265 (.184)
English Canadian	.692* (.274)	.714* (.276)	.186 (.278)	.108 (.279)
French Canadian	.171 (.277)	.663* (.291)	.105 (.300)	.225 (.299)
Hispanic	−2.031* (.175)	−.567 (.213)	−913* (.217)	−.659* (.222)
Foreign-born		−.284 (.134)	−.351* (.136)	−.229* (.138)

TABLE 7.10 (continued)

Variables	Model 1 Log Odds Ratio (Std. Error)	Model 2 Log Odds Ratio (Std. Error)	Model 3 Log Odds Ratio (Std. Error)	Model 4 Log Odds Ratio (Std. Error)
Parental English Ability		1.798* (.117)	1.797* (.120)	1.625* (.123)
South			−1.154* (.053)	−1.030* (.055)
Small Cities			.273* (.061)	.243* (.064)
Medium Cities			.530* (.101)	.533* (.105)
Big Cities			.343* (.093)	.392* (.098)
Parental Literacy				−.605* (.053)
Owns Home				.506* (.047)
Salesman				.234 (.162)
Clerical				.350 (.248)
Service				.561* (.219)
Farm				−.113 (.113)
Craft				.329* (.122)
Operative				.339* (.127)
Self-employed				.217* (.072)
Father Present				.372* (.110)
Proportion Reduction in Chi-Squared	.115	.149	.174	.188

*p < .05.

TABLE 7.11
Logistic Regression Models of Enrollment for Children Ages 14–18

Variables	Model 1 Log Odds Ratio (Std. Error)	Model 2 Log Odds Ratio (Std. Error)	Model 3 Log Odds Ratio (Std. Error)	Model 4 Log Odds Ratio (Std. Error)
Intercept	.366* (.013)	−.782* (.095)	−.639* (.096)	−1.693* (.106)
Black	−.802* (.034)	−.807* (.034)	−.755* (.037)	−.387* (.040)
American Indian	−.154 (.182)	.061 (.187)	−.093 (.188)	.152 (.192)
British	−.521* (.074)	−.463* (.075)	−.351* (.076)	−.294* (.078)
Irish	−.430* (.066)	−.407* (.066)	−.218* (.068)	−.073 (.070)
Scandinavian	−.321* (.065)	−.254* (.066)	−.299* (.067)	−.360* (.069)
German	−.864* (.048)	−.827* (.048)	−.756* (.049)	−.838* (.051)
Italian	−1.192* (.083)	−.713* (.090)	−.508* (.092)	−.413* (.096)
Jewish	−.471* (.075)	−.106 (.083)	.172* (.086)	.045 (.091)
Polish	−1.361* (.094)	−1.053* (.097)	−.897* (.099)	−.834* (.102)
Russian	−.576* (.139)	−.223* (.145)	−.204 (.147)	−.352* (.152)
Other N. European	−.745* (.128)	−.635* (.130)	−.595* (.131)	−.672* (.135)
Other S. European	−1.084* (.075)	−.727* (.080)	−.609* (.081)	−.573* (.084)
English Canadian	.111 (.091)	.221* (.093)	−.270* (.094)	.266* (.097)
French Canadian	−1.477* (.132)	−1.249* (.135)	−1.120* (.136)	−1.002* (.138)
Hispanic	−1.243* (.166)	−.248 (.183)	−.287* (.183)	−.090 (.186)
Foreign-born		−.541* (.060)	−.508* (.061)	−.278* (.062)

250

TABLE 7.11 (*continued*)

Variables	Model 1 Log Odds Ratio (Std. Error)	Model 2 Log Odds Ratio (Std. Error)	Model 3 Log Odds Ratio (Std. Error)	Model 4 Log Odds Ratio (Std. Error)
Parental English Ability		1.158* (.095)	1.224* (.096)	1.039* (.097)
South			−.214* (.028)	−.161* (.029)
Small Cities			−.340* (.029)	−.245 (.031)
Medium Cities			−.341* (.040)	−.166 (.043)
Big Cities			−.528* (.036)	−.326* (.039)
Parental Literacy				.399* (.037)
Owns Home				.393* (.024)
Salesman				.050 (.071)
Clerical				.029 (.108)
Service				−.333* (.093)
Farm				−.359* (.057)
Craft				−.529* (.057)
Operative				−.629* (.058)
Self-employed				.291* (.039)
Father Present				1.041* (.052)
Proportion Reduction in Chi-Squared	.027	.034	.040	.080

*$p < .05$.

Summary

Among the many empirical results in the preceding analysis, we think five findings are the most noteworthy. First, our evidence confirms the disadvantage of blacks relative to European immigrant groups in 1910. Blacks trailed foreign-born whites in attendance rates at all ages, and were even farther behind second-generation immigrants. We show that this result holds for each of twelve groups of European stock. In a companion paper, we show that the black enrollment disadvantage is evident in the South, the Midwest, and the West, but not in the Northeast (Greene and Jacobs 1992).

Second, young women and men had virtually the same chances of being enrolled in school. This finding is true for virtually every race, ethnic, and age subgroup we examined, with the notable exception of an enrollment advantage for young black women. This finding is in accord with other evidence based on census data (Perlmann 1988, p. 60), but differs from a number of reports based on school records, which find lower schooling rates among immigrant girls (U.S. Immigration Commission 1911; Olneck and Lazerson 1974). These discrepancies warrant further inquiry.

Third, the relatively high enrollment rates of immigrant children under age 14 are a striking result. Olneck and Lazerson (1974) report data showing that immigrant children under 13 had higher enrollment rates than native whites, but they downplay this finding. They judged the immigrant and native white rates to be essentially the same. (They report that 93 percent of second-generation immigrant children under 13 were in school in 1910 versus 88 percent of native whites, which translates into an odds-ratio advantage for the immigrants of 1.81.) We find a pattern of immigrant parity or advantage for most immigrant group children aged 5–9 that persists after recent immigration, location, and socioeconomic controls are introduced.

Fourth, we find that immigrant teens were less likely to be enrolled in school than native whites. The addition of controls in the multivariate analysis generally reduces this disadvantage, especially for recent immigrants. Also of note is the fact that the Northern and Western European groups—the British, the Scandinavians, the Germans, and Other Northern Europeans—had lower enrollment chances than native whites, chances that did not greatly differ from those of Eastern and Southern Europeans after controls were imposed.

Fifth, we show that both parental literacy and parental ability to speak English increased schooling rates in 1910. Locational considerations were also important factors in schooling rates, with the South trailing the rest of the country, and cities promoting schooling among young children but not among teenagers. Socioeconomic considerations are most notable among teenagers, who had economically productive alternatives to school to consider.

Discussion

What light do these results shed on the debate regarding socioeconomic resources and culture in influencing schooling patterns? There is evidence both sides can point to. The culturalist can point to the fact that there are differences between groups that are not explained when the available measures of recent immigration, location, and socioeconomic resources are controlled. The Poles, for example, trail native whites significantly at all age levels even after controls are imposed, while Jews surpass native whites until age 14, after which age no difference remains.

Yet there are five findings that are particularly supportive of the view that the principal differences across groups are rooted in social and economic resource constraints. First, we believe that the immigrants' interest in education is evident in the high rates of schooling of children under age 14. For these children, there was no economically productive alternative to school. In other words, in the absence of economic trade-offs, immigrant children were as likely if not more likely than native whites to attend school. We view this as strong evidence in favor of the view that schooling rates principally reflect the social and economic resources of families. Further, it may be the case that the teenage deficit for immigrant groups was merely a mirror image of their advantage at earlier ages. High school attendance remained low and high school completion remained exceptional in 1910, with the completion of a basic elementary education still the norm. If immigrant parents' main objective was obtaining a basic elementary education for their children, and if this goal had been accomplished by an earlier age, then it would be understandable that a "deficit" in the enrollment of the teenage children of immigrants would have been observed.

Second, the evidence indicates that, for the majority of the "new" immigrant groups, differences between native whites and immigrant groups are attenuated by measures of the recency of immigration, location, and socioeconomic resources. The Italians are often cited as a group lacking in a cultural commitment to schooling (Covello 1967), yet the evidence suggests that no difference remains between them and native whites after measures of recent immigration are taken into account (except among teenagers, for whom controls explained the majority of the enrollment gap).

Third, among teenagers, several of the Northern and Western European groups were actually at a net enrollment deficit. If the new immigrants were seen as insufficiently committed to schooling, the same charge may be leveled at earlier immigrant groups. In short, those who would rush to offer cultural explanations for the Italian, Jewish, and Polish results must be prepared to offer cultural-deficiency explanations for the British, Scandinavian, and German groups as well. We suspect that these cases may involve particular sets of opportunities that provided financially attractive alternatives to schooling. If these explanations are borne out by subsequent research, it may be possible to pursue similar explanations for the enrollment gaps found for other groups as well.

Fourth, the variables related to social and economic resources behave as expected. Foreign birth, parental literacy, parental ability to speak English, homeownership, and father's self-employment all have direct, sizable effects on schooling rates, which generally have the effect of attenuating differences across groups. Father's occupation has a clear effect, especially among teenagers, which we view as evidence that teenage enrollment was particularly sensitive to socioeconomic influences. Additional analyses of family structure and the availability of job opportunities would likely further reduce the interethnic differentials. There are several other identifiable but unavailable measures that would likely make a difference in enrollments. These include return migration for the Italians and especially the Hispanics and low southern-school expenditures for blacks. (The likelihood of return migration would tend to reduce one's interest or desire to obtain the skills needed for success in the United States, although unrelated individuals may have been more likely to return than families with children.)

Fifth, the lack of sex differences among the immigrant groups is another piece of evidence regarding the adaptability of cultures to circumstances. Because none of the traditional European cultures greatly stressed education for girls, the lack of strong gender differentials in schooling indicates that these cultural impediments to schooling for girls gave way after arrival in the United States.[9]

The points underscore the importance of social structure in influencing school enrollment rates. We nonetheless recognize that the com-

[9]Data on sex differences in schooling in Europe at the turn of the century are not easily found. However, available evidence from Britain (Dures 1971; Lawson and Silver 1973), Italy (Mazzocchi and Rubinacci 1975), and France (Prost 1968) all indicate that girls, especially teenagers, were at a disadvantage compared to boys in schooling rates during this period.

plexities of schooling cannot be entirely accounted for by such an analysis, and that a role for group strategies will inevitably need to be part of a complete explanation of enrollment rates.

The evidence presented in this chapter indicates the extent to which differences in schooling between race and ethnic groups were the result of differences in social and economic resources. Differences across groups diminished when control variables were added to the analysis, yet notable differences remained even after the entire set of variables at our disposal was included. We hope these results help to provide a context for local studies of the schooling and employment of teenagers, and stimulate further research on the complexities of schooling in 1910.

TABLE 7A.1

Definitions of Ethnicity Employed

A. Definitions Based on Place of Birth

British	Respondent or mother born in England, Wales, or Scotland.
Irish	Respondent or mother born in Ireland.
Russian	Respondent or mother born in Russia or Russian Poland.
Other Northern European	Respondent or mother born in Holland, Belgium, France, Switzerland, or Luxembourg.
Other Southern European	Respondent or mother born in Austria, Austrian Poland, Hungary, Austria-Hungary, Bohemia, Croatia, Serbia, Montenegro, Romania, Bulgaria, Greece, Spain, Portugal, Atlantic Islands, Azores, Turkey, Turkey in Europe, or Other European Countries.
Hispanic	Respondent or mother born in Mexico, Cuba, Central America, West Indies, South America, Bermuda, or Puerto Rico.

B. Definitions Based in Part on Mother Tongue

French Canadian	Respondent or mother born in Canada; mother tongue French.
English Canadian	Respondent or mother born in Canada; mother tongue English.
Scandinavian	Respondent or mother born in Iceland, Norway, Sweden, Denmark, or Finland; mother tongue (or mother's mother tongue) Icelandic, Norwegian, Swedish, Danish, or Finnish.
German	Respondent or mother born in Germany or German Poland; mother tongue (or mother's mother tongue) German.
Italian	Respondent or mother born in Italy; mother tongue (or mother's mother tongue) Italian.
Jewish	Respondent or mother foreign-born; mother tongue of respondent or mother given as Yiddish.
Polish	Respondent or mother born in Poland; or respondent or mother foreign-born and mother tongue of respondent or mother given as Polish.

C. Definitions Based in Part on Race

Black	Respondent's race given as Negro or mulatto.
American Indian	Respondent's race given as Indian.
Native White	Respondent and mother born in United States, including those born in any of what became the fifty states, those born in the U.S. but state unknown, and U.S. citizens born abroad, but excluding Puerto Rico and the Philippines, and respondent's race given as white.
Excluded	Those born at sea, birthplace unknown, birthplace illegible, birthplace blank; those born in Africa (if race not black); those born in Australia and New Zealand.

256

8

THE INDUSTRIAL AFFILIATION
OF WORKERS:
DIFFERENCES BY NATIVITY
AND COUNTRY OF ORIGIN

Ann R. Miller

IN THE CONTEXT of this volume, it is interesting to note that one aspect of population increase over the decade 1900–1910 bears a striking resemblance to growth in the most recent intercensal intervals. Of the total ten-year increase, 22 million in 1980–1990, 23 million in 1970–1980, 16 million in 1900–1910, 20–25 percent is accounted for by an increase in the foreign-born population. None of the intervening decades shows anything remotely like this relationship (Table 8.1).

Although the underlying mechanisms are quite different, associated as they are with the precipitous decline in natural increase of the native population in the recent as compared to the earlier period, and although the regions of origin of the foreign-born differ dramatically, this "coincidence" presents a rather intriguing point of departure for what is the focus of the present chapter and of the more general study of which it is a part. How has the industrial structure of employment in the United States been transformed? More specifically, who in the population made the adaptations that brought us from the agricultural-based rural economy that dominated most of our history to the present point, when virtually the entire country can be viewed as urban and agriculture includes less than 3 percent of the labor force?[1]

We concentrate on industrial structure because there is general

[1]This chapter has benefited from the comments of many people; I am particularly grateful to Claudia Goldin, Jerry Jacobs, Walter Licht, Andrew Miller, Suzanne Modell, Ewa Morawska, Sylvia Pedraza-Bailey, Herbert Smith, Susan Watkins, and Michael White. My thanks also go to Mark Keintz and Fred Thompsen for supervising the computer work and to Sharon Hooks for preparing the figures and the manuscript.

TABLE 8.1

Nativity Components of Population Increase, U.S.: 1900–1990

Census Date	Population						Components of Change						
	Number (1000s)			Percent			Decade	Number (1000s)			Percent		
	Total	Native-born	Foreign-born	Total	Native-born	Foreign-born		Total	Native-born	Foreign-born	Total	Native-born	Foreign-born
1990	248,710	228,943	19,767	100.0	92.1	7.9	1980–90	22,164	16,477	5,687	100.0	74.3	25.7
1980	226,546	212,466	14,080	100.0	93.8	6.2	1970–80	23,336	18,875	4,461	100.0	80.9	19.1
1970	203,210	193,591	9,619	100.0	95.3	4.7	1960–70	23,884	24,003	−119	100.0	100.5	−0.5
1960	179,326	169,588	9,738	100.0	94.6	5.4	1950–60	28,481	29,175	−693	100.0	102.4	−2.4
1950	150,845	140,413	10,431	100.0	93.1	6.9	1940–50	18,680	19,905	−1,226	100.0	106.6	−6.6
1940	132,165	120,508	11,657	100.0	91.2	8.8	1930–40	8,962	11,589	−2,626	100.0	129.3	−29.3
1930	123,203	108,919	14,283	100.0	88.4	11.6	1920–30	17,181	16,918	263	100.0	98.5	1.5
1920	106,022	92,001	14,020	100.0	86.8	13.2	1910–20	13,793	13,403	390	100.0	97.2	2.8
1910	92,229	78,598	13,630	100.0	85.2	14.8	1900–10	16,017	12,831	3,185	100.0	80.1	19.9
1900	76,212	65,767	10,445	100.0	86.3	13.7							

SOURCE: U.S. Bureau of the Census 1983, 1992.

agreement that this is the "demographic" component in the measure of economic development. Indeed, Colin Clark, one of the pioneers in the field, complained rather bitterly that historical censuses only gave him occupation data whereas what he needed was industry (Clark 1960, Chapter 9); over the years considerable effort has been expended in trying to manipulate occupation data in order to transform them into industry estimates (see, e.g., Carson 1949; Kuznets 1966; Lebergott 1964, 1966; Miller 1960). It is obvious that occupation structure also changes dramatically with economic development, but for a number of reasons the processes by which this occurs are more nebulous and, in fact, generally dependent on what is happening to the industry structure. One major asset of the 1910 Public Use Sample (PUS) is that it provides our first access to the industry data collected in the 1910 census, enabling the user to arrange them according to current concepts and to examine the geographic and demographic distributions of workers' industrial affiliations.

According to Clark, Sir William Petty, the seventeenth-century English statistician, was the first to observe that increased economic advancement brought a relative decline in the numbers of persons in agriculture and an increase in the numbers in manufacturing, and that then, in turn, the numbers in manufacturing began to decline relative to the numbers in services (Clark 1960, p. 492). Nowadays there is some dispute as to the timing of the relative increases in secondary versus tertiary industries in developing economies—and the empirical evidence from third world countries today is certainly mixed—but there seems to be no dispute that declines in proportions in agriculture are a necessary concomitant of the development process, and few would deny that the rapid industrial growth that characterized the late nineteenth and early twentieth centuries in the United States was a key component in the nation's rising economic power.

In 1910 we were still at the eve of the full flowering of the mass production system, which some recent analyses have proposed as the cause of what they hold to be the present malaise of the American economy (e.g., Dertouzos et al. 1989). Nevertheless, a number of large-scale industries were already well established in the Northeast and East North Central areas, and over 70 percent of all workers were wage earners.[2]

The emphasis in this chapter, then, is to examine the contribution of the foreign-born to the altered industrial structure of the work force.[3]

---

[2]Another advantage of the 1910 PUS is that it provides previously unavailable data on the first attempt to collect "class of worker" on a comprehensive basis in the U.S. census.

[3]Several fine studies on the occupations of the foreign-born are available (e.g., Hutchinson 1956; Lieberson 1980). The focus in those studies is on comparative occupational

The structural reference is the distribution of the total work force, but the comparative reference group—the "controls"—are the native whites of native parentage (NWNP). Although data for black workers are included in the tables, only occasional reference is made to these data in the text. This is in recognition of the situation that existed in 1910 and for many decades after: with few exceptions black workers were systematically excluded by the society in which they lived from the opportunities and benefits of economic development.

Within this framework, the second section is the heart of this chapter. Utilizing the major industrial divisions used in the 1980 Census of Population and other current household surveys, we examine the distributions among these industries for all foreign-born white workers, for each of ten immigrant groups by country or region of birth, for the NWNP, and for black workers. Except for the NWNP, for whom both total and male distributions are included, the discussion in the second section refers to data for all workers regardless of gender.[4]

A third section looks briefly at the distributions for women who reported themselves engaged in market work, again highlighting the differences among foreign-born groups and between the foreign-born and the native-born. This is followed by a section on the relationship between duration of residence in the United States and industrial affiliation in 1910 for specific immigrant groups, with considerable emphasis on the problems in interpreting such data.

Finally, a concluding section returns to the findings of the second section and offers some speculations on the issues these raise.

Definitions of Population Groups

The definitions of population groups in this chapter differ in varying degrees from those used in other sections of the volume:

(1) Native whites of native parentage (NWNP) here refer to persons whose mother and father were both native whites, whereas the category in the volume's Appendix B is based on mother's nativity only.

(2) Blacks here include persons reported as mulatto, shown sep-

---

attainment and social-economic status of immigrants (and their children) vis-à-vis the native-born, rather than, as here, the respective contributions of each in changing the nation's industrial structure.

[4]Tables 8.3a and 8.3b present industry distributions at the national level for males and females in each of the population groups.

arately in the volume's Appendix B; also included here are the very small number of blacks born abroad.

(3) The foreign-born groups distinguished here differ from the standard described in Chapter 2 and shown in the volume's Appendix B primarily because only reported place of birth is used as the defining variable (see Appendix 8C, this chapter). A major result is that three categories identified in other sections of the volume are not shown in the main text of this chapter: persons reporting Italian, Polish, or Yiddish as their mother tongue are combined with those who shared the same geographic origin but reported another mother tongue. Two considerations governed this departure from the standard procedure: first, the limited size of the sample when the emphasis is, as here, on the geographic divisions of the country, and, second, the possible effect of biases in the reporting of mother tongue.

As noted above, the focus in this chapter is on increasing our understanding of how the industrial structure of employment in the United States was transformed. Over time, a key component of this transformation has been the increasing similarity of structure throughout the country, that is, the clear trend toward convergence among the states (Miller 1960).

In this context, then, analysis of national data is insufficient; it is necessary to look at smaller geographic units. Because the size of the 1910 PUS does not permit disaggregation to the state level except for a few of the largest states, the divisional level has been used. As the next section shows, even at this level the sample does not provide enough cases in the South Atlantic, East South Central, and West South Central divisions for a number of the groups identified here. If we had disaggregated further by using mother tongue, these "blank" distributions would have been multiplied greatly.

The second consideration is more ambiguous: the reliability of the mother tongue data in identifying the group to which an individual "belongs." As Chapter 4 points out with respect to Yiddish-speakers, it is generally recognized that Jews in some European countries were likely to have the national language as the mother tongue, and therefore may not be identifiable as Jews in the census. The extent to which similar conflicts between "national" and "ethnic" languages may exist, particularly in the assorted political entities of Eastern and Central Europe at the turn of the century, is difficult to determine. Of course, the same difficulties may affect reports on country of birth, but grouping the countries of Central Europe (or Eastern Europe) together presumably reduces this problem.

Perhaps more to the point for the present discussion is the possible effect of place of destination on reported mother tongue. Those who settled in areas with sizable communities who share their mother tongue may be more likely to report that language than those who are dispersed, a possibility that may introduce a systematic bias into divisional differences. Although this may not be a problem for the national-level analyses in most of the other chapters of this volume, such a bias could seriously compromise the divisional analysis presented here. As far as I know, there has been no attempt to study this. It does mean, however, that given a choice between classifying the foreign-born either by country of origin or by mother tongue, the former seems more reliable in analyses at the subnational level.

In recognition of the considerable interest in the activities of three of the mother tongue categories—Polish, Yiddish, and Italian speakers—Appendix 8B, this chapter, presents national data for workers reporting these languages.

(4) Two groups of workers are not identified separately in this chapter (both are included in the totals shown for the United States and each region/division). These are persons reported as "other races" (i.e., not black, mulatto, or white) and, a much larger category, native whites of foreign or mixed parentage. Future work will examine the contribution of the latter category in the changing structure of employment; including them here would add further complexity to an already detailed description. Since they generally dominate the "omitted category" in every division, some indication of their aggregate impact can be obtained by noting the difference between line 1 and the sum of lines 2–4 for each geographic category in Appendix Table 8A, this chapter.

Definitions of Industry Groups

Industry entries on the 1910 PUS schedules were coded according to the classification system developed for the 1980 Census of Population and currently used in other household surveys (U.S. Bureau of the Census 1982). In general, the major industrial groups of that system are used here (see Appendix 8D, this chapter), but some modifications have been introduced: several groups have been combined in a residual "other services" category and wholesale and retail trade are treated as a single group. Sample frequencies in certain components of the categories are too small to warrant separate identification. Conversely, for two of the major divisions, manufacturing and personal services, two subcategories are identified. In manufacturing, nondurable and durable goods production are often assumed to represent "traditional" versus "modern" processing activities, although this is, of course, a crude oversimplification. A further consideration is that, historically, nondurable goods—and particularly textiles and apparel—were usually the main areas of women's manufacturing activities, whereas very few were employed in durable goods. The separation of private household workers from those working in other personal services is also common practice; they have often been treated as two independent major groups in recognition of widespread differences in working conditions.

Finally, data here exclude members of the armed forces, other persons living on military reservations, persons under 10 years of age, and a few persons not reporting sex.

The Relative Distribution of Natives and Immigrants among Industries

Overall, one-third of the working population was in agriculture in 1910, with regional variations that ranged from 10 percent in the Northeast to 57 percent in the South, and divisional concentrations that rose to 63 percent in the East South Central (Appendix Table 8A). These agricultural workers were predominantly male, of course; even if we control for the differences between male and female participation in 1910, 36 percent of male workers were in agriculture as contrasted with 23 percent of female workers (Tables 8.3a and 8.3b). More interesting is the dominance of agriculture by native white males, among whom 39 percent are in this industry (data not shown). Moreover, the native children of the foreign-born are dampening this proportion: if we look at native white males by parentage, 45 percent of those with native parents are in agriculture (Table 8.3a), as contrasted with 24 percent (not shown) of those with foreign parents; the dominance of natives cannot be entirely attributed to the very recent inflows of immigrants to the urban areas of the North. Even among the foreign-born groups that we think of as coming primarily for agricultural settlement—the Scandinavians and Germans, for example—substantially smaller proportions are in farming at the national level than is true of natives.

These points are graphically illustrated in Figure 8.1, which shows,

FIGURE 8.1

Percentage of Workers in Agriculture, Forestry, and Fisheries

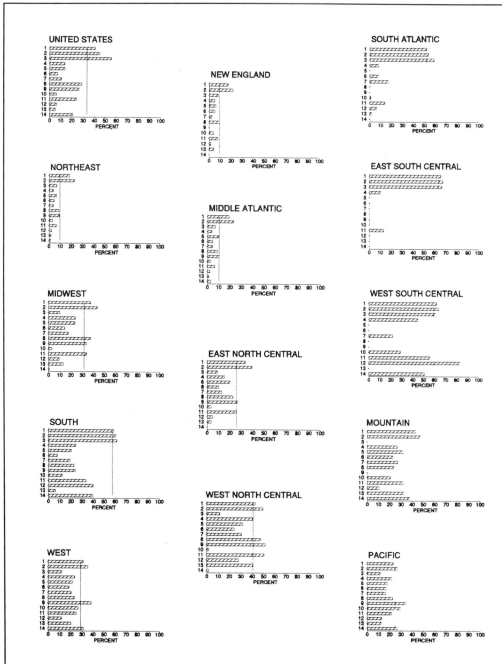

264

for each of fourteen specified nativity categories, the proportion of total workers in agriculture (including forestry and fisheries) in 1910 for the country as a whole, and for each of the four regions and nine divisions into which it is now customarily divided.[5] The vertical line in each segment of Figure 8.1 represents the proportion of all workers in the particular region/division who were in agriculture at the census date.

The assumption underlying this approach is that the distribution of all workers among industries represents, in crude fashion, the structure of the demand for labor. Obviously, such an assumption is a simplification of the many diverse factors associated with the industrial structure of the work force, but it is an assumption widely made in discussions of the distribution of employment by industry sectors. Specifically in the present case, we interpret the proportion of all workers in a given industry (i.e., the vertical line) as representing the demand for labor in that industry relative to the demand in all other industries. Deviations from this proportion by the demographic components we are examining become a measure of the differential response of the particular component to the general demand: if the bar for a group ends to the right of the "average" line, that group is overrepresented in the industry; if it falls short of the average, its members are less likely to be working in the industry than we would expect. For the country as a whole (the top-left segment of each figure) the picture is of overall differentials; for each region/division the measure is related to the structure of demand in that specific geographic entity. The preferred geographic entity is the division because there are substantial intraregional differences in structure (see particularly the differences between the East and West North Central divisions). However, the limited number of cases for certain for-

---

[5]Underlying data for figures are shown in Table 8A.1. The vertical line in each panel represents the total percentage for each area. Bars in each panel represent the percentage for each of the fourteen population groups in the following order:

1. Native white, native parentage, both sexes.
2. Native white, native parentage, males.
3. Black, both sexes.
4. Foreign-born white, total, both sexes.
5. Born in Canada, both sexes.
6. Born in Ireland, both sexes.
7. Born in Great Britain, both sexes.
8. Born in Scandinavia, both sexes.
9. Born in "Other Western Europe," both sexes.
10. Born in Southern Europe, both sexes.
11. Born in Germany, both sexes.
12. Born in Central Europe, both sexes.
13. Born in Eastern Europe, both sexes.
14. Other foreign-born white, both sexes.

For country content of groups see Appendix 8C. A blank bar denotes that sample contains fewer than fifty workers in the group in the specified region/division.

eign-born groups in several divisions results in a base too small to warrant examination of the distributions; even at the regional level, the samples in the South and West regions are very small for some groups. In the figures no bar is shown when the total number of workers for the group in the division is fewer than fifty (Table 8A.1, this chapter, shows N's for each bar). Using these proportions as indicators of differential response to the changing structure of demand is, of course, particularly questionable in subnational areas because it ignores the movement of workers among these areas. Future work will attempt to develop some indications of such movement, but for the present the role of internal migration is swept under the carpet of our assumption.

Figure 8.2 is the complement of Figure 8.1, showing the proportion of workers in all nonagricultural industries combined. At the national level, only the three native components, native whites of native parentage (bar 1), native white males of native parentage (bar 2), and blacks (bar 3), have higher than average proportions in agriculture, while each of the ten foreign-born groups and the total for all foreign-born workers (bar 4) are disproportionately concentrated in nonagricultural activities. With a few exceptions (notably, the West North Central), the same phenomenon can be observed when region/division of residence is held constant: more or less everywhere and for each of the immigrant groups we have identified, the proportion of workers in nonagricultural industries is higher than average, and especially higher than that for the NWNP.

That immigrants provided labor for some of the expanding nonagricultural sectors, particularly in the Northeast and East North Central areas, hardly comes as a surprise; it is part of the long tradition of the literature on immigration. But if we turn the issue around, a different question emerges: why did the native population apparently *not* respond to these basic structural changes in the economy, or at least not respond in the proportions that would have kept the distribution of its activities closer to the national average? We will return to this question later, but first we will examine certain major nonagricultural sectors more closely, and in particular the relative shares of each of the foreign groups identified.

In manufacturing (Figure 8.3a), a situation opposite to that in agriculture seems to prevail for the native control group. Except in the states of the old South (the South Atlantic and East South Central divisions), the NWNP are less likely to work in manufacturing than the proportion of labor in the industry would lead one to expect. For the foreign-born, however, the picture is somewhat more complex. Overall, for the United States as a whole, the Irish (bar 6) and the Scandinavians (bar 8) have about the expected proportions in the industry; for other groups, the national data indicate generally high concentrations in manufacturing.

FIGURE 8.2
Percentage of Workers in Nonagricultural Industries

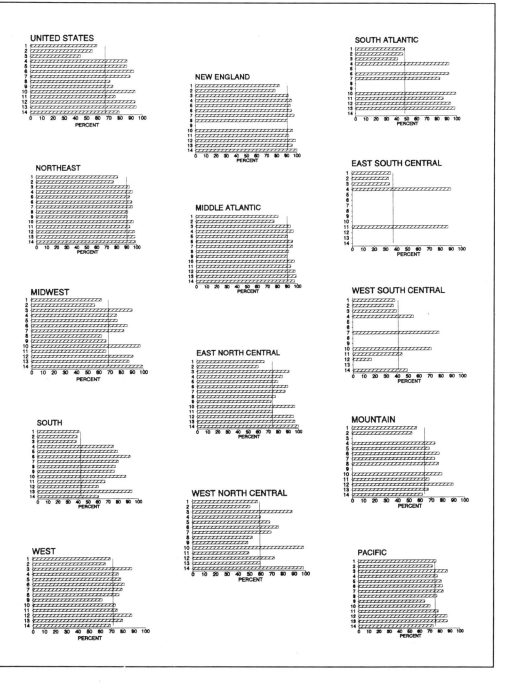

267

FIGURE 8.3A
Percentage of Workers in All Manufacturing Industries

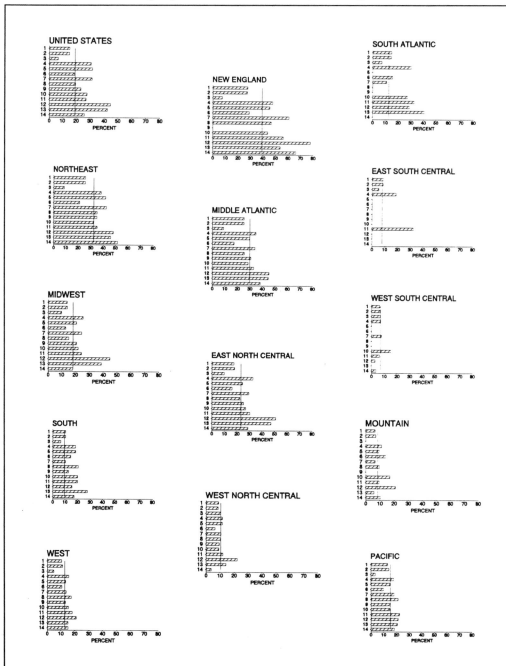

Rather surprisingly the concentration (relative to the average) for almost all groups is highest in the South, more specifically in the South Atlantic and East South Central divisions. As Table 8A.1 indicates, the samples for foreign-born workers in the South are very small, reflecting the historic dearth of immigrants to the region. Still, for the region as a whole the sample includes over 1,500 foreign-born workers, a fairly firm base as these things go, so the high proportion shown in bar 4 can probably be taken as an indication that those of the foreign-born who did find their way south were disproportionately employed in manufacturing.

Outside the South, the Irish (bar 6) were generally the least likely to be in manufacturing. Their average proportion at the national level (18.8 percent) does not reflect a general "propensity" to enter the industry but, rather, is associated with their geographic concentration in the areas with very high levels of manufacturing; 83 percent of Irish immigrants lived in the Northeast and East North Central states, and, therefore, although their proportions in manufacturing are relatively low in these areas, as Figure 8.3a indicates, the sheer weight of their numbers affects their national average. The heaviest concentration in manufacturing, on the other hand, is among those we have grouped together as "Central Europe" (bar 12), and their concentration is *not* associated with their location; in each of the areas (again, outside the South) the probability that a Central European immigrant is a factory worker is substantially higher than average, and generally higher than that for immigrants of other origin.

Closest to the Central Europeans (in terms of geographic origin as well as manufacturing proportions) are those from Eastern Europe (bar 13), the only other group that, at the national level, is more than twice as likely as average to be in manufacturing. As Figures 8.3b and 8.3c suggest, however, the two groups differ in their type of manufacturing activity: the Central Europeans are primarily in durable goods production (durable 27.7; nondurable 16.9), and the Eastern Europeans primarily in nondurable goods production (durable 17.8; nondurable 24.8); in general, this distinction is maintained throughout the country. That is, although both groups are disproportionately represented in both sectors, their relative degree of concentration between the two sectors differs.

The only other group with sharp differences in sectoral attachment within manufacturing are the Scandinavians (bar 8). Like the Irish, the Scandinavians appear to be in manufacturing at average proportions at the national level (19.5). Unlike the Irish, however, this is not associated with geographic concentration. Although the Scandinavians do not approach the levels for Central Europeans, they resemble them in the distinctions between durable and nondurable goods production: they are

FIGURE 8.3B
Percentage of Workers in Nondurable Goods Manufacturing

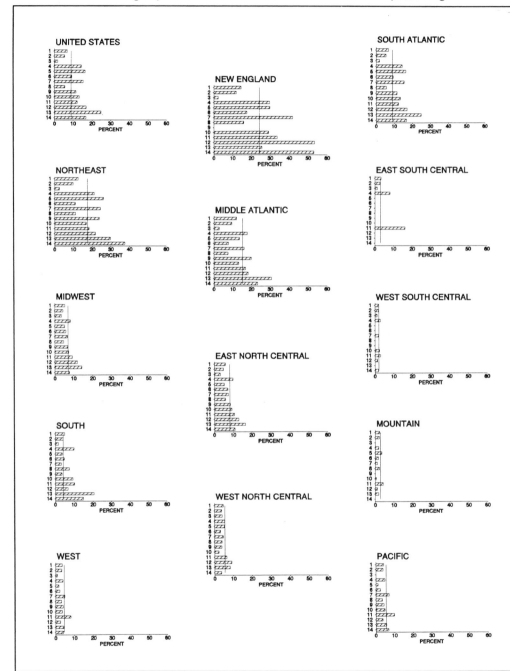

270

FIGURE 8.3C
Percentage of Workers in Durable Goods Manufacturing

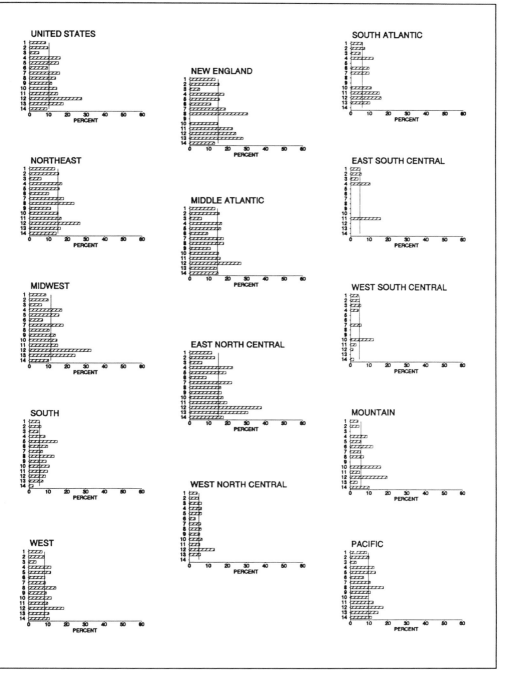

much more likely to be in the durable goods sector (13.8) than in the nondurable sector (5.7), with the differential persisting regardless of their location.

The durable/nondurable dichotomy does not emerge clearly for any of the other four large groups we have identified. Overall, the Canadians (bar 5), the British (bar 7), the Germans (bar 11), and the Southern Europeans (bar 10) have above-average proportions in manufacturing and in both of its subsectors, but there are some interesting geographic results. The Southern Europeans are less concentrated in manufacturing in the Northeast (where two-thirds of the group live) than are the British or Germans, with the differences more marked in New England than in the Middle Atlantic states.

The proportions for Canadians (bar 5) present a rather chaotic picture: although at the national level they show substantial overrepresentation in manufacturing (31.6 percent) and in both of its sectors (durable = 16.4, nondurable = 15.2), this balance is not generally characteristic of the regions or divisions within the country. One factor possibly associated with the unclear picture is that two distinct immigrant groups from Canada exist—a flow of French Canadians to the nondurable "heart" of the United States, New England, and a flow from the English-speaking provinces that has quite different industrial affiliations. Disaggregation of the durable sector indicates that Canadian males are much more likely than most foreign-born men to be in a subcategory, "lumber, furniture, stone, clay, glass," designed to represent more traditional U.S. durable goods industries. Only the Scandinavians resemble the Canadians in this. For other foreign-born groups durable goods employment is overwhelmingly in a second subcategory, "metals, machinery, transportation equipment," designed to represent the growing new industrial base (data not shown).

Overall, for the country as a whole, the importance of foreign-born workers in manufacturing receives substantial support from these new data. As the fourth bars in Figures 8.3A, 8.3B, and 8.3C indicate, taken as a group they are substantially more likely to be in the industry, and in each of its two sectors, than the average. In 1910, about a fifth of all workers were foreign-born, but they constituted almost one-third of all factory workers.

Their importance in the two other secondary industry groups is also notable. They form 30 percent of construction workers; in mining they are 44 percent of total.

As one would expect, the proportion of workers in mining is generally very small, with only the Middle Atlantic and Mountain states having more than 3 percent in the industry, so differences are particularly subject to sampling error. Nevertheless, the distinct patterns shown in Figure 8.4 are worth attention. Again, as in manufacturing, the Cen-

FIGURE 8.4
Percentage of Workers in Mining

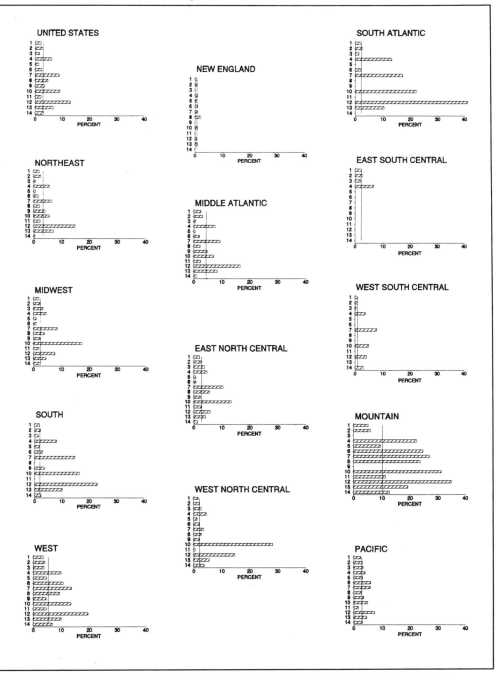

273

tral (bar 12) and Eastern Europeans (bar 13) show high levels of concentration, but they are joined here by the British (bar 7) and by the Southern Europeans (bar 10). One-third of all mine workers in the country were immigrants from these countries, and, in general, these origin patterns prevailed for all subnational areas.

Except for low levels in the South, the proportion of workers in construction is relatively stable among the regions/divisions. Moreover, this is the first of the nonagricultural industries we have discussed where native white males of native parentage play a (relatively) important role; bar 2 in Figure 8.5 is generally greater than the average and, for some areas, longer than the bar (4) for the total foreign-born. A possible hypothesis to be considered here is that construction, unlike the previously considered secondary sectors, engages a substantial proportion of traditionally skilled craft workers, and the strong showing of native heritage males represents this element in the industry's occupational structure. Construction also, of course, includes a number of what are generally termed unskilled laborers; the hypothesis, then, includes the proposition that the importance of certain foreign worker groups in the industry reflects this "unskilled" element. This hypothesis will be examined in future work when we begin to study the occupation-by-industry matrix that the 1910 sample yields.

Fairly distinct group patterns emerge among the foreign-born in construction. The Central (12) and Eastern Europeans (13), so strongly represented in manufacturing and mining, are clearly less likely to be in this industry (relatively speaking), while the other important mining groups, the British (7) and, particularly, the Southern Europeans (10) are again important components here. The Canadians (5) and the Irish (6) play a larger role here than in mining; for the Irish, construction is alone among the secondary industries in attracting above-average proportions. The Scandinavians (8) also tend to be overrepresented in construction, particularly in the Middle Atlantic and East North Central divisions, but the Germans (11), on the other hand, are not well represented except in the East North Central and South.[6]

Transportation (Figure 8.6) is variously considered to be in the secondary (industrial) or tertiary (service) sector, so that it forms a convenient transitional focus. In the 1980 census classification we are using here, employment in the communications and other public utilities industries is included, but the transportation segment dominates the sector everywhere in the present data; within transportation, railroad employment is the major component in 1910 except in the Pacific division.

---

[6]Sample size for Germans in the South is considerably larger than for most foreign groups (N = 347), so data are somewhat more firmly based.

FIGURE 8.5
Percentage of Workers in Construction

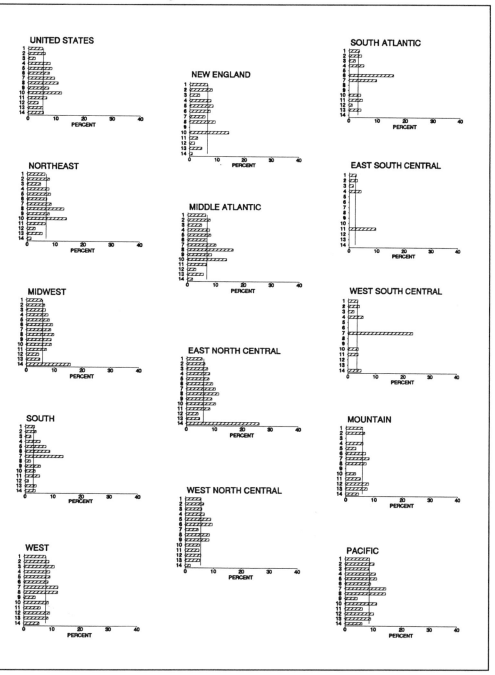

FIGURE 8.6

Percentage of Workers in Transportation, Communications, and Other Public Utilities

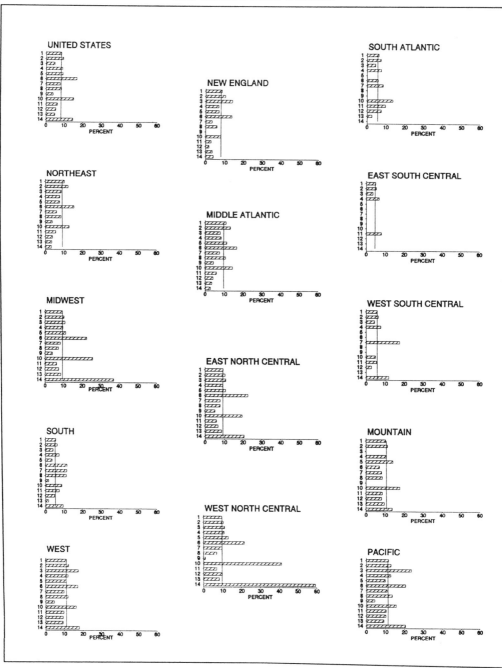

Like construction workers, transportation workers tend to be a fairly stable proportion of the total; levels are lower in the South, somewhat higher in the West, but (at least as compared to the wide variations in agricultural and manufacturing employment) each division is more or less well represented. The industry has a second similarity to construction: once again the NWNP—and particularly the males—hold their own and, in fact, are better represented than the foreign-born (as a whole) in most subnational areas.

If we disregard the small samples in the South, only two of the foreign groups have high relative concentration in transportation, the Irish and the Southern Europeans.[7] This pairing occurred for construction also and may, in fact, be associated with construction in transportation. It is probable that a considerable portion of railroad work was construction labor, that is, work in building and repairing track. Insofar as such persons are employed by the railroad (as opposed to being employed by independent contractors), they are considered transportation workers. On the other hand, other foreign groups in construction, the British, the Scandinavians, and the Canadians, do not show a consistent importance in transportation.

With trade we move indisputably into the service sector of the economy. At the national level it is the third largest of the major industry groups we are examining here, exceeded only (although by substantial margins) by agriculture and manufacturing. Trade maintains, or betters, this relative magnitude throughout the country; in fact, it is larger than agriculture in the two Northeast divisions and somewhat larger than manufacturing in the West North Central, West South Central, and Mountain states. The latter is in line with expectations; trade is in general the leading nonagricultural industry in predominantly agricultural areas, so the surprise is that manufacturing exceeds trade in the South Atlantic and (particularly) the East South Central states.[8]

In the South the foreign-born of all groups are in trade.[9] Outside the South, the Germans (bar 11) are in the Middle Atlantic and Western states, the Canadians (bar 5) and Central Europeans (bar 12) are in the West, and there is some concentration of British (bar 7) in the West

---

[7]The residual "other foreign-born" also shows a high concentration outside the Northeast; however, this small, heterogenous group needs a different approach from that used here in order to be interpreted.

[8]Roughly 40 percent of manufacturing employment in the East South Central states is in the subcategory "lumber, furniture, stone, clay, glass"; much of this is probably in lumber and forest products.

[9]The peak is reached in the East South Central states, where the small sample of foreign workers $(N = 208)$ shows that 31 percent are in trade. One is tempted to propose that the reason for the previously noted unexpected "deficit" in trade proportions in this division is that not enough foreign-born came.

North Central. Virtually everywhere, however, by far the highest relative concentration is among the Eastern Europeans (bar 13). Nearly one-quarter (24.1 percent) of immigrant workers from Eastern Europe were in this industry in 1910, a proportion very substantially higher than for any other of the groups identified here, as Figure 8.7 indicates. A number of studies have noted the importance of Jewish immigrants in the development of trade (Morawska 1990, p. 197). Since 45 percent of immigrant workers from Eastern Europe report Yiddish as their mother tongue (see Appendix 8B), we can tentatively propose the hypothesis that the data for Eastern Europeans are presenting us with "hard" evidence on this topic.

The "personal services" category, with its dominating "private household" subcategory (60 percent of the total), is the only industry group identified here that is predominantly female. We will postpone discussion of the private household sector (91 percent female) until a later (brief) look at female workers, dealing here only with the small "other personal services" group (Figure 8.8).

The subcategory includes a heterogeneous collection of generally small-scale (in 1910) personal services: hotels, boardinghouses, laundries, dressmaking and shoe repair shops, barber shops, and undertaking establishments. Here also the majority (55 percent) of workers are females, probably reflecting the relative importance of boardinghouses and dressmaking. Although there are scattered relatively high concentrations for each of the immigrant groups, the only generalization that emerges (aside from the usual situation in the South) is the persistently high proportion for Southern Europeans (bar 10), except in the Mountain states. Hutchinson (1956, pp. 125, 258)[10] has noted the very high concentration of barbers among Italians in 1890 and 1950, and perhaps that is what we have here. In any case, as Figure 8.8 indicates, outside the South the contribution of the foreign-born to other personal services is not particularly noteworthy.

Finally, we come to the residual "other service industries" group (Figure 8.9). Included here are the 1980 major industry groups "finance, insurance, and real estate," "business and repair services," "public administration," and, the major component, "professional services, recreation, and entertainment." The last is by far the largest sector, including over 60 percent of the group total.

As comparison between Figure 8.9 and Figures 8.3–8.8 shows, this is the only one of the nonagricultural industry groups we are examining where, outside the South, the total foreign-born contribution (bar 4) is

[10]Because Hutchinson had to rely on published occupation data for censuses before 1950, no figures for barbers at intervening dates are available.

FIGURE 8.7
Percentage of Workers in Wholesale and Retail Trade

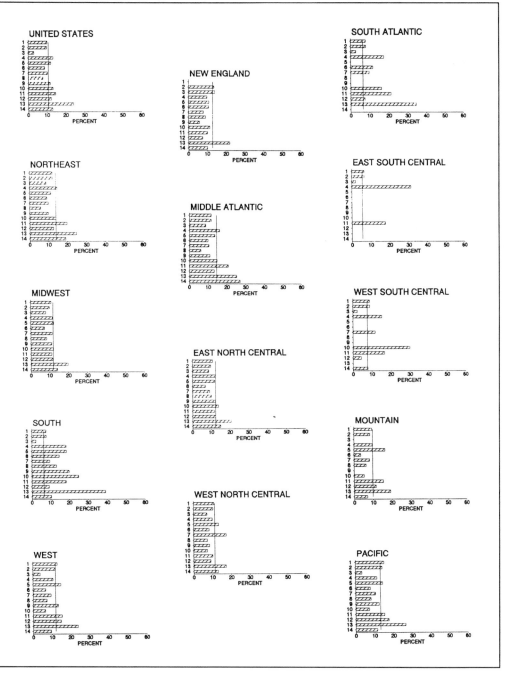

FIGURE 8.8

Percentage of Workers in Personal Services (excluding private households)

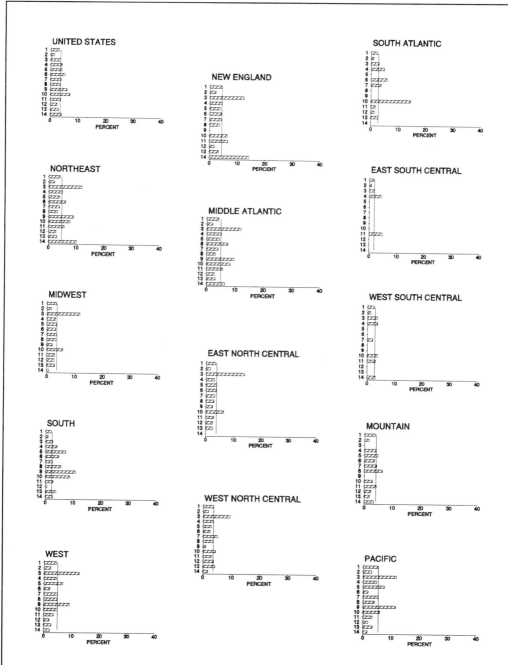

FIGURE 8.9

Percentage of Workers in Other Services (including finance, insurance, real estate, and public administration)

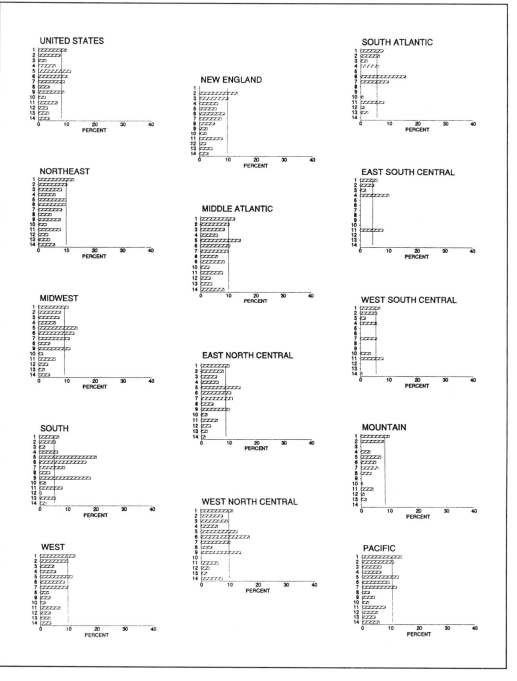

consistently and substantially below average. It is also the first in which the three English-language heritage groups—Canadians (partly English), Irish, and British (bars 5–7)—tend to act together and in contrast to virtually all other immigrant workers (only the small Other Western European group approaches them). Although the present level of analysis allows us only to guess at why the patterns for this industry differ so markedly, it seems likely that the high concentration of traditional professional practitioners included—doctors, lawyers, teachers, clergy—has weighted the distribution in the direction of those who are natives (or, rather, white natives) or whose language background—and perhaps education—are sufficiently like those of natives to enter these professions.

In this section, although we have seen that immigrants have contributed more than their expected share to all but one of the nonagricultural industries identified, we have also seen distinct differences among immigrant groups in the patterns of this contribution. Moreover, these differences are generally consistent across the several geographic entities at which we have looked despite the heterogeneity among these areas in the industrial structure of their work forces.

Almost without exception, the small group of foreign-born who found their way to the South by 1910 were concentrated in greater than expected numbers in every nonagricultural sector, regardless of their country of origin. The foreign-born, however, were only 3 percent of the region's work force, so it is basically to the other regions and their divisions that we must look for evidence of distinctive patterns. Among the eight major origin groups identified, no two have identical patterns of industrial concentration, as the following summary indicates: [11]

Bar	Origin	Industries of Concentration
5	Canada	Construction; Manufacturing (especially durable goods)
6	Ireland	Construction; Transportation
7	Great Britain	Mining; Construction; Manufacturing (especially durable goods)
8	Scandinavia	Construction; Durable goods manufacturing

[11]The two groups with fewer than 1,000 cases at the national level, "Other Western Europe" and "Other Foreign-born," are omitted from this summary. Not only are numbers small, but they, unlike other groups, do not have high concentrations from one or two countries (see Appendix 8C). The category "private households" is also excluded from this summary for reasons cited above; see the next section for discussion.

Bar	Origin	Industries of Concentration
10	Southern Europe	Mining; Construction; Manufacturing (especially durable goods); Other personal services
11	Germany	Manufacturing
12	Central Europe	Mining; Manufacturing (both sectors but especially durable goods)
13	Eastern Europe	Mining: Manufacturing (especially non-durable goods); Trade

The early pages of this section raised the question of why the native-born of native parentage did not respond to the structural shift from agriculture to nonagricultural industries in sufficient numbers to "hold their own" in the distribution between the two sectors. The evidence presented since shows this "failure to hold their own" occurred throughout the nonagricultural sector (at least with regard to the broad segments examined), with the single exception of the professional services group. It was particularly notable for what is generally considered the secondary sector—mining, manufacturing, and (less dramatically) construction—but can be observed also in most of the tertiary industries.

The data have, however, raised a second question: why did the major components of the immigrant population respond differently, displaying varying patterns that, by and large, remained consistent even when area of residence was controlled?

This, then, is another issue to be returned to later.

The Industrial Distribution
of Native and Immigrant Women Workers

Although it is our conceit in this chapter to regard the demand for labor as independent of supply—and therefore to be, among other things, gender-neutral—a nagging realism forces us to consider, at least briefly, that the structure of market employment for women in 1910 was rather dramatically different from the picture we have been examining. In this section, therefore, we temporarily assume that this difference for women has some meaning and look at how the foreign-born groups we have identified fall into (or out of) the general female situation.

Unfortunately, the sample is too small for us to follow the region/

division framework used previously. As the first line of Table 8.2 indicates, the largest group of immigrant women workers, the Irish, have fewer than 900 cases, and N's for other groups fall rapidly away from this level. The only concession to regional differences is to separate the black and the native-parentage white women into South and non-South. Because the proportion of foreign-born female workers in the South is extremely small (less than 4 percent of total), the native non-South women seem a better basis for comparison.

The low numbers of immigrant working women are in part related to the high sex ratios in the foreign-born population: among the immigrants as a whole there are 131 males for every 100 females in the population 10 years of age and over; only for the Irish is the ratio below 100 (82). In addition, the low proportion of immigrant women reported as workers reduces available sample size even further. Although in almost all groups the proportion exceeds that for native-parentage whites, none of them come anywhere near the work rate for black women (see last line Table 8.2). The validity of census measures of the proportion of women at work has, of course, long been questioned; apropos of the 1870 census, Francis Walker observed, "It is taken for granted that every man has an occupation . . . [but it] is precisely the other way with women. . . . The assumption is . . . that they are not engaged in remunerative employments . . . and it follows, from a plain principle of human nature, that [enumerators] will not unfrequently forget or neglect to ask the question" (Ninth Census 1872, p. 375, n.). In this regard, the 1910 census has sometimes been considered to have been more successful in counting women workers than the preceding or succeeding censuses (Jaffe 1956). Because the concern in this paper, however, is not with levels of participation but with structural differences, we make the general assumption that these structural differences are not significantly affected by whatever deficiencies in levels may exist.

Only six industry categories are discussed: agriculture, nondurable manufacturing, trade, private households, other personal services, and other services. Together these six include over 88 percent of workers in each of the sixteen columns of Table 8.2 and over 90 percent in most of them (including the total; as column 1 shows, they include 93 percent of all women workers in 1910). With so few categories and such major differences, the figures used to illustrate the previous discussion seem unnecessary; we focus, therefore, on comparing percentages.

Although, as noted, the concentration of women in these six categories is pervasive, patterns within the total are remarkably varied. The most extreme range is in the line showing proportions in agriculture: roughly half of native-parentage whites and over half of blacks in the South work in this industry, in stark contrast to all the other groups

TABLE 8.2

Female Workers 10 Years of Age and Over in Selected Industries

	(1)	(2)	(3)	(4)	(5)	(6)	(7)	(8)	(9)	(10)	(11)	(12)	(13)	(14)	(15)	(16)
		NWNP		Black			Foreign-Born White									
	Total	South	Non-South	South	Non-South	Total	Canada	Ireland	Gt. Britain	Scandinav.	Oth. W. Europe	So. Europe	Germany	Cen. Europe	E. Europe	Other For.-Bn.
Total (N)	32,623	4,328	7,824	7,381	794	4,865	615	879	459	498	145	311	643	611	624	80
Percent	100.0	100.0	100.0	100.0	100.0	100.0	100.0	100.0	100.0	100.0	100.0	100.0	100.0	100.0	100.0	100.0
Agr.	22.8	49.2	5.1	57.9	0.4	5.0	2.1	2.0	2.6	7.8	9.0	4.8	13.2	4.7	2.1	7.5
Nond.	13.9	9.8	15.2	0.8	1.9	22.8	25.5	8.1	27.2	6.2	14.5	46.9	10.4	30.4	47.0	15.0
Trade	10.0	7.0	14.0	0.6	3.5	11.4	13.3	5.1	11.3	7.8	7.6	11.6	11.8	14.1	18.6	17.5
Prv. Hs.	23.4	8.6	18.4	34.0	73.0	32.3	18.7	54.4	24.2	52.2	33.1	9.3	36.7	31.3	12.5	30.0
Oth. Prs. Serv.	9.6	8.1	13.0	3.7	13.9	11.7	11.5	12.1	13.1	16.5	17.2	13.5	11.7	8.3	7.5	11.3
Oth. Serv.	13.1	12.7	23.3	1.9	4.8	10.4	19.8	14.4	13.3	5.8	17.2	2.9	11.4	4.6	3.2	13.8
Percentage of Women 10 Years of Age and Over Working	23.8	16.8	17.6	57.1	45.2	21.9	26.2	29.4	21.0	22.3	22.0	16.4	14.3	25.1	24.1	19.2

identified. Because, however, the foreign-born are only marginally present in the South, we can pass over this in the present context.

Among the ten immigrant groups, the contrast between two industries stands out: nondurable manufacturing employs 47 percent of all Southern and Eastern European women workers but less than 10 percent of the Irish and Scandinavians, whereas private households engage over 50 percent of the latter two groups and relatively minimal proportions of the first two. Because the Irish and the Southern and Eastern Europeans are all heavily concentrated in the Northeast, these sharp differences cannot be associated with geographic differences in available opportunities.[12] The same two industry categories—which, between them, employ 55 percent of all immigrant female workers (column 6, Table 8.2)—share roughly equal proportions of British and Central European workers. About a quarter of Canadian women are in nondurable manufacturing, but for the remaining immigrant groups proportions in this category are moderate, roughly at the national level for all women.

The relatively low proportions of Irish and Scandinavian and relatively high proportions of Eastern European women in trade are in line with differences observed earlier for all workers, as are the low proportions in other personal services for Central and Eastern Europeans. Although differences in the residual "other services" category do not attain the levels of the two largest nonagricultural groups, there is more variation among immigrant groups for this than for trade or other personal services; in particular, it is the one category in which the relative concentration of native-parentage whites in the non-South (23 percent) is greater than for any foreign-born group. For women this category is dominated by hospitals and, especially, educational institutions. It is doubtless the schoolteachers who account for most of the high proportion of native whites and perhaps (assuming British heritage) for Canadians also. The association with English as a native tongue is not, however, as clear-cut across the groups as one might have expected. Although the four groups with below-average proportions, the Scandinavians and the Southern, Eastern, and Central Europeans, are also the four with the highest proportions of female immigrant workers arriving since 1900, and may therefore be expected to have language difficulties that precluded their entry to work in the educational (and probably also the

---

[12]Although we are not dealing with age differences in this chapter, it may be relevant to note that Irish women workers are, on average, considerably older (by 10–14 years) than those from Southern and Eastern Europe. On the other hand, Central Europeans, who seem to find private households and nondurable manufacturing about equally attractive (available), have, like those from Southern and Eastern Europe, an average age in the early 20s. We cannot, therefore, associate the differences with the greater attraction (availability) of factory work to the young, at least not at this stage of our analysis.

health care) system, neither the Irish nor the British, with English as a native language, nor the Germans, with the smallest proportion of recent immigrants, seem to have entered these systems in large numbers.[13]

The great variations in the structure of female employment observed in this section pique one's interest in further exploration of associated factors. One recent study has stressed the importance of women's traditional economic and social status in the home country as a factor in Irish women's willingness to enter domestic service (Diner 1983). But without considerably more comparative work it seems too early to dump the sharp differences shown by the data of Table 8.2 into the lap of "cultural differences."

The Association Between Duration of Residence and Industrial Affiliation in 1910

The literature on immigration, and particularly that appearing in the early decades of the century, is replete with references to the "old" versus the "new" immigrants, a distinction drawn on the basis of European country of origin. Carpenter (1969 [1927], p. 85) appears to be virtually unique among his contemporaries in pointing out that at least some of the "old" immigrants are recent arrivals and some of the "new" have been in the United States a substantial period of time. Moreover, later studies have noted sharp changes over time in the characteristics of emigrants from countries of the "old" immigration (e.g., Erickson 1972; Semmingsen 1960), findings that are clearly relevant to the issue of differential response to change in the structure of demand in the United States. Whatever the merits of the distinction between "old" and "new" and the discussions that surround it, in the context of this chapter it would be of considerable interest if we could measure the extent to which the differential patterns we have observed among immigrant groups are associated with the date of arrival in this country, and, especially, whether the behavior of recent arrivals dominates these patterns regardless of country of origin. With respect to the issue of native- versus foreign-born we can propose the hypothesis that it is new entrants into the labor market who lead the structural shifts in employment; if immigrants are considered "new entrants," regardless of their pre-migration

[13]The duration of residence variable unfortunately includes a substantial "not reported" component, particularly for females (12 percent for total immigrant female workers), but the differences here are substantial enough to permit these general statements.

status, then evidence that recent arrivals are the foreign-born component associated with the differences between immigrants versus natives might be taken as support for the hypothesis.

The 1910 census inquiry on duration of residence in the United States seems, at first glance, to provide a tool with which to deal with these issues. Unfortunately, there are a number of problems, both conceptual and technical, that cloud its interpretation. As with most discussions of migration data, the impact of these factors can be in some cases to overstate and in others to understate the measures under consideration. The following discussion briefly notes certain of the problems but cannot be summarized to indicate the possible overall effect.

First (and probably the most basic) in this array is that what we have is the pattern of employment in 1910. So when we find, as we do, that even the foreign-born males who have been here the longest are less likely to be in agriculture and more likely to be in manufacturing than native-born, native-parentage males, we cannot know the extent to which this reflects their initial distribution (i.e., when they first entered the U.S. labor market) or whether, in fact, it is the outcome of "job mobility" during the period in which they were here. The issue is further complicated by the fact that date of immigration cannot be equated with entrance into the labor market, even for males. A remarkable proportion of immigrants arrived as children; a minimum of 18 percent were below age 10 and another (also minimum) 13 percent were 10–15 at immigration. Although at least theoretically one might control for this in a more complex analysis, we are not attempting it here.

A second factor affecting these "retrospective distributions" is differential mortality. It seems to be quite firmly established that death rates were significantly lower in rural than in urban areas in the late nineteenth and early twentieth centuries (Preston et al., Chapter 3, this volume). So when we find, as we do, that the earlier the date of arrival the more likely the immigrant is to be in agriculture in 1910, we cannot know how much of this differential arises from differential survival.[14]

Analogous to the differential survival issue is the differential retirement issue. Although we have not yet examined the PUS data on this topic, evidence that farmers—as well as other self-employed workers—remain at work until an older age than do the waged and salaried is very widespread. With an average age at immigration of about 20, it is clear that the earlier immigrants include the great majority of older workers.

---

[14]This is not to raise questions about the direction of the differential—it seems clear from cumulative historical evidence that agriculture was a more important destination earlier than later—but only to caution about the differential's magnitude.

Differentials in age at retirement among the industries may also therefore be affecting the over-time comparisons.

These factors—job mobility, death, and retirement—are most relevant to the consideration of patterns for men. For immigrant women the retrospective distributions may have some element of the same effects, but the major problem is the very high concentration of work in the young adult years. The PUS data show that, among foreign-born women, two-thirds of the 16–19, 45 percent of the 20–24, and one-quarter of the 25–29-year-olds were reported as workers in 1910. Beyond age 30, fewer than 20 percent of women in every age group are reported at work. The situation can be summarized by noting that the ages 16–29 include 28 percent of all immigrant women 10 years of age and over in 1910, but 51 percent of those at work. Presumably at an earlier date many of the older women were working, but we do not, of course, know what they were doing. Moreover, in a situation of "mass" exodus from the work force when a cohort reaches ages 20–29, it is likely that those who remain are a selected group whose activities are not representative of the distribution at a previous date. For these reasons the retrospective distributions for women are of limited value for our purposes, and it is necessary to treat the two genders separately.

Finally, we come to the basic difficulty besetting all migration research that must rely on duration of residence as a measure: what we have are the immigrants who stayed. Although we have no firm data on the volume of return migration—and certainly none on the economic activities of the returnees before they left the United States—there is a general consensus that there were return flows and that these probably varied substantially among the several origin groups (Morawska 1990, p. 195). It seems unlikely that even within origin groups the returnees would have been randomly distributed among the industrial categories we are using.[15]

In summary, then, our retrospective distributions are unlikely to bear close resemblance to what cross-sectional analysis of immigrant workers at these earlier dates would have shown and are dubious representations of what even the workers in our sample had been doing at those dates. Tables 8:3a and 8:3b must be interpreted in this context: our interest is to examine the extent to which the distinctive patterns we have observed are, *in 1910*, the special contribution of recent immigrants.

[15]Recent research on return migration among internal migrants does suggest that return migrants are more likely to be randomly distributed than other migrant types (DeVanzo 1983; Miller 1977), but the applicability of this finding to international migration eighty years ago would require a tremendous leap of faith!

Two total columns are shown on Table 8.3 (a and b) because of one more problem with the duration of residence variable: in general, fairly substantial proportions of the sample, particularly among women, failed to report date of immigration. Overall, the "not reported" category is 6 percent of men and 12 percent of women workers, but there are differences among the immigrant groups, ranging up to 11 percent for Canadian men and 18.5 percent for German women. As comparisons between the distributions in the "Total" and "Total Reporting" rows indicate, the not-reported appear to be fairly randomly distributed among industries—no startling differences between the two rows emerge—and one can only hope the same is true decade by decade.[16]

For women, the most recent decade shows the highest number among the four time periods distinguished for all immigrant groups except the Germans (Column 1, Table 8.3b). This concentration is in large part associated with the special importance among workers of the youngest women, as discussed above. Women who have been in the United States longer will, on average, be older than the most recent immigrants and, therefore, less likely to be working in 1910. For men, the distribution among the decades is more equitable, or, rather, more in line with expectations. The countries of what is often referred to as the "new immigration"—Southern, Eastern, and Central Europe—have well over two-thirds arriving in the most recent period; the other origins have considerably less than one-third. Overall, 43 percent of male immigrant workers and 51 percent of women who reported the date of immigration had arrived in 1900 or later.

As the earlier summary of patterns of concentration showed, there are no clear distinctions in concentration that differentiate the "new" from the "old" immigration groups; for example, all three of the "new" are in mining, but so are the British; all of the "old" except the Germans are in construction, but so are the Southern Europeans. Abstracting from the decade of arrival, then, as we do here, keeps the picture of the persistence (or its lack) over time free of the muddying influence of differences in timing among the immigrant groups.

Unfortunately, the sample is too small to permit looking at the distributions within the subnational areas examined earlier.[17] As we saw there, the national distributions can sometimes be misleading because of the disparate industry structures and geographic distributions of origin groups among the regions/divisions of the country. A prime example

[16]Preliminary examination of the "not reported" for the population suggests that it is at particularly high levels for persons in the youngest and oldest age groups in 1910. The relative magnitudes among decades (first column of table) may therefore be affected.

[17]The subnational/origin group disaggregation could be done for a few selected categories, but it has seemed best to stick with the general picture for now.

TABLE 8.3A

Male Workers, with Decade of Immigration for Foreign-born Whites: Industry in 1910

Decade of Immigration	Total (N)	Percent	Agr.	Nonag.	Min.	Con.	Manufacturing Total	Nond.	Dur.	Trans.	Trade	Prs. Serv.	Other Serv.	NA
Total Males	119,584	100.0	36.0	64.0	3.5	6.7	19.8	7.7	12.1	9.9	11.0	2.8	6.9	3.3
NWNP	56,905	100.0	44.7	55.3	2.5	6.0	15.1	5.5	9.6	9.5	9.9	1.8	7.8	2.7
Black	12,464	100.0	57.5	42.5	2.4	4.0	10.4	2.5	8.0	8.0	4.5	5.2	3.1	4.9
Foreign-born Whites Total	26,143	100.0	15.3	84.7	7.1	9.2	31.3	12.9	18.5	10.5	13.8	3.7	5.2	3.9
Total Rptg.	24,656	100.0	14.9	85.1	7.2	9.1	31.9	13.2	18.8	10.3	13.9	3.6	5.1	3.9
Pre-1880	3,751	100.0	29.2	70.8	3.1	9.1	21.6	9.3	12.3	8.9	13.3	3.2	7.7	3.9
1880–89	5,402	100.0	19.5	80.5	4.9	9.8	27.5	12.4	15.1	9.5	15.7	3.1	6.5	3.4
1890–99	4,871	100.0	13.4	86.6	6.9	8.4	29.8	13.1	16.6	9.6	18.1	4.3	6.1	3.5
1900–10	10,632	100.0	8.1	91.9	10.0	9.2	38.8	14.9	23.9	11.6	11.2	3.8	3.1	4.3
Canada	2,192	100.0	17.2	82.8	1.6	10.8	31.9	13.8	18.1	11.5	12.0	2.8	9.2	3.1
Total Rptg.	1,957	100.0	16.6	83.4	1.5	10.8	33.2	14.4	18.8	11.7	11.5	2.8	8.9	3.1
Pre-1880	469	100.0	27.9	72.1	2.3	10.7	25.2	11.1	14.1	9.8	10.7	2.8	9.0	1.7
1880–89	538	100.0	16.2	83.8	1.5	12.6	32.7	14.9	17.8	9.9	12.1	2.4	8.7	3.9
1890–99	536	100.0	10.3	89.7	0.9	10.4	36.2	14.0	22.2	13.4	13.2	3.2	9.3	3.0
1900–10	414	100.0	12.3	87.7	1.4	9.2	38.9	17.9	21.0	13.8	9.4	2.7	8.7	3.6
Ireland	2,088	100.0	9.9	90.1	3.2	10.8	22.6	9.9	12.7	23.4	10.5	4.7	8.5	6.3
Total Rptg.	1,944	100.0	9.5	90.5	3.0	11.0	23.5	10.3	13.1	23.5	10.8	4.4	8.4	6.0
Pre-1880	624	100.0	14.3	85.7	2.9	10.9	22.0	8.8	13.1	18.6	11.1	3.0	9.1	8.2
1880–89	563	100.0	7.1	92.9	4.6	12.3	25.2	11.2	14.0	21.8	12.4	3.2	7.6	5.7
1890–99	370	100.0	5.7	94.3	3.0	10.5	24.6	10.8	13.8	25.9	10.3	4.9	10.5	4.6
1900–10	387	100.0	9.0	91.0	1.0	9.6	22.2	11.1	11.1	31.5	8.3	7.8	6.5	4.1
Gt. Britain	2,454	100.0	12.5	87.5	10.4	11.2	31.4	13.2	18.1	8.8	10.1	4.1	8.6	2.9
Total Rptg.	2,265	100.0	11.7	88.3	10.6	11.3	32.0	13.5	18.5	8.9	10.2	4.1	8.3	2.9
Pre-1880	578	100.0	19.6	80.4	8.5	9.7	26.6	10.7	15.9	8.3	12.1	2.9	9.3	2.9
1880–89	726	100.0	9.8	90.2	12.9	9.9	32.8	13.4	19.4	9.6	10.9	3.6	8.3	2.2
1890–99	424	100.0	8.7	91.3	10.1	8.3	33.7	14.6	19.1	9.7	12.0	4.2	9.0	4.2
1900–10	537	100.0	8.2	91.8	10.1	17.3	35.2	15.6	19.6	7.8	6.0	6.0	6.9	2.6

TABLE 8.3A (*continued*)

Decade of Immigration	Total (N)	Total Percent	Agr.	Nonag.	Min.	Con.	Manufacturing Total	Manufacturing Nond.	Manufacturing Dur.	Trans.	Trade	Prs. Serv.	Other Serv.	NA
Scandinavia	2,842	100.0	32.5	67.5	5.4	12.5	21.5	5.6	15.9	10.0	7.9	2.1	3.6	4.4
Total Rptg.	2,662	100.0	32.3	67.7	5.5	12.4	21.9	5.6	16.3	9.8	8.0	2.1	3.6	4.3
Pre-1880	418	100.0	50.7	49.3	2.4	6.9	10.8	3.6	7.2	7.2	11.5	2.4	4.5	3.6
1880–89	826	100.0	38.7	61.3	2.9	11.7	18.2	6.4	11.7	9.7	9.2	2.1	3.9	3.6
1890–99	573	100.0	28.4	71.6	6.1	12.9	23.7	6.3	17.5	10.1	7.5	1.9	5.6	3.7
1900–10	845	100.0	19.4	80.6	9.2	15.5	29.7	5.2	24.5	11.0	5.6	2.2	1.5	5.8
Oth. W. Europe	763	100.0	29.5	70.5	4.1	8.9	24.8	11.0	13.8	4.7	12.6	4.8	7.6	3.0
Total Rptg.	723	100.0	29.5	70.5	4.1	9.1	24.9	11.2	13.7	4.3	12.4	5.1	7.6	2.9
Pre-1880	154	100.0	35.7	64.3	0.6	12.3	14.3	7.1	7.1	2.6	12.3	3.2	14.3	4.5
1880–89	201	100.0	29.9	70.1	5.0	8.0	26.4	10.9	15.4	2.5	16.9	2.0	6.5	3.0
1890–99	147	100.0	29.3	70.7	5.4	6.8	26.5	12.2	14.3	6.8	17.7	3.4	3.4	0.7
1900–10	221	100.0	24.9	75.1	5.0	9.5	29.9	13.6	16.3	5.4	5.0	10.4	6.8	3.2
So. Europe	3,816	100.0	6.7	93.3	9.7	12.9	25.5	10.6	14.9	16.3	13.5	7.0	2.5	5.8
Total Rptg.	3,681	100.0	6.7	93.3	9.8	12.8	25.8	10.8	15.1	15.9	13.6	7.2	2.5	5.8
Pre-1880	76	100.0	21.1	78.9	5.3	6.6	11.8	2.6	9.2	9.2	21.1	13.2	6.6	5.3
1880–89	310	100.0	13.5	86.5	4.8	13.5	14.2	7.7	6.5	9.4	24.2	10.3	7.1	2.9
1890–99	640	100.0	6.9	93.1	7.8	11.1	21.6	11.1	10.5	8.3	23.4	11.7	4.2	5.0
1900–10	2,655	100.0	5.4	94.6	11.0	13.3	28.6	11.3	17.3	18.7	9.7	5.5	1.4	6.4
Germany	4,345	100.0	25.7	74.3	2.5	7.8	29.2	12.5	16.7	7.2	15.2	3.3	6.1	3.0
Total Rptg.	4,041	100.0	25.3	74.7	2.4	7.8	29.8	12.8	17.0	7.1	15.3	3.1	6.1	3.1
Pre-1880	1,212	100.0	34.4	65.6	1.4	7.8	23.3	10.5	12.9	6.5	14.2	3.2	6.1	3.1
1880–89	1,485	100.0	23.6	76.4	2.2	8.4	30.9	13.6	17.3	7.7	15.7	2.6	5.7	3.1
1890–99	802	100.0	21.1	78.9	2.7	7.4	33.0	13.3	19.7	6.7	16.6	3.1	6.0	3.4
1900–10	542	100.0	15.5	84.5	4.6	7.0	36.3	14.8	21.6	6.8	14.9	4.4	7.6	2.8

Cen. Europe	3,499	100.0	6.9	93.1	15.3	4.3	46.3	14.6	31.7	6.3	12.0	2.0	3.0	3.9
Total Rptg.	3,418	100.0	6.6	93.4	15.4	4.3	46.6	14.7	31.9	6.1	12.1	1.9	3.0	3.9
Pre-1880	108	100.0	30.6	69.4	1.9	7.4	25.0	13.0	12.0	2.8	18.5	4.6	6.5	2.8
1880–89	365	100.0	11.2	88.8	11.5	4.1	34.0	15.9	18.1	4.9	23.6	2.2	4.7	3.8
1890–99	590	100.0	9.3	90.7	16.6	5.1	35.1	14.6	20.5	6.6	18.0	2.2	3.7	3.4
1900–10	2,355	100.0	4.2	95.8	16.3	4.0	52.5	14.7	37.8	6.3	8.5	1.7	2.4	4.1
E. Europe	3,454	100.0	6.0	94.0	7.9	6.2	40.7	20.8	19.9	5.6	25.1	2.6	3.8	2.2
Total Rptg.	3,351	100.0	5.9	94.1	8.0	6.2	40.7	20.9	19.8	5.6	25.0	2.6	3.8	2.2
Pre-1880	72	100.0	26.4	73.6	2.8	9.7	15.3	9.7	5.6	0.0	37.5	0.0	5.6	2.8
1880–89	334	100.0	7.5	92.5	3.9	6.9	27.5	19.5	8.1	3.3	37.4	2.1	9.0	2.4
1890–99	688	100.0	6.5	93.5	8.3	4.1	30.4	18.8	11.6	5.4	35.6	3.1	4.8	1.9
1900–10	2,257	100.0	4.8	95.2	8.7	6.6	46.6	22.2	24.4	6.2	19.6	2.7	2.6	2.3
Oth. For.-Born	690	100.0	22.2	77.8	3.5	6.2	27.0	17.0	10.0	16.4	12.6	4.2	2.8	5.2
Total Rptg.	614	100.0	21.7	78.3	3.7	6.0	28.2	17.8	10.4	16.0	13.0	4.4	2.4	4.6
Pre-1880	40	—	—	—	—	—	—	—	—	—	—	—	—	—
1880–89	54	100.0	35.2	64.8	1.9	1.9	16.7	13.0	3.7	13.0	13.0	9.3	1.9	7.4
1890–99	101	100.0	20.8	79.2	5.9	5.9	27.7	14.9	12.9	8.9	19.8	5.0	2.0	4.0
1900–10	419	100.0	19.6	80.4	3.3	6.2	31.3	19.8	11.5	19.3	10.5	3.3	1.9	4.5

is the Irish, who show up in Table 8.3A as having substantial proportions in manufacturing although (as we saw above) their relative employment in the industry is considerbly below average in virtually all subnational areas.

With these cautions firmly in mind we can proceed to examine the data of Table 8.3A. Among foreign-born males as a whole there is a clear decline for proportions in agriculture as decade of arrival advances: 29 percent of those arriving before 1880, 19.5 percent of those coming in the 1880s, 13 percent of the 1890s arrivals, and only 8 percent of the most recent immigrants are in agriculture in 1910. Aside from minor reversals for the Canadians and Irish in the 1900s, this pattern can be observed for each of the origin groups identified. Among the thirty-nine cells involved in this observation, however, only one, Scandinavians arriving before 1880, shows a proportion (51 percent) exceeding that for all native white, native-parentage males in 1910 (45 percent); none of the other distributions are even close to the native white share. Whatever the roles played by the several factors considered above, it seems reasonable to suggest that the "march out of agriculture" of the country's economy owed much to the behavior of its foreign-born workers regardless of how long they had been here.

For manufacturing, the opposite emerges, although the picture is not quite as clear: generally, the longer the foreign-born have been here, the less likely they are to be in the industry in 1910, but the differences are less dramatic than those for agriculture: 22 percent for pre-1880 arrivals, 39 percent among the most recent. Again, at the national level, proportions in manufacturing are higher for the immigrants than for native white, native-parentage men in 1910 (15 percent) for each foreign-born group regardless of duration of residence, but there are a few more exceptions: the pre-1880 Scandinavians, Other Western Europeans, Southern and Eastern Europeans, and the Southern Europeans who arrived in the 1880s all have lower shares in manufacturing in 1910 than the native group.[18] For the other secondary sectors there is more variability. In mining the British have high concentrations in 1910 regardless of when they came, while for the Central, Southern, and Eastern Europeans—the other groups having two to four times the expected proportions in 1910—mining is more characteristic of later than of earlier

[18]Data not presented here show that the Southern and Other Western Europeans had higher proportions (than other foreign groups) among earlier arrivals who were living in the Pacific division in 1910. For Southern Europeans (but not for Other Western) the proportion drops off sharply after 1890. This, together with the sharp change in agricultural proportions shown in Table 8.3a, suggests the effects of geographic distribution on the proportions in manufacturing in 1910.

immigrants. For construction, decade of arrival makes little difference for the Canadians or the Irish; for Scandinavians and Southern Europeans the proportions become high only for workers coming after 1880; for the British, although the proportion is above average for all arrival dates, it is particularly high for those coming after 1900.[19] For a few groups there is some indication that *earlier* arrivals are more likely to be in construction in 1910, but the bases for these are usually quite small. On balance, for immigrants as a whole the proportions in construction are quite stable regardless of arrival date.

All Irish males show a high concentration in transportation, but for the other group that the previous discussion placed disproportionately in this industry, the Southern Europeans, only those arriving since 1900 show such concentration. In contrast, the high proportion of Southern Europeans that the earlier section found in "personal services" is here seen to derive largely from those who arrived *before* 1900. Some sectors of "personal service" share with trade the characteristic of having many small-scale independent enterprises operated by older men, and it may be that which is bringing the sharp break in the proportion for this group. It is also possible that we have here an indication of selectivity among those who remain; those who had established themselves in a business were probably less likely to return to their country of origin (and therefore be "missing" from the 1910 census) than those whose economic roots in this country were looser.

The same phenomenon—sharp declines among those arriving after 1900—can be observed in trade for most origin groups. Even among the Eastern Europeans, whose proportion in trade (20 percent) is notably high for those arriving after 1900, the level for these recent immigrants is very substantially lower than for those arriving before the turn of the century (36/37 percent). There appears to be general agreement that return migration was relatively low for Eastern Europeans—and particularly for the Jewish component—so selectivity among stayers may not be so important here. Only among the Germans is decade of arrival apparently irrelevant to the proportion in trade. Close to half of all foreign-born men in trade are self-employed in 1910 (data not shown), so it is likely that the clear and generally consistent distinction between the most recent and the pre-1900 immigrants is at least in part reflecting

---

[19]Erickson's (1972) examination of the ship lists for British immigrants shows high proportions reporting occupations in the building trades in the 1880s (in contrast to mid-century distributions); much of this was apparently seasonal. This finding raises further ambiguities about the "retrospective distributions" we are discussing here: not only may seasonal migrants distort the distributions, but it is also in general not clear what those who made multiple trips back and forth to the United States may have reported as date of immigration.

the effect of duration of residence on the ability to accumulate the resources needed to become a "proprietor."

The association between decade of arrival and probability of being
in the "other services" category (mostly professional) is straightforward
only for the total foreign-born males; at that level it declines as date of
arrival moves forward, in line with expectations. For most origin groups,
the newest immigrants are the least likely to be in the industry, but the
pattern is not as consistent as one might expect. For example, recent
German immigrants are more likely to be in "other services" than are
those who came before 1900. This may be indicating an increasing selectivity among immigrants from Germany; only 13 percent of German-
origin male workers reporting date of arrival have come after 1900, a far
lower proportion than for any other group, and it is possible that the
decline of "mass" emigration from the country had the effect of increasing the representation of the more highly educated or artistically tal-
ented in the flow.

As noted above, data on decade of immigration are of limited use-
fulness for women. In addition to the problems mentioned previously,
only for the Irish and the Germans do we have as many as 100 cases for
each of the four periods, and for three of the eight large origin groups—
the Central, Southern, and Eastern Europeans—numbers exceed 50 in
the last two periods only. Among the groups for which more than two
decades can be observed, recent arrivals from Germany, Scandinavia, and
Ireland are more likely to be in private households than earlier immigrants, Canadians are less likely, and period of arrival makes no difference for the British. In general, recent immigrant women workers are
more likely to be in manufacturing and less likely to be in "other services," but this is not true for the Irish and only partly so for the Canadians. "Other personal services" shows about the same pattern as we
have seen for men—declines as we move forward in time—and probably
for the same reasons: this is the only industry category with a substantial proportion of self-employed women.

To summarize the findings of this section, insofar as we can see,
there seems to be sufficient consistency to suggest that the distinctive
patterns observed in previous sections are not exclusively the result of
the behavior of the most recent immigrants.

Conclusion

Much of the literature on immigration to the United States has been
concerned with "assimilation," and often the standard used to assess

TABLE 8.3B

Female Workers, with Decade of Immigration for Foreign-born Whites: Industry in 1910

Decade of Immigration	Total (N)	Total Percent	Total Agr.	Total Nonag.	Min.	Con.	Manufacturing Total	Manufacturing Nond.	Manufacturing Dur.	Manufacturing Trans.	Trade	Prs. Serv Total	Prs. Serv Prv. H	Prs. Serv Oth.	Other Serv.	NA
Total Females	32,623	100.0	22.8	77.2	0.1	0.2	16.9	13.9	3.0	2.0	10.0	33.0	23.4	9.6	13.1	1.9
NWNP	12,152	100.0	20.8	79.2	0.1	0.3	16.1	13.2	2.9	3.3	11.5	26.1	14.9	11.2	19.5	2.3
Black	8,175	100.0	52.3	47.7	0.0	0.1	1.3	0.9	0.3	0.1	0.9	42.5	37.8	4.7	2.2	0.7
Foreign-born Whites Total	4,865	100.0	5.0	95.0	0.3	0.2	26.6	22.8	3.8	1.0	11.4	43.9	32.3	11.7	10.4	1.2
Total Rptg.	4,293	100.0	4.8	95.2	0.3	0.2	28.1	24.1	4.0	1.0	11.4	42.9	31.8	11.1	10.3	1.1
Pre-1880	454	100.0	15.0	85.0	0.0	0.0	13.0	10.8	2.2	0.7	10.4	42.3	27.5	14.8	17.2	1.5
1880–89	743	100.0	8.6	91.4	0.0	0.3	17.4	14.9	2.4	2.0	12.5	43.5	29.5	14.0	14.5	1.2
1890–99	896	100.0	4.5	95.5	0.2	0.2	26.7	21.3	5.4	1.3	15.1	40.0	28.7	11.3	9.8	2.2
1900–10	2,200	100.0	1.5	98.5	0.5	0.3	35.4	31.0	4.3	0.5	9.7	44.0	34.8	9.2	7.7	0.5
Canada	615	100.0	2.1	97.9	0.0	0.0	30.6	25.5	5.0	1.5	13.3	30.2	18.7	11.5	19.8	2.4
Total Rptg.	532	100.0	2.3	97.7	0.0	0.0	32.1	26.9	5.3	1.3	12.8	30.3	19.0	11.3	19.0	2.3
Pre-1880	68	100.0	8.8	91.2	0.0	0.0	14.7	10.3	4.4	1.5	16.2	42.6	25.0	17.6	14.7	1.5
1880–89	109	100.0	4.6	95.4	0.0	0.0	25.7	22.0	3.7	0.0	11.0	34.9	22.0	12.8	19.3	4.6
1890–99	158	100.0	0.6	99.4	0.0	0.0	39.9	32.9	7.0	2.5	16.5	26.6	14.6	12.0	10.8	3.2
1900–10	197	100.0	0.0	100.0	0.0	0.0	35.5	30.5	5.1	1.0	9.6	26.4	18.8	7.6	26.9	0.5
Ireland	879	100.0	2.0	98.0	0.1	0.1	9.9	8.1	1.8	0.9	5.1	66.4	54.4	12.1	14.4	0.9
Total Rptg.	766	100.0	2.0	98.0	0.0	0.1	9.9	8.1	1.8	1.0	4.3	66.7	55.1	11.6	15.1	0.8
Pre-1880	140	100.0	9.3	90.7	0.0	0.0	17.1	14.3	2.9	0.7	8.6	45.7	32.1	13.6	17.9	0.7
1880–89	180	100.0	0.0	100.0	0.0	0.0	11.7	9.4	2.2	2.8	3.9	65.6	52.8	12.8	15.6	0.6
1890–99	180	100.0	0.6	99.4	0.0	0.6	8.3	6.1	2.2	0.0	4.4	71.7	57.2	14.4	12.8	1.7
1900–10	266	100.0	0.4	99.6	0.0	0.0	6.0	5.3	0.8	0.8	2.3	75.2	67.3	7.9	15.0	0.4
Gt. Britain	459	100.0	2.6	97.4	0.0	0.4	31.4	27.2	4.1	1.7	11.3	37.3	24.2	13.1	13.3	2.0
Total Rptg.	396	100.0	2.0	98.0	0.0	0.3	33.3	29.0	4.3	1.5	11.9	35.9	23.7	12.1	13.1	2.0
Pre-1880	67	100.0	7.5	92.5	0.0	0.0	14.9	11.9	3.0	1.5	9.0	43.3	22.4	20.9	20.9	3.0
1880–89	93	100.0	3.2	96.8	0.0	1.1	26.9	23.7	3.2	2.2	19.4	32.3	20.4	11.8	12.9	2.2
1890–99	76	100.0	0.0	100.0	0.0	0.0	36.8	26.3	10.5	2.6	13.2	30.3	25.0	5.3	13.2	3.9
1900–10	160	100.0	0.0	100.0	0.0	0.0	43.1	40.6	2.5	0.6	8.1	37.5	25.6	11.9	10.0	0.6

TABLE 8.3B (continued)

Decade of Immigration	Total		Agr.	Nonag.	Min.	Con.	Manufacturing			Trans.	Trade	Prs. Serv			Other Serv.	NA
	(N)	Percent					Total	Nond.	Dur.			Total	Prv. H	Oth.		
Scandinavia																
Total Rptg.	498	100.0	7.8	92.2	0.4	0.6	7.8	6.2	1.6	0.4	7.8	68.7	52.2	16.5	5.8	0.6
	435	100.0	7.8	92.2	0.5	0.7	8.0	6.2	1.8	0.5	7.6	68.7	53.3	15.4	5.5	0.7
Pre-1880	31	—	—	—	—	—	—	—	—	—	—	—	—	—	—	—
1880–89	89	100.0	15.7	84.3	0.0	1.1	7.9	4.5	3.4	2.2	11.2	50.6	24.7	25.8	10.1	1.1
1890–99	71	100.0	5.6	94.4	1.4	0.0	11.3	8.5	2.8	0.0	11.3	63.4	46.5	16.9	5.6	1.4
1900–10	244	100.0	1.6	98.4	0.4	0.8	7.8	6.6	1.2	0.0	4.5	80.3	69.3	11.1	4.1	0.4
Oth. W. Europe																
Total Rptg.	145	100.0	9.0	91.0	0.0	0.0	15.9	14.5	1.4	0.0	7.6	50.3	33.1	17.2	17.2	0.0
	121	100.0	6.6	93.4	0.0	0.0	15.7	14.9	0.8	0.0	7.4	52.1	34.7	17.4	18.2	0.0
Pre-1880	11	—	—	—	—	—	—	—	—	—	—	—	—	—	—	—
1880–89	33	—	—	—	—	—	—	—	—	—	—	—	—	—	—	—
1890–99	23	—	—	—	—	—	—	—	—	—	—	—	—	—	—	—
1900–10	54	100.0	1.9	98.1	0.0	0.0	14.8	14.8	0.0	0.0	3.7	61.1	40.7	20.4	18.5	0.0
So. Europe																
Total Rptg.	311	100.0	4.8	95.2	1.6	0.3	55.0	46.9	8.0	0.0	11.6	22.8	9.3	13.5	2.9	1.0
	297	100.0	4.7	95.3	1.7	0.3	55.9	47.8	8.1	0.0	11.4	22.2	9.1	13.1	3.0	0.7
Pre-1880	3	—	—	—	—	—	—	—	—	—	—	—	—	—	—	—
1880–89	21	—	—	—	—	—	—	—	—	—	—	—	—	—	—	—
1890–99	56	100.0	8.9	91.1	1.8	0.0	42.9	33.9	8.9	0.0	23.2	17.9	5.4	12.5	5.4	0.0
1900–10	217	100.0	2.8	97.2	1.8	0.5	62.7	53.9	8.8	0.0	7.8	21.2	8.8	12.4	2.3	0.9
Germany																
Total Rptg.	643	100.0	13.2	86.8	0.0	0.0	13.2	10.4	2.8	0.9	11.8	48.4	36.7	11.7	11.4	1.1
	524	100.0	13.5	86.5	0.0	0.0	13.0	10.3	2.7	1.0	10.7	47.9	37.4	10.5	12.6	1.3
Pre-1880	118	100.0	20.3	79.7	0.0	0.0	7.6	7.6	0.0	0.0	8.5	42.4	28.8	13.6	18.6	2.5
1880–89	148	100.0	19.6	80.4	0.0	0.0	10.1	8.8	1.4	2.7	14.9	37.2	25.0	12.2	15.5	0.0
1890–99	131	100.0	11.5	88.5	0.0	0.0	20.6	13.7	6.9	0.8	9.2	48.1	35.9	12.2	7.6	2.3
1900–10	127	100.0	2.4	97.6	0.0	0.0	13.4	11.0	2.4	0.0	9.4	65.4	61.4	3.9	8.7	0.8

	N	1	2	3	4	5	6	7	8	9	10	11	12	13	14	15
Cen. Europe	611	100.0	4.7	95.3	0.5	0.0	35.2	30.4	4.7	0.8	14.1	39.6	31.3	8.3	4.6	0.5
Total Rptg.	573	100.0	4.4	95.6	0.5	0.0	36.6	31.8	4.9	0.9	14.5	37.9	29.5	8.4	4.7	0.5
Pre-1880	10	—	—	—	—	—	—	—	—	—	—	—	—	—	—	—
1880–89	40	100.0	9.8	90.2	0.0	0.0	34.8	30.4	4.3	1.1	16.3	22.8	16.3	6.5	13.0	2.2
1890–99	92	100.0	1.9	98.1	0.7	0.0	37.4	32.0	5.3	0.9	11.8	44.1	35.0	9.0	3.0	0.2
1900–10	431															
E. Europe	624	100.0	2.1	97.9	0.3	0.6	52.7	47.0	5.8	1.3	18.6	20.0	12.5	7.5	3.2	1.1
Total Rptg	591	100.0	2.0	98.0	0.3	0.7	53.6	47.5	6.1	1.4	19.5	18.4	11.7	6.8	3.0	1.0
Pre-1880	3	—	—	—	—	—	—	—	—	—	—	—	—	—	—	—
1880–89	17	100.0	3.9	96.1	0.0	1.0	37.3	33.3	3.9	3.9	34.3	11.8	5.9	5.9	4.9	2.9
1890–99	102	100.0	1.1	98.9	0.4	0.6	58.4	51.8	6.6	0.4	16.4	20.0	12.8	7.2	1.9	0.6
1900–10	469															
Oth. For.-born	80	100.0	7.5	92.5	0.0	0.0	17.5	15.0	2.5	1.3	17.5	41.3	30.0	11.3	13.8	1.3
Total Rptg.	58	100.0	8.6	91.4	0.0	0.0	19.0	17.2	1.7	0.0	17.2	39.7	25.9	13.8	13.8	1.7
Pre-1880	3	—	—	—	—	—	—	—	—	—	—	—	—	—	—	—
1880–89	13	—	—	—	—	—	—	—	—	—	—	—	—	—	—	—
1890–99	7	—	—	—	—	—	—	—	—	—	—	—	—	—	—	—
1900–10	35	—	—	—	—	—	—	—	—	—	—	—	—	—	—	—

this is to measure how closely the behavior of immigrants parallels that of the native-born. Taken at face value, the findings of this chapter are that a pronounced dissimilarity in the industrial affiliation of workers existed between the native-born of native parentage and the foreign-born in 1910, and that in terms of a traditional measure of economic development, the shift away from agriculture to secondary and tertiary activities, it was indeed fortunate for the economic progress of the United States that this difference occurred. If we were writing twenty years ago in the heyday of counterfactual economic history, it might be intriguing to push our findings further to estimate what the difference implied for GNP per capita and other measures of economic growth would have been in the absence of the immigrants' contribution to industrial change.

Why, then, was the transformation of the labor force in the period prior to 1910 so "dependent" on foreign immigration? One may speculate that rapid growth created a demand for labor that natural increase of the native population was not large enough to respond to—or at any rate, not large enough within the confines of the limits imposed on women's participation at that period. But why did natives not at least come closer to holding their own in the expanding growth sectors?

For blacks, one may say that their systematic exclusion from the benefits of material progress provides an explanation. By and large, they were not allowed by the larger society to participate in this transformation. But what of the native whites? Although there were undoubtedly some prosperous agriculturists, for most life on the farm was probably difficult. Comparisons between the incomes of farm and non-farm workers are always fraught with peril, particularly so with the crude estimates that must be made for this early period. Among other issues, obviously, is the extent to which cash income measures the "comforts" of life— the adequacy of food, shelter, and clothing. Descriptions of life in the slums of large cities, buttressed by measures of the continuing mortality differentials between urban and rural areas (Preston et al., Chapter 3, this volume), suggest that at least for some components of the urban population life was grim indeed. Nevertheless, the magnitude of income differentials for those dates at which estimates have been attempted (Easterlin 1960; Preston and Haines 1991; U.S. Department of Labor 1934) seems to justify a conclusion that for much of the rural population the economic gains to be achieved by joining the growing industry sectors would have been substantial.[20] Distance is often a barrier to migration,

[20]For example, the U.S. Department of Labor (1934, p. 229) estimated that monthly wages without board for male farm laborers in 1910 averaged $19.75 in the South Atlantic and $21.90 in the South Central (East and West combined) divisions (wages with board were, of course, lower); these very low levels presumably are strongly influenced by the wages for blacks, but even for Pennsylvania ($29) and Illinois ($32.90) the levels are gen-

but it is hard to believe that the trip from North Carolina to Pennsylvania would have been more arduous than that from Russia.

Earlier, the hypothesis that new entrants to the labor market may make the "adjustment" to the changing structure of demand was proposed. In the context of that remark our interest was in the extent to which recent immigrants carried the burden. But new entrants, of course, come from the native population also. We have not yet examined the age structure of industries, as available from the PUS, in detail, but our preliminary look suggests that in the United States in 1910, as virtually everywhere over the last 100 years, young native male workers are less likely to be in agriculture than are older males. Similar findings emerged from the 1900 PUS (Miller 1986). The differentials among natives by age are, however, less striking than those between the native white and the foreign-born presented here, and it is probably relevant to note also that median age for native white, native-parentage male workers (32.9 years) is four years below that for the foreign-born (37.2 years) in 1910. It seems unlikely, therefore, that age will prove the key variable in the difference between natives and immigrants.

An obviously important factor distinguishing the United States in the nineteenth century from the industrializing countries of Western Europe and from most third world countries today is the "settlement" process. Although, broadly speaking, the occupation of new territory was essentially completed by 1910, in certain areas of the country the opening of new lands was still very recent history. Insofar as settlement of new territory was disproportionately the task of native whites, one might expect higher proportions in agriculture, which was, by and large, the "settlement" industry.[21] Future work, which will attempt to relate structural shifts and internal migration, may throw further light on this issue. But, again, it is unlikely that this will prove the key.

Finally, at least for the present discussion, we come to what we can call, by way of shorthand terminology, the "Jeffersonian tradition," the view of farming as a way of life that has a special value and that is to be relinquished only in desperate circumstances. This is a theme that pervades our history, and whose parallel can be found in many other areas of the world, both in the past and today. As anyone with acquaintances who grew up on a farm will know, the view is not universally

---

erally less than half the implied monthly earnings for hod carriers in Boston, New York, Philadelphia, Chicago, and other cities, as reported in the same source (pp. 182–184). In the context of present-day discussions of rural-urban migration in the third world, with their emphasis on anticipated (often unachieved) gains, the 1910 situation in the United States looks even more perplexing.

[21]As evidence, it can be noted that in several of the Mountain states the proportion of workers in agriculture was still increasing after 1910 (Miller 1960, p. 82).

subscribed to. Still, it merits consideration as an unquantifiable variable affecting our findings. Perhaps the ultimate gift of the immigrants to their hosts was to allow them the privilege of staying "down on the farm" for a few decades more.

We come now to the second issue that arose, somewhat unexpectedly, in the course of our examination of industrial structure: the differentials among the foreign-origin groups identified with regard to concentration in the several nonagricultural sectors and the general persistence of these regardless of area of residence in 1910. Although recruiting for specific employments by American agents abroad undoubtedly played a role in some industries, it is unlikely to have had a direct impact on the mass of immigrants (Erickson 1984). Rather, the major operating mechanism that suggests itself is "chain migration," that is, the process by which friends, relatives, neighbors, and word of mouth alert the potential emigrant to possible contacts with immigrants already in the United States. A number of studies of specific groups have emphasized the importance of this factor, and the apparently widespread existence of ethnic concentrations in rural as well as urban areas provides additional evidence. Not only did such communities provide a place to go to, but presumably the contacts found there also provided entree into the job market (Morawska 1990, pp. 194, 204ff). Moreover, at least one recent study has suggested a considerable geographic mobility among ethnic communities within the United States (Puskás 1986). In this context, then, our findings are probably not unexpected; they are merely providing aggregate evidence to support the generalization of more specialized research.

Many excellent historical studies have been done on particular communities, particular industries, and particular ethnic groups. These provide insights into the processes of change, and the distribution of its costs and rewards, that the limited data available in censuses can never yield. What the Public Use Samples give us, however, is the framework within which these specific studies can be placed.

Appendix 8A

TABLE 8A.1

Working Population 10 Years of Age and Over, by Industry and Residence in 1910

	Total				Min.	Con.	Manufacturing			Trans.	Trade	Personal Services			Other Serv.	NA.
	(N)	Percent	Agr.	Nonag.			Total	Nond.	Dur.			Total	Prv. H.	Oth.		
United States																
Both Sexes	152,207	100.0	33.2	66.8	2.8	5.3	19.2	9.0	10.2	8.2	10.8	9.2	5.5	3.7	8.2	3.0
NWNP	69,057	100.0	40.5	59.5	2.0	5.0	15.3	6.9	8.4	8.4	10.2	6.1	2.9	3.2	9.9	2.6
Black	20,639	100.0	55.4	44.6	1.4	2.4	6.8	1.9	4.9	4.9	3.1	20.0	16.2	3.7	2.8	3.2
For.-born Wh.	31,008	100.0	13.7	86.3	6.0	7.8	30.6	14.4	16.2	9.0	13.4	10.0	5.6	4.3	6.0	3.5
Canada	2,807	100.0	13.9	86.1	1.2	8.4	31.6	16.4	15.2	9.3	12.3	8.8	4.5	4.3	11.5	3.0
Ireland	2,967	100.0	7.6	92.4	2.3	7.7	18.8	9.4	9.5	16.8	8.9	23.0	17.6	5.4	10.3	4.7
Gt. Britain	2,913	100.0	11.0	89.0	8.8	9.5	31.4	15.4	15.9	7.7	10.3	9.3	5.3	4.0	9.3	2.7
Scandinavia	3,340	100.0	28.8	71.2	4.7	10.7	19.5	5.7	13.8	8.6	7.9	12.1	8.4	3.7	3.9	3.8
Oth. W. Eur.	908	100.0	26.2	73.8	3.4	7.5	23.3	11.6	11.8	4.0	11.8	12.1	5.9	6.2	9.1	2.5
So. Eur.	4,127	100.0	6.5	93.5	9.1	12.0	27.7	13.3	14.4	15.1	13.3	8.2	0.9	7.3	2.5	5.4
Germany	4,988	100.0	24.1	75.9	2.1	6.8	27.1	12.2	14.9	6.4	14.8	9.1	5.2	3.9	6.8	2.8
Cen. Eur.	4,110	100.0	6.5	93.5	13.1	3.6	44.6	16.9	27.7	5.5	12.3	7.6	5.0	2.7	3.3	3.4
E. Eur.	4,078	100.0	5.4	94.6	6.7	5.4	42.5	24.8	17.8	5.0	24.1	5.3	2.1	3.1	3.7	2.0
Oth. For.-born	770	100.0	20.6	79.4	3.1	5.6	26.0	16.8	9.2	14.8	13.1	8.1	3.8	4.3	3.9	4.8
Male-NWNP	56,905	100.0	44.7	55.3	2.5	6.0	15.1	5.5	9.6	9.5	9.9	1.8	0.3	1.5	7.8	2.7
Northeast																
Both Sexes	44,514	100.0	9.9	90.1	3.5	6.8	32.3	17.6	14.7	9.3	14.0	11.0	6.1	4.9	10.0	3.4
NWNP	16,407	100.0	18.5	81.5	2.1	6.3	26.0	12.7	13.3	10.4	12.2	8.6	4.3	4.3	12.6	3.2
Black	1,163	100.0	7.0	93.0	0.6	4.7	8.9	2.8	6.1	8.8	8.9	44.7	32.7	12.0	8.3	8.1
For.-born Wh.	15,835	100.0	4.1	95.9	5.8	7.8	38.2	21.0	17.2	8.0	14.7	12.2	7.2	5.0	6.0	3.1
Canada	1,559	100.0	6.9	93.1	0.6	8.4	41.9	26.1	15.8	8.0	11.5	9.7	5.7	4.0	10.0	3.0
Ireland	2,122	100.0	4.8	95.2	1.6	7.1	21.3	11.2	10.1	15.6	9.3	26.9	20.5	6.3	9.6	3.9
Gt. Britain	1,519	100.0	3.9	96.1	6.6	8.6	42.5	24.4	18.1	6.3	10.1	10.9	6.8	4.1	8.4	2.6
Scandinavia	626	100.0	8.9	91.1	2.2	13.1	35.0	11.3	23.6	8.6	6.1	18.7	15.3	3.4	4.6	2.7
Oth. W. Eur.	287	100.0	9.4	90.6	4.2	8.0	34.8	23.7	11.1	3.8	10.1	19.5	10.5	9.1	8.0	2.1

TABLE 8A.1 (continued)

	Total						Manufacturing			Trans.	Trade	Personal Services			Other Serv.	NA.
	(N)	Percent	Agr.	Nonag.	Min.	Con.	Total	Nond.	Dur.			Total	Prv. H.	Oth.		
So. Eur.	2,739	100.0	3.2	96.8	5.7	14.0	32.0	16.9	15.1	12.9	13.9	9.1	1.1	7.9	2.9	6.2
Germany	1,638	100.0	6.7	93.3	2.3	6.5	35.0	18.3	16.7	5.7	19.8	13.7	7.9	5.9	7.9	2.4
Cen. Eur.	2,366	100.0	2.1	97.9	15.0	2.9	48.4	21.6	26.8	4.0	12.7	9.1	6.3	2.8	3.4	2.4
E. Eur.	2,774	100.0	1.9	98.1	7.1	5.5	46.2	29.8	16.4	3.6	24.7	5.8	2.6	3.2	4.1	1.1
Oth. For.-born	205	100.0	1.5	98.5	0.5	1.5	51.7	37.6	14.1	3.4	19.0	14.1	3.9	10.2	5.9	2.4
Male-NWNP	12,852	100.0	22.6	77.4	2.6	8.0	25.7	10.1	15.6	12.5	12.3	2.7	0.6	2.1	10.2	3.3
Midwest																
Both Sexes	46,338	100.0	31.4	68.6	2.5	5.8	18.4	7.1	11.3	9.4	11.9	8.0	4.2	3.7	9.1	3.5
NWNP	21,110	100.0	37.2	62.8	2.0	5.5	14.2	5.4	8.7	9.5	10.8	7.0	3.5	3.4	10.6	3.3
Black	1,138	100.0	10.0	90.0	3.4	6.8	10.1	3.6	6.5	10.9	8.1	34.5	22.7	11.9	7.3	8.9
For.-born Wh.	10,304	100.0	23.7	76.3	4.7	7.7	25.6	8.4	17.2	9.7	11.5	7.2	3.9	3.2	6.1	3.8
Canada	859	100.0	23.3	76.7	0.9	8.3	21.0	5.2	15.7	11.3	12.2	6.5	2.9	3.6	13.7	2.8
Ireland	521	100.0	14.4	85.6	1.2	9.4	13.1	6.0	7.1	22.3	7.3	13.2	10.0	3.3	12.7	6.5
Gt. Britain	752	100.0	17.4	82.6	8.6	8.8	24.6	6.6	18.0	8.4	11.3	6.4	2.8	3.6	11.0	3.5
Scandinavia	1,980	100.0	37.2	62.8	3.9	9.8	15.3	4.7	10.5	7.3	8.5	10.2	6.8	3.3	4.0	3.9
Oth. W. Eur.	394	100.0	33.5	66.5	2.3	8.9	20.8	7.1	13.7	4.1	11.2	5.8	3.8	2.0	11.2	2.3
So. Eur.	648	100.0	2.9	97.1	17.4	9.0	22.1	7.4	14.7	25.5	12.0	6.2	0.3	5.9	1.5	3.4
Germany	2,645	100.0	33.6	66.4	2.0	7.3	24.3	9.3	15.0	6.3	11.1	6.4	3.5	2.9	5.9	3.1
Cen. Eur.	1,389	100.0	9.5	90.5	7.7	4.5	44.9	12.2	32.8	7.4	11.7	6.2	3.5	2.7	3.2	4.9
E. Eur.	989	100.0	13.0	87.0	4.6	4.9	38.6	14.4	24.3	8.6	19.7	4.1	1.2	2.9	2.1	4.3
Oth. For.-born	127	100.0	0.8	99.2	2.4	15.7	18.1	7.9	10.2	37.0	14.2	3.1	2.4	0.8	3.9	4.7
Male-NWNP	17,642	100.0	43.4	56.6	2.3	6.5	14.3	4.4	9.9	10.4	10.0	1.9	0.3	1.6	7.9	3.4

South

Category	Number														
Both Sexes	48,808	100.0	57.3	42.7	1.8	2.9	9.6	4.2	5.5	5.4	6.5	9.1	6.7	2.4	5.3	2.0
NWNP	26,249	100.0	58.8	41.2	1.8	3.3	10.5	5.1	5.4	5.8	7.8	3.6	1.6	2.0	7.0	1.6
Black	18,236	100.0	61.6	38.4	1.3	2.0	6.5	1.7	4.8	4.2	2.4	17.4	14.8	2.7	2.1	2.5
For.-born Wh.	1,547	100.0	24.4	75.6	8.1	5.2	18.5	10.0	8.5	7.6	18.4	8.7	4.5	4.3	6.7	2.3
Canada	54	100.0	20.4	79.6	1.9	7.4	18.5	3.7	14.8	3.7	18.5	9.3	1.9	7.4	20.4	0.0
Ireland	102	100.0	7.8	92.2	2.9	8.8	14.7	4.9	9.8	11.8	14.7	18.6	13.7	4.9	16.7	3.9
Gt. Britain	155	100.0	19.4	80.6	14.8	13.5	10.3	3.2	7.1	11.6	9.7	9.7	7.1	2.6	9.0	1.9
Scandinavia	53	100.0	22.6	77.4	0.0	1.9	20.8	7.5	13.2	11.3	13.2	22.6	17.0	5.7	3.8	3.8
Oth. W. Eur.	55	100.0	23.6	76.4	3.6	5.5	12.7	3.6	9.1	1.8	20.0	12.7	1.8	10.9	18.2	1.8
So. Eur.	224	100.0	12.1	87.9	16.5	3.6	20.1	9.4	10.7	8.9	25.0	9.4	0.4	8.9	2.2	2.2
Germany	347	100.0	33.1	66.9	0.0	5.2	20.2	10.4	9.8	7.5	18.4	7.2	4.3	2.9	8.1	0.3
Cen. Eur.	161	100.0	39.8	60.2	23.0	1.2	15.5	6.8	8.7	5.0	9.3	3.1	2.5	0.6	0.6	2.5
E. Eur.	176	100.0	6.3	93.8	10.2	4.0	27.8	20.5	7.4	1.7	39.2	4.5	0.6	4.0	5.7	0.6
Oth. For.-born	220	100.0	39.5	60.5	2.3	3.6	17.3	15.0	2.3	9.5	10.5	8.2	5.5	2.7	2.3	6.8
Male-NWNP	21,921	100.0	60.6	39.4	2.1	3.9	10.4	4.2	6.2	6.5	7.9	1.0	0.2	0.8	5.9	1.6

West

Category	Number														
Both Sexes	12,547	100.0	28.5	71.5	5.4	7.7	12.9	4.5	8.4	11.1	12.0	8.5	3.5	5.0	9.8	4.1
NWNP	5,291	100.0	30.9	69.1	3.6	7.6	10.6	3.5	7.1	11.2	12.9	7.1	2.4	4.7	12.5	3.6
Black	102	100.0	11.8	88.2	3.9	10.8	4.9	1.0	3.9	17.6	3.9	35.3	22.5	12.7	4.9	6.9
For.-born Wh.	3,322	100.0	23.5	76.5	10.1	9.2	15.6	3.9	11.7	12.1	10.8	8.6	4.0	4.6	5.6	4.6
Canada	335	100.0	21.5	78.5	4.8	9.3	13.4	1.8	11.6	11.0	14.9	10.1	3.3	6.9	11.3	3.6
Ireland	222	100.0	18.5	81.5	10.8	8.6	10.8	2.3	8.6	17.1	6.8	10.8	8.6	2.3	8.6	8.1
Gt. Britain	487	100.0	20.3	79.7	13.8	12.1	13.8	4.9	8.8	9.9	9.7	8.6	3.7	4.9	9.9	2.1
Scandinavia	681	100.0	23.1	76.9	9.5	12.0	17.5	3.1	14.4	12.0	7.5	10.7	5.9	4.8	2.9	4.7
Oth. W. Eur.	172	100.0	38.4	61.6	4.7	4.1	13.4	4.1	9.3	4.7	13.4	14.0	4.7	9.3	3.5	4.1

TABLE 8A.1 (continued)

| | Total | | | | | | Manufacturing | | | | | Personal Services | | | Other | |
	(N)	Percent	Agr.	Nonag.	Min.	Con.	Total	Nond.	Dur.	Trans.	Trade	Total	Prv. H.	Oth.	Serv.	NA.
So. Eur.	516	100.0	26.6	73.4	13.6	8.7	15.5	3.5	12.0	16.3	6.6	6.0	1.0	5.0	1.7	5.0
Germany	358	100.0	24.9	75.1	4.7	5.9	18.2	8.1	10.1	9.8	15.4	9.5	5.9	3.6	7.0	4.7
Cen. Eur.	194	100.0	11.9	88.1	19.6	9.3	21.1	2.6	18.6	9.3	14.9	3.6	1.5	2.1	3.6	6.7
E. Eur.	139	100.0	20.1	79.9	10.1	8.6	15.1	4.3	10.8	9.4	23.7	4.3	1.4	2.9	3.6	5.0
Oth. For.-born	218	100.0	31.2	68.8	6.9	5.5	15.1	4.1	11.0	17.9	9.6	5.0	2.8	2.3	3.7	5.0
Male-NWNP	4,490	100.0	35.1	64.9	4.2	8.8	11.2	3.2	8.0	12.3	11.9	2.8	0.4	2.4	9.9	3.7
New England																
Both Sexes	11,700	100.0	9.2	90.8	0.6	6.5	39.2	24.2	14.9	8.0	12.8	10.1	5.7	4.4	9.7	3.7
NWNP	4,147	100.0	17.0	83.0	0.6	6.3	27.9	14.5	13.3	8.6	13.6	8.8	4.4	4.3	13.3	4.1
Black	171	100.0	8.2	91.8	0.0	3.5	7.6	2.3	5.3	14.0	9.9	38.0	25.7	12.3	6.4	12.3
For.-born Wh.	4,303	100.0	4.9	95.1	0.8	7.7	47.7	29.7	18.0	6.9	10.9	11.6	7.2	4.5	5.9	3.6
Canada	1,205	100.0	6.1	93.9	0.7	8.5	45.4	29.8	15.6	7.0	10.9	9.5	5.6	3.9	8.7	3.3
Ireland	738	100.0	5.1	94.9	0.9	7.5	28.9	17.6	11.2	13.7	8.0	22.9	18.7	4.2	7.7	5.3
Gt. Britain	488	100.0	2.5	97.5	0.8	5.5	60.7	41.8	18.9	3.5	9.2	10.2	6.1	4.1	5.3	2.3
Scandinavia	281	100.0	9.3	90.7	2.1	9.3	46.6	16.0	30.6	6.0	6.0	15.3	11.7	3.6	2.8	2.5
Oth. W. Eur.	41	—	—	—	—	—	—	—	—	—	—	—	—	—	—	—
So. Eur.	629	100.0	4.0	96.0	1.0	14.3	43.9	29.3	14.6	7.9	11.4	8.1	1.7	6.4	2.4	7.0
Germany	137	100.0	8.0	92.0	0.0	2.9	56.2	33.6	22.6	2.9	10.2	10.2	3.6	6.6	8.0	1.5
Cen. Eur.	221	100.0	1.4	98.6	0.5	1.8	77.8	53.4	24.4	1.8	7.7	5.0	3.2	1.8	2.3	1.8
E. Eur.	465	100.0	4.3	95.7	0.9	4.5	53.8	25.6	28.2	3.7	21.9	5.6	2.4	3.2	4.5	0.9
Oth. For.-born	98	100.0	0.0	100.0	0.0	1.0	66.3	53.1	13.3	4.1	10.2	14.3	0.0	14.3	3.1	1.0
Male-NWNP	3,150	100.0	21.4	78.6	0.8	8.1	27.5	11.9	15.5	10.3	14.0	3.3	1.1	2.2	10.1	4.6
Middle Atlantic																
Both Sexes	32,814	100.0	10.1	89.9	4.5	6.9	29.8	15.2	14.6	9.7	14.4	11.3	6.3	5.0	10.0	3.2
NWNP	12,260	100.0	19.1	80.9	2.6	6.3	25.4	12.1	13.3	11.0	11.7	8.6	4.3	4.3	12.4	2.9
Black	992	100.0	6.8	93.2	0.7	4.9	9.1	2.8	6.3	7.9	8.8	45.9	33.9	12.0	8.7	7.4
For.-born Wh.	11,532	100.0	3.8	96.2	7.7	7.8	34.7	17.8	16.9	8.4	16.1	12.5	7.2	5.2	6.1	2.9

Canada	354	100.0	9.6	90.4	0.6	8.2	29.9	13.6	16.4	11.3	13.6	10.5	5.9	4.5	14.4	2.0
Ireland	1,384	100.0	4.6	95.4	2.0	6.9	17.3	7.7	9.5	16.6	10.0	29.0	21.5	7.4	10.5	3.2
Gt. Britain	1,031	100.0	4.6	95.4	9.4	10.1	33.9	16.2	17.7	7.7	10.5	11.3	7.2	4.1	9.8	2.8
Scandinavia	345	100.0	8.7	91.3	2.3	16.2	25.5	7.5	18.0	10.7	6.1	21.4	18.3	3.2	6.1	2.9
Oth. W. Eur.	246	100.0	10.2	89.8	4.9	8.5	30.9	19.9	11.0	4.5	11.0	19.9	10.2	9.8	8.5	1.6
So. Eur.	2,110	100.0	2.9	97.1	7.2	13.9	28.5	13.2	15.3	14.4	14.7	9.3	0.9	8.4	3.1	6.0
Germany	1,501	100.0	6.5	93.5	2.5	6.8	33.0	16.9	16.2	6.0	20.7	14.1	8.3	5.8	7.9	2.5
Cen. Eur.	2,145	100.0	2.2	97.8	16.6	3.0	45.3	18.3	27.0	4.2	13.2	9.5	6.6	2.9	3.5	2.4
E. Eur.	2,309	100.0	1.4	98.6	8.4	5.7	44.7	30.6	14.1	3.6	25.2	5.8	2.6	3.2	4.0	1.2
Oth. For.-born	107	103.0	2.8	97.2	0.9	1.9	38.3	23.4	15.0	2.8	27.1	14.0	7.5	6.5	8.4	3.7
Male-NWNP	9,702	100.0	23.0	77.0	3.2	7.9	25.2	9.5	15.6	13.3	11.7	2.6	0.5	2.1	10.2	2.9
East North Central																
Both Sexes	28,801	100.0	25.8	74.2	2.8	6.0	23.2	8.1	15.1	9.3	12.4	8.2	4.5	3.8	8.8	3.5
NWNP	12,896	100.0	33.8	66.2	2.2	5.4	17.6	5.9	11.7	9.4	10.8	7.4	4.0	3.4	10.2	3.3
Black	639	100.0	8.9	91.1	3.9	7.5	9.9	3.3	6.6	10.8	8.8	36.0	22.2	13.8	5.6	8.6
For.-born Wh.	6,810	100.0	15.4	84.6	4.8	8.2	32.7	10.0	22.7	9.2	12.3	7.2	4.2	3.1	6.2	4.0
Canada	625	100.0	20.2	79.8	0.8	8.0	24.5	5.3	19.2	10.7	11.8	7.0	3.2	3.8	14.1	2.9
Ireland	363	100.0	10.2	89.8	0.8	9.4	16.0	7.2	8.8	22.6	6.9	16.0	12.4	3.6	10.7	7.4
Gt. Britain	555	100.0	12.8	87.2	10.5	10.3	29.5	7.4	22.2	7.9	9.2	5.8	2.7	3.1	11.4	2.7
Scandinavia	813	100.0	22.6	77.4	5.7	11.6	22.4	5.9	16.5	7.9	10.1	11.6	8.6	3.0	4.3	3.9
Oth. W. Eur.	287	100.0	26.8	73.2	2.4	9.1	25.1	8.4	16.7	5.2	12.2	6.6	4.2	2.4	10.1	2.4
So. Eur.	471	100.0	3.4	96.6	13.4	10.4	27.0	9.3	17.6	19.5	13.8	6.8	0.4	6.4	2.1	3.6
Germany	1,788	100.0	25.6	74.4	2.7	8.4	30.3	10.7	19.6	6.0	11.6	6.7	3.9	2.8	5.9	2.9
Cen. Eur.	1,101	100.0	4.7	95.3	5.9	4.2	50.9	13.0	37.9	6.8	12.4	6.2	3.7	2.5	3.4	5.6
E. Eur.	734	100.0	3.5	96.5	4.2	4.8	47.1	16.5	30.7	8.7	20.6	3.5	1.1	2.5	2.2	5.3
Oth. For.-born	73	100.0	0.0	100.0	1.4	26.0	28.8	11.0	17.8	20.5	15.1	1.4	1.4	0.0	1.4	5.5
Male-NWNP	10,719	100.0	39.6	60.4	2.6	6.5	18.0	4.8	13.2	10.4	9.8	1.8	0.3	1.5	8.0	3.3

TABLE 8A.1 (continued)

	Total						Manufacturing			Trans.	Trade	Personal Services			Other Serv.	NA.
	(N)	Percent	Agr.	Nonag.	Min.	Con.	Total	Nond.	Dur.			Total	Prv. H.	Oth.		
West North Central																
Both Sexes	17,537	100.0	40.5	59.5	2.1	5.5	10.5	5.4	5.1	9.6	11.2	7.5	3.8	3.6	9.8	3.5
NWNP	8,214	100.0	42.6	57.4	1.6	5.5	8.9	4.7	4.2	9.5	10.9	6.3	2.9	3.5	11.3	3.2
Black	499	100.0	11.4	88.6	2.8	5.8	10.4	4.0	6.4	11.0	7.2	32.7	23.2	9.4	9.4	9.2
For.-born Wh.	3,494	100.0	40.0	60.0	4.5	6.7	11.7	5.3	6.4	10.8	10.0	7.0	3.5	3.5	5.9	3.4
Canada	234	100.0	31.6	68.4	1.3	9.0	11.5	5.1	6.4	12.8	13.2	5.1	2.1	3.0	12.8	2.6
Ireland	158	100.0	24.1	75.9	1.9	9.5	6.3	3.2	3.2	21.5	8.2	7.0	4.4	2.5	17.1	4.4
Gt. Britain	197	100.0	30.5	69.5	3.6	4.6	10.7	4.6	6.1	9.6	17.3	8.1	3.0	5.1	10.2	5.6
Scandinavia	1,167	100.0	47.4	52.6	2.7	8.6	10.3	3.9	6.3	6.9	7.4	9.2	5.6	3.6	3.9	3.9
Oth. W. Eur.	107	100.0	51.4	48.6	1.9	8.4	9.3	3.7	5.6	0.9	8.4	3.7	2.8	0.9	14.0	1.9
So. Eur.	177	100.0	1.7	98.3	28.2	5.1	9.0	2.3	6.8	41.2	7.3	4.5	0.0	4.5	0.0	2.8
Germany	857	100.0	50.4	49.6	0.5	4.9	11.9	6.4	5.5	6.8	10.0	6.0	2.7	3.3	6.0	3.6
Cen. Eur.	288	100.0	27.8	72.2	14.6	5.6	22.2	9.0	13.2	9.7	9.0	6.3	2.4	3.8	2.8	2.1
E. Eur.	255	100.0	40.4	59.6	5.5	5.1	14.1	8.2	5.9	8.2	17.3	5.9	1.6	4.3	2.0	1.6
Oth. For.-born	54	100.0	1.9	98.1	3.7	1.9	3.7	3.7	0.0	59.3	13.0	5.6	3.7	1.9	7.4	3.7
Male-NWNP	6,923	100.0	49.2	50.8	1.9	6.5	8.5	3.8	4.7	10.3	10.4	2.0	0.2	1.8	7.7	3.4
South Atlantic																
Both Sexes	20,713	100.0	52.0	48.0	2.2	3.2	12.6	6.4	6.2	5.7	6.5	10.3	7.6	2.6	5.7	2.0
NWNP	10,734	100.0	51.8	48.2	2.1	3.6	14.8	8.5	6.3	6.3	7.9	3.9	1.7	2.2	7.9	1.7
Black	8,521	100.0	58.9	41.1	1.3	2.3	7.2	2.2	5.0	4.5	2.7	18.4	15.6	2.8	2.3	2.4
For.-born Wh.	659	100.0	7.9	92.1	13.1	5.3	30.0	17.9	12.1	7.6	17.6	10.9	6.1	4.9	6.4	1.2
Canada	17	—	—	—	—	—	—	—	—	—	—	—	—	—	—	—
Ireland	51	100.0	7.8	92.2	2.0	15.7	15.7	5.9	9.8	5.9	11.8	21.6	15.7	5.9	15.7	3.9
Gt. Britain	82	100.0	17.1	82.9	17.1	9.8	11.0	1.2	9.8	8.5	9.8	17.1	13.4	3.7	9.8	0.0
Scandinavia	19	—	—	—	—	—	—	—	—	—	—	—	—	—	—	—
Oth. W. Eur.	8	—	—	—	—	—	—	—	—	—	—	—	—	—	—	—

So. Eur.	118	100.0	0.8	99.2	22.0	4.2	27.1	16.1	11.0	13.6	16.1	15.3	0.8	14.4	0.8	0.0
Germany	123	100.0	13.8	86.2	0.0	4.9	32.5	17.1	15.4	9.8	21.1	8.9	7.3	1.6	8.1	0.8
Cen. Eur.	80	100.0	6.3	93.8	41.3	1.3	28.8	12.5	16.3	7.5	7.5	2.5	1.3	1.3	1.3	3.8
E. Eur.	116	100.0	1.7	98.3	10.3	4.3	40.5	30.2	10.3	2.6	34.5	3.4	0.9	2.6	2.6	0.0
Oth. For.-born	45	—	—	—	—	—	—	—	—	—	—	—	—	—	—	—
Male-NWNP	8,762	100.0	53.8	46.2	2.5	4.4	14.4	6.9	7.5	7.3	8.1	1.0	0.2	0.8	6.6	1.7
East South Central																
Both Sexes	14,140	100.0	63.2	36.8	2.3	2.2	7.9	3.0	5.0	4.6	5.6	8.3	6.5	1.8	4.4	1.4
NWNP	7,741	100.0	65.3	34.7	2.3	2.5	8.6	3.4	5.2	4.9	6.5	3.1	1.6	1.6	5.9	0.9
Black	5,640	100.0	66.2	33.8	2.1	1.5	5.3	1.4	3.9	3.5	2.0	15.5	13.7	1.8	2.0	2.1
For.-born Wh.	208	100.0	10.1	89.9	6.7	4.3	18.8	8.2	10.6	6.7	31.3	9.1	4.8	4.3	10.1	2.9
Canada	14	—	—	—	—	—	—	—	—	—	—	—	—	—	—	—
Ireland	23	—	—	—	—	—	—	—	—	—	—	—	—	—	—	—
Gt. Britain	22	—	—	—	—	—	—	—	—	—	—	—	—	—	—	—
Scandinavia	10	—	—	—	—	—	—	—	—	—	—	—	—	—	—	—
Oth. W. Eur.	10	—	—	—	—	—	—	—	—	—	—	—	—	—	—	—
So. Eur.	26	—	—	—	—	—	—	—	—	—	—	—	—	—	—	—
Germany	62	100.0	12.9	87.1	0.0	9.7	32.3	16.1	16.1	8.1	17.7	11.3	6.5	4.8	8.1	0.0
Cen. Eur.	10	—	—	—	—	—	—	—	—	—	—	—	—	—	—	—
E. Eur.	23	—	—	—	—	—	—	—	—	—	—	—	—	—	—	—
Oth. For.-born	8	—	—	—	—	—	—	—	—	—	—	—	—	—	—	—
Male-NWNP	6,505	100.0	67.1	32.9	2.8	3.0	8.7	2.8	5.9	5.3	6.6	0.8	0.1	0.7	4.8	1.0
West South Central																
Both Sexes	13,955	100.0	59.2	40.8	0.9	3.3	7.0	2.1	4.9	5.8	7.6	8.2	5.4	2.8	5.5	2.6
NWNP	7,774	100.0	61.9	38.1	0.8	3.5	6.4	2.1	4.3	5.9	8.9	3.6	1.3	2.3	7.0	2.1
Black	4,075	100.0	60.7	39.3	0.4	2.1	6.7	1.2	5.6	4.4	2.3	18.1	14.5	3.6	1.9	3.4
For.-born Wh.	680	100.0	44.9	55.1	3.8	5.4	7.2	2.9	4.3	7.8	15.3	6.5	2.8	3.7	5.9	3.2

TABLE 8A.1 (continued)

		Total					Manufacturing					Personal Services				
	(N)	Percent	Agr.	Nonag.	Min.	Con.	Total	Nond.	Dur.	Trans.	Trade	Total	Prv. H.	Oth.	Other Serv.	NA.
Canada	23	—	—	—	—	—	—	—	—	—	—	—	—	—	—	—
Ireland	28	—	—	—	—	—	—	—	—	—	—	—	—	—	—	—
Gt. Britain	51	100.0	21.6	78.4	7.8	23.5	7.8	2.0	5.9	17.6	11.8	2.0	0.0	2.0	5.9	2.0
Scandinavia	24	—	—	—	—	—	—	—	—	—	—	—	—	—	—	—
Oth. W. Eur.	37	—	—	—	—	—	—	—	—	—	—	—	—	—	—	—
So. Eur.	80	100.0	28.8	71.3	5.0	3.8	15.0	2.5	12.5	5.0	30.0	3.8	0.0	3.8	3.8	5.0
Germany	162	100.0	55.6	44.4	0.0	3.7	6.2	3.1	3.1	5.6	16.7	4.3	1.2	3.1	8.0	0.0
Cen. Eur.	71	100.0	83.1	16.9	4.2	0.0	2.8	1.4	1.4	2.8	4.2	2.8	2.8	0.0	0.0	0.0
E. Eur.	37	—	—	—	—	—	—	—	—	—	—	—	—	—	—	—
Oth. For.-born	167	100.0	50.9	49.1	3.0	4.8	3.6	1.8	1.8	12.0	7.8	9.6	6.6	3.0	0.6	7.8
Male-NWNP	6,654	100.0	63.3	36.7	1.0	4.0	6.8	2.0	4.9	6.5	8.9	1.2	0.2	1.0	6.0	2.2
Mountain																
Both Sexes	4,333	100.0	35.9	64.1	10.1	5.9	8.5	2.7	5.8	10.7	9.8	7.1	3.0	4.1	8.4	3.7
NWNP	2,065	100.0	42.9	57.1	5.1	5.9	6.6	2.4	4.3	10.4	9.5	6.0	2.2	3.8	10.1	3.5
Black	43	—	—	—	—	—	—	—	—	—	—	—	—	—	—	—
For.-born Wh.	1,089	100.0	26.6	73.4	22.3	6.1	11.1	1.8	9.3	10.7	9.6	7.2	3.1	4.0	3.3	3.2
Canada	85	100.0	31.8	68.2	9.4	3.5	9.4	3.5	5.9	14.1	16.5	5.9	1.2	4.7	7.1	2.4
Ireland	57	100.0	22.8	77.2	24.6	7.0	14.0	1.8	12.3	7.0	3.5	10.5	7.0	3.5	5.3	5.3
Gt. Britain	182	100.0	26.9	73.1	26.9	8.2	6.6	1.1	5.5	8.2	8.2	7.1	2.7	4.4	6.0	1.6
Scandinavia	220	100.0	23.6	76.4	23.6	7.3	9.5	2.3	7.3	8.6	6.4	11.8	5.5	6.4	3.6	5.5
Oth. W. Eur.	34	—	—	—	—	—	—	—	—	—	—	—	—	—	—	—
So. Eur.	170	100.0	20.6	79.4	31.2	3.5	17.1	0.6	16.5	17.6	5.3	3.5	0.6	2.9	0.6	0.6
Germany	116	100.0	31.9	68.1	11.2	5.2	9.5	4.3	5.2	8.6	15.5	8.6	4.3	4.3	4.3	5.2
Cen. Eur.	86	100.0	10.5	89.5	34.9	8.1	20.9	1.2	19.8	8.1	11.6	3.5	1.2	2.3	1.2	1.2
E. Eur.	52	100.0	32.7	67.3	19.2	7.7	5.8	1.9	3.8	9.6	19.2	1.9	0.0	1.9	1.9	1.9
Oth. For.-born	87	100.0	37.9	62.1	12.6	4.6	10.3	0.0	10.3	13.8	6.9	6.9	3.4	3.4	0.0	6.9
Male-NWNP	1,804	100.0	47.2	52.8	5.9	6.7	7.1	2.3	4.8	11.3	8.5	1.8	0.3	1.6	8.0	3.5

Pacific

Both Sexes	8,214	100.0	24.5	75.5	2.9	8.6	15.3	5.5	9.8	11.4	13.2	9.2	3.8	5.4	10.6	4.3
NWNP	3,226	100.0	23.2	76.8	2.6	8.6	13.1	4.2	8.9	11.7	15.2	7.8	2.5	5.4	14.0	3.7
Black	59	100.0	11.9	88.1	3.4	8.5	3.4	0.0	3.4	23.7	3.4	32.2	20.3	11.9	6.8	6.8
For.-born Wh.	2,233	100.0	21.9	78.1	4.1	10.7	17.8	4.9	12.9	12.8	11.4	9.3	4.4	4.9	6.7	5.3
Canada	250	100.0	18.0	82.0	3.2	11.2	14.8	1.2	13.6	10.0	14.4	11.6	4.0	7.6	12.8	4.0
Ireland	165	100.0	17.0	83.0	6.1	9.1	9.7	2.4	7.3	20.6	7.9	10.9	9.1	1.8	9.7	9.1
Gt. Britain	305	100.0	16.4	83.6	5.9	14.4	18.0	7.2	10.8	10.8	10.5	9.5	4.3	5.2	12.1	2.3
Scandinavia	461	100.0	22.8	77.2	2.8	14.3	21.3	3.5	17.8	13.7	8.0	10.2	6.1	4.1	2.6	4.3
Oth. W. Eur.	138	100.0	34.8	65.2	3.6	4.3	15.2	4.3	10.9	4.3	12.3	15.9	4.3	11.6	4.3	5.1
So. Eur.	346	100.0	29.5	70.5	4.9	11.3	14.7	4.9	9.8	15.6	7.2	7.2	1.2	6.1	2.3	7.2
Germany	242	100.0	21.5	78.5	1.7	6.2	22.3	9.9	12.4	10.3	15.3	9.9	6.6	3.3	8.3	4.5
Cen. Eur.	108	100.0	13.0	87.0	7.4	10.2	21.3	3.7	17.6	10.2	17.6	3.7	1.9	1.9	5.6	11.1
E. Eur.	87	100.0	12.6	87.4	4.6	9.2	20.7	5.7	14.9	9.2	26.4	5.7	2.3	3.4	4.6	6.9
Oth. For.-born	131	100.0	26.7	73.3	3.1	6.1	18.3	6.9	11.5	20.6	11.5	3.8	2.3	1.5	6.1	3.8
Male-NWNP	2,686	100.0	27.0	73.0	3.1	10.2	14.0	3.8	10.2	13.0	14.1	3.5	0.4	3.1	11.2	3.8

Appendix 8B: Industrial Distribution for Foreign-born White Workers Reporting Mother Tongue as Italian, Polish, or Yiddish

The main body of this chapter has focused on country/region of birth for immigrant workers. There is, however, a widespread interest in identifying "ethnic groups," particularly among those coming from continental Europe; the respondent's report on mother tongue has usually been the measure used in an attempt to establish this. Although the extent to which the variable successfully identifies all persons in the specific group is open to question, we present here the data on industrial affiliation as reported in the PUS for three major mother tongue categories: Italian, Polish, and Yiddish.

The great majority (83 percent) of immigrant workers from Southern Europe were from Italy. The proportion reporting Italian as mother tongue who were born in Southern Europe is, as one would expect, even higher—98.6 percent. Consequently, the industrial distributions of each of these categories—total born in Southern Europe, total foreign-born reporting Italian mother tongue, and Italian mother tongue reporters born in Southern Europe—are very similar (see Table 8B.1); the distinctive work patterns discussed for Southern Europe in the text—relatively high concentrations in mining, construction, manufacturing, and other personal services—apply equally to those who reported an Italian mother tongue.

The same overlap between birthplace and mother tongue does not occur for the other two categories. Although the proportion reporting Yiddish mother tongue shows a very high geographic concentration—83 percent were born in Eastern Europe—these respondents do not dominate that birthplace origin because only 45 percent of those born in Eastern Europe reported Yiddish as their mother tongue. For those reporting Polish as mother tongue, the overlap is even less notable. As the following table indicates, half were born in Eastern Europe, another one-third in Central Europe, and 15 percent gave Germany as place of birth:

Immigrant Workers 10 Years of Age and Over
Reporting Polish or Yiddish as Mother Tongue, by Place of Birth

	Total	Germany	Central Europe	Eastern Europe	Other
Total all Foreign-born	X	4,988	4,110	4,078	X
Polish Mother Tongue	2,336	353	793	1,172	18
Yiddish Mother Tongue	2,192	18	331	1,816	27

Although the sample is small, those reporting Polish mother tongue and birth in Germany (col. 5, Table 8B.1) show an interesting difference from other Polish mother tongue reporters: they are more likely to be in agriculture and less likely to be in manufacturing. Their proportions in these industries fall roughly midway between the total Polish mother tongue reporters (col. 4) and the total German born (col. 11). Moreover, their residence in the United States differs markedly from the total Polish mother tongue group—25 percent in the Northeast and 70 percent in the Midwest, as compared to 56 percent and 39 percent—and they are on average considerably older (data not shown). Both of these attributes suggest an earlier immigration date, a factor that may be associated with their differential industry distribution.

Those reporting Polish mother tongue born in Central Europe (col. 6) differ from others reporting Polish primarily in the high proportion in nondurable goods manufactures, a proportion that raises the total in manufacturing to a level much higher than that for any other group in Table 8B.1. Because, however, concentration in nondurable goods also distinguishes them from others with a similar birthplace (col. 12), and neither 1910 residence nor age is notably out of line with the general picture, the present level of analysis offers no hypothesis on factors associated with this concentration.

As noted above, one-half of immigrant workers reporting Polish mother tongue were born in Eastern Europe. Not surprisingly, therefore, distributions for these two categories (cols. 4 and 7) are quite similar. The industrial distribution of Eastern European-born Polish reporters differs substantially, however, from the total Eastern European group (col. 13) for several important industrial segments. Because the Yiddish-speaking component of Eastern Europeans is even larger than the Polish-speaking, we will discuss these groups jointly.

Among those reporting Yiddish mother tongue, differences in origin are not associated with differences in industrial affiliation (cols. 8, 9, and 10 are quite similar) and they are not associated with differences in destination: well over 80 percent of both origin categories resided in the Northeast, primarily in the Middle Atlantic division (data not shown).

In the context of this chapter, with its focus on differential industry concentration by place of birth, the most interesting aspects of Table 8B.1 are the variations between cols. 7 and 10, the Polish and Yiddish mother tongue components of immigrants from Eastern Europe. Together, these two groups include 73 percent of Eastern European workers in the United States in 1910, and the substantial differences between them illuminate further the distribution for all Eastern Europeans. The concentrations in mining and in durable goods manufacturing are associated with Polish-speakers; the concentrations in nondurable goods and in trade are associated with those reporting Yiddish as mother tongue.

TABLE 8B.1

Foreign-born Workers 10 Years of Age and Over with Selected Mother Tongues, by Industry and Place of Birth, Both Sexes

	(1)	(2)	(3)	(4)	(5)	(6)	(7)	(8)	(9)	(10)	(11)	(12)	(13)
	Italian Mother Tongue		Total Born So. Eur.	Polish Mother Tongue				Yiddish Mother Tongue			Total Born in		
Industry 1910	Total	Born So. Eur.		Total	Born Germany	Born Cen. Eur.	Born E. Eur.	Total	Born Cen. Eur.	Born E. Eur.	Ger-many	Cen. Eur.	East Europe
Total (N)	3,483	3,435	4,127	2,336	353	793	1,172	2,192	331	1,816	4,988	4,110	4,078
Percentage	100.0	100.0	100.0	100.0	100.0	100.0	100.0	100.0	100.0	100.0	100.0	100.0	100.0
Agr.	5.6	5.6	6.5	5.9	14.2	3.4	5.1	0.4	0.0	0.4	24.1	6.5	5.4
Nonag.	94.4	94.4	93.5	94.1	85.8	96.6	94.9	99.6	100.0	99.6	75.9	93.5	94.6
Min.	10.9	10.3	9.1	10.4	6.2	8.6	13.0	0.1	0.0	0.1	2.1	13.1	6.7
Con.	13.4	13.5	12.0	4.8	9.1	3.4	4.5	5.6	3.3	6.2	6.8	3.6	5.4
Mfg.	26.6	26.9	27.7	51.0	39.9	59.0	48.8	44.3	40.2	45.2	27.1	44.6	42.5
Nond.	11.8	11.9	13.3	19.6	12.7	29.9	14.6	36.4	30.2	37.7	12.2	16.9	24.8
Dur.	14.9	15.0	14.4	31.4	27.2	29.1	34.2	7.8	10.0	7.5	14.9	27.7	17.8
Trans.	14.4	14.5	15.1	6.5	6.2	5.9	7.1	2.0	2.1	1.9	6.4	5.5	5.0
Trade	12.3	12.3	13.3	10.9	11.9	9.0	11.6	36.1	38.4	35.7	14.8	12.3	24.1
Prs. Ser.	8.2	8.2	8.2	5.2	4.8	5.4	5.2	4.7	6.3	4.4	9.1	7.6	5.3
Prv. H.	0.9	0.8	0.9	3.2	3.1	3.2	3.2	1.2	3.9	0.7	5.2	5.0	2.1
Oth.	7.4	7.5	7.3	2.0	1.7	2.3	2.0	3.6	2.4	3.7	3.9	2.7	3.1
Oth. Ser.	2.6	2.6	2.5	2.1	3.4	2.5	1.4	6.0	8.8	5.3	6.8	3.3	3.7
NA	5.9	5.9	5.4	3.3	4.2	2.8	3.3	0.9	0.9	0.8	2.8	3.4	2.0

NOTE: As Appendix 8C, this chapter, shows, Romania has been included in Eastern Europe; as a result the number of persons reporting Yiddish mother tongue is higher in Eastern (and lower in Central) Europe here than in other chapters and in Appendix B of this volume.

314

Relative to total distributions in the three divisions where the samples include over 100 cases—New England, Middle Atlantic, and East North Central—the patterns tend to be similar; the Polish mother tongue group's concentration in mining is particularly striking in the Middle Atlantic states, while its concentration in durable goods manufacturing, although relatively high in all three divisions, is greatest in the East North Central; for Yiddish-speakers, the proportion in nondurables is about average in New England, but extremely high in the other divisions, while trade, which engages 33 percent of those in the Middle Atlantic area, shows even higher proportions for the small samples in other divisions.

These distinct differences in patterns of employment for immigrants from Eastern Europe according to reported mother tongue appear to provide further support for the importance of chain migration.

Appendix 8C: Country Content of Foreign-born Groups

Data for the foreign-born presented in this chapter refer only to persons whose race was reported as "white." Table 8C.1 shows the country content for each of the first nine foreign-born groups used in this chapter. Percentages in the last column are based on the sample frequencies presented in the 1910 PUS documentation (Strong et al. 1989, pp. 155–156). These frequencies include all cases reporting a specified country of birth regardless of race; but for the countries in groups 1–9 virtually all persons had "white" as race, so the proportions shown can be considered a good reflection of the country content of our groups. They are not, however, a precise reflection because they include all cases, whereas the data presented here are only for persons 10 years of age and over who were workers in 1910. Insofar as there are substantial age-sex differences among the countries within a given group, the within-group proportions in this chapter may differ from those shown below, but it is highly unlikely that significant differences exist. An early tabulation for white workers separated Russians from other Eastern Europeans and Italians from other Southern Europeans; in that tabulation Russians were 93.2 percent and Italians 84.0 percent of the respective totals.

Group 10 includes workers from all other foreign countries, but because these countries include substantial proportions of persons of "other races," the documentation frequencies cannot be used as an indicator. The early tabulation referred to above separated those from Western Hemisphere countries (except Canada) from others; over half of the residual group come from the Western Hemisphere, and it seems safe to assume that at least those in the West South Central and Western states (half the total group) have come predominantly from Mexico.

TABLE 8C.1

Country Content of Foreign-born Groups

Group Title and Reported Countries Included	Percentage of Group Total in Specified Country
1. Canada	100.0
Canada	100.0
2. Ireland	100.0
Ireland	100.0
3. Great Britain	100.0
England	72.5
Scotland	20.7
Wales	6.7
4. Scandinavia	100.0
Sweden	47.5
Norway	28.1
Denmark	14.4
Finland	10.0
Iceland	0.0
5. Other Western Europe	100.0
Switzerland	30.2
France	28.6
Holland	27.9
Belgium	12.4
Luxemburg	0.9
6. Southern Europe	100.0
Italy	85.9
Greece	7.2
Portugal	4.3
Spain	1.4
Atlantic Islands	1.0
Azores	0.2
7. Germany	100.0
Germany	100.0
German Poland	0.0
8. Central Europe	100.0
Austria	67.8
Hungary	31.0
Austria-Hungary	1.0
Bohemia	0.2
Austrian Poland	0.1
Croatia	0.0
9. Eastern Europe	100.0
Russia	93.3
Romania	3.9
Poland	1.5
Bulgaria	0.6
Montenegro	0.2
Russian Poland	0.2
Serbia	0.1
10. Other Foreign-born	See text above
Persons reported as "white" born in all other foreign countries, including Puerto Rico. Excludes "U.S. citizen, [born] abroad."	

Appendix 8D

TABLE 8D.1
Industry Groups

Nomenclature in this Chapter	1980 Census Industrial Classification Equivalent (Codes)[a]
1. Agriculture (Agr.)	1. Agriculture, Forestry, and Fisheries (010–031)
2. Nonagriculture (Nonag.)	2. Sum of All Categories Below (040–990)
3. Mining (Min.)	3. Mining (040–050)
4. Construction (Con.)	4. Construction (060)
5. Manufacturing (Mfg.)	5. Manufacturing (100–392)
6. Nondurable (Nond.)	6. Nondurable Goods (100–222)
7. Durable (Dur.)	7. Durable Goods (230–392)
8. Transportation (Trans.)	8. Transportation, Communications, and Other Public Utilities (400–472)
9. Trade	9a. Wholesale Trade (500–571) 9b. Retail Trade (580–691)
10. Personal Services (Prs. Serv.)	10. Personal Services (761–791)
11. Private Households (Prv. H.)	11. Private Households (761)
12. Other Personal Services (Oth.)	12. Other Personal Services (762–791)
13. Other Services (Other Serv.)	13a. Finance, Insurance, and Real Estate (700–712) 13b. Business and Repair Services (721–760) 13c. Entertainment and Recreation Services (800–802) 13d. Professional and Related Services (812–892) 13e. Public Administration (900–932)
14. NA	14. Industry Not Reported (990)

[a] SOURCE: U.S. Bureau of the Census 1982.

AFTERWORD

AMERICA'S IMMIGRANTS IN THE 1910 CENSUS MONOGRAPH: WHERE CAN WE WHO DO IT DIFFERENTLY GO FROM HERE?

Ewa Morawska

A S HE SET out to write a history of immigrants in America, Oscar Handlin realized that "immigrants *were* American history," and since his classic *The Uprooted* (1951), immigration and ethnicity have become permanent themes in mainstream American historiography. Earlier, studies of the diversity of immigrants' lifestyles and institutions, and prognoses about the pace of their assimilation to the dominant society and culture, formulated by University of Chicago scholars at the beginning of the century, laid the foundations of contemporary American sociology (R. E. Park 1916; R. E. Park and Miller 1969 [1921]; Bulmer 1980; Persons 1987; Lal 1983).

In the last two-and-a-half decades, newly intensified immigration (nearly 20 million entrants since 1965, not counting *indocumentados;* the majority from Asian and South American countries) reinvigorated interest among social scientists in immigrants' adaptation to American society, the educational and occupational opportunities they encounter, as well as their own impact on national and regional economies and on the ecology of American cities. Immigration studies, written and taught in college classrooms, have been proliferating, and a section on this field in the American Sociological Association is quickly growing in membership.

A century before, after the flow from Western Europe abated, the two and a half decades preceding World War I witnessed the arrival on American shores of over 17 million people, mostly from the ethnically differentiated lands of Southern and Eastern Europe, and, as a corollary of this influx, accelerated expansion of American industries and urban development. The ways in which newcomers accommodated themselves in the environments where they settled have attracted the attention, counting "from Handlin," of what is now three generations of immigration historians. They have produced a plethora of studies dealing with one or more immigrant groups in particular locations, on issues such as—to mention the most researched themes—chain migration and spatial mobility out of and within the United States; residential clustering and the development of ethnic institutions, both religious and secular; group support networks in the neighborhoods and at work; family and kin economic strategies; occupational mobility; educational achievement (of immigrants' children); and, more recently, gender, and specifically women's roles in the private and public spheres of immigrants' lives. Of course, immigrants and their offspring appear also—whether "implicit" or identified as such—in the investigations of other historical subfields covering many aspects of American society: as part of the demographic cohorts in the American population, as urban residents, workers, school attendees, family members, churchgoers, voters, or recipients of charity.

The 1910 census monograph *After Ellis Island* adds to this large and varied collection of studies on American society at a time when the country was undergoing profound economic and demographic transformation. The volume will certainly please demographers: reports on infant mortality, fertility, and the family structure of black and white native-born Americans, and immigrant groups recently incorporated into the American population, have been prepared by a highly qualified team, and bring new and useful information for specialists on this period as well as for comparativists. Without doubt, the book will also find a permanent place among others of a similar genre, to be used in time-series comparisons of national-level data: with the 1920 census monograph on immigrants and their children (Carpenter 1969 [1927]) and the 1980 census report on racial and ethnic groups in America (Lieberson and Waters 1988; Bean and Tienda 1987; Farley and Allen 1987). Most directly, however, it adds to a collection of studies on turn-of-the-century immigration, and I was asked to focus on this particular contribution as an ethnic historian.

The source and methods of *After Ellis Island* are of a specific kind, and so are the findings: (1) the monograph presents a general overview of the American population in 1910, based on a national random sample drawn from the manuscript schedules of the census conducted in that year; (2) it provides descriptions of the racial and nationality groups—the "average [native-born] Americans," the "average Irish (Germans, Italians, and so on)," including those identified by mother tongue, which in previously published summary tabulations appear, or *disappear*, rather, under the names of their multiethnic countries of birth—by selected characteristics that the census inquired about; and (3) for the major (largest) groups, it offers statistical analyses performed on individual-level data, identifying factors recorded in the census schedules that may have accounted for intergroup differences on measures such as infant mortality, fertility, family and household structure, residential segregation, and school enrollment.

While the authors of particular chapters do not spell out the methodological premises of their analyses, they share the positivist approach to the study of social reality dominant in American sociology. Historically minded researchers have traditionally used different ways of collecting and interpreting data, and of arriving at a more general knowledge. Obviously, the historically minded among social scientists are a quite varied group, who use diverse lenses and methods of investigation—micro- and macroscopic, single case and comparative, interpretative and variable-oriented—and engage in polemics on methodological issues (occasionally pretty sharp, e.g., Zunz 1987). But in this heterogeneous group there exists, it seems, a minimum consensus on a few epistemological basics (though they may be spelled out in more or less stringent versions).

One is the indispensable "variable" in history-sensitive research: time (see Abbott 1983, 1988; Aminzade 1992; Isaac and Griffen 1989). The specificity of the source the present volume has relied on—a single census—permits the inference of longitudinal changes only from cross-sectional data analyses (the authors of particular chapters acknowledge that limited information recorded in the census and its "snapshot" nature impose considerable, if unavoidable, constraints). The other fundamental of social-historical investigation is a general heuristic conception of how to seek understanding of the social world, be it by means of single case or comparative, interpretative, or variable-oriented methods. This guiding idea has two aspects, both concerning the rules of explanatory or interpretative construction, but at its different stages.

The first emphasizes as necessary (though not sufficient) a multi-level contextual approach, seeking to specify the set of conditions under which a given interpretation will best account for the phenomena studied; the (re-)constructed contexts can have a more or less macro- or microscopic range, depending on the researcher's theoretical assumptions, the questions investigated, and the available evidence. (On the central place of contextual analysis in sociohistorical and historical sociological research, see Himmelfarb 1987; Ragin 1987; Skocpol 1984; Sztompka 1986). The other aspect of this heuristic guideline suggests a preferred way to acquire increasingly general knowledge about conditions or causal configurations that shape social processes; namely, by an accumulation of compare-and-contrast-type contextual investigations of diverse social settings in which people act. Such investigations can well include, as building blocks in construction, analyses of varied sorts of location- and time-specific sampled data arranged in categories that can be adjusted in size should concrete, historical reasons suggest it. (The authors of *After Ellis Island* acknowledge that the adequate—that is, large enough—sample sizes required for statistical operations used in their studies often imposed historically "insensitive" analytical categories.)

I am a committed adherent to and practitioner of the historical approach to the study of social worlds as outlined above, and so when the editor of the volume prepared in so different a manner asked me to write the introduction to it (it grew and swelled, and eventually became the concluding chapter), I was at first hesitant. A beaver among rabbits, I thought, praising carrots and thinking fish. Our initial exchange, after I browsed through the manuscript, seemed to confirm my feeling that mixing species did not make sense. To my announcement "but we [immigration historians] have already known much of it, so what's in there for us?" (there is a good deal, as it turned out upon my subsequent readings, about which below), she replied, obviously pleased: "It is very well then, you have known these things from local studies and now you have a confirmation!" "No no, the other way round"—said the beaver to the rabbit—"it is you [national random samplers] who can relax when your findings are confirmed by our studies."

Eventually though, in part she convinced me and in part I convinced myself that assuming this task would be a good thing. On the part of the editor and authors, the invitation shows appreciation for historical studies, and more generally, for different research methodology. On my part, I reasoned, it might be a valuable exercise to try and see what a beaver-like immigration historian-sociologist could find in this representative national record, reflect on, and possibly turn into research in her own kind of way.

The 1910 census monograph does indeed "confirm" at a national level a good deal of what has been reported in historical studies of turn-of-the-century racial and ethnic groups in various localities in different regions of the United States. For instance, it demonstrates that the existential circumstances of blacks were on the whole significantly more disadvantaged than the immigrants' situations, as reflected in such important areas of life opportunities as infant mortality and schooling, and that foreign-borns from "new" immigration groups had many children, and that those numbers decreased—apparently adjusted somehow—in the American-born generation, approaching the lower fertility rates of the "old" immigrant and native-born white native-parentage population. It shows, too, that "new" immigrants were at that time highly endogamous, and that in the initial phase of their stay in American cities they kept boarders, usually of the same nationality; that they tended to form ethnic residential clusters, which in the bigger cities with large numbers of immigrants were separate from the settlements of native-born Americans; and that they also concentrated in particular industries, and, within these, often in specific branches, relying for that purpose on ethnic support networks they created themselves, commonly with encouragement from employers, and which often incorporated the next generation.

However, it is not the confirmation by reports based on a national random sample of some familiar general trends that I find exciting about *After Ellis Island.* And not its conclusion that, on the whole, ethnicity mattered in the America of 1910, either. Rather—my inclination brings out in the offering what is personally most tasty—it is what I see reflected throughout the monograph: the immense differentiation and complexity of American society in 1910, without and also with all the intricate statistical "controls." By suggesting that the same variable may operate differently for one group than for another, and that similar sets of factors may have varied effects contingent on what it is that they are supposed to exert an effect on, the reports, or the implications thereof, beg the questions of "why" and "how" of the contexts—the domain proper, the fishpond of history-minded research.

What follows summarizes the major findings of particular reports contained in the volume and presents a selection from my reading notes of "whys" and "hows" that could be taken up as possible themes or directions for future research on the early twentieth-century American immigration and ethnicity. Some of these research questions can draw, or redraw rather, on the 1910 census Public Use Sample (PUS) data file available at the Population Studies Center at the University of Pennsylvania, while some others would require gathering, and incorporating, additional information from external sources. While commenting on the reports' findings, I also noted possibilities of different theoretical and methodological approaches to particular problems dealt with in the book; some of these reformulations, again, can be worked out with the already existing 1910 PUS census data, while others would require more, and different, information. All that follows is deliberately selective, subjective, and unrepresentative: another immigration historian, I am sure, would have selected many, and other, different fish.

Infant Mortality

Although there have been studies of infant mortality in research on turn-of-the-century immigration (besides contemporary reports, e.g., Lieberson 1980; Dwork 1981; Toll 1982; Zunz 1982), this problem, unlike fertility, for instance, has not been part of a shared "consciousness" in the field. And it should be, I became convinced after having read the Preston et al. chapter in this volume, because of the breadth of its economic and sociocultural contexts and implications. Since I have undergone a "turn of mind" of sorts, like a good convert I will first and disproportionately dwell on this theme. (Let me also note for those interested that comparable analyses of infant mortality in different racial and ethnic groups, based on a national sample from the 1900 census, can be found in Preston and Haines 1991; since that census did not ask about mother tongue, however, Eastern European nationalities were subsumed under much broader country categories).

Having children overseas (the analyses distinguish between children born to mothers who married before and after coming to the United States) was more hazardous—the report indicates—than having them here, even in urban immigrant ghettos, whose unsanitary and grim living conditions so appalled contemporary social workers (e.g., Riis 1957 [1890]; de Forest and Veiller 1903; Woods and Kennedy 1911, 1913; Breckenridge and Abbott 1910. See also Ward 1971 [1925].). But once in this country, immigrant parents generally had a better chance of seeing their newborns survive by settling away from the big cities in the Northeast (New York City turned out to be the most deadly). Still, their babies died at rates greater than children born to native-born white Americans of native parentage; infant mortality in the "new" immigrant groups (Polish, Italian, French Canadian) was also higher than that among "old," Western European, stock.

Controlling for socioeconomic position and residence eliminated, that is, rendered statistically insignificant, most of the original differences in rates of infant mortality among nationality groups, suggesting the reported variation was effected primarily by "structural" rather than "cultural" (child care practices) factors. Since the authors of particular reports in *After Ellis Island* differently operationalized the general concepts used in the interpretations of findings, the reader should be reminded that the mortality chapter included literacy (not necessarily English) and English-speaking ability together with occupational status and residence as socioeconomic or structural influences, and used the thus-constructed cluster as a control to see whether cultural (or "ethnic"; in Chapter 3 this concept implies value and behavioral patterns of the old-country origin, or non-American) effects would persist.

Interestingly, however, given the above findings, in the 1920 census report analysed by Niles Carpenter (1969 [1927]), Polish and Italian immigrants still had higher infant mortality than others. By that time, factors found in 1910 as having significantly depressed infant mortality (increased length of stay in the United States and ability to speak English) should have exerted their influence owing simply to the passage of time. The mass flow from Europe almost stopped with the outbreak of war in 1914 and never resumed after 1918 on a larger scale, and so the group caught by the 1920 national census was basically the same as in 1910, plus the arrivals between 1910 and 1914, and the now-adult foreign-born men and women who came to America as children at the turn of the century but by 1920 were already married and parents. Unless this discrepancy is due to some simple (or complex) technical problem, such as incomparability of 1910 and 1920 data or methods of analysis, looking into the underpinnings of this disappearing/reappearing social problem may be worth the trouble for someone.

One possible avenue of inquiry, suggested by contemporary sources, might be a closer inspection of the acculturation dynamics of group health care practices (potentially relevant for infant and other kinds of mortality). For instance, a Russian doctor in Chicago reported during World War I that Slavic immigrants frequently used the services of "advertising quacks," whom they did not distinguish from regular physicians (Davis 1921, p. 146). The former were usually American or had American-sounding names (a perusal of the foreign-language press of that period indicates that such advertisements were indeed quite common). This "cultural effect" could be interpreted as an absorption of certain parts of mainstream American "consumer" culture into Slavic immigrant group health care practices. Rather than assimilation—a concept that in the classical model presumes a discrepancy between the immigrant (old-country) and dominant or American sociocultural patterns, and the eventual dislodgement of the former—this development may be called *ethnicization* (cf. Greene 1975; Sarna 1978). Ethnicization in this context suggests blending, in varying configurations depending on the concrete historical circumstances, the dominant American and the immigrant group's own traditions and lifestyles. What is interesting in the case of the "quacks" just described, however, and perhaps worth looking at in other contexts as well, is that the contribution of the dominant (American) culture to the well-being of new immigrants, and concretely to their infant mortality rates, might have been harmful (following the classical assimilation model, the report implicitly assumed the dominant American culture to have been uniformly beneficial).

It is of interest to note in this context contemporary ethnographic reports on some southern Italian folkways related to pregnancy and child care that persisted in the immigrant settlements in America (Davis 1921; Woodbury 1925; Williams 1938). Unless the 1910 PUS mortality results for Italians or ethnographic reports are unrepresentative for some (which?) segments of this ethnic group, could it be that customs reportedly still widespread in the Italian-American colonies, such as avoiding bathing during pregnancy, and the waning practice of having intercourse with one's wife as she was going into labor "for strength" (oy gevalt! exclaimed in terror my elderly Jewish friend from New York upon hearing this, as if confirming the divergent health practices of these two immigrant groups); or a quite stubborn custom, feeding babies very sweet black coffee "to make them feel good" (nursing mothers sipped this beverage, too), were health-neutral cultural residuals? Someone surely should look into this much more closely (on German-American folkways in child care that diverged from contemporary medical standards, see Aykroyd 1971).

But for some other groups investigated in Chapter 3, "ethnic effects" persisted despite controls for socioeconomic position, residential location, literacy, and speaking English: the Jews (in both generational groups), who scored much lower than anyone else; the French Canadians (foreign- and U.S.-born), who scored the opposite; and the Irish immigrant families, whose babies still died at significantly higher rates. For each group a different conjunction of factors, both, to stay with the terminology used in the volume, cultural and structural in character, seems to have been at work.

Irish immigrants, as the authors note, were reported in generally very poor health by contemporary surveys in big northeastern cities where they heavily concentrated, and especially so Irish immigrant females, who frequently suffered from tuberculosis, an illness known as a "baby-killer." This predicament, combined with the disadvantages of big-city living and congested housing, accounted, according to this report, for the persistently high infant mortality in this group, despite socioeconomic controls. On the basis of contemporary and current studies, more factors could be added to this unfortunate configuration. Alcoholism, which the authors dismissed too early, I believe, was widespread among Irish immigrant city-dwellers, and women appeared to drink more in this country, at least in places such as Boston or New York, than in their native Ireland (see Diner 1983 for a discussion of contemporary reports; see also Bales 1944). In addition, as various historical studies on the Irish family structure show (see Miller 1985 for a review), and Chapter 5 (on the family and household structure) in this volume reports, too, there were among Irish immigrants at the beginning of the century disproportionately high, as compared with other groups, numbers of female-headed households (Appendix 3B, in Chapter 3, controls for widowed/husband absent status of foreign-born women, but not for the Irish, or any other immigrant groups specifically). Add to this, from the local sources, the following: widespread poverty among Irish female household heads, especially those deserted and widowed, and very likely with children, that occasionally pushed them to beggary (noted, for example, in New York); in complete families, apparently common wife battering (probably related to alcohol abuse); and perhaps also the fact—reported in the fertility chapter—that Irish women had their children comparatively late in life, which could have made both mothers and babies biologically weaker. Such disadvantages, even when fragmentarily combined, seem sufficient to have kept immigrant Irish infant mortality high, and there could have been others. For instance, how popular among Irish mothers was a "child care practice," reported by a New York social worker (Herzfeld 1905), of adding a small daily portion of whiskey to their babies' milk, to keep them quiet? Or a different question, which could lead to an entire project: since local studies (Doyle 1976) reported Irish immigrants settled in the Midwest at the turn of the century as generally having much better living conditions and economic situations than their compatriots in the East Coast urban centers (and where, we may add, the temperance movement was particularly strong), could such intragroup comparative opportunity advantages have translated into significantly lower infant mortality rates? The constellation of factors potentially relevant for infant mortality seems to have been different yet in small Montana mining towns: there, while mortality among Irish immigrants was reported the highest of all groups, it was apparently men, not women, whose health condition was poorer, and Irish families were quite stable and congenial (Emmons 1989; on the demographic characteristics of immigrant and native-born American miners and their families in the Pennsylvania anthracite region in 1860–1880s, see Haines 1977).

And now for the Jews. That they had a generally low level of mortality in comparison with groups among whom they settled has been systematically reported since the nineteenth century, from Europe (including Russia) as well as the United States (see Dwork 1981 for a review of research), and so the findings from the 1910 census are not much of a surprise. The authors also provide a cogent discussion of factors, reported in various studies conducted in American cities at the beginning of the century, as likely to have accounted for this phenomenon regarding mortality of infants: the generally good health of Jewish mothers (considerably better, for that matter, than of Jewish men—cf. the 1902 Charity Organization Survey in New York City—cit. after Dwork 1981; Schereschewsky 1915); the low occurrence of out-of-home work during pregnancy; breast-feeding practices; unusual attention to hygienic and nutritious food, motivated in great part by religious norms; and, perhaps framing all this, several hundred years of experience with the hazards of urban life (Fishberg 1901; interestingly, Yemenite Jews, who had traditionally lived in agricultural settings where tuberculosis was almost unknown, upon settling in American cities were found to suffer from this disease at considerably higher rates than Ashkenazi Jewish immigrants from Europe).

Since the Preston et al. report did not test interaction effects of city type and particular ethnic groups (should anyone wish to, it can be done on the 1910 PUS census data set), we don't know whether residence in New York City, generally found to increase infant mortality rates, would show a similarly negative effect in the Jewish group; or would it be outbalanced perhaps by positive health and child care practices? Surveys conducted on the Lower East Side of New York City at the turn of the century indicate that Jewish infant mortality was the lowest among all immigrant groups there (1890, 1903—reviewed in Dwork 1981), and my own rough estimation from comparing the above with nationwide Jewish figures reported for 1890 (Billings 1894) seems to suggest that for Jewish babies New York was no more deadly than other urban locations in the country. It might have been that because sanitary conditions were so bad on the Lower East Side *and* because the Jewish community in New York City was institutionally much more developed than in other places (including German-Jewish organizations, well-established and solidly middle class by the 1900s, and active in community and "Americanization" work among East Europeans), redoubled efforts were made, using group resources, to combat the risk of life-threatening diseases: by 1900, one-half of the city's bathhouses were in Jewish hands (and crowded), and neighborhood dispensaries proliferated (Bernheimer 1948; Dwork 1981). A recent study of how such neighborhood miniclinics, providing both general and obstetrical care, functioned in New York before World War I, and who used them, showed that while other new immigrants were hesitant, Jews—especially women—came very eagerly (Dye 1987; on deeply mistrustful attitudes toward medical doctors and hospitals among Slavic and Italian immigrants in that period, see Herzfeld 1905; Davis 1921; Williams 1938).

French Canadians were found at the opposite end of the spectrum, with the highest infant mortality in the foreign-born group, about equal to that of the blacks, who also remained disadvantaged despite all available controls. Using existing historical studies (especially Hareven 1982), the authors explain this result primarily by factors of structural or derivative character (although it could be argued that behind the structural lay cultural motives): a higher proportion of women in the labor force than among other immigrant groups (and employed also during pregnancy), and, resulting from it, a short period of breast-feeding and reduced time for child care. Outside employment of women during pregnancy and infant care appears to have had an evident negative impact on small children's survival (see Chapter 3, Tables 3.2–3.5). Given these telltale data, the effects of women's employment should have been looked at separately in the regression models (Table 3.8). Preston et al. explained that the reason for this omission was that the variable could not be sufficiently specified: outside employment led to increased risk of infant mortality, but it could also work in the reverse direction—from child death to women's joining the labor force (see, however, the 1900 census analysis in Preston and Haines 1991). But did working outside the home have the same bad influence on mortality levels of babies born to immigrant mothers in other ethnic groups—for instance, Hungarians and Lithuanians—who showed (Appendix B, this volume) high rates of female employment similar to the French Canadians, and similar high rates of infant mortality? Here's a good research question that could be started from the 1910 PUS data set (but see below for further elements of this puzzle).

Or take the Italians. It is widely assumed (and Preston et al. repeat, explaining factors that could have contributed to the elimination of statistically significant difference in infant mortality between Italians and the dominant-American group) that married Italian women did not work outside the home. Indeed, various censuses from the period record much lower rates of employment among Italian than among other married immigrant women. But local studies have shown that Italian wives, particularly on the East Coast, regularly worked in unreported seasonal jobs, especially in the canneries. They were accompanied, and at the same time socially supervised, as custom required, by a whole network of cousins, aunts, and children, while small babies slept nearby under the watchful eyes of the whole caring crowd (Yans-McLaughlin 1977). If unrecorded by census takers, women's employment obviously cannot be considered for its effects on child care in a report like this monograph.

It is possible, however, to expand the PUS 1910 census data set by adding contextual variables to check on potentially significant effects "above" the individual-level information. In the case discussed here, it might be useful to introduce the type of industry(ies) prevailing in the county (or city, if it is large) and proportions of women employed, to get a general "check" on the regional/local economic structure. (In Philadelphia, for example, 28 percent of all women 16+ years of age were in the labor force in 1900, 15 percent in Buffalo, but only 8 percent in Pittsburgh: Golab 1977; see also Stern 1987.) Interesting also could be a variable on types of occupations available to women: a comparison of mortality indexes for different occupational groups under "women employed" in Table 3.2 of the mortality chapter suggests that certain jobs might have been less detrimental than others for infant mortality. In addition, on the basis of what has been reported in previous studies of the matter, some other measures could be added, such as housing congestion (proportions of families, or of people, per house or apartment); perhaps also, in immigrant sections, numbers of dispensaries or Anglo-Protestant-sponsored settlement houses with their Americanization programs in health and hygiene; and, finally, some measure of intragroup ethnic institutional "density," particularly in regard to social work and educational resources. Such contextual variables could well contribute more than the one (and only) used in the mortality chapter: median state earnings, which did not have statistically significant effects for the foreign-born groups in any case. And not at all surprisingly, considering the enormous fluctuations in American industries that employed immigrants, especially at the unskilled level. This chronic arrhythmia was reflected directly in workers' biweekly paychecks, but not in state wage censuses gathered from averaged reports by manufacturing companies. A historically more accurate indicator of the "structural context" of the economic well-being of immigrant daily laborers and semiskilled industrial workers in that period could be the "average number of days in operation [factory] per annum," data regularly published by the Labor Department.

Fertility

Like its predecessor, Chapter 4 brings more detailed demographic information on the subject matter than has been so far available in published reports of a similar kind; in particular, by accounting for both age and parity, it provides a much finer description of the fertility experience of the women. It is a pity that the authors included for comparisons neither French Canadian nor black women—two groups whose record was so unusual in infant mortality. A research project extending comparisons by looking at these women would certainly be worthwhile, and could be done from the 1910 PUS census data set (perhaps even more analyses beyond straight fertility rates would be possible on "little groups" reported in Appendix B, this volume?).

According to the reported findings, patterns of birth by age and parity among immigrant groups of Western European origin, and among native-born white Americans of native parentage (the comparative reference group for all others), looked very much alike, and fertility levels in both groups indicate the practice of some form of birth control. On the other side of the spectrum among new immigrant groups, Poles and Italians had similar, high marital fertility (in addition, both Poles and Italians married much earlier than members of "old," Western European and native white American groups, so the former's total fertility scored even higher). After controlling for urban/rural residence and father's occupational position, duration in the United States, and ability to speak English, urban living was shown to have had the strongest effect in reducing fertility for all ethnic groups (including native-born white Americans of native parentage). But even after introducing all these controlling variables, intergroup differences remained quite large: in making babies, ethnicity clearly mattered (similar results were reported in Detroit by Zunz 1982).

Readers should keep in mind, however, that the definitional looseness of the concept of ethnicity employed in Chapter 4 allows for different interpretations of the reported "ethnic effects": it could be some combination of religious, pre-emigration folk beliefs and practices, or—the product of ethnicization—a mélange of the above with elements absorbed from American mass culture. A more general comment concerning the underlying theoretical assumptions and the choice of interpretative frameworks used by this and other reports in *After Ellis Island* may be of interest here. The book does not proceed from an explicit and theoretically elaborated option for a particular conceptualization of the "contents" and direction of the processes of immigrants' adaptation (for a review of the commonly used approaches in contemporary immigration and ethnic studies in the United States, see Scott 1990 and Kivisto 1990; cf. also Thernstrom 1982; McKay 1982; Archdeacon 1985). But the reference framework that the authors actually use in measuring and comparatively evaluating investigated phenomena—native-born white Americans of native parentage—implies the choice of the classical assimilation model, namely, adoption of sociocultural patterns of the dominant group (in infant mortality, fertility, family and household structure, and education) and contact with its representatives (in residence).

Other theoretically arguable and historically reasonable options, however, could be taken using the same 1910 census data supported by the existing studies, and the results could be interpreted differently, measured by different yardsticks. In the fertility analysis, take, for instance, the rates of the "new," South and East European immigrants, and the "old," West European groups. Among the former, Slavic Catholics, unless they married among themselves (the great majority), were at the beginning of the century most likely to espouse their fellow religionists a step higher in the American status order as seen from their own low position: the Irish and, better yet, the Germans (Pagnini and Morgan 1990). Since it is known from data on subsequent decades that the same pattern of ethnic intermarriage persisted and strengthened (Carpenter 1969 [1927]; Kennedy 1944; Herberg 1955; Lieberson 1963; Greeley 1971), the fertility rates of West European Catholic groups— those with whose members the Slavs were most inclined to establish families once they became more settled in this country—could, with good historical sense, be used as a yardstick of "reproductive assimilation" in 1910. At the same time, the fertility of Western European immigrants, closer, as we know from contemporary sources and historical studies, to the dominant American group on the social and cultural distance scale, could have been measured against that of the latter. The whole picture, although by necessity static (1910), would thus have acquired a certain potential dynamism, as it were, a perspective of movement through "stages," or along different "paths," depending on the interpretative framework. An issue deserving the specific attention of those interested could be to identify the historically most meaningful and theoretically tenable comparative reference groups for "reproductive assimilation" of blacks.

The authors identified four distinct patterns of fertility: that of white non-Southern native-born women of native parentage; Poles and Italians; Irish women, and Yiddish-speakers. I will comment here on the immigrant groups. Among Italians and Poles, the authors concluded, there was very little fertility control: they simply went on having children, without any apparent strategy. It may be noted, though, that a study of Southern Italian folkways in the immigrant colonies in America at the beginning of the century (Williams 1938) reported that some married couples used separate beds in an attempt to avoid unwanted pregnancies, referring among themselves to this practice as "sleeping the American way." (Such attempts, by the way, could be considered either as a sign of cultural assimilation or as an "ethnicization effect.") Sexual relations of ethnic couples have thus far been studied very little by immigration historians (see Weinberg 1988 on Jews). It might be interesting to try to find out in an ethnographic study whether the above-mentioned practice was really implemented in Italian or Polish marriages, how common this "birth control method" was, and whether its practitioners shared any distinct socioeconomic characteristics.

Irish women having babies presented another kind of a specific pattern, part of which "puzzled" authors of the fertility report. I lined up for a rapid telephonic consult three friends knowledgeable on matters of Irish-American history (I wish to thank Hasia Diner, Kerby Miller, and David Doyle for their time and insights). They all "needed to see more specific context," but nevertheless offered some ideas.

Here they are: a "puzzle" the authors pondered on was who were the Irish women, married and past the age of 40, who according to the 1910 census stayed at 0 or the next-lowest parities; in other words, they had either no children or 1.5 of them, while the then-prevailing sociocultural norm in this immigrant group was to have several children. My consulting network was also surprised at this finding: "strange," they have not encountered such a phenomenon in their research (which includes oral histories, immigrant press, memoirs, and novels). Possible answers, they reasoned, depend in good part on finding out when these 40+ childless or minimum-parity women got married (it can be calculated, the authors told me, from the PUS data set). If they married shortly before the 1910 census, then the wait-and-see approach would seem most reasonable—in other words, hold your explanatory urge, since carrying around a pregnant abdomen well after the age of 40 was perfectly acceptable and not at all a "shame" in Irish immigrant society (understandably so, considering how late women tended to marry). If, however, this group of 40+ women in question married several years before the 1910 census, they could have been sterile, not unlikely as a result of (common among Irish females) poverty combined with chronic illness, especially tuberculosis, which was known to be bad for fertility.

Interestingly though, my collocutors were unanimous in suggesting that the women's *own choice* not to marry at all or—what is of concern here—if married, not to have children, should be seriously considered. The latest to marry were usually longtime domestics: unlike their fellow ethnics employed in industries and crowded in immigrant tenements, they were generally in good health, and especially much less exposed to tuberculosis (cf. Ward 1971 on comparative rates of tubercular patients in American middle-class and immigrant city neighborhoods in that period); they could, therefore, be less likely to have had problems with conception or successfully completing pregnancy. But since they had supported themselves for so long, and faced the American world alone, as it were, outside the security and dependency of the immigrant community, these women often developed a strong sense of self-reliance. This, and a fear of establishing one more "unhappy Irish home" (often described in immigrant novels and memoirs, and echoed in urban social surveys of the time) appears to have motivated a number of these women not to marry at all (Crum 1890; Kuczynski 1901—cited in Diner, 1983). Those who did could have made a similar negative choice regarding children. A *concilium*, including Hasia Diner, the pioneer in the field, was also in accord that the matter of Irish women and their marital and birth control choices certainly needs further research.

Poles and Italians multiplied above the dominant white American fertility rate despite (statistical) controls. Why would duration in the United States and English-speaking ability matter for infant mortality among these peoples, but not for women's fertility? The authors of the mortality report implicitly assumed the following causal order of developments (I am reconstructing only one link): longer stay in the United States and speaking English—learning habits of hygiene or health care (cultural diffusion through "media," e.g., pamphlets dropped in the neighborhoods, or in contacts with natives, e.g., via settlement houses and their Americanization programs, which strongly emphasized daily hygiene and food preparation)—practice of the above at home, and thus—decrease in infant mortality rates. A similar scheme is apparently implied in the fertility chapter, where the authors propose a "diffusion through contact" hypothesis. But hygiene and health care habits had a much lighter "value load" than contraception, and under the Comstock Law of 1873 instruction in birth control methods was considered illegal.

There were a few devoted supporters of legal and medically supervised family planning among left-leaning liberal reformers like practicing nurses Margaret Sanger or Lillian Wald and among radical anarchists, vocal campaigners for free love and contraceptives for all, like "Red" Emma Goldman and Rose Pastor Stokes (Sanger 1938; Wald 1915; Goldman 1983; see also Kennedy 1970; Daniels 1989). But respectable Anglo-Protestant ladies, conducting Americanization classes for immigrants in settlement houses, eagerly taught there cleanliness and nutrition, but not birth control methods.

As for personal contacts, since formality and social distance between teachers and students were generally pronounced, and since new immigrants, certainly Slavic peasants, saw sexual matters between husband and wife as embarrassing and strictly private (Thomas and Znaniecki 1927), I do not think this was the channel through which new arrivals learned about American methods of birth control.

As written and oral records (letters, memoirs, novels, life stories) created by immigrant women suggest, some of them were indeed intrigued by "American tricks" that freed wives from ceaseless pregnancies, but my educated intuition from these sources is that at that time those "tricks" were largely alluded to or whispered about among Slavs and Italians rather than learned in a more systematic manner. Well, perhaps "sleeping the American way" was practiced, but considering the data on Italian fertility we have just been presented with, that trick does not seem to have helped much. On second thought, separate marital beds as a contraceptive device could have been the only birth control method respectable and law-abiding Protestant ladies from settlement houses actually taught their pupils.

Unlike Poles and Italians, Jews practiced birth control, and apparently with some strategy in mind: a common practice, a precursor of planned parenthood of sorts, was apparently to have the number of children a wife/husband couple wished one after another, and after that, sharply to reduce (control) fertility. But let me note that Jewish parity, generally lower than among other "new" immigrants, must have varied depending on a complex of local circumstances. My study in small coalmining towns in western Pennsylvania reveals, for instance, a higher (by

1.3) average number of children born to Jewish immigrants than shown in the 1910 census national sample (the data are from local manuscript schedules for the same year, and personal interviews). Jewish families' "parity preferences" around Johnstown were different from those of their fellow ethnics in Portland, Oregon, for instance (Toll 1982).

Here are some general comments on the issue of immigrant fertility provoked by the Jewish case as discussed in Chapter 4: the hypothesis of cultural diffusion (of the dominant standards) via social interaction between immigrants and native-born white Americans of native parentage has not been supported when proxy-measurements available in the census and used in statistical analyses turned out to be of negligent significance for ("new") immigrant fertility levels. But as suggested before, the search could have moved in the wrong direction. The Jewish situation, although specific, provides a good illustration of the general idea where, one can argue, lay at that time the primary locus of cultural diffusion: namely, not the interactions with "Anglos," but, rather, *within the immigrant communities* and by means of their native languages. Take the *enfant terrible* Emma Goldman, a Russian immigrant. For the majority of Jewish Lower East Siders at the turn of the century, she was *meshuge*, crazy, and yet she was "one of ours," brilliant, unconventional, a great speaker, and her public appearances, including outrageous calls for "free love and free contraception for all," attracted enormous crowds (*Red Emma Speaks* 1983). "Modern ways" in sexual mores were in the air, loudly spoken of by fellow immigrant Jews, crazy as those ideas might appear. A popular health magazine, *Unzer gezund*, published by Dr. Ben-Zion Liber, an immigrant from Romania, openly advocated birth control. Also, there widely circulated on the Lower East Side a sex education guidebook by Margaret Sanger, translated into Yiddish: *Vos yedde meydl darf visn* (What every girl should know). A practicing nurse herself, Sanger inaugurated in 1916 a contraceptive-dispensing clinic in Brooklyn and sent around advertising leaflets in Yiddish and Italian. I do not know about Italian women, but the clinic quickly acquired a large Jewish clientele (Kennedy 1970; Lederhendler 1991). The enormously popular Yiddish-language daily, *Forverts*, more conventional in these matters than *Unzer gezund* or *Red Emma*, nevertheless openly came to the defense of "modern American life," in this case meaning smaller families, quality children, and so on.

In contrast, similar talk of contraception or even allusions to it in the mainstream Slavic-language press or other publications in that period (and, as a matter of fact, in the following decades either) is nonexistent. Explicit religious prohibitions, particularly in Catholicism (in this regard Judaic teachings were rather implicit, and thus open to various interpretations), combined with control over large areas of immigrant public life by the church hierarchy and its lay representatives, obviously played an inhibitive role. But there was, as my Johnstown study suggests, and ethnic composition and social contexts in the immigrant settlements in larger cities make likely, in any case for Slavic women, another avenue of learning birth control practices. It was through diffusion, though not directly from Americans, but by information passed on from members of a group more "modernized" in this regard, and with whom Slavs had close residential and economic contacts: the Jews. Slavic girls commonly worked as maids in Jewish homes, and, in part because they did not have a sufficient number of their own, and in part because of a special trust in Jewish skills, immigrants from practically all East European groups routinely used the services of Jewish doctors, and with the passage of time, increasingly also of women's specialists and obstetricians. No English was required, since they communicated in old-country tongues. (On this enduring proximity and service exchange between the two groups, transplanted from Eastern Europe into American cities, see Morawska 1987.)

It could make for an interesting and novel study to look at various areas of possible "assimilative effects" of different intermediary groups positioned in the middle of the dominant society's social hierarchy between native-born white Americans and turn-of-the-century new immigrants (we shall come back to this issue in the next section). Or, to reverse a perspective: what did happen to modern and "Americanized," that is, controlled and respectably low, fertility rates of, say, Germans (Catholic) when they intermarried with (Catholic) Poles? Up? The same? And who made the decisions? How much—or how many, rather—depended on whether the couple made their home in the German or the Polish ethnic community?

One last comment on the fertility report, regarding its possible amelioration by adding contextual variables. The following readily come to mind: type(s) of industry in the region/county-city; occupational structure and proportion of women in the labor force; ethnic composition and intergroup residential segregation (aggregate, preferably city level); proportion of naturalized citizens per immigrant group; religion (perhaps number of churches in neighborhood/city/county or per immigrant group; the 1890, 1906, and 1915 U.S. Religious Censuses could be used for regional and city-level data); number of ethnic newspapers in the English language (per immigrant group; although, as suggested before, "assimilation" could very well proceed in the foreign languages inside ethnic networks). However, the *sine qua non* for a good study of such ground-level (bedroom) subjects is ground-level research (on the significance of "community variables" in intergroup fertility differences, see Hareven and Vinovskis 1975; Haines 1977).

Family and Household Structure

Major findings of Chapter 5 confirm by and large what has been reported in studies conducted at the local level. The immigrants, particularly new ones, differed from native-born white Americans of native parentage—the comparative reference group in the study—in terms of household structure (boarders, of course; cf. Bodnar, Simon, and Weber 1982; Zunz 1982; Hareven 1982), while blacks were similar in this respect to white Americans. In family structure, however, it was blacks who were different, while immigrants resembled the pattern of the dominant group.

Black Americans are found to have had a large proportion of female-headed single-parent households—apparently a pattern much preceding in time what is a widespread phenomenon in present-day urban ghettos (Pagnini and Morgan 1990). The census data also show an uncommonly high proportion of foster children in black families, which the authors interpret—interestingly, but in my opinion not convincingly enough in terms of supportive data—as the persistence of African family culture.

Compared with other groups, Jews seem to have had the "tightest" families, that is, the highest proportion of households headed by a couple and the lowest percentage reporting "missing," that is, absent, children. When informed that the spouse was absent, the census takers simply recorded this fact without specifying the cause (and so did the authors of Chapter 5), but it is reasonable to think it could have been desertion. In the Jewish case, the low proportion of missing husbands reported in the 1910 census would then lend support to recently raised doubts about the actual scale of family desertions, which in the overviews of Jewish American history (e.g., Howe 1976; Hertzberg 1989) are presented as a widespread phenomenon in immigrant settlements at the beginning of the century. (Considerably diminished figures based on the recalculated statistics of the National Desertion Bureau of the United Hebrew Charities are found in Friedman 1982; see also Felder 1986; Goren 1990). Why, then, such a persistent perception of family desertions as a widespread social problem? There might have been several reasons, which are listed below (I thank Jonathan Sarna for throwing in his ideas, lucid as usual, into what follows).

Indeed, the *Forverts* and other Yiddish papers often published announcements of wives looking for their vanished husbands. But perhaps precisely because it was such uncustomary behavior in Jewish society, and because of the miserable position Jewish religious law assigned the *agunah* (a woman whose husband disappeared for whatsoever reason), she remained "tied," that is, unable to establish another family, until he sent her a *get* (bill of divorce), or else until there was proof of his death. Hence, a "statistically insignificant" problem, so to speak, was perceived as, and made into, a widespread social evil. (At the beginning of the century there circulated among Jewish Lower East Siders a popular song, *"Mentshen fresser"* [Men-eaters], that spoke about dreadful tubercular microbes and bacilli—killers of tenement residents [Slobin 1982]. The song's very popularity reflected a shared perception of the seriousness of the situation in the Jewish community, even though, compared with other immigrant groups, tuberculosis among Jewish immigrants in New York City was the lowest.) On the other hand, it is known that since the status of the *agunah* was not only personally painful and economically costly to the woman, but also highly embarrassing socially, deserted women frequently lied about their situation, claiming that their husbands were "away at work" (Wald 1915; Dwork 1981). It is, therefore, quite probable that they said the same to the census takers.

It could have been, too, that many of the "find me my husband" appeals published in the Yiddish papers in America involved men who abandoned, that is, did not bring over, their wives left in Europe, or wives who came over by themselves in search of their husbands, who could have in the meantime remarried. The Yiddish press at that time repeatedly noted the presence in large immigrant settlements such as New York City of a number of unscrupulous reverends who made a business of performing marriages without adequate checking of the candidates' backgrounds. Unless this problem, too, was considerably exaggerated, a common occurrence of remarriage without a proper Jewish divorce could have "covered up" some of the desertions in the census data. Finally, it is possible that a number of the *agunahs* decided to return to Europe to live in their parents' homes rather than endure embarrassment in America. Except for a couple of studies quoted earlier (Goren's is a review essay), not much historical research has yet been done on this interesting problem.

As to the boarders. Very likely a number of them were kin, but since they paid regular board (and explaining to a census taker the intricacies of a relationship for which there was often no term in American English, with its "modernized," much attenuated vocabulary of kinship, was impossible), they were thus recorded as mere lodgers. Let me also note that the census, and therefore the family report in *After Ellis Island*, did not record quite common interhousehold kinship, that is, families who lived next door or at the end of the block (see, e.g., Gabbaccia 1984; Smith 1985; Morawska 1985).

The report, accurately according to historical studies, presents boarding as a correlate of recency of immigration. But it does not consider what the existing research has shown to have been another significant factor: its stage in the family life cycle. Interestingly, patterns of lodger-keeping were not the same for all immigrant groups: Polish families, for example, tended to eliminate this source of income when children reached the age of employment, but not so Italian families, who expanded it (Hareven and Model 1977). Information on family life stages is calculable from the PUS 1910 census data set, and could be used by those interested in ethnic family history, and especially immigrants' economic strategies and gains and losses related to particular options. Take Lithuanians, for example (Appendix B, this volume): the 1910 census shows them to have had the highest proportion of augmented (boarder-keeping) households, whether headed by men (65 percent) or by women (59 percent) among "new" immigrant groups (the Poles registered 48 percent and 34 percent, respectively). At the same time, the same data indicate a very high infant mortality rate in Lithuanian immigrant families, equaling that of the French Canadians. The latter, however, are shown by the 1910 census information to have kept boarders at a much lower proportion: 21 percent and 20 percent, respectively. Yet the two groups, as already commented on in the mortality chapter, had a similar, high proportion of women in the labor force. Did Lithuanian infants, therefore, have an enhanced mortality risk from overcrowded quarters and mothers' outside employment? But perhaps it was in a specific region where Lithuanian women worked outside the home? A large proportion of Lithuanian immigrant families, but not French Canadian ones, resided in small towns in the coal-mining region of Pennsylvania (Greene 1975). There was in that location no employment for women, but plenty of coal dust (see Haines 1977 and Emmons 1989 on increased mortality among immigrant miners). Quite a puzzle, all this, suggesting that different constellations of factors could have accounted for higher rates of infant mortality in the French Canadian than in the Lithuanian case, and possibly within the latter group as well, depending on residence, industry, and, reflecting these structural conditions, family economic strategies.

Among some other interesting issues for further investigation based on the already existing research and data reported in Chapter 5 are female heads of households: their demographic and ethnic characteristics, and economic position (see Gabbaccia 1989 for an updated bibliography of studies on immigrant women). The report treats outmarriage, particularly that upward on the status ladder of the dominant American society, as an indicator of assimilation. The idea is, of course, reasonable, but there are caveats. First, as Zunz demonstrated in his Detroit study (1982), outmarriage could have been a result of demographic imbalance within one's own ethnic group (in other words, not enough people to marry) and did not necessarily mean a move toward assimilation. Second, and obversely, even almost complete endogamy did not preclude quick assimilation (understood, as does the classical model, as the absorption by immigrants of the dominant social norms, cultural values, and practices): take Sephardic Jews in Colonial America (Marcus 1970; see Cohen 1981 on Jewish fertility at that time: high and matching in level the dominant Anglo-American group), or German Jewish immigrants in the nineteenth century (Baltzell 1958; Cohen 1984), or even East European arrivistes in the early twentieth (Birmingham 1984). It might be interesting to try to time-, place-, and group-contextualize a relationship between ethnic endo- and exogamy and assimilation/ethnicization.

A theme already noted is that of "assimilation intermediaries": the lowest degree of ethnic endogamy within the immigrant households is shown to be for employee status. It was much more often women, occupied as servants, than men who were domestic employees. Studies have shown the role that such employment, usually in Anglo-American homes, played in the cultural assimilation of Irish women (Woods and Kennedy 1913; see also Diner 1983), and I have suggested a similar role played by Jewish households for immigrant Slavic maids. A general issue of interest in this context is the role of women in the assimilation process of immigrants: its channels as well as spheres (for a fascinating account of Jewish women's creative adaptation—ethnicization, precisely—of middle-class American material culture, see Braunstein and Joselit 1990. Cf. also Heinze 1990).

Residential Segregation

The report is based on individual-level data (an approach the authors believe gives their analyses an explanatory advantage over conventional measurements of residential segregation that use aggregate units), and, following the classical assimilation model, treats immigrants' proximity to native-born white Americans of native parentage as a yardstick of residential assimilation. Many readers, I am sure, found this approach convincing and the material useful. In my opinion, however, it would be historically more meaningful to handle the problem in a different way.

To begin with, it does not seem persuasive to apply an individual-level analysis of residential patterns at a time in American urban and immigration history when masses of people were moving and settling *in groups,* by choice as well as because of different kinds of necessities. Second and related to these necessities, or opportunity structures, is that where and how members of these immigrant groups settled, and who their neighbors were (for mingling), were in great part contingent on what individual-level data analyses do not capture: the type of industry in a particular location (city); its ecology, and especially business centers; and population (racial and ethnic) composition. (On "causal effects" of the above factors on ethnic residential processes, see, e.g., Lieberson 1963, 1980; Zunz 1982; Bodnar, Simon, and Weber 1982; Hershberg 1981; Yancey, Erikson, and Juliani 1976. The authors cite all these studies, and agree that such contextual variables "influence the statistics," but proceed with their own method.)

From a theoretical viewpoint, a different interpretative framework, that of ethnicization, might have been more adequate than the classical assimilation model, at least for a great number of recent immigrants in larger settlements in bigger American cities. As Park and Miller observed three-quarters of a century earlier about immigrant neighborhoods in Chicago (R. E. Park and Miller 1969 [1921]), and Stanley Lieberson repeated in his longitudinal study of ethnic residential patterns in American cities (1963), *ethnic clustering* precisely, or—using terminology from Chapter 5—immigrant residential concentration, was *at that time* a measure of the newcomers' having progressed in the assimilation process (the "first step" for advocates of the classical linear model, a "path" for proponents of the ethnicization perspective). On the other hand, on similar premises as in the case of fertility, integration into American society of the "old," that is, West European, immigrants, could be conceptualized, and then measured, as the extent of residential intermingling ("association" in Chapter 6) with native-born white Americans of native parentage. For the blacks, again (treated in the report by the same measurements as white immigrants) it would be necessary to find some other, distinct approach, since neither ethnic residential concentration nor association with the dominant group as indices of a way or aspect of assimilation seem adequate.

There was, as mentioned already, a category of immigrants whose individual "mingling" with members of the dominant group on a regular basis could be construed as a pattern of sociocultural assimilation, and these were immigrant domestics and other servants employed in Anglo-American households; but then again, Slavs commonly worked in Jewish homes, and those were in the immigrant neighborhoods.

The report's major findings are that "new" immigrants were in 1910 more concentrated, and isolated residentially from native-born white Americans of native parentage, than were members of "old" immigrant groups; that similar indices for blacks were (still) generally statistically insignificant (cf. Lieberson 1963; Hershberg et al. 1981); that mulattoes were found to have been more segregated (but there were only $N = 87$ in a sample); and that magnitudes of all these measurements varied by cities.

For "old," West European immigrants, controlling for socioeconomic position, measured by occupational status and homeownership, reduced their residential segregation from native-born white Americans of native parentage (the standard reference category) to statistical insignificance. Not so, however, for "new" immigrants: neither increased occupational status nor homeownership appeared to have been influential in bringing new arrivals spatially (and, as the report has it, by implication socially) closer to Anglo-Americans, while duration in the United States and American citizenship actually "removed" them from the dominant group. A puzzle, isn't this? For those interested in looking into this matter in a more historically grounded manner, here are some suggestions for a possible reconceptualization of the general approach to the problem (assimilation), and, as a result of this cognitive rearrangement, recalculation of the statistics (from the same 1910 PUS census data file).

Theoretical assumptions and explanatory analyses concerning "old" Western European immigrants could be left as they are in Chapter 5. Their economic and social-cultural situation in America by 1910 was incomparably more proximate to Anglo-dominant standards than that of recent arrivals from Southern and Eastern Europe, and so using residential intermingling as a measure of assimilation seems reasonable. Looking at the adaptation of new immigrants at the beginning of this century, however, one could proceed from a different conceptual framework: for these people, as argued before, it was *ethnic concentration* that signaled the processes of assimilation at work. Moving now to the analysis of factors that by 1910 could have affected the thus-defined assimilation of Poles, Italians, Jews, Ukrainians, Lithuanians, Hungarians, and others, I would run a logistic regression model on ethnic residential concentration, instead of proximity to Anglos. It may turn out that some of the variables found insignificant in the proximity model will display more explanatory muscle when put to a different use.

Take homeownership, for instance, to which the authors automatically ascribe Anglo-American middle-class attributes. It is defined as a sign of economic wealth/mobility, and, therefore, expected to act as a facilitator of residential mixing with the dominant group. For recent immigrants from Southern and Eastern Europe, a great many of whom came to America with an intention of returning home some day, buying a home—usually after some years in the United States ("duration")—signaled an intent of staying, if not firmly for good, then for a "we'll see" period of time (see review of return migration literature in Morawska

1991). And when such immigrants stayed on, often still hestitating for years about whether they shouldn't go back after all, much more often than not they stayed among their fellow countrypeople. And so did their homes. Local studies of Slavic immigrants have shown that it did not take much capital for an immigrant to erect a simple house for himself and his family in the 1900s: commonly, he drew for help on his friends in the neighborhood, all of whom usually had some carpentry and other useful skills from the old country, and they built the house together, on weekends. Quite a number of immigrants, not at all economically afflu-ent, became homeowners in this way in Detroit, Pittsburgh, and Johns-town. (Zunz 1982; Bodnar, Simon, and Weber 1982; Morawska 1985).

Now occupation. Here's an Italian, Polish, or Jewish immigrant pro-fessional in 1910, still with a pronounced accent, and perhaps some mannerisms strange to the Anglo-Protestant eye. Such professionals would at that time have been most likely to work in or around the immigrant colonies: they were needed there, they enjoyed greater status inside eth-nic communities than outside them, and they generally did not feel they "really belonged" to that dominant Anglo-American world (new immi-grants' letters, memoirs, and novels from that period are good witnesses of both the immersion in ethnic communities and the social alienation from mainstream America).

And naturalization, also assumed in the report to increase proxim-ity, did not bring new American citizens of 1910 closer to the dominant group either, not in residence. The path, rather, led again back into the immigrant neighborhoods. At that time, naturalized immigrants com-monly became leaders of their own ethnic communities, organizers of "American Citizens' Clubs" in parochial basements, often also inter-mediaries between the immigrants and vote-seeking politicians from city hall. (Generally on immigrant leadership in that period, see Higham 1978; Green 1987; Smith 1971; Bodnar 1985; Jews naturalized much earlier and on a much greater scale than did Slavs or Italians, but they re-mained in their ethnic neighborhoods, busy assimilating themselves from the inside, as it were.) Such an altered conceptualization and differently programmed statistical analysis can be tried, should anyone be tempted, on the basis of information contained in the PUS 1910 census data set (the chapter on residence does use a measure of ethnic "concentration"; it's just that cause-testing analysis was performed on "segregation" from white Americans of native parentage). What is troubling, however—and there appears to be no easy answer—is the following: given the enor-mous residential transiency of (new) immigrants during the decades 1880s–1910s (in some places nearly two-thirds of the neighborhood's population turned over within one year), *whom* are we talking about when we deliberate on individual residential proximity and its effects on assimilation from "mingling"? (On immigrants' intense residential migrations in that period, see, e.g., Thernstrom and Knight 1970; Kopf 1977; Coleman 1962; Golab 1977; Bodnar, Simon, and Weber 1982.) Take one Haraszti Janos, for example: after six months in Baltimore (where his sister and her husband lived; he first stayed with them after he came to America), he moved to Pittsburgh (there was a nice Hungarian community there, and he heard the steel mills paid pretty good wages), and after a year he traveled on to Detroit (a friend found him a cleaner job). Many thousands of others were likewise on the move, and, quite likely, a good number of them were "caught" in the 1910 census PUS data set. From this, the White team calculated assimilation rates of our transients in a place where they happened to be during the census-taking months of 1910. Then they moved on. These three cities had different residential patterns, and, as Table 6.2 in the report shows, different segregation indexes. Are we creating frames of a sort, as if for pictures, calling them "Pittsburgh Hungarians," "Baltimore Hungarians," "Detroit Hungarians," and so on, that were filled every year with *different* contents as people came and went? Then who was mingling?

Schooling

The authors see their report as a revisitation of Lieberson's terrain (*A Piece of the Pie: Blacks and White Immigrants Since 1880*, 1980), but adding new vistas gained from expanded statistical analyses examining patterns of schooling in different age categories in new and old immigrant groups and comparing them to those of native white and black Americans. They proceed within a more explicit theoretical model than do the authors of the other chapters, dichotomizing the structural and cultural explanations and arguing for the former. In my view, however, possibly because I conceive of structure and culture as aspects of each other, and not as disjunctive, the patterns revealed form an intricate mosaic of complex multidirectional links, some thick, some barely visible, among different categories of age, nativity, and other attributes of individuals receiving education.

The report's evidence confirmed Lieberson's (1980) argument about the educational disadvantage of blacks relative to white immigrant groups in 1910, but another analysis by the same authors (Greene and Jacobs 1990) and based on the same 1910 census data shows this not holding true in the Northeast—a finding that very likely will interest researchers and generate more comparative studies within that region.

Of interest to students of gender-related issues should be the finding that young men and women from groups included in the report's analyses had by and large equal chances of being enrolled in school (excepting blacks; in this group, as previously reported, girls were found to have been receiving more schooling than boys). An inspection of "little groups" in Appendix B, this volume, however, reveals large gender differences to young men's advantage in school enrollments in the 14–18 age category, among Hungarians, Slovaks, Russians, and Slovenians. Since these subsamples are small, only a suggestion can be offered here that could be pursued in a more focused investigation using the same 1910 data set: namely, that all these groups had large (20 percent–35 percent, larger than Poles and Italians) proportions of immigrants in rural areas, and it might have been that in such places the peasant tradition of not educating women beyond the required minimum survived more strongly than elsewhere.

Just how important contexts were in influencing "new" immigrants' schooling, however, is demonstrated by a study of East European immigrants in Minnesota's Iron Range (Chyatt et al., research in progress; the study actually deals with Jews, but the authors gathered some interesting information on other groups as well). The Jacobs and Greene report finds urban location to have been a significant facilitator of schooling. But immigrants in the Range lived in unincorporated places, far away from the bustling urban civilization of the 1900s. Yet the progressive educational system, introduced into the public schools of the entire state by Populist politicians, a system that provided financial resources for intellectually stimulating extracurricular academic activities and stipends for students from working-class families, enabled immigrant adolescents of both sexes to develop an aspiration for extended schooling. Willingly supported by their parents, and encouraged by Slovenian, Polish, and Croation ethnic leaders (active also in local Populist politics), Iron Range Slavic high school graduates enrolled in college "at amazing rates" even at the beginning of the century. It seems to have been a happy conflation of "structural" and "cultural" influences indeed.

A word about elementary schools. As the authors note, some immigrant children were receiving public, and some parochial, education (the census did not specify). The findings reported in the chapter show that Polish, but not Italian, children's underenrollment persisted after controls, and it has been also known from these groups' ethnic histories that the Poles had an extensive parochial school system (as did French Canadians, Slovaks, and Catholic Hungarians), and the Italians did not. Could this have been one of the reasons? The skimpy evidence that exists on the functioning of Slavic parochial schools is inconclusive: in some, pupils stayed longer than in public educational institutions; in others they dropped out sooner, sometimes even with a note from the priest stating that the underage child (boy) was old enough to work (Chalasinski 1935; Roucek 1969; Smith 1969; Miaso 1971; Parot 1971; Bodnar 1976; Stolarik 1985; Morawska 1985. Generally on the history of Catholic education in the United States, see Burns and Kohlbrenner 1937). Or did the length of parochial education vary by city, depending on its industrial profile (employability of youth) and/or the intensity of prejudice, if not open racism, toward new immigrants in American public institutions, including schools? Or did it also, and to what extent, depend on an even more particular context: commitment to children's continued education by the priest-director of the parochial school or its team of teaching nuns? A comparison of rates of retention of immigrant children in public versus parochial schools certainly awaits research. (Perlmann's [1988] study of high school enrollments among white immigrants and blacks in Providence, Rhode Island, at the beginning of the century contains some such data for the Irish.) Such a comparative investigation, however, should incorporate contextual variables into the analysis, especially for "structural" arguments.

An inspection of schooling data in Appendix B, this volume, shows that a greater proportion of Russian than Austro-Hungarian Jewish youth was found to continue schooling beyond the age of 14 (even though, on the whole, Russians were more recent arrivals than Austro-Hungarians, and one could expect a greater percentage of children in the former, less established, group to go to work as soon as they finished mandatory schooling). Funny, at first sight. Perhaps, quite simply, the two groups had different age distributions in the 14+ category. After the age of 15 there was at that time a steep attrition of students, and so if Austro-Hungarian Jews (who according to the 1910 census sample data [Appendix B, this volume] had generally been in the United States longer) had a larger proportion of 17- and 18-year-olds than did the Russian group, the difference in enrollments could be reasonably accounted for.

But if the age distribution in the 14–18 category in these groups was similar, could it be that the Litvaks—as legend has it, more intellectually oriented than the Galicianers (and more still than the sub-Carpathian Jews influenced by mystical Hassidic ideas)—rubbed some of it off on their American-born offspring? Not very likely. Perhaps, then, if not owing to different age distributions, the reported finding reflects a composition of the Jewish subsample in the 1910 census national sample: a considerably larger *proportion* of Austro-Hungarians than Russians resided in New York City (in total numbers, Russian Jews were of course a much larger group). In New York City at that time, a great many Jewish youth dropped out of school early and went to work to help their families: I am persuaded here more by the "structuralist" emphasis of Berrol's (1976) contextual argumentation than by Kessner's (1977) "culturalism" and occupational analysis (to mollify Kessnerites, however, it should be noted that in those years one did not need a high school education to be a white-collar worker or even an elementary school teacher).

And a last comment on Jews and New York City. According to the Jacobs and Greene analysis (data not included in Chapter 9), residence in New York City did not exert any special booster effect on Jewish school enrollments (for all age categories combined). In 1910, it makes sense. As a matter of fact, as the earlier argument about possible reasons for Austro-Hungarians' lower enrollments suggests, residence in New York City might even have had a negative impact on the schooling of young people beyond elementary education (the effects of residence in New York City on enrollments of this particular age category 14–18 can be calculated from the 1910 census national sample data set, for Jewish as well as other larger ethnic group samples). However, it could be argued on the basis of "soft" information (memoirs, novels, oral histories) and comparative enrollment data on Jewish educational pursuits in the 1920s and 1930s in Johnstown, Pennsylvania, and in New York City (my own study), that New York City was *about to begin to act as just such a booster*, as Jews were moving out of the Lower East Side and garment-making shops, and as the city's postsecondary schooling system was rapidly expanding.

As for Germans, who are found to be persistently low in school enrollments in the 14+ age group, different factors could have accounted for this result (I thank Kathy Conzen for discussing them with me, and pointing out, of course, that they should be considered "in specific contexts"). The following two seemed of particular importance. The first can be reconstructed from the PUS 1910 census data set by anyone interested in finding out for oneself. The controls used in the report did not include regions, while contemporary and historical studies show that in small- and medium-size towns in the Midwest, German boys after elementary school still traditionally went into the crafts like their fathers (and forefathers). This pattern persisted also in large cities among many a first-generation urbanite in this region. (On the persistence at the beginning of this century of the family craft tradition among Germans residing more to the east, in Erie County, New York, see Stern 1987.) The second reason that German youths' school enrollment in the 14–18 age category could have lagged behind the rate of native white Americans could not be retrieved from the census data, and from other sources only partially and at the cost of terribly painstaking research; namely, that German Catholics and fundamentalist Lutherans, about one-third of the entire German stock in the United States, had traditionally low school enrollments beyond the mandatory age. One could, of course, go to Cincinnati, for instance, where there was a large group of German Catholics, get their turn-of-the-century parochial school records, and then trace the alumni in local high schools, comparing the results with a "control group" of non-Catholic Germans. Having struggled for months with mountains of dusty and chaotic school records in my little Johnstown, I would not recommend such an exercise, even for a doctoral dissertation. But this low educational performance of some groups within the large ethnic category of Germans should be noted.

Finally, two variables in the report showed strong positive effects on immigrant children's school enrollments: homeownership and parental literacy. The authors classified both factors as "structural" (i.e., not "cultural," taking the dichotomizing approach, and so their explanatory model appears to be supported). One can disagree, but readers must by now have made up their own minds on how to interpret these findings. A word about homeownership, though: as in the analysis of residence (Chapter 7), in this case, too, one could take homeownership of new immigrants not, or not necessarily, as an indicator of economic position, but as a sign of intent to stay in this country for good. So understood, homeownership could, logically, be expected to correlate with duration in the United States—the most forceful of enrollment facilitators in the Jacobs and Greene analysis. Now immigrant parents who bought or built (in the way described earlier) a house, a little hut even, when they decided to stay in this country, would be more likely, wouldn't they, to send their children to an American school? This, of course, would not preclude positive effects on schooling of economic improvement in the immigrant families: better-skilled occupations and owned homes (statistical interaction of these two was not tested in the report). Anyone interested? All this—reconceptualization and reanalysis—can be tried with the PUS 1910 census data set.

Industrial Affiliation

The report by and large confirms what labor and immigration historians have gathered from contemporary sources and case or comparative investigations. Mainly, that those of foreign stock concentrated in nonagricultural sectors of the economy, and that there was a marked variation within the foreign stock in their concentrations in particular sectors of industries, persisting over time, and transferred from the immigrant to the American-born generation (cf. Bodnar, Simon, and Weber 1982; Smith 1985; Yans-McLaughlin 1977; Rischin 1977; Zunz 1982; Hareven 1982; Puskas 1982; Golab 1977; Hershberg 1981; Stolarik 1980; Benkart 1980; Barton 1975; Model 1985, 1988. And of course *Harvard*

Encyclopedia of American Ethnic Groups, 1980; and also Lieberson 1980).

I found two very useful elements in what this chapter has to say about immigrants in American industries in 1910. One is a reminder of an obvious but too often overlooked economic and social fact, namely, that the category of "foreign-born" actually covers people who left their homelands and arrived in this country at different times, and that it was, or could have been, significant for their subsequent adaptation. A tabulation (Tables 8A.3A and 8A.3B) of immigrants' industrial employment by decades of their arrival in the United States well illustrates this variation. Obviously, the immigrants' situation in 1910 reflected, to name just a few factors: skills brought over from the old country (whose economy was not static); emigration waves that were not evenly distributed over the land; the structure of an American economy that was rapidly being reshaped; and the duration of a person's stay in America with all its social and cultural implications. Other useful, and new, information can be gathered by inspecting industrial distributions of such "little groups" (in Appendix B, this volume) as Lithuanians, Croatians, Slovenians, or Russians (without, or almost without, Jews this time). As could be expected, considering that immigrants entered industrial sectors following one another and forming small and larger ethnic "niches" therein, these concentrations were not identical. Perhaps some research projects could be started from this.

But the greater contribution of this report lies elsewhere in that it does not quite belong, really, to the rest of the book and thus offers a different perspective. It is like an inverse telescope: in whatever has been discussed, mortality, fertility, family structure, or schooling, everyone else focused an eye on *the immigrants,* while this report centered on the *American economy*—fed, fueled, and restructured by the mass influx of immigrant labor during the five decades preceding World War I. It is not that we have not known this in immigration studies. Of course we have, and Lieberson's magisterial *A Piece of the Pie* (1980) has been a welcome reminder. But there is a difference between knowledge and awareness. It is generally good for intellectual processes that, while looking at things from one perspective, we remain aware that other ways of viewing, and therefore other views, are possible and could be helpful. As just such a consciousness-raiser with its reversed view on immigration, the industrial affiliation report is especially fitting as the closing chapter.

*   *   *

Here end my notes on *After Ellis Island.* Although it has been thought out and executed in ways very different from mine, the book brings heuristically useful orientation data (because of my interests, especially on the "little groups" from Eastern Europe that until now "did not exist" in the national censuses of that period; and the Yiddish-speakers, finally separated from Russians). In addition, and perhaps more importantly, I have discovered in the reports on particular subjects a number of hunches that look both interesting and promising for further research in immigration history, local and comparative. And I am convinced that readers have found several more.

APPENDIX A

AN INTRODUCTION TO THE PUBLIC USE SAMPLE OF THE 1910 U.S. CENSUS OF POPULATION

Michael A. Strong
Samuel H. Preston
Mark C. Hereward

THIS APPENDIX is a brief introduction to the Public Use Sample (PUS) of the 1910 United States Census of Population that was created at the University of Pennsylvania and recently released to the public. The PUS is a nationally representative sample of the household and individual records from the 1910 census. It was drawn from the microfilmed records of the original enumeration forms of the forty-six states, the territories of Arizona and New Mexico, the District of Columbia, Alaska, and Hawaii, and from the forms of overseas military personnel. Puerto Rico, which was enumerated in 1910, is not included in the Public Use Sample. A 1-in-250 sampling fraction was used, producing a total of 88,814 households and 366,239 individuals.

The 1910 Census of Population

The 1910 Census of Population was the thirteenth official national enumeration of the U.S. population.[1] An act of Congress, passed in July

SOURCE: *Historical Methods* 22(2) (Spring 1989):54–56. Reprinted by permission of the Helen Dwight Reid Educational Foundation. Published by Heldref Publications, 1319 Eighteenth Street, N.W., Washington, D.C. 20036-1802. Copyright © 1989.

[1]This section is drawn primarily from Durand, E. D. 1909. Report of the Director of the Census. *Annual Report of the Secretary of Commerce.* Washington: U.S. Government Printing Office; and *ibid.* 1910. Report of the Director of the Census. *Annual Report of the Secretary of Commerce.* Washington: U.S. Government Printing Office.

1909, authorized the enumeration to be taken as of April 15, 1910. This mid-April date was six weeks earlier than previous national censuses. Congress authorized the change in date after officials from the Census Bureau argued that changes in lifestyles, particularly in urban areas, made it inadvisable to enumerate the population in the summer when increasing numbers of people were away on vacation.

The collection of birth and death statistics was dropped from the list of census items. Census Bureau officials believed that the information on births and deaths collected by enumerators was somewhat inaccurate, and that this task could best be accomplished by improving state collection programs.

Census operations remained largely unchanged from those of the 1900 census. Approximately 70,000 enumerators personally visited all dwellings in each of their enumeration districts within an officially prescribed period of time. In urban areas, the enumerators were instructed to complete their task within two weeks; in rural areas, they were allowed thirty days. In most large urban areas, a sample form was mailed out a few days before the census. This served to both alert the citizenry to the impending visit of the enumerator and allow them to prepare the necessary information, if they so wished.

Changes in the census schedule reflected changing governmental concerns and refinements in survey techniques. The more important revisions included (1) the reappearance of a color (race) classification, last used in 1890, that included the category "mulatto"; (2) deletion of the month and year of birth; (3) the appearance of questions on the mother tongue of the respondent and of the respondent's parents; and (4) information on the type of industry and class of worker. Not all of these changes were incorporated in the Alaskan questionnaire, which looks more like the 1900 than the 1910 instrument. Both the 1900 and 1910 censuses included questions asked of married women regarding the number of children they had borne and the number who were still living.

The Public Use Sample

The 1910 Public Use Sample is a 1-in-250 sample of households and individuals appearing in the manuscripts of the 1910 United States Population Census. Sample selection was designed so that each household and each individual in the manuscript population had an equal probability of being selected. As a consequence, the sample is self-weighted. The final PUS is actually made up of two 1-in-500 samples. The first of these was funded by the National Institute of Child Health and Human Development and the second by the National Science Foundation.

Original census manuscript records for the forty-six states, the territories of Arizona and New Mexico, the District of Columbia, Alaska, Hawaii, and overseas military personnel were copied onto 1,756 reels of microfilm. These microfilmed records made up the sample domain. At the time that the manuscripts were filmed by the Census Bureau, each reel was divided into one to four parts, or sequences, each normally containing records from a single county (or parish in Louisiana) and numbering 250–300 pages. Populous counties required multiple sequences on several reels of microfilm.

Each of the original enumeration sheets, or pages, was divided into 100 lines, 50 lines on each side, with one line allocated for each enumerated individual. Some lines were left blank because enumerators were required to start a new form in a variety of situations.

For each of the 1-in-500 samples, the sample design divided the sample into strata. Each stratum consisted of a group of five pages within one of the 1,756 reels. One examination line was chosen within each stratum. There were 100 lines per page; thus, a sample point was chosen for every 500 lines. Thus, pages 1 through 5 of each reel would contain one line to be examined, as would pages 6–10, 11–15, 16–20, and so forth.

Within each five-page (i.e., 500-line) segment, a random number was generated and converted into a page and line number identifier, termed the "examination line," using information initially provided by the data entry operators on the number of sequences and pages within each sequence. The page number corresponded to a numeral appearing at the top of each page, which was stamped on the original document at the time of microfilming. The line number generated referred to a line on the particular page selected, from 1 to 100.

Our objective was to produce a household sample; therefore, we devised a scheme that would give each household, regardless of size, an equal probability of selection. That is, we ensured that a six-person household would not be oversampled relative to a one-person household. Entering the entire household each time any person in the household was randomly selected would result in an oversampling of large households simply because there are more potential examination points in larger households.

Census families with twenty or fewer nonfamily members and a head or head equivalent were included in the PUS sample as a household only if the head or head equivalent (in most cases, the first person enumerated in the census family—"a group of persons living together in the same dwelling place") appeared on the examination line. When that happened, the entire census family, including all nonfamily members (e.g., companions, boarders, servants, hired hands), was entered into the sample and became a PUS household. If any other members of this type of census family appeared on the examination line, the census family was rejected, and the data entry operators proceeded to the next examination line.

A census family with twenty-one or more nonfamily members and a head or a head equivalent was regarded as a collection of smaller households. One of these households contained all family members related to the head. This household was entered into the PUS if the head appeared on the examination line; nonfamily members were excluded. If a relative of the head appeared on the examination line, the household was excluded from the sample. Each of the nonfamily members in such a census family was considered a separate one-person household and was included in the sample if he or she appeared on the examination line. Only that person was taken, even if he or she had relatives within the census family. For example, if the examination line contained a male boarder with a wife and two children, only the male boarder was included in the sample; if it contained one of the boarder's children, only the child was taken.

When no head or head equivalent was present in a census family, all individuals in the unit were considered one-person households to be sampled individually, regardless of the size of the group. This situation was characteristic of trailing household fragments, parts of census families that were initially missed by enumerators and later entered on enumerator forms at the end of the enumeration district. This situation typically occurred when lodgers or boarders who were absent from the census family on the first canvass were enumerated on a subsequent canvass of the district. They were not integrated into the body of the household by the census enumerators but were listed separately.

Rather than present a data file that was as close as possible to the original records, we elected to correct some of the most obvious errors of enumerators and respondents. We eliminated as many operator errors as possible through an extensive rechecking procedure, then re-examined the remaining inconsistencies. In the end, the solution to a particular problem depended upon its frequency and importance and upon the quality and quantity of the related evidence that could be used in determining the probable "correct" response. For many variables, the problem was rare and appeared to pose little threat to data analysis. In other instances, the information available did not allow us to identify a correct response; in these cases, the entry was left unaltered.

On occasion, enumerators entered information on the schedule that violated their instructions. This type of problem included cases in which a marriage frequency number greater than two was entered; in which information on reading and writing for children under age ten was supplied; and in which alien status was indicated for anyone other than foreign-born males age twenty-one or older. The PUS staff believed that including this information would not diminish the quality of the file and that it might prove useful to some researchers, provided that they were aware that the data could hardly be regarded as representative.

On the PUS, household records contain fields indicating the state, county, and ward of residence; the size and type of location; the population of the county of residence in 1890, 1900, and 1910; the type and funding of group quarters; the number of family members in the household; the number of people in the household; and the number of person records following the household record. They also contain indicators to show whether or not the household is a fragment; whether the home is owned or rented and, if owned, whether owned outright or mortgaged; whether or not the household lives on a farm; how many different farm schedules were filled out for members of this household; and, finally, the microfilm reel, sequence, page, and line numbers of the sample point of this household.

The person records have information on surname indicators, relation to head of household, sex, race, age, marital status, number of marriages, years married, number of children ever born and surviving, the place of birth and mother tongue of the respondent and his or her parents, the language the respondent speaks, the year of immigration and naturalization status of immigrants, occupation and industry coded according to 1910 and 1980 classification schemes, two unemployment variables, literacy, schooling of children, blindness, deaf and dumb status, farm-schedule indicators, information on Civil War veterans, and created variables showing links between the respondent and his or her mother and/or wife.

These linkages were created to indicate whether a person was the biological child or the husband of a woman in the household. Linkages were made or rejected in a three-stage process.

1. Simple links—Linkages were constructed through relation-to-head codes in the most obvious cases, providing that certain other conditions were met.

2. Probability links—Linkages that could not definitely be accepted or rejected as "simple links" were evaluated based on a probability linking system that examined many relationships between the potential members of the linked pair. Characteristics of these relationships had been weighted by their ability to distinguish links from nonlinks in a hand-linked subset of the data. A total score was calculated for each potentially linked pair. If the score exceeded a prespecified minimum,

the link was accepted; if it fell short of a prespecified maximum, it was rejected. Scores in a grey area triggered the third procedure.

3. Hand linking—Linkages were accepted or rejected by virtue of re-examination of the original microfilm records for the household. This re-examination was conducted independently by two project staff members. If they agreed on the disposition of a household, no further investigation was needed. If they disagreed, a conference was held in front of the microfilm image for the household, and the outcome was decided jointly.

The 1910 Census Public Use Sample is available from the ICPSR at the University of Michigan.

APPENDIX B

A TABULAR PRESENTATION OF IMMIGRANT CHARACTERISTICS, BY ETHNIC GROUP

Susan Cotts Watkins
Arodys Robles

THIS APPENDIX presents basic information on the demographic, so-cial, and economic characteristics of many of the ethnic and ra-cial groups in the United States in the 1910 Public Use Sample (PUS). The tables that follow begin with the presentation of this infor-mation for the largest of the groups, those that form the basis of the analysis in the preceding chapters (Table B.1). Information for the sec-ond generation of these large groups follows (Table B.2). We then present this information for smaller groups: first (Table B.3) those defined by both place of birth and mother tongue, then (Table B.4) those defined by mother tongue only, and finally (Table B.5) those defined by place of birth only. An individual can be a member of only one of the ethnic groups within each table, but may appear in more than one table.[1]

The list of smaller groups is not exhaustive, since some of the groups had too few members to make the calculations of these measures reli-able. We omitted groups with a total of less than 200 foreign-born indi-viduals in the 1910 PUS.[2] A blank means that there were no cases in

[1]For example, a Polish-speaker from Russia-Poland will appear as a Polish-speaker in Table B.1, as well as in the "Russia-Polish" category in Table B.3.

[2]The following mother tongue groups had fewer than 200 individuals in the 1910 PUS and thus were not examined separately: Romanian (136), Armenian (109), Ruthenian (108), Syrian (96), Gaelic (82), Bulgarian (70), American Indian (68), Serbian (55), Eskimo (51), Belgian (40), Turkish (28), Little Russian (20), Dalmatian (15), Montenegran (15), Ar-abic (14), Moravian (9), Hindi (7), Albanian (6), Korean (5), Basque (1), Filipino (1), Rhaeto-Romansch (1), and Maltese (1). The following place of birth designations had fewer than 200 individuals in the 1910 PUS and thus were not examined separately: Turkey in Asia (198), Turkey in Europe (115), West Indies (105), Poland (105), Spain (87), Cuba (70), Atlan-tic Islands (66), Austria-Hungary (65), Australia and New Zealand (51), Bulgaria (44), Korea (29), Turkey (25), Africa (19), India (18), Montenegro (17), Azores (15), Russian Poland (15), Other Asian (12), Bohemia (10), Central America (10), Serbia (8), Syria (8), Philippine Is-lands (8), Pacific Islands (7), Puerto Rico (7), Austrian Poland (6), Iceland (2), Bermuda (1), Croatia (1), German Poland (1).

that ethnic group in that category (unless otherwise noted). It is important to note that the numbers in our sample in a particular category for which percentages are given may, nonetheless, be quite small. Thus, when the total number in the ethnic group is small, comparisons across ethnic groups in a particular category may be unwarranted. Where similarities among two or more ethnic groups justify combining the groups, we did so; where this was considered problematic, we omitted the groups rather than combining them. We note that the 1910 PUS is available for those who wish to make calculations omitted here.

The measures presented in Tables B.1, B.3, B.4, and B.5 describe the foreign-born, except the measures of schooling which also include the children of the foreign-born (and the total count of the second generation). In Table B.1 we also show these measures for native-born blacks, mulattoes, and native Americans (all three groups as they were defined by the 1910 census, where native Americans were called "Indians") and native-born whites of native parentage. Table B.2 describes the second generation (native-born but with a foreign-born mother). The generational status and ethnicity of a child are defined by his or her mother.[3] Thus, the native-born child of an English-born mother but an American-born father would be considered second-generation English; a native-born child of an American-born mother but an English-born father would be considered a native of native parentage.

In order to limit the size of the following tables, the numbers (N's) in the Public Use Sample in each ethnic group are given only for the totals in each panel; each cell then shows the percentage of the total in a particular category. In most panels the N's are the totals for whom information is available; when other criteria apply, this will be stated. The total number in a panel will not necessarily be the same as the total number in the first generation (or the second generation). In some cases, this is because information was missing from the census schedules, while in other cases it is because the information in the panel refers only to a subset of the foreign-born in that ethnic group.[4]

Most of the measures were calculated from the PUS by Arodys Ro-

[3]Second-generation immigrants could be defined as those who were native-born but whose (a) mother, (b) father, or (c) both parents were foreign-born. By excluding native-born children with a native-born mother and a foreign-born father, we are thus excluding 16,024 persons, or about 8 percent of the total native-white population.

[4]Since residence was assigned by the Census Bureau, the panels on residence by size of place, residence by division, and residence in the ten largest cities have no missing information. For some panels (e.g., date of immigration), the extent of missing data can be estimated by comparing the total with the totals given in the panels on residence. For other panels, (e.g., alien status, which was asked only of those age 21 and over) the N's are smaller than the total in the residence panels because the question was only asked of a subset of the population, and the extent of missing data cannot be estimated from the information presented here.

bles. The measures that are central to each chapter were calculated for this appendix by an author of that chapter: the mortality index and the fertility rates by Doug Ewbank, household structure and relation to head of household by Philip Morgan and Ellen Kramarow, workers by industry by Ann R. Miller, and school enrollment by Margaret Greene.[5]

Socioeconomic Measures

The measures presented below were chosen by two criteria. Some we believe to be of general interest to those interested in the characteristics of the foreign-born in the United States (e.g., the percentage married at ages 20–29). Others are used in the analyses in at least one of the chapters in this volume but are presented there only for a subset of the ethnic groups. Some of this information is available from the published volumes of the 1910 census, but most is not.

First generation. Those who were born outside the United States. Here the United States also includes Alaska and Hawaii, those born in the United States where the state is unknown, and U.S. citizens born abroad. Those born in Puerto Rico and the Philippine Islands were considered to be foreign-born. Those for whom place of birth or sex were unknown, illegible, or blank are excluded. Foreign-born includes all races identified in the census.

Second generation. Those who were born in the United States (defined as above) but at least whose mother was foreign-born.

Year of immigration. As is conventional, year of immigration is given by decade. While the number missing a date of immigration is relatively small (as shown by a comparison of the total foreign-born for each group with those for whom a year of immigration was given), the missing values vary substantially by age, and to a lesser degree by sex.[6] There is considerable heaping on years of immigration ending in 0 (e.g., 1890, 1900) and to a lesser extent on years of immigration ending in 5.

[5]We are grateful to Nikolai Botev for his assistance in preparing the tables.
[6]Of the total foreign-born aged 0–9 in 1910, 28.9 percent of the males and 29.2 percent of the females were missing a year of immigration; of those aged 10–15 in 1910, 16.9 percent of the males and 18.0 percent of the females were missing a year of immigration. There is also considerable variation across ethnic groups. In general, information on year of immigration is less likely to be missing for those in immigrant groups whose major migration streams occurred late in the nineteenth century and between 1900 and 1910 than in the ethnic groups whose major migration streams were earlier.

Age structure. We have used here the conventional breakdown between those who are under 15, those 15–64, and those 65 or older. Enumerators were instructed to get approximate age if it was impossible to get the exact age.

Percentage married at ages 20–29. The percentage married at ages 20–29 is a reasonable indicator of the marriage patterns in the population, since it is largely determined by the age at first marriage and little influenced by marital disruption from divorce or death.[7] The N's are the total number (all marital statuses) in the age group 20–29.

Residence by size of place. Since definitions of "urban" and "rural" vary, this information is presented by size of place. The census defined places of less than 2,500 inhabitants as rural. "Other" refers to military installations, Indian reservations, or blank/illegible. While most unincorporated places are small, in some cities the sections where the black population mainly lived were unincorporated (Chapter 5, this volume, footnote 3).

Residence in ten largest cities. The percents in this panel are the percentage living in one of the ten largest cities, for each ethnic group. The total percentage of those living in the ten largest cities is also given.

Residence by division. The divisions are as defined by the census. **New England:** Maine, New Hampshire, Vermont, Massachusetts, Rhode Island, and Connecticut. **Mid-Atlantic:** New York, New Jersey, and Pennsylvania. **East North Central:** Ohio, Indiana, Illinois, Michigan, and Wisconsin. **West North Central:** Minnesota, Iowa, Missouri, North Dakota, South Dakota, Nebraska, and Kansas. **South Atlantic:** Delaware, Maryland, District of Columbia, Virginia, West Virginia, North Carolina, South Carolina, Georgia, and Florida. **East South Central:** Kentucky, Tennessee, Alabama, and Mississippi. **West South Central:** Arkansas, Louisiana, Oklahoma, and Texas. **Mountain:** Montana, Idaho, Wyoming, Colorado, New Mexico, Arizona, Utah, and Nevada. **Pacific:** Washington, Oregon, California, Hawaii, and Alaska. Both Arizona and New Mexico were territories at the time.

Males in the labor force, by age. Those for whom an occupation and/or industry was given were considered to be in the labor force. The census schedule says, "Trade or profession of, or particular kind of work

---

[7]The enumerators were instructed to determine the marital status as of April 15, although a person who was single on that date may have married before the visit of the enumerator.

done by this person, as spinner, salesman, laborer, etc.", and, in a separate column, "General nature of industry, business or establishment in which this person works, as cotton-mill, dry-goods store, farm, etc." This information was supposed to be asked of every person enumerated, and enumerators were instructed to write "none" if the person had no occupation. However, nearly half of the entries for this column were blank (see Strong et al. 1989), evidence that the instructions to enumerators were ignored.[8] Individuals who were reported as currently unemployed but who had an occupation listed are included here. Some for whom an occupation was not given were nonetheless identified as workers through their relationship to the head of the household (e.g., servant, employee) (see Strong et al. 1989). We included these in the labor force. Note that published census tables include only persons 10 years old and over. The table shows the distribution of all men in the labor force, by age. The N here refers to total male workers.

Proportion of females aged 10–64 in the labor force, by marital status. The determination of labor force status was made as described above for males. N here, however, refers to the total female population aged 10–64; it is not a count of workers. It has been noted by many that censuses usually underestimate the extent to which women worked (for a fuller discussion, see A. R. Miller, Chapter 8, this volume, and Watkins, Chapter 2, this volume; see also Conk 1980). The table presents for each marital status the proportion of women who were listed as having an occupation. The total refers to the percentage of women aged 10–64 who were in the labor force.

Occupations of males aged 10–64. These are the most usual working ages, although the panel on males in the labor force shows both younger and older workers. The category **Managerial, Professional** is currently called "Managerial and Professional Specialty Occupations"; the category **Technical, Sales** includes clerical occupations, and its full title is "Technical, Sales, and Administrative Support Occupations"; the category **Farming and Forestry** also includes fishing; the category **Crafts** includes precision production, craft workers, and repair occupations; **Operators, Laborers** includes fabricators; **Other** is not reported, those in the armed forces, and those in service occupations. We have used here the major occupational divisions, recognizing that for other purposes other categories would be more useful. Occupation categories are as defined

[8]The enumerators probably roughly followed the 1900 procedure, which was to ask occupation of those aged 10 or over. However, in 1910 enumerators clearly asked it of some younger than 10; the numbers under 10 with an occupation are particularly large for those in agriculture in the South (Ann R. Miller, personal communication).

by the U.S. Bureau of the Census in its 1980 classification system.[9] The N here refers to male workers aged 10–64. These data refer only to civilian workers.

Workers aged 10 and over by industry. Workers were defined as above. For males, three industries are distinguished: **Agriculture** (including forestry and fisheries), **Manufacturing,** and **Trade.** For females, there are also three: **Agriculture, Manufacturing,** and **Private Household Services.** We note that for a third of the ethnic groups there are fewer than fifty cases for females, and for another 20 percent the number of cases is between fifty and ninety-nine; thus comparisons across ethnic groups must be made with caution. The industrial divisions are those used in the 1980 census and other current household surveys in order to facilitate comparability over time. For males, these three industries were chosen because, with a few exceptions, they include well over half of male workers in each ethnic group.[10] Note that the percentages in the table are the percent of all workers in the specific industry: because not all industries are included, the percentages do not add up to 100. These data refer to civilians only (the armed forces are excluded).

Alien status. This question was to be asked only of foreign-born males aged 21 or older. There are three possible categories: **Naturalized** were those who were born abroad but had become full citizens by taking out the second (or final) papers of naturalization, or through the naturalization of parents while the person was under age 21; **Aliens** were those who had "taken no steps towards becoming an American citizen," while **Papers** was the category for those who had declared their intention to become American citizens and had taken out "first papers" (U.S. Bureau of the Census 1910, p. 31). The N is all those for whom information on alien status was given.

Those aged 10 and over who speak English. This question was to be asked only of persons aged 10 and over. As discussed in Chapter 2, it is not possible to tell the proficiency of the individual. The N is the number aged 10 and over.

Those aged 10 and over who are able to read. This question was also to be asked only of those aged 10 and over. The enumerators were

[9]In the 1910 PUS two sets of occupational codes are given, those that correspond to the coding scheme of the Census Bureau in 1910 and those that correspond to the coding scheme of the Census Bureau in 1980. In this table we have used the 1980 occupational codes in order to facilitate comparison with modern censuses.

[10]The exceptions reflect high concentrations in Mining (Finns, Welsh), Transportation (Irish, Italians, Mexicans), or general dispersion (French-speakers born in Europe).

instructed to write "Yes" for those "who can read any language, whether English or some other" (U.S. Bureau of the Census 1910, p. 38). Again, it is not possible to infer the literacy competence of the individual. The N is the number aged 10 and over.

Homeownership. This table is based on questions about home-ownership and mortgage status, both put only to heads of households. The N is the number of household heads. The homeownership question asked whether the home was owned or rented; the mortgage question asked whether the home was owned free or was mortgaged. The instructions to the enumerators say that "If a dwelling is occupied by more than one family it is the home of each of them, and the question should be answered with reference to each family in the dwelling" (U.S. Bureau of the Census 1910, p. 39). In about 2 percent of the responses to the homeownership question, the enumerator entered a check mark in the column "home owned or rented," and in a similarly small proportion the enumerator entered check marks for the mortgage question. These were coded separately in the 1910 PUS. The home was considered to be owned if it was owned either wholly or in part by the head, his wife, a son or daughter, or other relative living in the same house with the head of the family. There are four categories: (1) **owns free** includes those who owned the house in response to the homeownership question and owned free in response to the mortgage status question; (2) the **owns mortgage** category includes those whose answers to the homeownership question were coded as "owns," those whose answers to the mortgage question were coded "mortgage," and those who answered the home-ownership question by saying they owned but where the mortgage status was indicated only by a check mark; (3) the **rents** category includes "rents" in response to the homeownership question, and blank in response to the mortgage question; and (4) **probably owned** includes those with a check mark for both the "home owned or rented" question and the "owned free or mortgaged" question.

Child mortality index. The index is the ratio of cumulative child deaths that a woman has experienced to her expected number of child deaths, where the expected deaths are based on prevailing mortality levels and the length of time her children were exposed to the risk of mortality. For the entire sample, the ratio of actual to expected deaths is 1.000. (For a more detailed discussion of this index, see Preston, Ewbank, and Hereward, Chapter 3, this volume.)[11] Where there were fewer than 50 women, the index was not calculated.

[11]These estimates may differ slightly from those in Chapter 3, owing to minor differences in coding.

Fertility rates. The Total Fertility Rate (**TFR**) is five times the sum of the five-year age-specific fertility rates. It thus represents the number of births a woman would have had if she had experienced the current age-specific rates over her entire reproductive period (ages 15–49). The numerator of the age-specific rate is the number of births to women in a given age group; the denominator is the number of women in that age group. The Total Marital Fertility Rate (**TMFR**) is an equivalent measure, save that the denominator is confined to married women. It is five times the sum of age-specific marital fertility rates. Because there are few women aged 45–49 for some of the ethnic groups, we have limited the TMFR to ages 20–44. Since unmarried women, who are less likely to have children than married women, are included in the denominators of the age-specific fertility rates, the TFR is generally lower than the TMFR. However, since the TMFR is based on fewer age groups, the TFR can exceed the TMFR if fertility is very high at ages 15–19 and 45–49. In these calculations, only births in the United States within the five years preceding the 1910 census are included. (For a further discussion, see Chapter 4, this volume.) We have not calculated marital fertility rates for blacks and mulattoes because it has been shown that marital status is reported less accurately for these groups (Preston, Lim, and Morgan 1992). Standard errors were calculated for these estimates; where they were too large for the estimates to be reliable, the estimates are not given.

Relationship to household head. This panel includes all except a small number of unclassifiable persons (e.g., homeless, transients). The **head** is the person listed as head of the household; others in the household are defined in relation to the head.[12] **Child** is defined by relationship, not by age, and includes persons listed as son, daughter, or child of the head, sons-in-law and daughters-in-law, and adopted and foster children. In Tables B.1, B.3, B.4, and B.5 all children are foreign-born; in Table B.2, all children are native-born of foreign mothers. **Kin** includes persons listed as parent,[13] or sibling of the head; grand-kin (e.g., grandparent, grand-niece); step-kin, adopted or foster kin; and other collateral kin such as aunts/uncles, nieces/nephews, cousins, in-laws, or persons who were simply listed as "family." **Boarder/Lodger** are persons listed

---

[12]Strictly speaking, the head was the individual on the first enumeration line for the census "family." In most cases that individual was listed as the "head." In some cases there was no "head" and the first person had an equivalent title such as "supervisor" or "manager"; they are not included in our tables as head of household (Strong et al. 1989). Household heads may live alone.

[13]The parent of the household head would thus be the grandparent of the household head's children, if any.

as a boarder, lodger, roomer, or renter, as well as the relatives of a boarder, lodger, roomer, or renter. **Employee** is a servant, housekeeper, maid, driver, cook, gardener, employee, nurse, laborer, farmhand, assistant helper, hired hand, caretaker, coachman, manager, overseer, governess, or the relative of one of the above. **No Relation** includes persons listed as a visitor, companion, friend, comrade, partner,[14] member, ward; it also includes those listed as inmate, patient, prisoner, orphan, military, student, or religious, most of whom were living in group quarters.

Household structure. **Living alone** were people listed as heads of households but with no one else in the household. **Nuclear** households were defined as those composed of no more than two generations of nuclear family members (e.g., parents and children). Included in this category are those who were married but with spouse absent, and married couples with no children (or no parents) present. **Extended** households were those with some non-nuclear kin, but no non-relatives (e.g., a household with an aunt but no boarders or employees would be extended). **Augmented** households were those with some non-relative (e.g., a boarder) but no non-nuclear kin. **Extended/Augmented** households included both non-nuclear kin and non-relatives (e.g., an aunt and a boarder). Members of the military, fragments, primaries, and those for whom no relationship was given—these were coded as missing (for the definition of primary individuals, see Strong et al. 1989, p. 51); all others living in group quarters were considered to be living in augmented households. This table is based on individuals, whereas in Chapter 5 (on females and households) some analyses are based on individuals while others are based on households.

School enrollment. The percentage of children enrolled in school, by age group. Census enumerators asked respondents if they attended school any time since September 1, 1909. Children are defined by age (5–18). Table B.1 includes foreign-born children and native-born children of foreign mothers; no information on school enrollment is given separately for native-born children of foreign parentage in Table B.2. The N's in the table are the total numbers aged 5–18 in each ethnic group; the percentages are the percent in each group (by sex and age) who are enrolled.[15] These were calculated only to one digit.

[14]"In the event that two or more unrelated people lived together on equal footing, enumerators were instructed to designate one as 'head' and the other as 'partner,' so the category of partner may include individuals designated by census takers as 'partners' as well as self-designated 'partners' " (Strong et al. 1989, p. 55).

[15]A slight discrepancy in the number of blacks and mulattoes between the panel in this appendix and Chapter 7 is due to the inclusion of foreign-born blacks and mulattoes in Chapter 7 and their exclusion here.

Ethnic and Racial Groups

Four groups are defined using the census definition of race: blacks, mulattoes, Native Americans, and native whites of native mothers (NWNM). All four groups are limited to those born in the U.S. The ethnic groups of the foreign-born are defined by using only two characteristics: place of birth and/or mother tongue (or, for the second generation, mother's place of birth and/or mother's mother tongue). Some groups are defined on the basis of both characteristics (Table B.3), others only on the basis of their mother tongue (Table B.4) or only on the basis of their place of birth (Table B.5). Race is not used as a criterion for the foreign-born or the children of the foreign-born.

We are limited to these two characteristics as they were reported in the census. Given the complexity of the map of Europe (particularly Central Europe) at the time, and boundary changes within the lifetimes of those counted in the census, uncertainty and thus inconsistency in recording was likely. The Census Bureau attempted to reduce ambiguity by specifying certain distinctions, as well as certain combinations (U.S. Bureau of the Census 1910, pp. 30–31; see also Chapter 2, this volume). The recorded places of birth and mother tongue do not, however, completely match the instructions to the enumerators, suggesting that some respondents or enumerators disregarded the census instructions.[16] In addition, there was some migration before coming to the United States: thus, for example, a person in our sample whose mother tongue is Polish, and who reported both parents with a mother tongue of Polish, could report England as a place of birth, although both parents were reported as born in Austria-Hungary (see Chapter 2).

In defining the ethnic groups presented here, we were guided by the literature, including the *Harvard Encyclopedia of American Ethnic Groups* and the 1910 published census volumes, and assisted by Ewa Morawska. Nonetheless, some may take issue with our decisions. We note again that the 1910 PUS is publicly available, so that it is possible to calculate our measures (and those of others) using alternative definitions.

Table B.1 and Table B.2: Large Groups

The first tables present the largest of the groups, those that are featured in the analyses in the preceding chapters. Table B.1 shows only the foreign-born, except for the figures on school enrollment (and blacks, mulattoes, Native Americans, and NWNMs). Table B.2 shows the

---

[16]For example, enumerators were instructed not to write "Austrian" as a mother tongue, but some did so.

native-born of foreign-born mothers. The two groups presented here that are defined entirely on the basis of mother tongue (Poles, as Polish-speakers, and Jews, as Yiddish-speakers) were selected first; thus the other groups do not include either Polish-speakers or Yiddish-speakers.

British.　Place of birth England, Wales, or Scotland.[17]

Irish.　Place of birth Ireland.[18]

Scandinavians.　Scandinavians are defined here by a combination of place of birth and mother tongue. Scandinavians are those with a combination of a Scandinavian mother tongue (Danish, Finnish, Norwegian, Swedish, or Icelandic) and a Scandinavian place of birth (Denmark, Finland, Norway, Sweden, or Iceland). They thus include Swedish speakers born in Norway, etc.[19]

Germans.　Place of birth Germany, mother tongue German.[20]

Italians.　Place of birth Italy, mother tongue Italian.[21]

Poles.　Mother tongue Polish.

Jews.　Mother tongue Yiddish.[22] Jews from Central Europe (roughly the Austrian-Hungarian Empire) included Yiddish-speakers born in Aus-

---

[17]Not all of these gave "English" as a mother tongue: there were some who gave "Scots" or "Celtic."

[18]Some of these gave "Irish" as their mother tongue.

[19]Some would question the inclusion of Finns in the category Scandinavians, given the quite different linguistic family of Finnish. We also note that this category excludes small numbers whose place of origin and language are not congruent, for example, Danish-speakers whose place of birth was Germany.

[20]An alternative would have been to define Germans as all those whose mother tongue was German no matter where they lived, as we did in our definition of Poles. We decided that for the purposes of further analysis of the Germans in the United States, the present definition was more useful, because there is reason to believe that the German-speakers from other areas of Eastern and Central Europe, as well as from Western European countries like Switzerland, would have had separate social institutions (e.g., churches, newspapers).

[21]If place of birth were the only criterion, there would have been 18 more Italians in our sample. Note that the category "Italians" excludes those whose mother tongue was Italian but who were born in Switzerland, Austria, and so on.

[22]This category includes small numbers whose language was reported as "Hebrew" or "Jewish." As noted in Chapter 2, this is an incomplete definition of Jews because those Jews who did not give Yiddish as a mother tongue are excluded from this category. Since the U.S. census did not ask religion, mother tongue is the only means of identifying Jews in the census. It is important to note that our definition of Jews excludes Jews whose place of birth was Germany and who gave their mother tongue as German, as well as Jews of Eastern European origin who did not give their mother tongue as Yiddish. For a fuller discussion, see Chapter 2.

tria, Hungary, Germany, Austria-Poland, and Romania. Jews from Eastern Europe (roughly Russia) included Yiddish-speakers born in Russia, Russia-Poland, and Poland. In our sample, there were no Yiddish-speakers who gave their place of birth as Austria-Hungary, Bohemia, Croatia, Germany-Poland, Serbia, Montenegro, or Bulgaria.

Native whites of native mothers.   Those whose race was given as white, who were born in the United States, and whose mothers were also born in the United States.

Foreign, not European.   Those born abroad in countries other than those of Europe. The category includes Puerto Rico, the Philippines, Canada, Mexico, Cuba, Central America, the West Indies, South America, Bermuda, Syria, China, Japan, Korea, India, Other Asia, Africa, Australia, New Zealand, Pacific Islands, Southwest Asia, and "At Sea."

Blacks.   Born in the United States, race given as "black" in the 1910 census.

Mulattoes.   Born in the United States, race given as "mulatto" in the 1910 census. Enumerators were instructed to include as "black" "all persons who are evidently full-blooded negroes, while the term 'mulatto' includes all other persons having some proportion or perceptible trace of negro blood" (U.S. Bureau of the Census 1910, p. 28). Note that it is left up to the enumerator to make this distinction, with appearance as a guide. (For a fuller discussion of this point, see A. T. Miller 1991.)

Native Americans.   Born in the United States, race given as "Indian" in the 1910 census.

Table B.3: Groups Defined by Mother Tongue and Place of Birth

Russian Polish.   Mother tongue Polish, place of birth Russia or Russia-Poland.

Austrian Polish.   Mother tongue Polish, place of birth Austria or Austria-Poland.

German Polish.   Mother tongue Polish, place of birth Germany.

French (Europe).   Mother tongue French, place of birth France, Belgium, Switzerland, Germany, Italy, Austria, England, Norway, Sweden, or Luxembourg.[23]

German I.   Mother tongue German, place of birth the Austrian-Hungarian Empire.[24]

German II.   Mother tongue German, place of birth Russia or Poland.[25]

German III.   Mother tongue German, born in northwestern Europe.[26]

French Canadian.   Mother tongue French, place of birth Canada.

English Canadian.   Mother tongue English, place of birth Canada.

Swedish.   Mother tongue Swedish, place of birth Sweden.

Norwegian.   Mother tongue Norwegian, place of birth Norway.

Danish.   Mother tongue Danish, place of birth Denmark.

Finnish.   Mother tongue Finnish, place of birth Finland.

Greek.   Mother tongue Greek, place of birth Greece.

Russian.   Mother tongue Russian, place of birth Russia.[27]

[23]Of the total 561 French-speakers from Europe, the vast majority (417) were born in France, with the next-largest groups from Belgium (75) and Switzerland (47).

[24]Most in this category gave their place of birth as Austria or Hungary, with small numbers from Austria-Hungary and Romania. There were no German-speakers from German-Poland, Bohemia, Croatia, Serbia, Montenegro, or Bulgaria.

[25]According to the *Harvard Encyclopaedia,* German-speakers in Russia typically had little to do with their Russian, Ukrainian, and Tatar neighbors (Rippley 1988, p. 426). Most were Protestants (14% Catholic, 4% Mennonite). In the United States they also kept to themselves, with community organizations separate from those of other German immigrants (Rippley 1988, p. 428). The German-speakers from Russia were predominantly farmers both in the United States and in Russia (Rippley 1988, p. 427).

[26]Most are from Switzerland, with small numbers from the other countries.

[27]The *Harvard Encyclopaedia* estimates, using the U.S. Census Bureau figures for 1910, 1920, and 1930, that only 17 percent of the 1.5 million immigrants who entered from Russia were actually Russians, and that this category often included Belorussians and Ukrainians as well (Magocsi 1988, p. 885). In making the 1910 PUS data tape, a few "White Russians" (4) were recoded as mother tongue Russian. Those who gave their mother tongue as Russian in the 1910 census probably include some other linguistic groups (United States 1913, p. 972). For example, the category is likely to include some Russian-speaking Jews and some Russian-speaking Poles, born in Russia, who gave their mother tongue as Russian, as well as Ukrainians.

Table B.4: Groups Defined by Mother Tongue Only

Magyars. Mother tongue Magyar.[28]

Bohemians and Moravians. Mother tongue Bohemian or Moravian.[29]

Slovaks. Mother tongue Slovak.[30]

Lithuanians and Letts. Mother tongue Lithuanian or Lettish. Here Lithuanians have been combined with Lettish-speakers, following the practice of the Census Bureau.[31]

Dutch/Flemish/Frisian. Dutch-speakers are combined with Flemish-speakers (most from Belgium) and Frisian speakers (most from Holland), on the grounds that the numbers are too small for separate analysis and the languages are said to be mutually intelligible.[32]

Slovenians. Mother tongue Slovenian.[33]

Croatians. Mother tongue Croatian.

Chinese. Mother tongue Chinese.

Japanese. Mother tongue Japanese.

[28]"Hungarian" was reported as mother tongue for 88 persons in the sample. These were coded in the 1910 PUS as Magyar speakers. In the 1910 PUS there is evidence that the enumerators did distinguish between Hungary as a place of birth and Magyar as a mother tongue, as they were explicitly instructed to do: there are 1,996 foreign-born individuals with a place of birth given as Hungary, but only 843 of these have a mother tongue of Magyar. Magyars were the dominant group within Hungary, and the Magyar language was the official language.

[29]Bohemian and Moravian were combined in the published volumes of the 1910 census; "returns showed that one had often been wrongly reported for the other" (United States 1913, p. 960). In the 1910 PUS, there were a total of 861 immigrants who gave Bohemian as a mother tongue, and 9 who gave Moravian. Most of the Bohemians in the sample were born in Austria; the next-largest group is from Germany.

[30]The Census Bureau believed the numbers of those with mother tongue Slovak to have a larger margin of error than perhaps any other in the regular classification. Slovak, they say, was sometimes confused with Slovenian; in addition, some who reported "Slav," "Slavic," "Slavish," or "Slavonian" should properly have been reported as Slovak or Slovenian (United States 1913, p. 961). Most Slovak-speakers came from the Austro-Hungarian Empire, the majority from parts ruled by Hungary, with another large group from Austria.

Table B.5: Groups Defined by Place of Birth Only[34]

Switzerland.   Place of birth Switzerland.

Scotland.   Place of birth Scotland.

Wales.   Place of birth Wales.

Portugal and Spain.   Place of birth Portugal or Spain.

Mexico.   Place of birth Mexico.

---

[31]There were a total of 517 foreign-born who gave Lithuanian as a mother tongue, and 87 who gave Lettish. Almost all the Lithuanians and Letts gave Russia as their place of birth.

[32]Dutch and Frisian were combined in the published volumes of the 1910 census, on the grounds that one was often wrongly reported for the other (United States 1913, p. 960). In addition, the Census Bureau believed that "some who have been reported as German in mother tongue no doubt should have been reported as Frisian, although it is believed that more of the latter have been reported as Dutch" (United States 1913, p. 960). In the 1910 PUS, there were 451 immigrants who gave Dutch as a mother tongue, 510 who gave Flemish, and 18 who gave Frisian.

[33]Most Slovenian-speakers came from lands under the political rule of Austria.

[34]There were no Polish-speakers or Yiddish-speakers in the 1910 PUS who gave these countries as a place of birth.

TABLE B.1
Large Ethnic Groups

First Generation	British	Irish	Scand.	German	Italian
All (N)	5,120	5,453	5,282	8,707	5,434
Male (N)	2,846	2,456	3,063	4,658	3,613
Female (N)	2,274	2,997	2,219	4,049	1,821
Year of Immigration					
N	4,490	4,865	4,768	7,638	5,261
Before 1860 (%)	7.06	11.28	1.41	10.28	6.46
1860–1879	20.38	26.25	16.55	26.25	1.56
1880–1889	28.98	26.17	30.10	34.25	7.72
1890–1899	17.39	18.71	20.26	16.90	18.72
1900–1910	26.19	17.60	31.69	12.32	65.54
Total	100.00	100.00	100.00	100.00	100.00
Age Structure (Males)					
N	2,841	2,445	3,053	4,658	3,613
Less than 15 (%)	5.03	0.78	2.56	1.72	8.50
15–64	82.54	81.15	90.30	81.06	89.95
65+	12.43	18.08	7.15	17.22	1.55
All	100.00	100.00	100.00	100.00	100.00
Age Structure (Females)					
N	2,271	2,988	2,215	4,045	1,821
Less than 15 (%)	6.25	0.80	3.75	1.56	14.00
15–64	80.27	81.16	87.97	79.68	84.02
65+	13.48	18.04	8.28	18.77	1.98
All	100.00	100.00	100.00	100.00	100.00
Married at Ages 20–29					
Male (N)	434	328	673	479	1,238
Female (N)	375	471	470	476	545
Married Males (%)	34.10	24.09	25.85	37.79	37.40
Married Females	57.07	35.24	52.34	65.55	86.97
Residence by Size of Places					
N	5,121	5,453	5,283	8,707	5,438
Unincorporated (%)	19.27	11.64	37.08	28.43	17.08
Less than 2,500	7.75	4.69	10.26	6.89	5.09
2,500–9,999	11.85	8.33	8.63	6.94	8.48
10,000–24,999	9.67	6.11	6.97	5.67	8.40
25,000+	51.42	69.19	36.97	51.97	60.89
Other	0.04	0.04	0.09	0.10	0.05
Total	100.00	100.00	100.00	100.00	100.00
Residence in Ten Largest Cities					
N	5,121	5,453	5,283	8,707	5,438
New York, NY (%)	8.77	18.47	4.49	11.17	24.22
Chicago, IL	3.48	5.13	7.19	6.78	2.80

Polish	Jews C.E.	Jews E.E.	NWNM[1]	FNE[2]	Blacks	Mul.	Native American
3,627	833	3,107	210,516	7,216	30,723	8,197	1,154
2,230	435	1,635	106,974	4,128	15,418	3,838	593
1,397	398	1,472	103,542	3,088	15,305	4,359	561
3,402	805	2,989	—	6,055	—	—	—
0.35	0.25	0.03	—	2.43	—	—	—
3.17	1.37	1.20	—	15.71	—	—	—
12.52	13.79	9.23	—	21.87	—	—	—
18.34	29.69	22.35	—	24.59	—	—	—
65.61	54.91	67.18	—	35.41	—	—	—
100.00	100.00	100.00	—	100.00	—	—	—
2,227	435	1,635	106,764	4,085	15,365	3,832	593
5.94	10.11	13.39	36.10	6.34	37.40	39.69	42.50
91.85	87.59	85.20	59.78	87.44	59.31	57.93	53.29
2.21	2.30	1.41	4.12	6.22	3.29	2.38	4.22
100.00	100.00	100.00	100.00	100.00	100.00	100.00	100.00
1,395	398	1,472	103,384	3,079	15,246	4,339	561
8.89	8.29	14.33	36.23	7.83	37.96	35.91	44.92
88.61	88.69	84.24	59.34	85.74	59.20	61.44	51.34
2.51	3.02	1.43	4.43	6.43	2.84	2.65	3.74
100.00	100.00	100.00	100.00	100.00	100.00	100.00	100.00
843	138	506	18,703	882	2,826	712	81
507	112	458	18,553	613	3,038	933	83
41.40	38.41	42.09	40.36	30.95	52.12	50.84	45.68
78.30	71.43	63.97	59.98	60.03	64.98	64.42	77.11
3,629	833	3,107	210,523	7,219	30,723	8,198	1,154
14.74	0.60	0.55	49.79	25.77	67.42	57.28	56.07
2.87	0.36	1.03	12.90	9.31	7.51	8.38	6.67
8.60	0.60	0.84	9.86	12.41	6.59	7.51	1.04
7.99	0.96	2.00	5.68	9.28	4.79	4.97	1.65
65.80	97.48	95.48	21.67	43.05	14.73	22.02	0.78
—	—	—	0.09	0.18	0.05	0.01	33.80
100.00	100.00	100.00	100.00	100.00	100.00	100.00	100.00
3,629	833	3,107	210,523	7,219	30,723	8,198	1,154
9.20	70.59	53.97	2.15	3.52	0.80	1.02	—
13.59	4.68	6.15	1.06	1.95	0.33	0.91	—

First Generation	British	Irish	Scand.	German	Italiar
Philadelphia, PA	3.67	5.76	0.40	2.77	2.9:
Saint Louis, MO	0.49	0.88	0.15	1.85	0.3!
Boston, MA	1.43	5.32	1.04	0.40	2.7
Cleveland, OH	1.25	0.75	0.21	1.27	1.1
Baltimore, MD	0.18	0.44	0.02	0.91	0.5:
Pittsburgh, PA	1.70	1.72	—	1.32	1.3
Detroit, MI	1.02	0.68	0.15	1.60	0.3:
Buffalo, NY	0.57	0.57	0.11	1.26	1.2.
Total % in 10 L. Cities	22.56	39.72	13.61	29.33	37.6
Other	77.47	60.28	86.24	70.67	62.3
Total	100.00	100.00	100.00	100.00	100.0
Residence, by Division					
N	5,121	5,453	5,283	8,707	5,43:
New England (%)	16.74	24.76	8.06	2.66	13.4
Mid-Atlantic	35.70	44.89	9.88	29.76	59.6
East North Central	19.84	13.53	25.23	35.60	9.9
West North Central	7.52	5.65	37.33	18.61	3.2
South Atlantic	2.62	2.07	0.57	2.48	2.5
East South Central	0.74	0.95	0.25	1.24	0.7
West South Central	1.58	0.95	0.80	3.12	2.0
Mountain	5.96	1.63	5.92	1.79	2.8
Pacific	9.30	5.54	11.89	4.66	5.5
Military	0.02	0.02	0.08	0.07	0.0
Total	100.00	100.00	100.00	100.00	100.0
Males in the Labor Force, by Age					
N	2,455	2,101	2,773	3,948	3,22
75+ (%)	1.06	1.57	0.79	1.95	0.1
65–74	7.21	8.71	3.43	8.08	0.8
35–64	60.24	62.87	57.74	66.39	35.8
15–34	31.16	26.42	37.65	23.51	62.1
10–14	0.16	—	0.07	0.05	0.5
Less than 10	0.16	0.43	0.32	0.03	0.5
Total	100.00	100.00	100.00	100.00	100.0
Females Ages 10–64 in the Labor Force, by Marital Status					
N	1,879	2,438	1,986	3,253	1,65
Single (%)	63.39	84.46	75.22	69.53	45.7
Married	7.65	7.10	3.96	5.81	7.3
Divorced	77.78	44.44	62.50	57.89	–
Widowed	35.35	34.52	39.47	25.49	28.4
Total	23.42	34.21	23.46	16.42	15.4

Polish	Jews C.E.	Jews E.E.	NWNM[1]	FNE[2]	Blacks	Mul.	Native American
3.03	5.04	8.56	1.17	0.40	0.89	0.83	—
0.58	0.24	1.32	0.56	0.28	0.43	0.81	—
0.80	2.04	3.83	0.35	2.99	0.11	0.22	—
2.42	1.68	1.42	0.27	0.69	0.08	0.10	—
0.96	—	2.00	0.54	0.14	0.94	0.98	—
2.40	0.48	1.38	0.40	0.07	0.27	0.20	—
4.99	0.36	0.19	0.29	2.69	0.01	0.01	—
2.12	0.60	0.55	0.26	1.15	—	0.09	—
40.09	85.71	79.37	7.05	13.88	3.86	5.17	—
59.91	14.29	20.63	92.94	86.12	96.14	94.84	100.00
100.00	100.00	100.00	100.00	100.00	100.00	100.00	100.00

Polish	Jews C.E.	Jews E.E.	NWNM[1]	FNE[2]	Blacks	Mul.	Native American
3,629	833	3,107	210,523	7,219	30,723	8,198	1,154
11.79	3.96	11.20	5.47	29.51	0.56	1.28	0.17
42.33	85.11	70.87	17.52	11.51	4.11	3.79	2.51
36.70	7.80	9.69	20.15	16.08	2.70	4.29	4.42
4.13	1.20	2.80	13.45	7.41	2.09	3.65	13.60
2.51	0.84	2.54	14.12	1.77	43.38	42.46	1.73
0.28	—	0.61	10.47	0.48	26.33	24.35	2.17
0.80	0.12	0.77	11.13	8.10	20.37	19.50	33.88
0.41	0.24	0.71	3.07	5.37	0.21	0.24	23.48
1.05	0.72	0.80	4.55	19.67	0.25	0.41	18.02
—	—	—	0.07	0.08	0.01	0.01	—
100.00	100.00	100.00	100.00	100.00	100.00	100.00	100.00

Polish	Jews C.E.	Jews E.E.	NWNM[1]	FNE[2]	Blacks	Mul.	Native American
2,031	361	1,360	62,980	3,627	10,165	2,349	255
0.15	—	0.15	0.77	0.85	0.96	0.64	0.39
1.08	0.28	1.10	3.30	3.50	3.33	2.43	3.53
34.22	40.72	37.57	40.47	53.35	35.29	34.10	45.49
64.20	59.00	60.81	51.20	40.86	49.49	54.15	46.27
0.20	—	0.29	3.60	0.25	8.97	7.49	1.96
0.15	—	0.07	0.66	1.19	1.96	1.19	2.35
100.00	100.00	100.00	100.00	100.00	100.00	100.00	100.00

Polish	Jews C.E.	Jews E.E.	NWNM[1]	FNE[2]	Blacks	Mul.	Native American
1,288	372	1,344	72,591	2,747	10,823	3,132	351
71.38	74.49	66.23	29.47	61.60	59.37	52.08	16.22
8.11	5.56	3.75	6.36	11.96	51.83	43.18	17.56
75.00	100.00	75.00	61.26	70.00	91.06	87.10	1.43
52.54	41.18	14.29	39.55	35.80	83.13	73.67	28.57
23.91	26.34	25.97	18.41	27.59	58.62	50.22	17.38

TABLE B.1 (continued)

First Generation	British	Irish	Scand.	German	Italian
Occupation of Males Ages 10–64					
N	2,248	1,876	2,647	3,551	3,172
Managerial, Profes (%)	8.76	5.65	3.70	7.18	2.14
Technical, Sales	13.26	9.75	5.25	10.42	6.69
Farming, Forestry	12.23	10.18	33.96	25.49	5.74
Precision, Craft	34.79	19.56	27.20	25.06	21.88
Operators, Laborers	25.09	42.43	25.73	25.06	55.49
Other	5.87	12.42	4.16	6.53	8.13
Total	100.00	100.00	100.00	100.00	100.00
Workers Ages 10–64, by Industry					
Males (N)	2,248	1,876	2,647	3,551	3,185
Agriculture (%)	11.39	8.26	31.85	24.78	5.46
Manufacturing	32.03	23.40	21.68	29.35	24.69
Trade	9.70	10.98	7.82	15.80	12.12
Females (N)	440	834	466	534	256
Agriculture (%)	2.27	0.96	6.44	12.36	4.40
Manufacturing	31.14	10.19	7.94	12.36	54.90
Private Household	24.32	55.28	53.65	37.64	7.03
Alien Status (asked only of males 21+)					
N	2,375	2,180	2,702	4,000	2,911
Naturalized (%)	69.60	77.43	64.84	80.43	18.79
Alien	22.61	15.87	21.17	11.25	73.48
Papers	7.79	6.70	13.99	8.33	7.73
Total	100.00	100.00	100.00	100.00	100.00
Those Ages 10 or Older Who Speak English					
Males (N)	2,756	2,434	3,005	4,616	3,426
Females (N)	2,185	2,977	2,169	4,012	1,672
Males (%)	99.42	99.59	91.15	90.36	48.86
Females	99.18	99.33	83.22	83.67	38.64
Those Ages 10 or Older Who are Able to Read					
Males (N)	2,756	2,434	3,005	4,616	3,426
Females (N)	2,185	2,977	2,169	4,012	1,672
Males (%)	98.55	95.81	97.87	96.58	65.27
Females	96.57	91.57	94.88	94.82	53.53
Homeownership					
N	2,030	2,038	2,000	4,001	1,477
Own Free (%)	27.78	27.67	35.70	37.77	9.75
Mortgage %	14.68	15.11	24.30	20.79	10.16

Polish	Jews C.E.	Jews E.E.	NWNM[1]	FNE[2]	Blacks	Mul.	Native American
2,003	360	1,342	60,000	3,426	9,530	2,249	239
1.85	8.89	9.31	7.48	7.44	1.15	3.07	2.51
4.29	30.56	28.81	13.71	9.78	1.07	2.36	1.67
6.19	—	0.67	43.16	25.13	60.88	49.76	77.82
21.32	32.22	30.48	13.83	15.88	4.37	6.80	4.18
63.95	23.89	27.50	18.28	33.68	24.35	24.19	12.97
2.40	4.45	2.24	3.55	8.09	8.17	13.83	0.84
100.00	100.00	100.00	100.00	100.00	100.00	100.00	100.00
2,003	360	1,342	60,000	3,426	9,530	2,249	239
5.84	—	0.60	42.64	23.47	59.49	48.82	75.31
52.87	35.27	39.41	15.91	25.49	10.51	10.76	3.35
10.08	44.17	39.79	10.33	11.33	4.13	6.40	1.67
308	98	349	13,365	758	6,344	1,573	61
4.55	—	—	18.67	6.33	55.80	40.75	32.79
41.88	60.20	67.33	17.20	26.25	1.20	1.78	24.59
22.08	14.29	3.15	14.63	22.96	35.88	42.91	32.79
1,831	320	1,173	276	3,185	70	18	10
23.10	45.31	33.42	94.20	41.60	98.57	100	10.00
68.87	38.44	47.49	3.99	54.38	1.43	—	90.00
8.03	16.25	19.10	1.81	4.02	—	—	—
100.00	100.00	100.00	100.00	100.00	100.00	100.00	100.00
2,147	416	1,528	80,063	3,939	11,383	2,757	403
1,323	384	1,365	77,163	2,945	11,256	3,247	372
46.34	81.25	77.81	98.71	74.08	98.90	98.88	67.00
43.69	70.09	62.86	98.65	78.37	98.82	98.74	59.08
2,147	416	1,528	80,063	3,939	11,383	2,757	403
1,323	384	1,365	77,163	2,945	11,256	3,247	372
73.22	89.18	90.18	95.59	84.36	65.71	79.11	56.58
70.07	74.74	74.80	95.65	86.42	63.99	78.66	50.14
1,062	245	916	41,972	2,438	6,953	1,598	219
13.47	2.86	2.62	34.54	22.19	14.14	20.17	58.90
16.20	8.57	10.48	15.40	13.17	5.84	7.88	9.59

First Generation	British	Irish	Scand.	German	Italian
Rent %	55.91	55.45	38.00	40.14	77.79
Probably Owns/Mortgage %	1.63	1.77	2.00	1.30	2.30
Total	100.00	100.00	100.00	100.00	100.00
Child Mortality Index					
Number of Women	816	897	889	1,514	970
Index	1.14	1.20	0.87	0.90	1.25
Fertility Rates					
TFR	2.96	2.63	3.92	3.94	6.93
TMFR	4.24	5.26	5.63	4.71	6.59
Relationship to Household Head					
Male (N)	2,846	2,456	3,063	4,658	3,613
Missing (%)	0.35	0.45	1.04	0.26	1.41
Head	62.33	60.99	59.97	73.19	39.72
Child	12.02	3.46	6.82	6.81	14.75
Kin	6.36	8.67	5.09	5.54	6.78
Boarder	14.79	20.28	20.08	9.96	32.83
Employee	2.57	2.08	5.09	2.00	1.80
No Relation	1.58	4.07	1.89	2.25	2.71
Total	100.00	100.00	100.00	100.00	100.00
Female (N)	2,274	2,997	2,219	4,049	1,821
Missing (%)	0.22	0.47	0.41	0.17	0.05
Head	11.87	18.39	7.93	15.24	2.75
Wife	54.22	44.74	61.78	61.84	64.85
Child	15.22	2.90	8.07	5.14	20.59
Kin	9.41	11.28	7.21	10.60	8.57
Boarder	3.87	4.34	2.93	2.12	2.14
Employee	4.18	14.91	10.55	3.68	0.44
No Relation	1.01	2.97	1.13	1.21	0.60
Total	100.00	100.00	100.00	100.00	100.00
Household Structure					
Male (N)	2,846	2,456	3,063	4,658	3,613
Missing (%)	5.80	9.28	8.10	4.81	8.22
Living Alone	2.42	2.36	3.53	2.62	1.02
Nuclear	48.07	41.65	43.39	56.78	31.08
Extended	17.15	17.71	11.62	15.54	12.96
Augmented	19.57	22.15	26.02	15.05	34.17
Ext/Aug.	6.99	6.84	7.35	5.20	12.55
Total	100.00	100.00	100.00	100.00	100.00
Female (N)	2,274	2,997	2,219	4,049	1,821
Missing (%)	2.51	5.47	2.12	2.10	0.99

Polish	Jews C.E.	Jews E.E.	NWNM[1]	FNE[2]	Blacks	Mul.	Native American
68.74	86.53	85.59	48.05	61.69	75.51	68.15	21.00
1.60	2.04	1.31	2.01	2.95	4.52	3.25	10.50
100.00	100.00	100.00	100.00	100.00	100.00	100.00	100.00
747	204	662	25,006	1,113	3,928	1,170	—
1.24	1.04	0.92	0.86	1.05	1.48	1.39	—
6.95	4.29	4.52	3.64	3.41	4.80	4.28	—
7.08	4.94	5.08	4.55	4.48	—	—	—
2,230	435	1,635	106,974	4,128	15,418	3,838	593
0.13	0.00	0.06	0.31	1.02	0.53	0.34	1.52
44.89	53.33	52.42	35.30	52.81	37.44	32.88	33.90
11.48	26.44	29.11	51.17	14.24	43.28	48.91	49.92
5.11	4.60	6.85	5.15	4.07	7.67	8.70	7.25
36.28	14.02	10.89	5.51	18.58	7.14	6.67	2.70
1.21	0.69	0.43	1.45	4.84	2.29	1.25	0.67
0.90	0.92	0.24	1.11	4.43	1.65	1.25	4.05
100.00	100.00	100.00	100.00	100.00	100.00	100.00	100.00
1,397	398	1,472	103,542	3,088	15,305	4,359	561
0.07	0.00	0.14	0.15	0.16	0.16	0.18	0.71
4.58	3.27	4.21	4.33	9.00	8.00	8.10	4.28
64.57	60.80	52.24	33.85	52.88	31.02	30.76	33.51
13.67	21.61	30.57	50.11	17.71	43.99	43.73	49.73
4.08	7.04	7.54	7.13	8.23	9.87	10.19	6.77
7.52	4.02	4.21	2.55	6.35	3.60	4.04	1.43
4.80	3.02	0.54	1.25	4.18	2.95	2.59	1.25
0.72	0.25	0.54	0.64	1.49	0.41	0.41	2.32
100.00	100.00	100.00	100.00	100.00	100.00	100.00	100.00
2,230	435	1,635	106,974	4,128	15,418	3,838	593
2.69	1.15	0.86	2.76	9.18	2.61	2.06	5.56
0.54	0.46	0.37	1.07	3.34	2.08	1.49	1.69
30.73	50.34	50.70	60.93	43.22	54.57	53.07	57.34
9.10	14.94	17.37	17.76	12.57	22.55	25.59	24.11
48.03	26.21	23.61	13.03	27.13	13.35	12.79	9.78
8.92	6.90	7.09	4.44	5.55	4.83	5.00	1.52
100.00	100.00	100.00	100.00	100.00	100.00	100.00	100.00
1,397	398	1,472	103,542	3,088	15,305	4,359	558
1.57	0.50	0.88	1.49	3.08	1.08	1.17	3.41

First Generation	British	Irish	Scand.	German	Italian
Living Alone	1.93	2.74	1.40	2.62	0.22
Nuclear	54.93	42.01	54.03	59.79	51.10
Extended	20.27	19.59	14.42	18.79	20.15
Augmented	14.82	21.35	20.87	12.18	19.82
Ext/Aug.	5.54	8.84	7.17	4.52	7.72
Total	100.00	100.00	100.00	100.00	100.00
School Enrollment					
Males (N)	956	1,134	1,296	2,360	1,165
5–9 (%)	73.3	79.2	68.1	74.8	65.2
10–13	94.6	98.2	95.2	95.8	90.3
14–18	45.1	47.4	48.3	38.8	28.1
Total	68.0	72.6	68.4	65.6	57.9
Females (N)	945	1,264	1,212	2,374	953
5–9 (%)	74.4	79.9	72.7	73.6	66.4
10–13	96.6	96.3	96.6	94.1	93.0
14–18	47.2	49.2	54.0	36.8	33.9
Total	69.8	71.8	72.3	63.3	63.9

[1] Native White of Native Mother.
[2] Foreign, not European.

Polish	Jews C.E.	Jews E.E.	NWNM[1]	FNE[2]	Blacks	Mul.	Native American
0.50	0.25	0.34	0.84	1.17	1.34	1.22	1.25
46.46	54.52	52.24	61.85	53.24	55.19	52.70	60.75
9.74	19.10	19.16	19.59	18.56	25.80	27.05	26.34
33.72	19.85	21.06	11.64	18.01	11.56	11.72	6.27
8.02	5.78	6.32	4.59	5.96	5.02	6.15	1.97
100.00	100.00	100.00	100.00	100.00	100.00	100.00	100.00
828	252	797	33,937	353	5,113	1,331	210
56.9	74.44	75.76	63.67	51.61	36.99	46.11	48.9
93.2	100.00	94.71	92.51	84.27	66.85	79.20	71.2
28.1	54.21	57.32	58.82	30.99	39.89	41.64	58.8
57.9	71.08	72.20	70.07	49.86	44.46	51.08	57.6
883	223	746	32,970	330	5,135	1,385	200
59.4	80.82	78.85	63.83	51.28	40.91	46.48	58.1
90.0	97.87	95.89	93.13	75.00	70.20	80.99	73.1
25.5	44.12	55.13	59.74	35.71	45.49	55.21	50.9
55.4	67.57	71.35	70.43	49.39	49.09	57.18	60.0

TABLE B.2
Large Ethnic Groups (second generation)

Second Generation	British	Irish	Scand.	German	Italian	Polish	Jews C.E.	Jews E.E.
All (N)	6,239	11,062	5,491	16,844	2,830	2,638	498	1,604
Male (N)	3,171	5,349	2,775	8,437	1,446	1,319	252	810
Female (N)	3,068	5,713	2,716	8,407	1,384	1,319	246	794
Age Structure (Males)								
N	3,171	5,349	2,775	8,437	1,446	1,319	252	810
Less than 15 (%)	26.02	20.23	46.34	24.11	79.05	73.31	72.62	77.04
15–64	70.96	77.64	53.59	74.73	20.95	26.69	27.38	22.96
65+	3.03	2.13	0.07	1.16	—	—	—	—
All	100.00	100.00	100.00	100.00	100.00	100.00	100.00	100.00
Age Structure (Females)								
N	3,068	5,713	2,716	8,407	1,384	1,319	246	794
Less than 15 (%)	25.95	19.81	45.18	23.60	81.94	75.21	71.54	77.96
15–64	70.34	78.07	54.82	74.97	17.99	24.72	28.46	22.04
65+	3.65	2.03	—	1.38	—	0.08	—	—
All	100.00	100.00	100.00	100.00	100.00	100.00	100.00	100.00
Married at Ages 20–29								
Male (N)	566	948	620	1,774	96	147	24	60
Female (N)	576	1,076	662	1,792	95	130	22	51
Married Males (%)	36.93	23.21	23.87	31.17	20.83	22.45	20.83	28.33
Married Females	57.29	33.36	40.48	53.35	65.26	59.23	45.45	33.33
Residence, by Size of Places								
N	6,239	11,062	5,491	16,845	2,830	2,638	498	1,604
Unincorporated (%)	23.77	13.13	45.29	30.20	12.86	17.85	0.20	0.56
Less than 2,500	10.00	5.94	11.05	7.17	3.60	4.06	0.60	0.94
2,500–9,999	13.13	9.05	9.00	7.52	7.99	9.97	1.41	1.81
10,000–24,999	8.72	7.45	5.66	5.97	7.21	8.07	1.41	3.49
25,000+	44.29	64.27	28.90	49.00	68.34	60.01	96.39	93.20
Other	0.10	0.17	0.09	0.14	—	0.04	—	—
Total	100.00	100.00	100.00	100.00	100.00	100.00	100.00	100.00
Residence in Ten Largest Cities								
(N)	6,239	11,062	5,491	16,845	2,830	2,638	498	1,604
New York, NY (%)	6.91	13.11	2.71	8.70	28.16	5.80	68.07	47.07
Chicago, IL	2.47	4.50	5.04	5.62	2.54	14.48	3.01	7.42
Philadelphia, PA	3.56	5.34	0.05	2.37	4.98	2.50	3.41	6.48
Saint Louis, MO	0.63	1.26	0.25	2.55	0.28	0.27	0.40	1.81
Boston, MA	1.03	4.07	0.33	0.28	2.23	0.61	2.81	4.99
Cleveland, OH	1.04	0.90	0.11	1.57	1.31	2.50	1.41	2.49
Baltimore, MD	0.19	0.55	—	1.13	0.42	1.14	—	2.31
Pittsburgh, PA	1.44	1.27	—	1.40	0.99	2.01	0.20	0.94
Detroit, MI	0.53	0.50	0.04	1.70	0.39	4.21	0.60	0.06
Buffalo, NY	0.67	0.92	0.07	1.34	1.48	3.07	0.20	1.00
Total % in 10 L. Cities	18.46	32.42	8.61	26.67	42.79	36.58	80.22	74.66
Other	81.53	67.58	91.39	73.33	57.21	63.42	19.88	25.44
Total	100.00	100.00	100.00	100.00	100.00	100.00	100.00	100.00

Second Generation	British	Irish	Scand.	German	Italian	Polish	Jews C.E.	Jews E.E.
Residence, by Division								
(N)	6,239	11,062	5,491	16,845	2,830	2,638	498	1,604
New England (%)	12.92	22.57	5.08	1.96	13.32	8.34	5.82	12.03
Mid-Atlantic	34.00	40.40	6.25	25.71	61.27	37.00	83.33	65.90
East North Central	21.98	16.24	25.28	38.98	9.93	43.67	7.83	11.72
West North Central	10.07	8.50	48.04	20.41	2.12	5.65	1.00	3.93
South Atlantic	2.71	2.20	0.49	2.78	1.77	2.50	—	3.37
East South Central	0.85	1.41	0.11	1.62	0.78	0.08	—	0.69
West South Central	1.86	1.56	1.09	3.32	3.67	1.52	0.20	0.50
Mountain	8.06	1.83	5.70	1.28	2.05	0.42	0.40	0.81
Pacific	7.45	5.14	7.87	3.82	5.09	0.80	1.41	1.06
Military	0.10	0.15	0.09	0.12	—	0.04	—	—
Total	100.00	100.00	100.00	100.00	100.00	100.00	100.00	100.00
Males in the Labor Force, by Age								
N	2,157	3,946	1,344	6,064	256	326	56	138
75+ (%)	0.46	0.13		0.07	—	—	—	—
65–74	2.09	1.77	0.15	1.01	—	—	—	—
35–64	48.40	54.84	19.49	45.18	7.81	3.37	5.36	5.80
15–34	47.98	42.47	76.86	52.14	89.06	92.33	94.64	90.58
10–14	0.74	0.46	3.20	1.47	1.95	3.99	—	2.90
Less than 10	0.32	0.33	0.30	0.13	1.17	0.31	—	0.72
Total	100.00	100.00	100.00	100.00	100.00	100.00	100.00	100.00
Females Ages 10–64 in the Labor Force, by Marital Status								
N	2,447	4,895	1,933	7,101	453	558	118	322
Single (%)	40.02	55.00	34.48	44.58	25.00	39.91	30.21	24.20
Married	5.09	6.11	3.85	4.71	8.82	6.19	—	2.94
Divorced	68.42	52.63	66.67	62.50	—	—	—	100.00
Widowed	30.37	39.90	41.38	37.80	33.33	50.00	—	100.00
Total	21.45	32.99	24.88	23.81	21.19	32.44	25.42	22.05
Occupation of Males Ages 10–64								
N	2,095	3,858	1,338	5,991	253	325	56	137
Managerial, Profes (%)	9.26	9.49	5.01	7.98	5.53	3.08	8.93	11.68
Technical, Sales	17.76	18.22	14.05	15.02	22.13	11.08	62.50	60.58
Farming, Forestry	20.29	13.58	47.68	27.86	7.11	16.00	—	—
Precision, Craft	24.68	20.97	13.15	19.71	19.76	17.54	14.29	9.49
Operators, Laborers	24.06	29.94	17.41	23.37	42.69	48.31	14.29	16.06
Other	3.96	7.80	2.69	4.47	9.88	4.00	—	2.19
Total	100.00	100.00	100.00	100.00	100.00	100.00	100.00	100.00
Workers Ages 10–64, by Industry								
Males (N)	2,095	3,858	1,319	5,991	253	325	56	137
Agriculture (%)	20.05	13.17	47.84	27.51	5.93	15.69	—	—
Manufacturing	25.11	13.59	15.32	26.44	31.62	47.69	28.57	26.28
Trade	10.93	14.15	12.13	16.02	20.16	10.18	42.86	46.72
Females (N)	525	1,615	474	1,691	96	181	30	71
Agriculture (%)	1.57	1.67	6.12	5.62	5.21	4.42	—	—
Manufacturing	28.38	33.07	14.76	28.50	59.38	49.17	36.67	32.39
Private Household	12.57	14.18	25.95	18.57	3.13	13.26	—	—

doesn't include Blacks or Native Am (none are "2nd generation")

Second Generation	British	Irish	Scand.	German	Italian	Polish	Jews C.E.	Jews E.E.
Those Ages 10 or Older Who Speak English								
Males (N)	2,648	4,686	1,951	7,220	496	552	123	339
Females (N)	2,559	5,011	1,933	7,217	453	559	118	322
Males (%)	99.24	99.25	98.56	98.43	96.98	96.01	99.19	97.35
Females	99.30	99.28	98.55	98.21	95.58	92.49	98.31	97.20
Those Ages 10 or Older Who Are Able to Read								
Males (N)	2,648	4,686	1,951	7,220	496	552	123	339
Females (N)	2,559	5,011	1,933	7,217	453	559	118	322
Males (%)	98.04	98.36	98.10	98.34	94.35	94.20	99.19	97.64
Females	98.59	98.10	97.83	97.88	93.60	94.63	95.76	97.20
Homeownership								
N	1,446	2,531	487	3,922	54	68	7	28
Own Free (%)	32.02	27.50	29.77	32.08	9.26	11.76	—	7.14
Mortgage	18.26	14.90	24.02	17.64	7.41	25.00	—	3.57
Rent	47.79	55.43	44.15	48.52	79.63	60.29	85.71	89.29
Probably Owns/Mort	1.94	2.17	2.05	1.76	3.70	2.94	14.29	—
Total	100.00	100.00	100.00	100.00	100.00	100.00	100.00	100.00
Child Mortality Index								
Number of Women	869	1,500	453	2,601	77	92	—	—
Index	0.89	0.99	0.59	0.76	1.17	0.80	—	—
Fertility Rates								
TFR	2.75	2.23	3.09	3.03	—	—	—	—
TMFR	3.71	4.43	4.60	4.29	—	—	—	—
Relationship to Household Head								
Male (N)	3,171	5,349	2,632	8,437	1,446	1,319	252	810
Missing (%)	0.32	0.60	0.38	0.17	0.41	0.30	0.00	0.12
Head (%)	40.43	39.09	17.10	41.80	3.32	4.85	2.78	3.33
Child	46.01	42.36	70.17	46.76	89.97	89.54	92.06	92.84
Kin	4.29	5.76	3.42	3.37	3.67	1.67	3.17	2.35
Boarder	6.46	8.41	5.28	5.50	1.87	2.05	0.79	0.99
Employee	1.10	1.35	2.62	1.45	0.07	0.45	0.00	0.00
No Relation	1.39	2.43	1.03	0.96	0.69	1.14	1.19	0.37
Total	100.00	100.00	100.00	100.01	100.00	100.00	99.99	100.00
Female (N)	3,068	5,713	2,550	8,407	1,384	1,319	246	794
Missing (%)	0.20	0.26	0.16	0.13	0.14	0.08	0.00	0.00
Head (%)	5.61	7.91	1.57	4.82	0.43	0.30	0.00	0.13
Wife	38.98	33.82	21.53	40.80	6.29	7.81	6.91	4.03
Child	43.68	41.15	66.86	44.47	87.86	87.04	91.06	92.44
Kin	6.13	8.63	3.06	5.28	3.47	2.20	1.63	2.27
Boarder	3.32	4.18	2.78	1.89	0.79	0.61	0.00	0.38
Employee	1.63	2.78	3.61	2.16	0.22	1.21	0.00	0.00
No Relation	0.46	1.26	0.43	0.44	0.79	0.76	0.41	0.76
Total	100.01	100.00	100.00	100.00	100.00	100.00	100.00	100.00

Second Generation	British	Irish	Scand.	German	Italian	Polish	Jews C.E.	Jews E.E.
usehold Structure								
Male (N)	3,171	5,349	2,632	8,437	1,446	1,319	252	810
Missing (%)	3.38	5.12	3.12	2.35	1.24	1.90	1.19	0.62
Living Alone	1.04	1.38	1.63	1.11	0.14	0.08	0	0.12
Nuclear	60.32	54.22	62.20	64.06	59.82	61.11	61.90	61.73
Extended	16.06	18.56	12.04	15.08	16.39	11.37	17.46	17.04
Augmented	14.89	15.03	16.53	13.74	16.53	21.30	16.67	18.15
Ext./Aug.	4.32	5.68	4.48	3.66	5.88	4.25	2.78	2.35
Total	100.00	100.00	100.00	100.00	100.00	100.00	100.00	100.00
male (N)	3,068	5,713	2,550	8,407	1,384	1,319	246	794
Missing (%)	1.27	2.94	1.61	1.11	1.23	1.14	0.41	1.01
Living Alone	1.01	0.82	0.27	0.59	0.07	0	0	0.13
Nuclear	61.54	54.52	63.95	65.39	62.79	61.11	59.35	64.36
Extended	16.85	22.16	13.14	17.13	16.18	12.36	15.45	15.37
Augmented	14.37	14.06	16.27	11.42	14.96	21.83	20.73	15.87
Ext./Aug.	4.95	5.50	4.75	4.37	4.77	3.56	4.07	3.27
Total	100.00	100.00	100.00	100.00	100.00	100.00	100.00	100.00

Groups Defined by Place of Birth and Mother Tongue

	Russian Polish	Austr. Polish	German Polish	French (Europe)	German 1	German 11	Germa 111
First Generation							
All (N)	1,672	1,156	689	561	880	498	45⬤
Male (N)	1,127	701	341	301	468	280	25⬤
Female (N)	545	455	348	260	412	218	20⬤
Second Generation							
(N)	843	587	1,142	642	530	460	64
Year of Immigration							
N	1,580	1,093	628	501	824	419	39⬤
Before 1860 (%)	0.06	0.37	1.11	8.38	0.85	0.95	7.2⬤
1860–1879	1.33	0.37	13.06	13.77	5.46	10.50	20.8⬤
1880–1889	6.71	5.12	39.01	22.36	14.20	14.56	34.5⬤
1890–1899	17.91	12.53	28.66	22.95	17.35	21.72	18.8⬤
1900–1910	73.99	81.61	18.15	32.53	62.14	52.27	18.5⬤
Total	100.00	100.00	100.00	100.00	100.00	100.00	100.0⬤
Age Structure (Males)							
Male (N)	1,127	701	341	301	468	280	25⬤
<15 (%)	6.65	5.99	4.11	3.99	10.26	14.64	2.7⬤
15–64	92.19	93.58	86.51	82.72	87.39	80.36	83.7⬤
65 +	1.15	0.43	9.38	13.29	2.35	5.00	13.4⬤
Total	100.00	100.00	100.00	100.00	100.00	100.00	100.0⬤
Age Structure (Females)							
Female (N)	545	455	348	260	412	218	20⬤
<15 (%)	13.03	7.25	4.60	5.00	6.31	17.43	1.4⬤
15–64	85.50	91.65	89.08	82.69	91.02	77.98	88.3⬤
65 +	1.47	1.10	6.32	12.31	2.67	4.59	10.1⬤
Total	100.00	100.00	100.00	100.00	100.00	100.00	100.0⬤
Married at Ages 20–29							
Male (N)	467	292	60	56	132	53	2⬤
Female (N)	216	204	67	47	132	50	3⬤
Married Males (%)	36.40	49.66	46.67	53.57	40.15	49.06	38.4⬤
Married Female	81.02	79.41	70.15	63.83	71.21	80.00	62.5⬤
Residence, by Size of Places							
N	1,674	1,156	689	561	880	498	458
Unincorporated (%)	12.66	15.82	18.87	21.39	16.36	56.22	40.17
<2,500	3.05	2.25	3.92	5.53	3.86	9.84	10.48
2,500–9,999	10.75	6.40	6.68	10.34	6.36	5.02	8.30
10,000–24,999	7.65	7.87	10.16	6.06	4.20	5.82	4.15
25,000 +	65.89	67.56	60.38	56.68	69.20	23.09	36.90
Other	—	—	—	—	—	—	—
Total	100.00	100.00	100.00	100.00	100.00	100.00	100.00

French-Canadian	English-Canadian	Swedish	Norwegian	Danish	Finnish	Greek	Russian
1,519	3,075	2,545	1,485	744	470	443	348
794	1,521	1,445	847	457	289	406	212
725	1,554	1,100	638	287	181	37	136
1,670	2,586	2,359	1,996	726	247	18	161
1,384	2,592	2,299	1,323	667	444	421	311
2.53	3.43	0.57	3.40	1.35	—	0.24	0.64
18.71	19.29	14.88	22.75	18.89	1.80	0.48	1.93
24.86	25.62	34.71	28.80	30.13	9.91	9.43	14.15
26.01	27.82	23.44	14.36	22.04	18.92	6.65	19.29
27.89	23.84	26.40	30.69	27.59	69.37	91.21	63.99
100.00	100.00	100.00	100.00	100.00	100.00	100.00	100.00
794	1,521	1,445	847	457	289	406	212
6.05	5.19	2.21	3.07	3.72	3.81	2.46	8.96
85.52	86.79	90.38	87.84	89.50	95.85	97.04	88.68
8.44	8.02	7.40	9.09	6.78	0.35	0.49	2.36
100.00	100.00	100.00	100.00	100.00	100.00	100.00	100.00
725	1,554	1,100	638	287	181	37	136
8.28	4.50	2.27	5.49	4.88	7.18	5.41	11.03
85.38	88.10	90.27	82.29	88.15	91.71	94.59	87.50
6.34	7.40	7.45	12.23	6.97	1.10	—	1.47
100.00	100.00	100.00	100.00	100.00	100.00	100.00	100.00
148	254	277	180	91	122	191	61
137	291	214	118	51	84	22	46
47.30	34.65	27.44	21.11	27.47	26.23	8.90	39.34
62.77	48.45	50.00	49.15	64.71	53.57	81.82	69.57
1,519	3,075	2,545	1,486	744	470	443	348
9.94	18.67	32.53	47.38	34.01	34.68	17.38	10.92
11.13	10.24	8.45	12.05	13.17	8.72	7.90	4.02
20.14	12.16	7.90	7.27	8.20	18.09	11.06	3.74
12.44	9.43	7.50	3.57	6.18	15.96	14.45	2.87
46.28	49.43	43.50	29.68	38.31	22.55	49.21	77.87
0.07	0.07	0.12	0.07	0.13	—	—	0.57
100.00	100.00	100.00	100.00	100.00	100.00	100.00	100.00

	Russian Polish	Austr. Polish	German Polish	French (Europe)	German 1	German 11	Germa 111
Residence in Ten Largest Cities							
N	1,674	1,156	689	561	880	498	45
New York, NY (%)	11.89	9.43	1.89	15.51	26.82	4.42	5.0
Chicago, IL	8.06	19.38	18.43	2.50	5.45	2.61	2.6
Philadelphia, PA	3.76	2.25	1.31	4.28	5.45	2.81	2.6
Saint Louis, MO	0.78	0.17	0.73	0.71	3.52	—	1.3
Boston, MA	1.49	—	—	0.89	0.11	0.80	0.2
Cleveland, OH	2.81	1.56	3.05	0.18	3.98	0.20	0.2
Baltimore, MD	0.96	0.52	1.74	—	0.68	—	0.6
Pittsburgh, PA	3.23	1.73	1.31	1.25	1.48	—	1.3
Detroit, MI	4.30	5.28	6.97	1.25	0.57	0.20	0.6
Buffalo, NY	1.25	1.30	5.66	0.89	0.57	0.80	0.2
Total % in 10 largest cities	38.53	41.62	41.09	27.46	48.63	11.84	14.8
Other	61.47	58.39	58.93	72.55	51.36	88.15	85.1
Total	100.00	100.00	100.00	100.00	100.00	100.00	100.0
Residence, by Division							
N	1,674	1,156	689	561	880	498	45
New England (%)	14.64	14.97	0.73	6.95	2.84	2.41	2.1
Mid-Atlantic	50.36	41.00	22.64	35.65	53.52	14.86	24.0
E. North Central	27.18	33.91	65.60	21.93	22.61	12.25	30.5
W. North Central	2.93	4.76	6.24	6.06	10.45	51.81	16.8
South Atlantic	2.99	2.08	2.32	1.43	2.27	—	1.3
E. South Central	0.54	0.09	—	1.96	0.91	—	1.5
W. South Central	0.30	0.95	1.74	8.73	1.93	2.81	2.4
Mountain	0.36	0.61	0.15	3.21	2.27	5.62	4.3
Pacific	0.72	1.64	0.58	14.08	3.18	10.24	16.8
Military	—	—	—	—	—	—	–
Total	100.00	100.00	100.00	100.00	100.00	100.00	100.0
Males in the Labor Force, by Age							
N	1,027	645	305	261	408	226	21
75 + (%)	0.10	—	0.66	2.30	—	0.88	–
65–74	0.49	0.16	5.25	5.36	2.21	3.54	7.3
35–64	29.31	29.61	60.33	56.70	43.63	46.90	70.3
15–34	69.43	70.23	33.77	35.25	53.43	46.46	22.3
10–14	0.39	—	—	0.38	0.74	2.21	–
Less than 10	0.29	—	—	—	—	—	–
Total	100.00	100.00	100.00	100.00	100.00	100.00	100.0
Proportion of Females Ages 10–64 in the Labor Force, by Marital Status							
N	494	432	315	219	384	185	18
Single	60.95	83.18	65.00	81.63	73.47	26.32	64.2
Married	5.01	14.65	3.98	11.94	13.85	8.63	11.0

French-Canadian	English-Canadian	Swedish	Norwegian	Danish	Finnish	Greek	Russian
1,519	3,075	2,545	1,486	744	470	443	348
0.66	3.64	4.20	4.64	4.03	5.96	7.45	41.09
1.65	3.22	9.51	5.59	6.99	—	10.16	3.74
—	0.49	0.51	0.20	0.40	0.21	0.45	2.87
0.07	0.39	0.20	0.07	0.27	—	0.23	—
0.66	6.11	1.45	0.67	0.81	0.21	1.58	0.57
0.07	1.24	0.28	0.20	0.13	—	—	2.01
—	0.20	0.04	—	—	—	1.13	0.57
—	0.10	—	—	—	—	0.45	—
1.32	4.98	0.04	0.13	0.67	—	2.26	—
0.13	2.34	0.16	0.13		—	0.23	—
4.56	22.71	16.39	11.63	13.30	6.38	23.94	50.85
95.46	77.30	83.61	88.36	86.69	93.62	76.06	49.14
100.00	100.00	100.00	100.00	100.00	100.00	100.00	100.00
1,519	3,075	2,545	1,486	744	470	443	348
72.81	30.37	11.28	1.95	5.91	13.40	12.87	5.46
6.32	16.00	11.55	7.00	9.95	9.15	14.90	59.20
13.30	25.92	25.89	23.76	25.27	27.23	30.47	16.09
3.82	9.89	33.36	50.20	32.53	24.47	16.70	3.74
0.26	1.11	0.63	0.20	1.08	0.64	3.16	3.16
—	0.65	0.43	0.07	0.13	—	1.13	0.57
0.26	0.91	0.90	0.40	1.48	0.43	1.13	1.72
1.32	3.61	4.44	4.17	11.16	11.49	9.71	—
1.84	11.48	11.43	12.18	12.37	13.19	9.93	9.48
0.07	0.07	0.08	0.07	0.13	—	—	0.57
100.00	100.00	100.00	100.00	100.00	100.00	100.00	100.00
688	1,334	1,322	749	410	270	387	182
1.60	0.67	0.76	1.20	0.73	—	—	0.55
3.78	4.87	3.56	4.14	3.66	0.37	—	1.65
54.80	61.24	60.36	57.81	62.68	37.41	18.60	42.31
39.39	32.91	35.17	36.58	32.68	60.37	80.62	54.95
0.29	0.07	0.08	—	—	0.37	0.26	—
0.15	0.22	0.08	0.27	0.24	1.48	0.52	0.55
100.00	100.00	100.00	100.00	100.00	100.00	100.00	100.00
645	1,401	1,001	537	263	173	36	123
73.18	64.14	79.65	73.55	56.36	80.36	80.00	83.33
14.56	8.65	4.30	1.93	3.80	9.17	20.00	4.82

TABLE B.3 (continued)

	Russian Polish	Austr. Polish	German Polish	French (Europe)	German 1	German 11	German 111
Divorced	100.00	—	—	—	100.00	—	50.0(
Widowed	53.85	66.67	45.45	62.86	34.78	42.86	52.6:
Total	20.24	33.10	14.60	35.62	30.99	13.51	23.7:

Occupation of Males Ages 10–64

	Russian Polish	Austr. Polish	German Polish	French (Europe)	German 1	German 11	German 111
N	1,018	644	287	241	399	216	20:
Manag./Profes (%)	1.77	0.47	3.83	11.62	6.27	4.17	5.9:
Technical, Sales	5.60	1.71	4.88	8.30	9.52	10.65	5.4:
Farming, Forestry	6.19	3.42	12.89	14.94	7.52	48.15	41.3:
Precision, Craft	22.59	18.01	21.95	27.39	29.32	12.50	21.1:
Operators, Laborers	62.08	72.98	54.70	26.56	37.09	23.15	22.1:
Other	1.77	3.42	1.74	11.20	10.27	1.39	3.9:
Total	100.00	100.00	100.00	100.00	100.00	100.00	100.0(

Workers Ages 10–64, by Industry

	Russian Polish	Austr. Polish	German Polish	French (Europe)	German 1	German 11	German 111
Males (N)	1,018	644	287	241	399	216	20:
Agriculture (%)	5.60	3.42	12.54	14.11	7.02	48.15	39.9(
Manufacturing	50.69	61.49	33.90	25.72	42.86	12.97	26.1:
Trade	11.30	6.99	11.85	16.60	18.55	13.89	10.8:
Females (N)	100	143	46	78	119	25	4:
Agriculture (%)	1.00	3.50	15.22	2.56	5.04	40.00	15.9:
Manufacturing	40.00	49.65	26.09	16.66	17.65	12.00	11.3(
Private Household	28.00	16.08	19.57	25.64	45.38	12.00	47.7:

Alien Status (asked only of males 21 +)

	Russian Polish	Austr. Polish	German Polish	French (Europe)	German 1	German 11	German 111
N	926	563	292	270	353	207	20(
Naturalized (%)	16.63	10.12	66.78	53.70	38.24	53.62	73.3(
Alien	76.13	83.30	19.52	36.67	48.16	31.40	12.1:
Papers	7.24	6.57	13.70	9.63	13.60	14.98	14.5(
Total	100.00	100.00	100.00	100.00	100.00	100.00	100.0(

Those Ages 10 or Older Who Speak English

	Russian Polish	Austr. Polish	German Polish	French (Europe)	German 1	German 11	German 111
Males (N)	1,082	675	332	292	438	260	24:
Females (N)	502	437	337	251	395	195	20(
Male (%)	46.03	32.44	72.29	80.14	66.21	65.38	92.7:
Female (%)	46.81	32.04	50.74	78.09	65.82	47.69	86.4:

Those Ages 10 or Older Who Are Able to Read

	Russian Polish	Austr. Polish	German Polish	French (Europe)	German 1	German 11	German 111
Males (N)	1082	675	332	292	438	260	24:
Females (N)	502	437	337	251	395	195	20(
Males (%)	71.44	71.26	81.33	96.58	96.35	90.00	95.1(
Females	65.34	66.82	80.12	88.84	91.14	84.62	96.1:

French-Canadian	English-Canadian	Swedish	Norwegian	Danish	Finnish	Greek	Russian
—	80.00	50.00	50.00	100.00	—	—	—
37.74	31.67	36.49	40.82	36.36	71.43	—	33.33
32.71	26.62	23.88	21.97	18.25	34.68	36.11	28.46
650	1,257	1,264	707	391	265	385	177
4.46	12.17	4.35	3.11	3.84	1.13	4.94	7.34
6.62	14.96	5.30	5.37	6.91	1.51	15.32	25.98
11.69	19.65	30.06	43.85	38.36	20.38	1.30	5.08
23.23	21.64	28.80	21.78	24.55	38.49	4.42	15.82
50.31	25.46	28.09	21.07	20.20	35.47	57.92	38.98
3.69	6.13	3.40	4.81	6.14	3.02	16.10	6.78
100.00	100.00	100.00	100.00	100.00	100.00	100.00	100.00
650	1,257	1,264	707	391	265	385	177
8.92	18.22	28.16	42.57	36.57	14.34	1.04	3.95
51.54	24.35	27.06	15.14	17.40	20.37	27.80	24.29
9.85	12.49	6.96	7.64	12.53	5.66	25.97	35.03
211	373	239	118	48	60	13	35
0.95	1.88	4.60	11.86	8.33	1.76	—	—
58.77	15.55	7.12	3.39	10.41	18.33	69.23	17.14
9.95	23.86	58.58	50.85	39.58	51.67	15.38	28.57
621	1,180	1,272	735	400	273	354	173
50.56	63.98	70.13	65.44	71.25	27.84	6.21	31.21
45.09	29.58	18.24	17.41	14.00	56.04	87.01	56.07
4.35	6.44	11.64	17.14	14.75	16.12	6.78	12.72
100.00	100.00	100.00	100.00	100.00	100.00	100.00	100.00
766	1,487	1,424	829	447	281	401	204
691	1,516	1,083	615	283	175	36	125
85.77	99.53	93.26	93.24	94.85	67.62	37.66	69.12
69.03	99.27	86.52	82.11	93.29	49.71	19.44	72.80
766	1,487	1,424	829	447	281	401	204
691	1,516	1,083	615	283	175	36	125
81.46	97.92	98.38	97.35	99.11	94.66	82.04	80.88
85.38	98.09	95.57	94.80	95.76	89.71	69.44	80.80

TABLE B.3 *(continued)*

	Russian Polish	Austr. Polish	German Polish	French (Europe)	German 1	German 11	Germ. 111
Homeownership							
N	465	290	279	202	267	178	18
Owns Free (%)	9.03	7.93	26.52	31.19	16.85	36.52	35.4
Mortgage	12.04	10.69	30.11	11.39	13.86	28.09	20.9
Rents	77.42	78.62	42.65	53.47	66.29	32.58	41.9
Probably Owns							
Mortgage	1.51	2.76	0.72	3.96	3.00	2.81	1.6
Total	100.00	100.00	100.00	100.00	100.00	100.00	100.0
Child Mortality Index							
Number of Women	304	243	176	86	187	106	8
Index	1.29	1.29	1.14	1.21	0.98	0.93	0.8
Fertility Rates							
TFR	—	—	7.62	—	3.92		
TMFR	6.84	6.80	7.87	4.27	4.63	—	—
Relationship to Household Head							
Male (N)	1,127	701	341	301	468	280	25
Missing (%)	0.09	0.29	0.00	0.66	0.43	0.00	1.1
Head	39.13	39.51	74.78	56.48	52.99	60.36	68.2
Child	11.98	8.13	15.25	9.97	17.52	22.14	7.1
Kin	4.79	5.71	4.69	8.97	4.91	4.64	3.5
Boarder	41.35	44.79	4.11	18.94	20.73	7.50	7.5
Employee	1.69	0.86	0.29	2.99	1.50	3.93	7.5
No Relation	0.98	0.71	0.88	1.99	1.92	1.43	4.7
Total	100.00	100.00	100.00	100.00	100.00	100.00	100.00
Female (N)	545	455	348	260	412	218	200
Missing (%)	0.00	0.22	0.00	0.77	0.00	0.00	0.4
Head	4.59	2.86	7.18	13.46	4.85	4.13	7.2
Wife	63.85	60.66	72.41	46.54	58.74	62.84	65.0
Child	16.70	9.89	12.36	9.62	15.78	25.69	4.8
Kin	4.59	3.96	3.45	9.62	7.04	5.50	10.1
Boarder	5.32	16.04	0.86	10.77	3.16	0.92	2.4
Employee	4.77	5.71	2.01	6.92	9.95	0.92	6.8
No Relation	0.18	0.66	1.72	2.31	0.49	0.00	2.9
Total	100.00	100.00	100.00	100.00	100.00	100.00	100.00
Household Structure							
Male (N)	1,127	701	341	301	468	280	252
Missing (%)	2.48	2.57	2.64	7.64	4.27	2.86	6.75
Living Alone	0.80	0	0.59	2.66	1.50	1.43	4.37
Nuclear	24.84	20.83	69.21	42.86	39.96	60.36	54.76
Extended	8.16	7.70	15.54	16.94	8.97	14.29	11.51

immigrants only

French-Canadian	English-Canadian	Swedish	Norwegian	Danish	Finnish	Greek	Russian
540	1,091	979	573	308	122	67	106
19.81	26.49	35.04	38.05	32.47	39.34	4.48	3.77
14.26	17.87	24.41	25.83	27.27	10.66	4.48	10.38
63.70	53.71	38.71	33.51	39.29	46.72	86.57	84.91
2.22	1.92	1.84	2.61	0.97	3.28	4.48	0.94
100.00	100.00	100.00	100.00	100.00	100.00	100.00	100.00
276	533	431	236	131	85	16	67
1.38	0.85	0.83	0.85	0.96	1.08	1.07	0.91
4.73	2.42	3.30	4.28	—	6.28	—	—
6.07	3.70	4.93	6.24	5.51	—	—	—
794	1,521	1,445	847	457	289	406	212
0.13	0.33	1.25	1.30	0.22	0.69	3.20	0.47
61.71	62.59	61.73	61.04	64.33	40.14	17.00	47.17
19.14	13.81	7.27	6.26	6.35	6.92	2.96	15.09
4.03	5.65	5.40	5.90	4.81	1.73	7.64	3.77
12.59	13.41	18.75	16.65	15.10	46.02	59.11	25.47
1.13	2.10	3.81	6.61	6.78	4.15	2.71	3.30
1.26	2.10	1.80	2.24	2.41	0.35	7.39	4.72
100.00	100.00	100.00	100.00	100.00	100.00	100.00	100.00
725	1,554	1,100	638	287	181	37	136
0.14	0.13	0.82	0.00	0.00	0.00	0.00	0.00
7.45	9.72	8.45	9.25	5.92	3.87	0.00	4.41
51.86	54.12	63.09	58.31	66.20	57.46	43.24	57.35
22.07	13.64	6.36	9.56	10.10	9.94	13.51	19.85
6.90	9.40	7.09	8.46	7.67	2.76	10.81	5.88
6.76	6.31	2.09	3.29	2.79	7.18	27.03	5.88
2.62	5.34	10.91	9.56	6.62	18.78	5.41	6.62
2.21	1.35	1.18	1.57	0.70	0.00	0.00	0.00
100.00	100.00	100.00	100.00	100.00	100.00	100.00	100.00
794	1,521	1,445	847	457	289	406	212
3.53	6.90	8.03	8.85	6.35	9.69	26.85	8.02
0.5	2.76	3.46	4.84	3.28	0.69	1.48	0.47
55.79	49.57	45.88	41.79	47.26	28.37	5.42	40.09
14.36	16.44	12.18	13.34	11.82	3.46	4.93	11.79

TABLE B.3 (*continued*)

	Russian Polish	Austr. Polish	German Polish	French (Europe)	German I	German II	Germa III
Augmented	54.04	57.49	11.14	24.58	34.40	18.93	16.2
Ext./Aug.	9.67	11.41	0.88	5.32	10.90	2.14	6.3!
Total	100.00	100.00	100.00	100.00	100.00	100.00	100.0(
Female (N)	545	455	348	260	412	218	20(
Missing (%)	0.73	2.20	2.01	5.38	1.21	0.46	4.8!
Living Alone	0.55	0	1.15	1.92	0.49	0.46	0.4!
Nuclear	40.73	33.85	72.13	45.00	44.90	72.48	59.2;
Extended	8.26	9.45	13.79	17.31	16.75	14.68	16.0;
Augmented	39.27	44.62	10.06	21.15	29.13	10.55	14.0!
Ext./Aug.	10.46	9.89	0.86	9.23	7.52	1.38	5.3
Total	100.00	100.00	100.00	100.00	100.00	100.00	100.0(
School Enrollment							
Males (N)	109	60	24	16	56	49	1]
5–9 (%)	68.97	58.82	28.57	42.86	66.67	46.67	75.0(
10–13	95.24	83.33	100.00	50.00	100.00	100.00	100.0(
14–18	23.73	16.13	16.67	42.86	45.45	42.11	50.0(
Total	49.54	41.67	37.50	43.75	66.07	61.22	72.7;
Females (N)	95	70	21	12	53	40	(
5–9 (%)	50.00	66.67	33.33	100.00	63.64	26.67	—
10–13	90.91	60.00	60.00	66.67	100.00	100.00	100.0(
14–18	27.91	12.50	—	40.00	21.21	53.85	50.0(
Total	49.47	28.57	28.57	66.67	43.40	57.50	66.6;

TABLE B.3 (continued)

French-Canadian	English-Canadian	Swedish	Norwegian	Danish	Finnish	Greek	Russian
21.16	17.82	23.74	24.09	23.63	46.71	42.61	34.91
4.66	6.51	6.71	7.08	7.66	11.07	18.72	4.72
100.00	100.00	100.00	100.00	100.00	100.00	100.00	100.00
725	1,554	1,100	638	287	181	37	136
2.34	3.28	2.27	2.35	1.74	1.10	0.00	1.47
0.69	1.48	1.82	1.25	0.7	0.55	0	0
55.86	50.90	54.64	52.35	59.23	46.41	21.62	56.62
17.52	19.76	14.18	17.24	16.38	3.87	8.11	12.50
19.72	17.44	20.00	19.91	17.77	35.36	37.84	24.26
3.86	7.14	7.09	6.90	4.18	12.71	32.43	5.15
100.00	100.00	100.00	100.00	100.00	100.00	100.00	100.00
78	102	45	41	21	11	42	21
77.78	66.67	80.00	60.00	75.00	100.00	33.33	83.33
100.00	100.00	90.00	85.71	100.00	100.00	100.00	100.00
15.56	52.17	20.00	15.79	41.67	37.50	7.89	40.00
46.15	71.57	55.56	43.90	61.90	54.55	11.90	80.95
86	100	40	46	24	19	7	29
71.43	61.90	84.62	66.67	100.00	60.00	—	88.89
90.91	88.46	85.71	100.00	75.00	100.00	100.00	100.00
12.00	58.48	10.00	22.22	33.33	37.50	16.67	23.53
41.86	67.00	47.50	56.52	58.33	63.16	28.57	51.72

TABLE B.4
Groups Defined by Mother Tongue Only

First Generation	Magyar	Bohemian + Moravian	Slovak	Lith Lett
All	960	870	820	6
Male (N)	588	463	547	3
Female (N)	372	407	273	2
Second Generation (N)	361	1,217	542	2
Year of Immigration				
N	908	798	772	5
Before 1860 (%)	—	1.50	—	
1860–1879	0.22	18.80	0.65	0.
1880–1889	5.62	28.57	9.20	4.
1890–1899	13.99	19.92	20.47	17.
1900–1910	80.18	31.20	69.69	77.
Total	100.00	100.00	100.00	100.
Age Structure (Males)				
Males (N)	588	463	547	3
Less than 15 (%)	7.99	6.48	7.13	4.
15–64	90.99	87.69	92.50	95.
65 +	1.02	5.83	0.37	
All	100.00	100.00	100.00	100.
Age Structure (Females)				
Females (N)	372	407	273	2
Less than 15 (%)	14.25	4.42	9.16	13.
15–64	84.41	89.43	90.11	86.
65 +	1.34	6.14	0.73	
All	100.00	100.00	100.00	100.
Married at Ages 20–29				
Male (N)	206	106	200	1
Female (N)	124	85	110	8
Married Males (%)	43.20	55.66	46.00	23.
Married Females	75.00	71.76	87.27	74.
Residence, by Size of Places				
N	960	870	820	6
Unincorporated (%)	20.52	30.57	32.80	10.
Less than 2,500	3.02	5.40	4.15	4.
2,500–9,999	10.83	4.60	17.80	11.
10,000–24,999	9.69	2.99	13.90	16.
25,000 +	55.94	55.98	31.10	57.
Other	—	0.46	0.24	
Total	100.00	100.00	100.00	100.

Dutch + Flem + Frisian	Slovenian	Croatian	Chinese	Japanese
519	332	242	237	258
319	216	191	226	238
200	116	51	11	20
648	201	62	85	16
476	315	236	211	213
6.51	—	—	0.47	—
17.65	1.27	—	23.70	—
25.63	5.71	2.97	46.92	1.41
16.60	18.73	9.32	18.48	12.68
33.61	74.29	87.71	10.43	85.92
100.00	100.00	100.00	100.00	100.00
319	216	191	226	238
7.52	7.41	2.62	1.33	10.08
81.19	92.59	96.34	95.13	89.92
11.29	—	1.05	3.54	—
100.00	100.00	100.00	100.00	100.00
200	116	51	11	22
12.50	11.21	7.84	18.18	5.00
74.50	88.79	92.16	81.82	95.00
13.00	—	—	—	—
100.00	100.00	100.00	100.00	100.00
53	89	91	11	112
27	49	25	2	8
33.96	39.33	32.97	27.27	0.89
81.48	89.80	92.00	100.00	75.00
519	333	242	239	258
36.80	24.92	29.34	12.13	42.25
5.97	3.00	5.37	0.42	7.75
13.29	18.02	11.57	4.60	8.14
5.20	5.41	12.81	8.37	11.24
38.54	48.61	40.91	74.48	29.84
0.19	—	—	—	0.78
100.00	100.00	100.00	100.00	100.00

First Generation	Magyar	Bohemian + Moravian	Slovak	Lith-Lettis
Residence in Ten Largest Cities				
N	960	870	820	60
New York, NY (%)	13.85	10.00	3.41	5.9
Chicago, IL	4.48	25.06	7.07	16.0
Philadelphia, PA	0.94	1.38	1.34	5.7
Saint Louis, MO	0.83	1.49	0.49	0.1
Boston, MA	0.31	0.11	—	0.9
Cleveland, OH	6.98	5.98	4.76	1.4
Baltimore, MD	0.52	1.72	—	1.9
Pittsburgh, PA	1.46	0.80	2.07	1.3
Detroit, MI	0.83	0.23	—	0.3
Buffalo, NY	0.83	—	—	—
Total %	31.03	46.77	19.14	34.1
Residence, by Division				
N	960	870	820	60
New England (%)	6.15	0.34	2.44	13.7
Mid-Atlantic	62.08	16.78	64.76	48.6
East North Central	24.79	46.67	26.95	27.4
West North Central	2.71	23.91	2.20	4.6
South Atlantic	2.50	2.41	2.32	2.4
East South Central	0.42	—	—	—
West South Central	0.10	8.05	0.37	1.4
Mountain	0.31	0.80	0.85	0.6
Pacific	0.94	1.03	0.12	0.8
Military	—	—	—	—
Total	100.00	100.00	100.00	100.0
Males in the Labor Force, by Age				
N	525	408	498	37
75+ (%)	0.19	—	—	—
65–74	0.38	2.70	0.20	—
35–64	37.9	55.64	32.13	33.0
15–34	61.33	40.69	66.87	65.0
10–14	—	0.74	0.20	—
Less than 10	0.19	0.25	0.60	1.3
Total	100.00	100.00	100.00	100.0
Females Ages 10–64 in the Labor Force, by Marital Status				
N	333	372	258	19
Single (%)	73.49	72.73	64.86	75.4
Married	10.48	7.07	7.66	10.5
Divorced	—	100.0	—	100.0
Widowed	36.84	27.27	33.33	50.00
Total	27.93	17.47	17.05	30.2

Table B.4 (*continued*)

Dutch + Flem + Frisian	Slovenian	Croatian	Chinese	Japanese
519	333	242	239	258
3.47	5.71	0.83	14.23	2.33
5.97	3.60	10.74	2.51	—
—	—	—	0.42	—
—	—	2.48	—	—
0.39	—	—	3.77	—
—	10.81	2.07	2.09	0.39
—	1.20	—	—	—
0.19	2.10	4.96	—	—
2.12	0.60	6.20	3.35	—
—	—	—	—	—
12.14	24.02	27.28	26.37	2.69
519	333	242	239	258
1.16	3.30	—	7.11	—
25.63	39.64	26.45	16.32	2.71
48.55	29.73	46.28	11.72	0.78
14.84	4.20	18.60	—	1.94
0.19	2.10	1.24	—	—
0.39	—	—	0.42	—
0.58	3.00	—	1.26	—
4.05	9.61	5.79	2.51	15.12
4.43	8.41	1.65	60.67	78.68
0.19	—	—	—	0.78
100.00	100.00	100.00	100.00	100.00
273	199	180	216	227
1.10	—	1.11	0.93	—
6.59	—	—	1.85	—
56.04	31.16	26.67	81.94	20.26
35.9	68.84	72.22	13.89	70.04
0.37	—	—	—	—
—	—	—	1.39	9.69
100.00	100.00	100.00	100.00	100.00
159	106	47	10	20
45.83	66.67	80.00	50.00	100.00
2.36	4.88	9.76	—	56.25
—	—	—	—	—
57.14	50.00	100.0	—	100.0
11.32	17.92	19.15	10.00	65.00

non-English one

First Generation	Magyar	Bohemian + Moravian	Slovak	Lith + Lettisl
Occupations of Males Ages 10–64				
N	521	396	494	36?
Manag/Profess (%)	1.15	3.03	0.40	1.0%
Technical/Sales	5.57	8.84	0.81	4.3(
Farming, Forestry	3.26	29.04	4.25	3.2?
Precision, Craft	26.49	26.01	28.14	33.2.
Operators Laborers	60.27	30.30	63.77	54.5(
Other	3.26	2.78	2.63	3.5.
Total	100.00	100.00	100.00	100.0(
Workers Ages 10–64 by Industry				
Males (N)	521	396	494	36?
Agriculture (%)	3.26	28.28	4.05	3.0(
Manufacture	48.56	28.53	50.60	50.6%
Trade	9.21	17.93	3.24	8.7?
Females	93	65	44	5%
Agriculture (%)	1.1	21.5	—	—
Manufacture	31.2	29.2	31.8	37.%
Private Household	46.2	23.1	40.9	24.
Alien Status (asked only of males 21 +)				
N	506	391	464	34?
Naturalized (%)	13.64	59.85	14.22	17.5%
Alien	75.89	24.55	79.09	73.7%
Papers	10.47	15.60	6.68	8.6?
Total	100.00	100.00	100.00	100.0(
Those Age 10 or Older Who Speak English				
Males (N)	566	446	523	38
Females (N)	338	397	260	19.
Males (%)	41.17	71.30	44.36	56.1
Female	52.96	57.93	40.77	45.8.
Those Age 10 or Older Who Are Able to Read				
Males (N)	566	446	523	38
Females (N)	338	397	260	19
Males (%)	89.58	92.15	81.07	76.1
Females	83.73	89.17	68.85	65.6.
Homeownership				
N	234	366	214	14
Owns Free (%)	4.70	34.15	12.62	10.2.
Mortgage	10.68	18.85	11.21	14.2.
Rents	81.20	45.90	72.43	74.8.
Probably Owns/Mortgage	3.42	1.09	3.74	0.6
Total	100.00	100.00	100.00	100.0(

Dutch + Flem + Frisian	Slovenian	Croatian	Chinese	Japanese
252	199	178	207	205
3.57	1.51	6.18	7.25	6.34
6.35	1.01	1.12	13.04	4.39
36.11	14.57	0.56	14.49	33.66
20.24	16.58	16.85	0.48	1.95
28.57	60.30	72.47	43.00	23.90
5.16	6.03	2.81	22.74	29.76
100.00	100.00	100.00	100.00	100.00
252	199	178	207	205
35.71	11.06	—	14.01	33.66
22.62	45.23	50.00	18.84	4.39
11.11	6.03	3.93	22.71	13.66
18	19	9	1	13
—	—	—	—	—
22.2	31.6	11.1	—	—
33.3	42.1	33.3	—	46.15
260	194	157	202	192
63.08	10.82	7.64	5.45	2.60
25.38	76.80	84.08	94.55	95.83
11.54	12.37	8.28	—	1.56
100.00	100.00	100.00	100.00	100.00
304	207	187	223	214
185	106	47	10	20
85.53	58.45	33.69	45.29	74.77
77.30	46.23	34.04	30.00	35.00
304	207	187	223	214
185	106	47	10	20
94.08	76.81	68.45	81.61	90.19
92.97	70.75	70.21	40.00	70.00
208	88	43	68	41
27.40	15.91	9.30	2.94	—
25.00	7.95	4.65	—	—
46.15	73.86	79.07	95.59	90.24
1.44	2.27	6.98	1.47	9.76
100.00	100.00	100.00	100.00	100.00

First Generation	Magyar	Bohemian + Moravian	Slovak	Lith + Lettish
Child Mortality Index				
Number of Women	174	217	178	112
Index	1.095	0.9055	1.2326	1.3049
Fertility Rates				
TFR	—	4.77	—	—
TMFR	—	—	—	—
Relationship to Household Head				
Male (N)	588	463	547	394
Missing (%)	0.17	0.22	0.18	0.25
Head	37.93	71.49	37.66	36.29
Child	12.41	13.39	11.52	5.84
Kin	4.42	4.10	6.40	3.55
Boarder	42.69	6.48	42.60	51.02
Employee	0.51	3.46	0.73	2.54
No Relation	1.87	0.86	0.91	0.51
Total	100.00	100.00	100.00	100.00
Female (N)	372	407	273	210
Missing (%)	0.00	0.74	0.37	0.00
Head	2.96	8.85	3.30	1.90
Wife	58.06	69.04	72.89	60.95
Child	19.35	9.09	9.52	15.7
Kin	3.49	6.63	3.66	2.84
Boarder	3.23	1.47	4.03	13.8
Employee	12.10	3.93	5.86	4.29
No Relation	0.81	0.25	0.37	0.48
Total	100.00	100.00	100.00	100.00
Household Structure				
Male (N)	588	463	547	39
Missing	4.76	3.02	2.01	2.2
Living Alone	0.34	1.94	0.00	0.00
Nuclear	28.91	67.39	26.51	16.7
Extended	9.01	11.88	5.30	4.8
Augmented	50.51	11.45	51.92	65.2
Ext./Aug.	6.46	4.32	14.26	10.9
Total	100.00	100.00	100.00	100.0
Female (N)	372	407	273	21
Missing	1.61	1.72	1.10	0.9
Living Alone	0.27	1.47	0.37	0.0
Nuclear	49.19	69.78	45.42	25.7
Extended	10.75	14.50	8.79	4.7
Augmented	29.84	9.09	35.90	59.5
Ext./Aug.	8.33	3.44	8.42	9.0
Total	100.00	100.00	100.00	100.0

Dutch + Flem + Frisian	Slovenian	Croatian	Chinese	Japanese
85	73	32	4	8
0.6764	1.0093	1.0004	0.3454	—
—	—	—	—	—
—	—	—	—	—
319	216	191	226	238
1.25	0.46	1.05	3.54	2.52
60.50	39.35	22.51	30.09	17.23
16.30	11.11	2.62	0.00	0.84
3.76	5.56	2.62	0.88	0.84
12.54	36.11	65.97	42.04	38.66
3.13	4.17	2.62	11.06	32.35
2.51	3.24	2.62	12.39	7.56
100.00	100.00	100.00	100.00	100.00
200	116	51	11	20
0.00	0.00	0.00	0.00	0.00
7.50	2.59	1.96	0.00	0.00
67.50	69.83	76.47	72.73	55.00
16.00	18.10	9.80	18.18	0.00
5.00	2.59	3.92	0.00	0.00
0.50	0.86	1.96	0.00	20.00
2.50	6.03	5.88	9.09	25.00
1.00	0.00	0.00	0.00	0.00
100.00	100.00	100.00	100.00	100.00
319	216	191	226	238
5.33	8.80	13.61	24.34	25.63
1.88	0.46	0.52	9.29	3.36
54.55	29.63	10.47	3.98	3.36
12.54	4.17	0.52	0.88	0.00
23.82	43.52	58.64	56.19	55.46
1.88	13.43	16.23	5.31	12.18
100.00	100.00	100.00	100.00	100.00
200	116	51	11	20
0.00	0.00	1.96	9.09	15.00
1.00	0.00	0	0	0
68.00	54.31	43.14	36.36	20.00
12.50	7.76	3.92	9.09	0.00
14.50	31.90	41.18	18.18	55.00
4.00	6.03	9.80	27.27	10.00
100.00	100.00	100.00	100.00	100.00

TABLE B.4 (continued)

First Generation	Magyar	Bohemian + Moravian	Slovak	Lith Letti
School Enrollment				
Males (N)	69	37	54	]
5–9 (%)	62.5	83.33	57.14	33.:
10–13	94.74	57.14	83.33	75.(
14–18	41.18	44.44	28.57	22.:
Total	62.32	67.57	51.85	42.]
Females (N)	77	23	30	:
5–9 (%)	62.96	50.00	71.43	66.(
10–13	92.86	100.00	100.00	100.(
14–18	13.89	25	—	18.]
Total	87.01	82.61	93.33	91.]

Dutch + Flem + Frisian	Slovenian	Croatian	Chinese	Japanese
32	23	7	3	4
72.73	28.57	50	—	—
100.00	100.00	—	—	—
25.00	33.33	—	66.67	50.00
62.50	52.17	14.29	66.67	25.00
27	17	6	2	3
69.23	42.86	66.67	—	100.00
100.00	100.00	0	100.00	100.00
28.57	14.29	—	—	—
85.19	76.47	83.33	100.00	100.00

Groups Defined by Place of Birth Only

First Generation	Switzerland	Scotland	Wales	Spain + Portugal	Mexico
All (N)	478	1,066	346	359	953
Male (N)	257	586	197	224	585
Female (N)	221	480	149	135	368
Second Generation (N)	639	1,310	566	298	573
Year of Immigration					
N	422	934	299	335	680
Before 1860 (%)	7.11	5.78	9.03	—	0.44
1860–1879	18.01	19.27	25.08	6.57	4.26
1880–1889	34.12	29.98	29.77	17.91	8.38
1890–1899	21.33	13.38	17.39	16.72	13.53
1900–1910	19.43	31.58	18.73	58.81	73.38
Total	100.00	100.00	100.00	100.00	100.00
Age Structure (Males)					
Males (N)	257	586	197	224	585
Less than 15 (%)	2.72	7.00	4.06	8.93	18.80
15–64	85.60	81.40	82.23	87.50	77.61
65+	11.67	11.60	13.71	3.57	3.59
All	100.00	100.00	100.00	100.00	100.00
Age Structure (Females)					
Females (N)	221	480	149	135	367
Less than 15 (%)	1.36	6.67	3.36	10.37	23.64
15–64	89.14	80.00	84.56	85.19	72.53
65+	9.50	13.33	12.08	4.44	3.80
All	100.00	100.00	100.00	100.00	100.00
Married at Ages 20–29					
Male (N)	26	105	36	71	16
Female (N)	36	89	22	44	7
Married Males (%)	38.46	29.52	33.33	39.44	31.1
Married Females	58.33	43.82	68.18	84.09	84.2
Residence, by Size of Places					
N	478	1,066	346	359	95
Unincorporated (%)	38.08	18.76	20.52	30.08	54.6
Less than 2,500	10.04	8.07	6.94	6.13	9.9
2,500–9,999	9.21	11.73	20.23	13.65	8.3
10,000–24,999	4.18	9.38	16.47	5.57	7.1
25,000+	38.49	52.06	35.84	44.57	19.5
Other	—	—	—	—	0.4
Total	100.00	100.00	100.00	100.00	100.0

First Generation	Switzerland	Scotland	Wales	Spain + Portugal	Mexico
Residence in Ten Largest Cities					
N	478	1,066	346	359	954
New York, NY (%)	4.81	9.10	0.29	1.95	0.21
Chicago, IL	2.51	5.16	1.45	—	0.10
Philadelphia, PA	2.72	4.50	0.58	—	—
Saint Louis, MO	1.26	0.75	0.29	—	0.10
Boston, MA	0.42	1.41	—	1.67	—
Cleveland, OH	0.63	1.13	0.58	0.28	—
Baltimore, MD	0.21	—	—	—	—
Pittsburgh, PA	1.26	2.16	3.47	—	—
Detroit, MI	0.84	1.50	0.58	—	—
Buffalo, NY	0.21	0.38	0.29	—	—
Total %	14.87	26.09	7.53	3.90	0.41
Residence, by Division					
N	478	1,066	346	359	954
New England (%)	3.14	17.35	4.34	39.55	—
Mid-Atlantic	24.06	33.86	55.49	3.06	0.42
East North Central	28.45	21.29	19.65	0.28	0.31
West North Central	13.18	7.88	6.65	—	8.49
South Atlantic	0.84	1.97	1.45	5.57	0.63
East South Central	1.46	1.13	0.29	0.28	—
West South Central	3.77	0.94	0.58	1.67	55.45
Mountain	5.23	4.88	3.76	5.85	17.71
Pacific	19.87	10.69	7.80	43.73	16.98
Military	—	—	—	—	—
Total	100.00	100.00	100.00	100.00	100.00
Males in the Labor Force, by Age					
N	224	506	170	200	464
75+ (%)	—	1.38	1.76	1.00	1.08
65–74	6.70	6.52	7.65	1.50	3.02
35–64	68.75	59.09	58.82	40.00	35.34
15–34	24.55	32.21	31.76	55.50	57.97
10–14	—	0.59	—	0.50	1.08
Less than 10	—	0.20	—	1.50	1.51
Total	100.00	100.00	100.00	100.00	100.00
Ages Females, 10–64 in the Labor Force by Marital Status					
N	200	396	130	123	305
Single (%)	71.05	70.54	64.00	62.50	23.61
Married	10.87	8.55	2.25	14.61	8.42

First Generation	Switzerland	Scotland	Wales	Spain + Portugal	Mexic
Divorced	50.00	100.00	—	—	100.0
Widowed	45.45	30.61	25.00	20.00	33.3
Total	26.50	29.04	16.92	24.39	15.0
Occupation of Males Ages 10–64					
N	209	465	154	192	43
Managerial, Prof (%)	5.74	9.68	11.04	1.56	1.1
Technical, Sales	5.74	13.55	12.34	3.65	2.7
Farming, Forestry	37.32	12.69	7.79	29.69	37.4
Precision, Craft	23.92	40.00	36.36	10.94	8.2
Operators, Laborers	22.01	20.00	29.22	45.83	47.2
Other	5.26	4.09	3.25	8.33	3.2
Total	100.00	100.00	100.00	100.00	100.0
Workers Ages 10–64, by Industry					
Males (N)	209	465	154	192	43
Agriculture (%)	35.89	11.40	7.79	29.69	34.2
Manufacture	25.83	30.75	20.78	36.45	9.1
Trade	10.05	11.18	9.09	6.25	4.1
Females (N)	53	115	22	30	4
Agriculture (%)	13.21	1.74	—	10.00	28.2
Manufacture	11.32	29.57	18.18	63.33	6.5
Private Household	49.06	24.35	45.45	16.67	43.4
Alien Status (asked only of males 21 +)					
N	213	482	178	187	38
Naturalized (%)	71.36	68.46	79.78	20.86	14.1
Alien	13.15	24.07	15.17	75.40	84.2
Papers	15.49	7.47	5.06	3.74	1.5
Total	100.00	100.00	100.00	100.00	100.0
Those Age 10 or Older Who Speak English					
Males (N)	254	562	192	212	5
Females (N)	221	460	148	129	3
Males (%)	92.91	99.11	97.40	57.08	12.9
Females	85.52	99.13	97.30	44.19	9.0
Those Age 10 or Older Who Are Able to Read					
Males (N)	254	562	192	212	5
Females (N)	221	460	148	129	3
Males (%)	95.28	99.11	97.40	66.98	46.9
Females	95.02	98.26	90.54	55.04	42.0

First Generation	Switzerland	Scotland	Wales	Spain + Portugal	Mexico
Homeownership (asked of household heads)					
N	186	415	141	119	254
Own Free (%)	35.48	26.27	29.79	21.85	21.26
Mortgage	20.97	16.39	13.48	17.65	2.36
Rent	41.94	56.14	55.32	53.78	67.72
Probably Owns/Mortgage	1.61	1.20	1.41	6.72	8.66
Total	100.00	100.00	100.00	100.00	100.00
Child Mortality Index					
Number of Women	90	162	60	73	137
Index	0.80	0.94	1.61	1.01	1.07
Fertility Rates					
TFR	—	—	—	—	—
TMFR	—	—	—	—	—
Relationship to Household Head					
Male (N)	257	586	197	224	585
Missing (%)	1.17	0.17	0.00	4.91	3.08
Head	64.98	61.60	62.94	49.11	38.29
Child	7.00	12.63	13.71	12.05	26.32
Kin	4.67	5.46	5.58	4.91	3.76
Boarder	8.95	14.68	16.75	22.77	19.83
Employee	8.95	3.92	0.51	4.91	2.39
No Relation	4.28	1.54	0.51	1.34	6.32
Total	100.00	100.00	100.00	100.00	100.00
Female (N)	221	480	149	135	368
Missing (%)	0.00	0.00	0.00	0.00	0.54
Head	9.05	11.46	11.41	6.67	8.70
Wife	61.09	48.13	57.72	58.52	46.74
Child	4.98	18.54	14.09	15.56	29.62
Kin	10.86	10.00	11.41	10.37	8.42
Boarder	2.71	5.00	0.00	6.67	3.80
Employee	8.60	5.63	4.03	2.22	1.36
No Relation	2.71	1.25	1.34	0.00	0.82
Total	100.00	100.00	100.00	100.00	100.00
Household Structure					
Male (N)	257	586	197	224	585
Missing (%)	7.39	6.14	3.55	13.39	11.79
Living Alone	3.89	2.05	2.54	2.68	3.76
Nuclear	51.36	46.08	52.79	40.18	42.05
Extended	12.06	16.38	13.20	10.71	14.19

First Generation	Switzerland	Scotland	Wales	Spain + Portugal	Mexic
Augmented	18.68	24.23	19.29	27.23	25.9
Ext./Aug.	6.61	5.12	8.63	5.80	2.2
Total	100.00	100.00	100.00	100.00	100.0
Female (N)	221	480	149	135	36
Missing (%)	4.52	3.75	0.00	1.48	2.9
Living Alone	0.90	1.67	2.01	0.74	1.3
Nuclear	56.11	52.50	59.06	55.56	55.7
Extended	15.38	18.96	22.82	20.00	22.0
Augmented	16.29	16.46	12.75	18.52	14.9
Ext./Aug.	6.79	6.67	3.36	3.70	2.9
Total	100.00	100.00	100.00	100.00	100.0
School Enrollment					
Males (N)	104	184	76	85	18
5–9 (%)	83.78	81.25	91.30	77.42	38.2
10–13	100.00	95.31	100.00	96.15	68.8
14–18	63.64	54.17	64.29	50.00	38.9
Total	82.69	75.54	84.21	74.12	48.4
Females (N)	108	166	55	75	18
5–9 (%)	91.43	83.93	85.71	70.00	35.3
10–13	100.00	96.08	95.24	100.00	54.8
14–18	61.54	50.85	50.00	54.17	38.1
Total	83.33	75.91	76.36	73.33	42.8

BIBLIOGRAPHY

Abbott, A. 1983. "Sequences of Social Events: Concepts and Methods for the Analysis of Order in Social Processes." *Historical Methods* 4:129–147.

—— 1988. "Transcending General Linear Reality." *Sociological Theory* 2:169–186.

Alba, R. 1985. *Italian Americans: Into the Twilight of Ethnicity.* Englewood Cliffs, NJ: Prentice-Hall.

—— 1990. *Ethnic Identity: The Transformation of White America.* New Haven, CT, and London: Yale University Press.

Aldrich, J. H., and F. D. Nelson 1984. *Linear Probability, Logit, and Probit Models.* Beverly Hills: Sage Publications.

Alisaukas, A. 1980. "Lithuanians." In *Harvard Encyclopedia of American Ethnic Groups,* S. Thernstrom, ed. Cambridge, MA, and London: The Belknap Press of Harvard University Press.

Allen, W. 1978. "The Search for Applicable Theories of Black Family Life." *Journal of Marriage and the Family* 40:117–129.

Alonso, W. 1987. "Identity and Population." In *Population in an Interacting World,* W. Alonso, ed., pp. 95–125. Cambridge, MA: Harvard University Press.

Aminzade, R. 1992. "Time and Historical Sociology." *Sociological Methods and Research* 20:456–480.

Anderson, M. J. 1988. *The American Census: A Social History.* New Haven: Yale University Press.

Anderton, D., and L. L. Bean 1985. "Birth Spacing and Fertility Limitation: A Behavioral Analysis of a Nineteenth Century Population." *Demography* 22 (2):169–184.

Angel, R., and M. Tienda 1982. "Determinants of Extended Household Structure." *American Journal of Sociology* 87:1360–1383.

Archdeacon, T. 1985. "Problems and Possibilities in the Study of American Immigration and Ethnic History." *International Migration Review* 19:112–135.

Ashby, H. 1922. *Infant Mortality.* Cambridge: Cambridge University Press.

Atwater, W. O., and C. D. Woods 1897. *Dietary Studies with Reference to the Food of the Negro in Alabama in 1895 and 1896.* U.S. Department of Agriculture, Office of Experimental Stations Bulletin 38. Washington, DC: U.S. Government Printing Office.

Aykroyd, W. R. 1971. "Nutrition and Mortality in Infancy and Early Childhood: Past and Present." *American Journal of Clinical Nutrition* 24:480–487.

411

Bales, R. F. 1944. "The 'Fixation Factor' in Alcohol Addiction: A Hypothesis Derived from a Comparative Study of Irish and Jewish Social Norms." Ph.D. diss., Harvard University, Cambridge, MA.

Baltzell, D. 1958. *Philadelphia Gentlemen*. New York: Free Press.

Barton, J. 1975. *Peasants and Strangers: Rumanians and Slovaks in an American City, 1890–1950*. Cambridge, MA: Harvard University Press.

Bean, F., and M. Tienda 1987. *The Hispanic Population of the United States*. New York: Russell Sage Foundation.

Beck, W. H. 1939. *Lutheran Elementary School in the United States*. St. Louis: Concordia Publishing House.

Becker, G. 1981. *A Treatise on the Family*. Cambridge, MA: Harvard University Press.

Bell, T. 1950. *Out of This Furnace*. New York: Liberty Book Club, Inc.

Benkart, P. 1980. "Hungarians." In *Harvard Encyclopedia of American Ethnic Groups*, S. Thernstrom, ed., pp. 462–471. Cambridge, MA, and London: The Belknap Press of Harvard University Press.

Bennett, T., G. Martin, C. Mercer, and J. Woollacott, eds. 1981. *Culture, Ideology and Social Process*. London: Open University Press.

Berkner, L. 1975. "The Use and Misuse of Census Data for the Historical Analysis of Family Structure." *Journal of Interdisciplinary History* 4:721–738.

Bernheimer, C. 1948. *Half a Century of Community Service*. New York: Association Press.

Berrol, S. 1976. "Education and Economic Mobility: The Jewish Experience in New York City, 1880–1920." *American Jewish Historical Quarterly* 65:257–272.

Bertson, J. 1953. "A Statistically Precise and Relatively Simple Method of Estimating the Bioassay with Quantal Response, Based on the Logistic Function." *Journal of the American Statistical Association* 48:565–599.

Billings, J. S. 1894. *Vital Statistics of the Jews in the United States*. Special Report for the Eleventh Census of the United States (Census Bulletin No. 19). Washington, DC: U.S. Government Printing Office.

Billingsley, A. 1968. *Black Families in White America*. New York: Touchstone.

Birmingham, S. 1984. *The Rest of Us: The Rise of America's East European Jews*. London: McDonald and Co.

Bledsoe, C. 1989. "Strategies of Child Fosterage Among Mende Grannies in Sierra Leone." In *Reproductive and Social Organization in Sub-Saharan Africa*, Ron Lesthaeghe, ed., pp. 442–469. Berkeley: University of California Press.

Blum, J. M. 1978. *Pseudoscience and Mental Ability: The Origins and Fallacies of the IQ Controversy*. New York: Monthly Review Press.

Bodnar, J. 1976. "Moralism and Morality: Slavic-American Immigrants and Education, 1890–1940." *Journal of Ethnic Studies* 1:1–21.

———— 1985. *The Transplanted: A History of Immigrants in Urban America*. Bloomington: Indiana University Press.

Bodnar, J., R. Simon, and M. P. Weber 1982. *Lives of Their Own: Blacks, Italians, and Poles in Pittsburgh, 1900–1960*. Urbana and Chicago: University of Illinois Press.

Borjas, G. J. 1985. "Assimilation, Change in Cohort Quality, and the Earnings of Immigrants." *Journal of Labor Economics* 3:463–489.

Braunstein, S., and J. Weissman Joselit 1990. *Getting Comfortable in New York: The American Jewish Home, 1880–1950.* New York: The Jewish Museum.

Breckinridge, S. P., and E. Abbott 1910. "Chicago's Housing Problem: Families in Furnished Rooms." *American Journal of Sociology* 16:289–308.

———— 1910. "Housing Conditions in Chicago, Illinois: Back of the Yards." *American Journal of Sociology* 16:433–448.

Bulmer, M. 1980. *The Chicago School of Sociology.* Chicago: University of Chicago Press.

Burgess, E. W. 1967[1925]. "The Growth of the City." In *The City,* Robert E. Park, Ernest W. Burgess, and R. D. McKenzie, eds. Chicago: University of Chicago Press.

Burns, J. 1912. *The Growth and Development of the Catholic School System in the United States.* New York: Benziger Brothers.

Burns, J., and B. Kohlbrenner 1937. *A History of Catholic Education in the United States.* New York: Benziger Brothers.

Burstein, A. N. 1981. "Immigrants and Residential Mobility." In *Philadelphia,* T. Hershberg, ed., pp. 174–203. New York: Oxford University Press.

Caldwell, C. V. 1974[1919]. "The Control of Midwifery." In *Standards,* W. L. Chenery and E. A. Merritt, eds. New York: Arno Press.

Caldwell, J. C. 1990. "Cultural and Social Factors Influencing Mortality Levels in Developing Countries." *Annals of the American Academy of Political and Social Science* 510:44–59.

Caroli, B. B. 1973. *Italian Repatriation from the United States, 1900–1914.* New York: Center for Migration Studies.

Carpenter, N. 1969[1927]. *Immigrants and Their Children, 1920.* New York: Arno Press.

Carson, D. 1949. "Changes in the Industrial Composition of Manpower since the Civil War." In *Studies in Income and Wealth,* vol. 11, pp. 46–134. New York: National Bureau of Economic Research, Inc.

Chalasinski, J. 1935. "Parafia i Szkola Parafialna Wsrod Emigracji Polskiej w Ameryce. Studium Dzielnicy Polskiej w Poludniowym Chicago." *Przeglad Socjologiczny, Warsaw* 3–4:633–771.

Chapin, C. V. 1974. "The Control of Midwifery." In *Standards of Child Welfare,* W. L. Chenery and E. A. Merritt, eds. New York: Arno Press. Reprint of U.S. Department of Labor, Children's Bureau, Standards of Child Welfare. Report of the Children's Bureau Conferences, May and June 1919. Bureau Publication No. 60. Washington, DC: Department of Labor.

Cheney, T. 1988. "Linguistic Assimilation of U.S. Immigrants, 1900–1920." Paper presented at the annual meeting of the Population Association of America, New Orleans, LA.

Cherlin, A. 1981. *Marriage Divorce Remarriage.* Cambridge, MA: Harvard University Press.

Chiswick, B. R. 1987. "The Effect of Americanization on the Earnings of Foreign Born Men." *Journal of Political Economy* 78:897–921.

Clark, C. 1960. *The Conditions of Economic Progress.* London: Macmillan.

Cleland, J., and C. Wilson 1987. "Demand Theories of the Fertility Decline: An Iconoclastic View." *Population Studies* 41:5–30.

Coale, A. J. 1986. "The Decline of Fertility in Europe since the Eighteenth Century as a Chapter in Human Demographic History." In *The Decline of Fertility in Europe,* A. J. Coale and S. Cotts Watkins, eds., pp. 1–30. Princeton: Princeton University Press.

Coale, A. J., and P. Demeny 1983. *Regional Model Life Tables and Stable Populations.* Princeton: Princeton University Press.

Coale, A. J., and N. W. Rives, Jr. 1973. "A Statistical Reconstruction of the Black Population of the United States, 1880–1970: Estimates of True Numbers by Age and Sex, Birth Rates, and Total Fertility." *Population Index* 39:3–36.

Coale, A. J., and R. Treadway 1986. "A Summary of the Changing Distribution of Overall Fertility, Marital Fertility, and the Proportion Married in The Provinces of Europe." In *The Decline of Fertility in Europe,* A. J. Coale and S. C. Watkins, eds., pp. 31–181. Princeton: Princeton University Press.

Coale, A. J., and J. Trussell 1974. "Model Fertility Schedules: Variations in the Age Structure of Childbearing in Human Populations." *Population Index* 40 (2):185–258.

Coale, A. J., and M. Zelnick 1963. *New Estimates of Fertility and Population in the United States.* Princeton: Princeton University Press.

Cohen, N. 1984. *Encounter with Emancipation: The German Jews in the United States, 1803–1914.* Philadelphia: The Jewish Publication Society of America.

Cohen, R. 1981. "Jewish Fertility in Contemporary America." In *Modern Jewish Fertility,* Paul Ritterband, ed., pp. 144–159. Leiden: E. J. Brill.

Coleman, P. 1962. "Restless Grant County: Americans on the Move." *Wisconsin Magazine of History* 3:16–20.

Condran, G. A., and E. A. Kramarow 1991. "Child Mortality among Jewish Immigrants to the United States." *Journal of Interdisciplinary History* XXII:223–254.

Condran, G. A., H. Williams, and R. A. Cheney 1984. "A Decline in Mortality in Philadelphia from 1870 to 1930: The Role of Municipal Services." *The Pennsylvania Magazines of History and Biography* 108:153–177.

Conk, M. A. 1980. *The United States Census and Labor Force Change: A History of Occupation Statistics, 1870–1949.* Ann Arbor, MI: UMI Research Press.

Conzen, K. N. 1975. "Patterns of Residence in Early Milwaukee." In *The New Urban History,* L. F. Schnore, ed. Princeton: Princeton University Press.

———1979. "Immigrants, Immigrant Neighborhoods, and Ethnic Identity: Historical Issues." *Journal of American History* 66:603–615.

Conzen, K. N., K. D. Gerber, E. Morawska, G. Pozzetta, and R. Vecoli 1990. "The Invention of Ethnicity: A View from the United States." *Altreitalie* (April):36–62.

Covello, L. 1967. *The Social Background of the Italiano-American School Child.* Leiden: E. J. Brill.

Cox, O. 1940. "Sex Ratio and Marital Status Among Negroes." *American Sociological Review* 5:937–947.

Daniels, D. 1989. *Always a Sister: The Feminism of Lillian Wald.* New York: Feminist Press.

Dart, H. M. 1921. "Maternity and Child Care in Selected Rural Areas of Mississippi." *Bureau of Rural Child Welfare Series* 5. Washington, DC: U.S. Government Printing Office.

DaVanzo, J. 1983. "Repeat Migration in the U.S.: Who Moves Back and Who Moves On?" *Review of Economics and Statistics* 65:552–559.

Davenport, D. 1985. "Duration of Residence in the 1855 Census of New York." *Historical Methods* 18(Winter):5–12.

David, P. A., and W. C. Sanderson 1987. "The Emergence of a Two-child Norm among American Birth-controllers." *Population and Development Review* 13(1):1–41.

Davis, M. M., Jr. 1921. *Immigrant Health and the Community.* New York: Harper and Brothers.

Denton, N. A., and D. S. Massey 1988. "Residential Segregation of Blacks, Hispanics, and Asians by Socioeconomic Status and Generation." *Social Science Quarterly* 69:797–817.

Dertouzos, M. L., T. K. Lester, and R. M. Solow 1989. *Made in America: Regaining the Productive Edge.* Cambridge, MA: The MIT Press.

Diner, H. R. 1983. *Erin's Daughters in America: Irish Immigrant Women in the Nineteenth Century.* Baltimore and London: Johns Hopkins University Press.

Doyle, D. 1976. *Irish Americans, Native Rights and National Empires.* New York: Arno Press.

Dublin, L. I., and W. B. Gladden 1920. "The Mortality of Race Stocks in Pennsylvania and New York, 1910." *Quarterly Publications of the American Statistical Association, vol. 17* 129:13–44.

DuBois, W. E. B. 1899. *The Philadelphia Negro.* Philadelphia: University of Pennsylvania Press.

—— 1908. *The Negro American Family.* New York: New American Library.

Duis, P. R. 1983. *The Saloon: Public Drinking in Chicago and Boston, 1880–1920.* Urbana and Chicago: University of Illinois Press.

Duncan, O. D., and S. Lieberson 1959. "Ethnic Segregation and Assimilation." *American Journal of Sociology* 64:364–374.

Dures, A. 1971. *Schools.* London: B. T. Batsford, Ltd.

Dwork, D. 1981. "Health Conditions of Immigrant Jews on the Lower East Side of New York, 1880–1914." *Medical History* 25:1–40.

Dye, N. S. 1987. "Modern Obstetrics and Working-Class Women: The New York Midwifery Dispensary, 1890–1920." *Journal of Social History* 20:549–564.

Easterlin, R. A. 1960. "Regional Growth of Income: Long Term Tendencies, 1880–1950." In *Population Redistribution and Economic Growth, United States, 1870–1950. II: Analysis of Economic Change,* S. Kuznets, A. R. Miller, and R. A. Easterlin, eds., pp. 141–203. Philadelphia: The American Philosophical Society.

Easterlin, R. A., and E. Crimmins 1985. *The Fertility Revolution.* Chicago: University of Chicago Press.

Emmons, D. 1989. *The Butte Irish: Class and Ethnicity in an American Mining Town, 1875–1925.* Urbana, Il: University of Illinois Press.

Erickson, C. J. 1972. "Who Were the English and Scottish Immigrants to the U.S.A. in the 1880's?" In *Population and Social Change*, D. V. Glass and R. Revelle, eds., pp. 347–381. London: E. Arnold.

———— 1984. "Why Did Contract Labor Not Work in the Nineteenth-Century United States?" In *International Labor Migration: Historical Perspectives*, S. Marks and P. Richardson, eds., pp. 34–56. Middlesex, U.K.: Maurice Temple Smith, Ltd.

Espenshade, T. 1985. "Marriage Trends in America: Estimates, Implications, and Underlying Causes." *Population and Development Review* 11:193–245.

Ewbank, D. C. 1987. "History of Black Mortality and Health Before 1940." *The Milbank Quarterly* 65A(Supplement 1):100–128.

———— 1989. "Estimating Birth Stopping and Spacing Behavior." *Demography* 26:473–483.

———— 1991. "The Marital Fertility of American Whites Before 1920." *Historical Methods* 24(4):141–170.

Ewbank, D.C., S. P. Morgan, and S. C. Watkins 1992. "The Fertility of the Foreign Born in the U.S., 1905–1909." Unpublished paper.

Fairchild, H. P. 1926. *The Melting Pot Mistake.* Boston: Little, Brown.

Farley, R. 1971. "Family Types and Family Headship: A Comparison of Trends Among Blacks and Whites." *Journal of Human Resources* 3:275–296.

———— 1977. "Residential Segregation in Urbanized Areas of the United States in 1970: An Analysis of Social Class and Race Differentials." *Demography* 14:497–518.

———— 1985. *Blacks and Whites: Narrowing the Gap?* Cambridge, MA: Harvard University Press.

———— 1991. "Residential Segregation of Social and Economic Groups Among Blacks, 1970 to 1980." In *The Urban Underclass*, C. Jencks and P. E. Peterson, eds., pp. 274–298. Washington, DC: Brookings Institution.

Farley, R., and W. Allen 1987. *The Color Line and the Quality of Life in America.* New York: Russell Sage Foundation.

Farley, R., and A. Hermalin 1971. "Family Stability: A Comparison of Trends Between Blacks and Whites." *American Sociological Review* 36:1–17.

Felder, O. B. 1986. "Family Desertion Among East European Jewish Immigrants: 1900–1930." Ph.D. diss., Columbia University, New York.

Feldman, D. M. 1974. *Marital Relations, Birth Control, and Abortion in Jewish Law.* New York: Schocken Books.

Fishberg, M. 1901. "Relative Infrequency of Tuberculosis Among Jews." *American Medicine* 1:655–699.

Fleming, M. E. 1980. "White Ethnic Fertility in the U.S.: Convergence, 1890–1975." Ph.D. diss., Princeton University, Princeton, N.J.

Foerster, R. 1919. *The Italian Immigration of Our Times.* Cambridge, MA: Harvard University Press.

Folbre, N., and M. Abel 1989. "Women's Work and Women's Households: Gender Bias in the U.S. Census." *Social Research* 56:544–569.

Forest, R. de, and L. Veiller 1903. *The Tenement House Problem.* New York: Macmillan.

Friedman, R. S. 1982. "Send Me My Husband Who Is in New York City: Husband Desertion in the American Jewish Immigrant Community, 1900–1926." *Jewish Social Studies* 1:1–19.

Frissell, H. B., and I. Bevier 1899. *Dietary Studies of Negroes in Eastern Virginia in 1897 and 1898.* Washington: U.S. Department of Agriculture, Office of Experiment Stations Bulletin 71, G.P.O.

Furstenberg, F. F., D. Strong, and A. G. Crawford 1979. "What Happened When the Census Was Redone: An Analysis of the Recount of 1870 in Philadelphia." *Sociology and Social Research* 63:475–505.

Gabaccia, D. R. 1984. *From Sicily to Elizabeth Street.* Albany, NY: State University of New York Press.

———— 1989. *Immigrant Women in the United States: A Selectively Annotated Multidisciplinary Bibliography.* Westport, CT: Greenwood Press.

Gauvreau, D. 1990. Centre Interuniversitaire de Recherches sur les Populations, Université du Québec a Chicoutimi, Canada. Letter to Samuel Preston.

Gjerde, J. 1985. *From Peasants to Farmers.* New York: Cambridge University Press.

Glanz, R. 1976. *The Jewish Woman in America: Two Female Immigrant Generations 1820–1929, vol. 1: The Eastern European Jewish Woman.* KTAV Publishing House, Inc., and National Council of Jewish Women.

Glazer, N. 1983. *Ethnic Dilemmas.* Cambridge, MA: Harvard University Press.

Glover, J. W. 1921. *United States Life Tables, 1890, 1901, 1910, and 1901–1910.* Washington, DC: U.S. G.P.O.

Glover, M. 1989. *Consumer Behavior and Immigrant Assimilation: A Comparison of the United States, Britain, and Germany, 1989/90.* National Bureau of Economic Research Working Paper Series on Historical Factors in Long Run Growth, Cambridge, MA.

Golab, C. 1977. "The Impact of the Industrial Experience on the Immigrant Family." In *Immigrants in Industrial America: 1850–1929,* Richard Ehrlich, ed., pp. 1–21. Charlottesville: University of Virginia Press.

Goldman, E. 1983. *Red Emma Speaks: An Emma Goldman Reader.* New York: Schocken Books.

Goldscheider, C. 1965. "Socio-Economic Status and Jewish Fertility." *The Jewish Journal of Sociology* 7:221–227.

Goldscheider, C., and A. S. Zuckerman 1984. *The Transformation of the Jews.* Chicago: University of Chicago Press.

Goldstein, A. 1981. "Some Demographic Characteristics of Village Jews in Germany: Nonnenweier, 1800–1931." In *Modern Jewish Fertility,* Paul Ritterband, ed., pp. 112–143. Leiden: E. J. Brill.

Goldstein, S. 1980. "Jews in the United States: Perspectives from Demography." In *The American Jewish Year Book, 1981,* pp. 3–59. New York: The American Jewish Committee.

Goody, E. 1982. *Parenthood and Social Reproduction: Fostering and Occupational Roles in West Africa.* Cambridge, MA: Cambridge University Press.

Gordon, M. 1964. *Assimilation in American Life.* New York: Oxford University Press.

——— 1973. *The American Family in Social-Historical Perspective.* New York: St. Martin's Press.

Goren, A. 1990. "Preaching American Jewish History." *American Jewish History* 4:538–552.

Gould, S. J. 1981. *The Mismeasure of Man.* New York: W. W. Norton.

Greeley, A. 1971. *Why Can't They Be Like Us? America's White Ethnic Groups.* New York: E. P. Dutton.

Green, V. 1987. *American Immigrant Leaders, 1800–1910.* Baltimore: Johns Hopkins University Press.

Greenberg, S. W. 1981. "Industrial Location and Ethnic Residential Patterns in an Industrializing City: Philadelphia, 1880." In *Philadelphia,* Theodore Hershberg, ed., pp. 204–231. New York: Oxford University Press.

Greene, M., and J. Jacobs 1990. "Urban Enrollments and the Growth of Schooling: Evidence from the U.S. 1910 Census Public Use Sample." Paper presented at the Eastern Sociological Society Meeting, Boston, MA.

Greene, V. 1975. *For God and Country: The Rise of Polish and Lithuanian Ethnic Consciousness in America.* Madison: State Historical Society of Wisconsin.

Guest, A. M. 1981. "Social Structure and U.S. Inter-State Fertility Differentials in 1900." *Demography* 18:465–486.

——— 1982. "Fertility Variation Among the U.S. Foreign Stock Population in 1900." *International Migration Review* 16:577–594.

Guest, A. M., and S. Tolnay 1983. "Urban Industrial Structure and Fertility: The Case of Large American Cities." *Journal of Interdisciplinary History* 13:387–409.

Gutman, H. G. 1976. *The Black Family in Slavery and Freedom 1750–1925.* New York: Vintage Books.

——— 1987. "The Black Family in Slavery and Freedom: A Revised Perspective." In *Power and Culture: Essays on the Working Class,* H. Gutman, ed., pp. 357–379. New York: Pantheon.

Gutmann, M. P., and K. H. Fliess 1988. "Culture and Fertility Decline in the American Southwest." Paper presented at the annual meeting of the Social Science History Association, November 3–6, Chicago, IL.

Guttentag, M., and P. Secord 1983. *Too Many Women?: The Sex Ratio Question.* Beverly Hills, CA: Sage Publications.

Haines, M. R. 1977. "Fertility, Marriage, and Occupation in the Pennsylvania Anthracite Region, 1850–1880." *Journal of Family History* 1:28–55.

——— 1980. "Fertility and Marriage in a Nineteenth Century Industrial City: Philadelphia, 1850–1880." *Journal of Economic History* 40(1):151–158.

——— 1989. "Consumer Behavior and Immigrant Assimilation: A Comparison of the United States, Britain, and Germany 1889/1890." Working Paper No. 6, Working Paper Series on Historical Factors in Long Run Growth. Cambridge, MA: National Bureau of Economic Research, Inc.

——— 1990. "Western Fertility in Mid-Transition: Fertility and Nuptiality in the United States and Selected Nations at the Turn of the Century." *Journal of Family History* 15(1):23–48.

Hamilton, A. 1909. "Excessive Child-bearing as a Factor in Infant Mortality." In *Prevention of Infant Mortality*, Conference on the Prevention of Infant Mortality. Under the auspices of the American Academy of Medicine. Conference in New Haven, pp. 74–80.

Hapgood, H. 1902. *The Spirit of the Ghetto: Studies of the Jewish Quarter in New York.* New York and London: Funk and Wagnalls Company.

Hareven, T. K. 1976. "Modernization and Family History: Perspectives on Social Change." *Journal of Women in Culture and Society* 2, 1:190–206.

———— 1982. *Family Time and Industrial Time: The Relationship Between Family and Work in a New England Industrial Community.* Cambridge: Cambridge University Press.

Hareven, T. K., and R. Langenbach 1978. *Amoskeag.* New York: Pantheon.

Hareven, T. K., and J. Modell 1977. "Urbanization and the Malleable Household." In *Family and Kin in Urban Communities 1700–1930*, Tamara K. Hareven, ed., pp. 164–186. New York and London: New Viewpoints: A Division of Franklin Watts.

———— 1980. "Family Patterns." In *Harvard Encyclopedia of Ethnic Groups*, S. Thernstrom, ed., pp. 345–354. Cambridge, MA, and London: The Belknap Press of Harvard University Press.

Hareven, T. K., and M. Vinovskis 1975. "Marital Fertility, Ethnicity, and Occupation in Urban Families: An Analysis of South Boston and the South End in 1880." *Journal of Social History* 1:69–94.

———— 1978. "Patterns of Childbearing in Late Nineteenth Century America: The Determinants of Marital Fertility in Five Massachusetts Towns in 1880." In *Family and Population in Nineteenth Century America*, T. K. Hareven and M. A. Vinovskis, eds., pp. 85–125. Princeton: Princeton University Press.

Hawley, A. 1950. *Human Ecology.* New York: Ronald.

Heinze, A. 1990. *Adapting to Abundance: Jewish Immigrants, Mass Consumption, and the Search for American Identity.* New York: Columbia University Press.

Herberg, W. 1955. *Protestant Catholic Jew: An Essay in American Religious Sociology.* Chicago: The University of Chicago Press.

Hereward, M., S. P. Morgan, D. Ewbank, and A. Miller 1990. *Oversample of Black-headed Households: 1910 United States Census of Population:* User's Guide. ICPSR, University of Michigan, Ann Arbor, MI.

Hershberg, T., ed. 1981. *Philadelphia: Work, Space, and Group Experience in the 19th Century.* New York: Oxford University Press.

Hershberg, T., et al. 1981. "A Tale of Three Cities: Blacks, Immigrants, and Opportunity in Philadelphia, 1850–1880, 1930, 1970." In *Philadelphia*, Theodore Hershberg, ed., pp. 461–492. New York: Oxford University Press.

Herskovits, M. 1928. *The American Negro.* Bloomington: Indiana University Press.

———— 1941. *The Myth of the Negro Past.* New York: Harper.

Hertzberg, A. 1989. *The Jews in America.* New York: Simon & Schuster.

Herzfeld, E. 1905. *Family Monographs.* New York: The James Kempster Printing Company.

Higham, J. 1978. *Ethnic Leadership in America.* Baltimore: Johns Hopkins University Press.

───── 1984. *Send These to Me: Immigrants in Urban America.* Baltimore and London: Johns Hopkins University Press.

───── 1988 [1955]. *Strangers in the Land: Patterns of American Nativism, 1865–1925.* New Brunswick, NJ: Rutgers University Press.

Hill, R. 1971. *The Strengths of Black Families.* New York: Emerson Hall Publishers.

Himmelfarb, G. 1987. *The New History and the Old: Critical Essays and Reappraisals.* Cambridge, MA: Harvard University Press.

Hirschman, C. 1983. "America's Melting Pot Reconsidered." *Annual Review of Sociology* 9:397–423.

Hodgson, D. 1991. "Ideological Origins of the PAA." *Population and Development Review* 17:1–34.

Hofferth, S. L. 1984. "Kin Networks, Race, and Family Structure." *Journal of Marriage and the Family* 46:791–806.

Hogan, D. J. 1985. *Class and Reform: School and Society in Chicago, 1880–1930.* Philadelphia: University of Pennsylvania Press.

Hollopeter, W. C. 1906. "The Pediatric Outlook." *Transactions of the Section on Disease of Children, American Medical Association, 1866–1932* II:15–18.

Howe, I. 1976. *World of Our Fathers.* New York: Simon and Schuster.

Hsu, F. L. K. 1943. "The Myth of Chinese Family Size." *American Journal of Sociology* 48:555–556.

Hunt, M. B. 1910. "The Housing of Non-Family Groups of Men in Chicago." *American Journal of Sociology* 16:145–170.

Hutchinson, E. P. 1956. *Immigrants and Their Children, 1850–1950.* New York: Wiley.

───── 1981. *Legislative History of American Immigration Policy 1798–1965.* Philadelphia: University of Pennsylvania Press.

Isaac, L. G., and L. Griffen 1989. "Ahistoricism in Time-Series Analyses of Historical Process: Critique, Redirection, and Illustrations from U.S. Labor History." *American Sociological Review* 6:873–890.

Isiugu-Abanihe, U. 1985. "Child Fosterage in West Africa." *Population and Development Review* 11:53–74.

Jacobs, J. A. 1990. "Ethnicity and Schooling in Providence: A Review Essay." *Historical Methods* 23:83–85.

Jaffe, A. J. 1956. "Trends in the Participation of Women in the Working Force." *Monthly Labor Review* 79(5):559–565.

Jasso, G., and M. R. Rosenzweig 1990. *The New Chosen People: Immigrants in the United States.* New York: Russell Sage Foundation.

Jenks, J., and W. J. Lauck 1913. *The Immigration Problem.* New York: Wagnalls.

Jones, J. 1986. *Labor of Love, Labor of Sorrow.* New York: Basic Books.

Katz, M. B. 1986. *In the Shadow of the Poorhouse.* New York: Basic Books.

Kennedy, D. 1970. *Birth Control in America: The Career of Margaret Sanger.* New Haven, CT: Yale University Press.

Kennedy, R. J. Reeves 1944. "Single or Triple Melting Pot? Intermarriage Trends in New Haven, 1920–1940." *American Journal of Sociology* 1:331–339.

Kermack, W. O., A. G. McKendrick, and P. L. McKinlay 1934. "Death Rates in Great Britain and Sweden: Some General Regularities and Their Significance." *Lancet* 226:698–703.

Kessner, T. 1977. *The Golden Door: Italian and Jewish Immigrant Mobility in New York City, 1880–1915.* New York: Oxford University Press.

King, M., and S. Ruggles 1990. "American Immigration, Fertility and Race Suicide at the Turn of the Century." *Journal of Interdisciplinary History* 20:347–369.

Kintner, H. J. 1987. "The Impact of Breastfeeding Patterns on Regional Differences in Infant Mortality in Germany, 1910." *The European Journal of Population* 3:233–261.

Kivisto, P. 1990. "The Transplanted Then and Now: The Reorientation of Immigration Studies from the Chicago School to New Social History." *Ethnic and Racial Studies* 4:455–481.

Kobrin, F. E. 1966. "The American Midwife Controversy: A Crisis of Professionalization." *Bulletin of the History of Medicine* 40:350–363.

Kopf, E. 1977. "Untarnishing the Dream: Mobility, Opportunity, and Order in Modern America." *Journal of Social History* 4:206–228.

Kuczynski, R. R. 1901. "The Fecundity of the Native and Foreign-Born Population in Massachusetts." *Quarterly Journal of Economics* 15:1–24.

Kuznets, S. 1966. *Modern Economic Growth: Rate, Structure, and Spread.* New Haven, CT: Yale University Press.

Ladner, J. 1971. *Tomorrow's Tomorrow.* Garden City, NY: Doubleday.

Lajos, V. 1922. *A Magyar Zsidosag Tortenete a Honfoglalastol a Vilaghaboru Kitoreseig.* Budapest.

Lal, B. B. 1983. "Perspectives on Ethnicity: Old Wine in New Bottles." *Ethnic and Racial Studies* 2:154–173.

Landes, W., and L. Solomon 1972. "Compulsory Schooling Legislation: An Economic Analysis of Law and Social Change in the Nineteenth Century." *Journal of Economic History* 32:54–97.

Laslett, P. 1970. "The Comparative History of Household and Family." *Journal of Social History* 4:75–87.

—— 1972. "Introduction: The History of the Family." In *Household and Family in Past Time,* P. Laslett and R. Wall, eds., pp. 1–89. Cambridge, MA: Cambridge University Press.

Lawson, J., and H. Silver 1973. *A Social History of Education in England.* London: Methuen and Co.

Leavitt, J. W. 1986. *Brought to Bed: Children in America, 1750–1950.* New York: Oxford University Press.

Lebergott, S. 1964. *Manpower in Economic Growth: The American Record Since 1800.* New York: McGraw-Hill.

—— 1966. "Labor Force and Employment, 1800–1960." In *Studies in Income and Wealth* 30:117–210. New York: National Bureau of Economic Research.

Lederhendler, E. 1991. "Guides for the Perplexed: Sex, Manners, and Mores for the Yiddish Reader in America." *Modern Judaism* 11(3):138–177.

Lieberson, S. 1961. "The Impact of Residential Segregation on Ethnic Assimilation." *Social Forces* 40:52–57.

——— 1963. *Ethnic Patterns in American Cities*. New York: Macmillan.

——— 1980. *A Piece of the Pie: Blacks and White Immigrants Since 1880*. Berkeley, CA: University of California Press.

Lieberson, S., and M. C. Waters 1988. *From Many Strands: Ethnic and Racial Groups in Contemporary America*. New York: Russell Sage Foundation.

Livi Bacci, M. 1961. *L'immigrazione e L'assimilazione degli Italiani negli Stati Uniti*. Milan: Dott A. Giuffre Editore.

——— 1977. *A History of Italian Fertility During the Last Two Centuries*. Princeton: Princeton University Press.

Loughran, M. E. 1921. *The Historical Development of Child-Labor Legislation in the United States*. Washington, DC: Catholic University of America.

Luebke, F. C. 1980. "Austrians." In *Harvard Encyclopedia of Ethnic Groups*, S. Thernstrom, ed., pp. 164–171. Cambridge, MA, and London: The Belknap Press of Harvard University Press.

McDaniel, A. 1990. "The Power of Culture: A Review of the Idea of Africa's Influence on Family Structure in Antebellum Africa." *Journal of Family History* 15:225–238.

McKay, J. 1982. "An Exploratory Synthesis of Primordial and Mobilizationist Approaches to Ethnic Phenomena." *Ethnic and Racial Studies* 5:395–421.

Magocsi, P. R. 1988. "Russians." In *Harvard Encyclopedia of Ethnic Groups*, S. Thernstrom, ed., pp. 885–894. Cambridge, MA, and London: The Belknap Press of Harvard University Press.

Marcus, J. R. 1970. *The Colonial Jew in America*. Detroit: Wayne State University Press.

Marini, M., and Burton Singer 1988. "Causality in the Social Sciences." *Sociological Methodology* 18:347–411.

Massey, D., and N. Denton 1987. "Trends in Residential Segregation of Blacks, Hispanics and Asians." *American Sociological Review* 52:802–825.

Massey, D., and B. P. Mullan 1984. "Processes of Hispanics and Black Spatial Assimilation." *American Journal of Sociology* 89:836–873.

Mazzocchi, L., and D. Rubinacci 1975. *L'istruzione Populare en Italia del Secolo XVIII ai Nostri Giorni*. Milano: Dott A. Giuffre Editore.

Meckel, R. A. 1990. *Save the Babies: American Public Health Reform and the Prevention of Infant Mortality, 1850–1929*. Baltimore: The Johns Hopkins University Press.

Meyerowitz, J. J. 1988. *Women Adrift: Independent Wage Earners in Chicago, 1880–1930*. Chicago: University of Chicago Press.

Miaso, J. 1970. *Dzieje Oswiaty Polonijnej w Stanach Zjednoczonych*. Warsaw: Panstwowe Wydawnictwo Naukowe.

——— 1971. "Z Dziejow Oswiaty Polskiej w Stanach Zjednoczonych." *Problemy Polonii Zagranicznej* 6:19–42.

Miller, A. R. 1960. "Labor Force Trends and Differentials." In *Population Redistribution and Economic Growth, United States, 1870–1950, II: Analysis of Economic Change*, S. Kuznets, A. R. Miller, and R. A. Easterlin, eds., pp. 7–101. Philadelphia: The American Philosophical Society.

———— 1977. "Interstate Migrants in the United States: Some Social-economic Differences by Type of Move." *Demography* 14:1–17.

———— 1986. "Internal Migration and the Changing Structure of Employment in the United States in 1900." In *Migration Across Time and Nations: Population Mobility in Historical Contexts*, I. A. Glazier and L. De Rosa, eds., pp. 336–355. New York: Holmes & Meier.

Miller A. T. 1991a. "Fosterage in the U.S.: Signs of an African Heritage." Paper presented at the National Conference on the Black Family in America, Louisville, KY.

———— 1991b. "Measuring Mulattoes: The Changing U.S. Racial Regime in Census and Society." Paper presented at the annual meeting of the Population Association of America, Washington, DC.

———— 1991c. "Looking at African American Families: Recognition and Reaction." Ph.D. diss., University of Pennsylvania.

Miller, K. 1985. *Emigrants and Exiles: Ireland and the Irish Exodus to North America.* New York: Oxford University Press.

Model, S. W. 1985. "Comparative Perspectives on the Ethnic Enclave: Blacks, Italians, and Jews in New York City." *International Migration Review* 19:68–82.

————1988. "Italian and Jewish Intergenerational Mobility in New York, 1910." *Social Science History* 12:31–48.

Modell, J. 1978. "Patterns of Consumption, Acculturation, and Family Income Strategies in Late 19th Century America." In *Family and Population in 19th Century America*, T. Hareven and M. Vinovskis, eds., pp. 206–240. Princeton: Princeton University Press.

Modell, J., and T. Hareven, 1973. "Urbanization and the Malleable Household." *Journal of Marriage and the Family* 35:467–479.

Morawska, E. 1985. *For Bread with Butter: The Lifeworlds of the East Europeans in Johnstown, Pennsylvania, 1890–1940.* New York: Cambridge University Press.

———— 1987. "A Replica of the 'Old Country' Relationship in the Ethnic Niche: East European Jews and Gentiles in Small-Town Western Pennsylvania, 1880s–1930s." *American Jewish History* 1:27–86.

————, ed. 1990. "The Sociology and Historiography of Immigration." In *Immigration Reconsidered: History, Sociology and Politics*, pp. 187–240. Oxford: Oxford University Press.

———— 1991. "Return Migration: Theory and Research." In *A Century of European Migrations, 1830 to 1930*, R. Vecoli, ed. Urbana: University of Illinois Press.

Morgan, S. P. 1991. "Late Nineteenth and Early Twentieth Century Childlessness among White Women in the United States." *American Journal of Sociology* 97:779–807.

Morgan, S. P., A. McDaniel, A. T. Miller, and S. Preston 1990. "Racial Differences in Household and Family Structure at the Turn of the Century." *American Journal of Sociology* 98:798–828.

Morgan, S. P., and S. C. Watkins 1992. "Ethnic and City Fertility Contexts: Immigrants and Natives at the Turn of the Century." Paper presented at a meeting of the International Union for the Scientific Study of Population, Vera Cruz, Mexico, May 18–23.

Nagnur, D. 1986. *Longevity and Historical Life Tables: 1921–1981.* Ottawa: Ministry of Supply and Services.

National Academy of Science 1988. *A Common Destiny: Blacks and American Society.* Washington, DC: National Academy Press.

National Child Labor Committee 1912. *The Child Labor Bulletin, vol. 12.* New York: J. J. Little & Ives Co.

Neidert, L., and R. Farley 1985. "Assimilation in the United States: An Analysis of Ethnic and Generational Differences in Status." *American Sociological Review* 50:840–849.

Nelli, H. S. 1983. *From Immigrants to Ethnics: The Italian Americans.* Oxford and New York: Oxford University Press.

Ninth Census 1872. *The Statistics of the Wealth and Industry of the United States, vol 3.* Washington, DC: U.S. Government Printing Office.

Nobles, W. 1974. "Africanity: Its Role in Black Families." *The Black Scholar* 5:10–17.

Notestein, F. 1931. "The Decrease in Size of Families from 1890 to 1910." *The Milbank Memorial Fund Quarterly Bulletin* 110:181–188.

Olneck, M. 1990. "Can Ethnicity Be Counted?" Review of *Ethnic Differences* by Joel Perlmann, *Contemporary Sociology* 19:183–185.

Olneck, M., and M. Lazerson 1974. "The School Achievement of Immigrant Children, 1900–1930." *History of Education Quarterly* 14:453–482.

Onyango, D. 1985. *The Sociology of the African Family.* New York: Longmans.

Orsi, R. A. 1985. *The Madonna of 115th Street: Faith and Community in Italian Harlem, 1880–1950.* New Haven, CT, and London: Yale University Press.

Ostergren, R. C. 1988. *A Community Transplanted: The Trans-Atlantic Experience of a Swedish Immigrant Settlement in the Upper Middle West, 1835–1915.* Madison: University of Wisconsin Press.

Osterman, P. 1980. *Getting Started: The Youth Labor Market.* Cambridge: MIT Press.

Page, H. 1989. "Childbearing Versus Childrearing: Coresidence of Mother and Child in Sub-Saharan Africa." In *Reproduction and Social Organization in Sub-Saharan Africa,* R. Lesthaeghe, ed., pp. 401–436. Berkeley: University of California Press.

Pagnini, D., and S. P. Morgan 1990. "Intermarriage and Social Distance Among U.S. Immigrants at the Turn of the Century." *American Journal of Sociology* 96(2):405–432.

Park, E. H., and E. Hoh 1903. "Report Upon the Results With Different Kinds of Pure and Impure Milk in Infant Feeding in Treatment Houses and Institutions of New York City: A Cultural and Bacteriological Study." *Archives of Pediatrics* 20(12):881–909.

Park, R. E. 1952. *Human Communities.* Glencoe, IL: Free Press.

—— 1967. "The City." In *The City,* R. E. Park, E. Burgess, and R. D. McKenzie, eds. Chicago: University of Chicago Press.

—— 1969. "The City: Suggestions for Investigation of Human Behavior in the

Urban Environment." In *Classic Essays on the Culture of Cities*, R. Sennett, ed., pp. 91–130. New York: Appleton-Century-Crofts.

Park, R. E., and H. A. Miller 1969 [1921]. *Old World Traits Transplanted*. New York: Arno Press.

Parot, J. 1971. "The American Faith and the Persistence of Chicago Polonia, 1870–1920." Ph.D. diss., Northern Illinois University, Chicago.

Passel, J., and B. Edmonston forthcoming. "Immigration and Race: Recent Trends in Immigration to the United States." In *Immigration and Ethnicity: The Integration of America's Newest Immigrants*, B. Edmonston and J. Passel, eds. Washington, DC: Urban Institute Press.

Pedraza-Bailey, S. 1990. "Immigration Research: A Conceptual Map." *Social Science History* 14(1):43–67.

Perlmann, J. 1988. *Ethnic Differences: Schooling and Social Structure among the Irish, Italians, Jews and Blacks in an American City, 1880–1935*. Cambridge: Cambridge University Press.

Persons, S. 1987. *Ethnic Studies at Chicago, 1905–45*. Urbana: University of Illinois Press.

Philpott, T. L. 1978. *The Slum and the Ghetto: Neighborhood Deterioration and Middle-Class Reform, Chicago, 1880–1930*. New York: Oxford University Press.

Portes, A., and L. Jensen 1989. "The Enclave and the Entrants: Patterns of Ethnic Enterprise in Miami Before and After Mariel." *American Sociological Review* 54:929–949.

Portes, A., and R. G. Rumbaut 1990. *Immigrant America*. Berkeley, CA: University of California Press.

Pozzetta, G. E. 1971. "The Italians of New York City, 1890–1940." Ph.D. diss., University of North Carolina at Chapel Hill, NC.

Preston, S. H., and M. Haines 1984. "New Estimates of Child Mortality in the United States at the Turn of the Century." *Journal of the American Statistical Association (386)* 79:272–281.

——— 1991. *Fatal Years: Child Mortality in Late Nineteenth Century America*. Princeton: Princeton University Press.

Preston, S. H., S. Lim, and S. P. Morgan 1992. "African-American Marriage in 1910: Beneath the Surface of Census Data." *Demography* 29(1):1–15.

Preston, S. H., and A. Palloni 1978. "Fine-tuning Brass-type Mortality Estimates with Data on Ages of Surviving Children." In United Nations, *Population Bulletin of the United Nations, 10-1977*, pp. 72–91. New York: United Nations.

Preston, S., and E. van de Walle 1978. "Urban French Mortality in the Nineteenth Century." *Population Studies* 32:275–297.

Prost, A. 1968. *Histoire de l'enseignement en France: 1800–1967*. Paris: Armand Colin.

Puskás, J. 1982. *From Hungary to the United States, 1880–1914*. Budapest: Akademiai Kiado.

——— 1986. "Hungarian Migration Patterns, 1880–1930: From Macroanalysis to Microanalysis." In *Migration Across Time and Nations: Population Mobil-*

ity in Historical Contexts, I. A. Glazier and L. De Rosa, eds., pp. 231–254. New York: Holmes & Meier.

Radcliffe-Brown, A. R. 1950. *African Systems of Kinship and Marriage.* New York: Oxford University Press.

Raftery, A. E. 1986. "Choosing Models for Cross-Classification." *American Sociological Review* 41:145–146.

Ragin, C. 1987. *The Comparative Method: Moving Beyond Qualitative and Quantitative Strategies.* Berkeley: University of California Press.

Ransom, R. L., and R. Sutch 1977. *One Kind of Freedom: The Economic Consequences of Emancipation.* Cambridge: Cambridge University Press.

Ravitch, D. 1974. *The Great School Wars, New York City, 1805–1973: A History of the Public Schools as Battlefield for Social Change.* New York: Basic Books.

Riis, J. 1957 [1890]. *How the Other Half Lives.* New York: Hill & Wang.

Rindfuss, R. R., S. P. Morgan, and G. Swicegood 1988. *First Births in America: Changes in the Timing of Parenthood.* Berkeley: University of California Press.

Ripley, L. V. J. 1988. "Germans from Russia." In *Harvard Encyclopedia of Ethnic Groups,* S. Thernstrom, ed., pp. 425–430. Cambridge, MA, and London: The Belknap Press of Harvard University Press.

Rischin, M. 1977. *The Promised City: New York's Jews, 1870–1914.* Cambridge, MA: Harvard University Press.

Robles, A., and S. C. Watkins 1993. "Immigration and Family Separation in the U.S. at the Turn of the Century, 1906." *Journal of Family History* 18:191–211.

Rosenwaike, I. 1971. "The Utilization of Census Mother Tongue Data in American Jewish Population Analysis." *Jewish Social Studies* 33(2–3):141–159.

Ross, E. 1913. *The Old World in the New.* New York: Century Co.

Roucek, J. 1969. "The Image of the Slav in United States History and in Immigration Policy." *American Journal of Economics and Sociology* 28:29–49.

Rubinow, I. 1907. *The Economic Condition of Jews in Russia: Bulletin of the Bureau of Labor,* No. 72. Washington, DC: U.S. Government Printing Office.

Ryan, W. 1971. *Blaming the Victim.* New York: Vintage.

Sallume, X., and F. W. Notestein 1932. "Trends in the Size of Families Completed Prior to 1910 in Various Social Classes." *The American Journal of Sociology* 37:398–498.

Sanders, R. 1969. *The Downtown Jews.* New York: Harper & Row.

Sanderson, W. C. 1979. "Herbert Gutman's The Black Family in Slavery and Freedom, 1750–1925: A Cliometric Reconsideration." *Social Science History* 3:66–85.

Sanger, M. 1938. *An Autobiography.* New York: W. Norton and Co.

Sarna, J. 1978. "From Immigrants to Ethnics: Toward a New Theory of 'Ethnicization.'" *Ethnicity* 5:370–378.

Sartorio, E. C. 1974 [1918]. *Social and Religious Life of Italians in America.* Clifton, NJ: Augustus M. Kelley.

Schereschewsky, J. W. 1915. "The Health of Garment Workers." *Public Health Bulletin,* 71:17–104.

Scott, G. 1990. "A Resynthesis of the Primordial and Circumstantial Approaches to Ethnic Group Solidarity: Towards an Explanatory Model." *Ethnic and Racial Studies* 2:147–171.

Seller, M. S. 1985. " 'Women's Interests' Page of the Jewish Daily Forward: Socialism, Feminism and Americanization in 1919." In *The Press of Labor Migrants in Europe and North America, 1880s to 1930s*, C. Harzig and D. Herder, eds., pp. 221–242. Bremen: Universiteit Bremen.

Semmingsen, I. G. 1960. "Norwegian Emigration in the 19th Century." *Scandinavian Economic History Review* 8:150–160.

Sharlip, W., and A. Owens 1928. *Adult Immigrant Education: Its Scope, Content and Methods.* New York: Macmillan.

Sharpless, J. B., and Ray M. Shortridge 1975. "Biased Underenumeration in Census Manuscripts." *Journal of Urban History* 1(4):409–439.

Shimkin, D., E. Shimkin, and D. Frate 1978. *The Extended Family in Black Societies.* The Hague: Mouton.

Simon, R. 1978. "The City-Building Process: Housing and Services in New Milwaukee Neighborhoods, 1880–1910." *Transactions of the American Philosophical Society* 68:1–64.

Simon, R. J. 1985. *Public Opinion and the Immigrant: Print Media Coverage, 1880–1980.* Lexington, MA: Lexington Books.

Skårdal, D. B. 1974. *The Divided Heart: Scandinavian Immigrant Experience Through Literary Sources.* Lincoln: University of Nebraska Press.

Sklare, M. 1971. *America's Jews.* New York: Random House.

Skocpol, T. 1984. " 'Sociology's Historical Imagination' and 'Emerging Agendas and Recurrent Strategies in Historical Sociology.' " In *Vision and Method in Historical Sociology*, T. Skocpol, ed. New York: Cambridge University Press.

Slobin, M. 1982. *Tenement Songs. The Popular Music of the Jewish Immigrants.* Urbana, IL: University of Illinois Press.

Smith, D. S. 1992. "The Meaning of Family and Household: Change and Continuity in the Mirror of the American Census." *Population and Development Review* 18(3):421–456.

Smith, J. E. 1985. *Family Connections: A History of Italian and Jewish Immigrant Lives in Providence, Rhode Island, 1900–1940.* Albany: State University of New York Press.

Smith, T. 1969. "Immigrant Social Aspirations and American Education, 1880–1930." *American Quarterly* 3:522–549.

——— 1971. "Lay Initiative in the Religious Life of American Immigrants." In *Anonymous Americans: Explorations in Nineteenth-Century Social History*, T. Hareven, ed. Englewood Cliffs, NJ: Prentice-Hall.

Sowell, T. 1981. *Ethnic America.* New York: Basic Books.

Spain, D., and L. H. Long 1981. *Black Movers to the Suburbs: Are They Moving to Predominantly White Neighborhoods?* Washington, DC: U.S. Bureau of the Census.

Spector, A. R., S. C. Watkins, and A. Goldstein 1991. "Family Planning Patterns Among Jewish and Italian Women in the United States, 1900–1940." Paper presented at the Social Science History Association meetings, October 30–November 3, 1991, New Orleans, LA.

427

Stack, C. 1974. *All Our Kin: Strategies for Survival in a Black Community.* New York: Harper & Row.

Stambler, M. 1968. "The Effect of Compulsory Education and School Attendance on High School Attendance in New York City, 1889–1971." *History of Education Quarterly* (8)2:189–214.

Steckel, R. H. 1991. "The Quality of Census Data for Historical Inquiry: A Research Agenda." *Social Science History* 15:579–599.

Steinberg, S. 1989. *The Ethnic Myth: Race, Ethnicity, and Class in America.* Boston: Beacon Press.

——— 1990. "Review of the Ethnic Differences by Joel Perlmann." *American Journal of Sociology* 95:1333–1334.

Stern, M. J. 1987. *Society and Family Strategy: Erie County, New York, 1850–1920.* Albany: State University of New York Press.

Stolarik, M. 1980. *Slovak Migration from Europe to North America, 1870–1918.* Cleveland, OH: Cleveland Historical Society.

——— 1985. *Growing Up on the South Side: Three Generations of Slovaks in Bethlehem, Pennsylvania, 1880–1976.* Lewisburg, PA: Bucknell University Press.

Strong, M. A., S. H. Preston, A. R. Miller, and M. Hereward 1989. *User's Guide, Public Use Sample, 1910 United States Census of Population.* Philadelphia: Population Studies Center, University of Pennsylvania.

Sudarkasa, N. 1981. "Interpreting the Africa Heritage in Afro-American Family Organization." In *Black Families,* H. McAdoo, ed., pp. 37–53. Beverly Hills, CA: Sage Publications.

Sweet, J., and L. Bumpass 1987. *American Families and Households.* New York: Russell Sage Foundation.

Sztompka, P. 1986. "The Renaissance of Historical Orientation in Sociology." *International Sociology,* 3:321–337.

Taeuber, K., and A. F. Taeuber 1964. *Negroes in Cities.* Chicago: Aldine.

Tentler, L. W. 1979. *Wage-Earning Women: Industrial Work and Family Life in the United States, 1900–1930.* Oxford and New York: Oxford University Press.

Theil, H. 1970. "On the Estimation of the Relationship Involving Qualitative Dependent Variables." *American Journal of Sociology* 76:103–154.

Thernstrom, S. E. 1964. *Poverty and Progress.* Cambridge, MA: Harvard University Press.

——— 1973. *The Other Bostonians.* Cambridge, MA: Harvard University Press.

——— 1982. *Concepts of Ethnicity.* Cambridge, MA: The Belknap Press of Harvard University Press.

Thernstrom, S. E., and P. Knight 1970. "Men in Motion: Some Data and Speculations about Urban Population Mobility in Nineteenth-Century America." *Journal of Interdisciplinary History* 3:9–32.

Thomas, W. I., and F. Znaniecki 1927. *The Polish Peasant in Europe and America.* Boston: Knopf.

Thompson, F. V. 1920. *Schooling of the Immigrant.* New York: Harper Brothers.

Thornton, P., and S. Olson 1990. "Infant Mortality and Fertility: Cause or Effect? Some Evidence from 19th Century Montreal." Paper presented at the annual meeting of the Population Association of America, Toronto.

Toll, W. 1982. *The Making of an Ethnic Middle-Class. Portland Jewry over Four Generations.* Albany: State University of New York Press.

Tolnay, S. 1984. "Black Family Formation and Tenancy." *American Journal of Sociology* 90(2):305–325.

Tolnay, S. E., and A. Guest 1982. "Childlessness in a Transitional Population: The United States at the Turn of the Century." *Journal of Family History* 7(2):200–219.

Tolnay, S., S. Graham, and A. Guest 1982. "Own-Children Estimates of U.S. White Fertility, 1886–99." *Historical Methods* 15:127–138.

–––––– 1984. "American Family Building Strategies in 1900: Stopping or Spacing." *Demography* 21:9–18.

Truesdell, L. E. 1965. *The Development of Punch Card Tabulation in the Bureau of the Census, 1890–1940.* Washington, DC: Bureau of the Census, U.S. Department of Commerce.

Trussell, J., and S. H. Preston 1982. "Estimating the Covariates of Childhood Mortality from Retrospective Reports of Mothers." *Health Policy and Education* 3:1–43.

Tyack, D. 1974. *The One Best System: A History of American Urban Education.* Cambridge, MA: Harvard University Press.

United Nations 1985. *Socioeconomic Differentials in Child Mortality in Developing Countries.* New York: United Nations.

United Nations Immigration Commission 1983. *Indirect Techniques for Demographic Estimation.* New York: United Nations.

United States 1913. *Thirteenth Census of the United States, volume 1.* Washington, DC: U.S. Government Printing Office.

U.S. Bureau of the Census 1904. *Negroes in the United States.* Bulletin 8. Washington, DC: U.S. Government Printing Office.

–––––– 1910. *Instructions to Enumerators.* Washington, DC: U.S. Government Printing Office.

–––––– 1922. *Fourteenth Census of the United States Taken in the Year 1920, volume 2, Population 1920.* Washington, DC: U.S. Government Printing Office.

–––––– 1945. *Differential Fertility, 1940 and 1910: Women by Number of Children Ever-Born.* Washington, DC: Government Printing Office.

–––––– 1960. *Nativity and Parentage.* Washington, DC: U.S. Government Printing Office.

–––––– 1975. *Historical Statistics of the United States Colonial Times to 1970: Part 1.* Washington, DC: U.S. Government Printing Office.

–––––– 1979. *Twenty Censuses: Population and Housing Questions, 1790–1980.* Washington, DC: U.S. Government Printing Office.

–––––– 1982. *Alphabetical Index of Industries and Occupations, Final Edition.* Washington, DC: U.S. Government Printing Office.

–––––– 1983. *1980 Census of Population. I. Characteristics of the Population PC80-1-C1.* Washington, DC: U.S. Government Printing Office.

U.S. Census Office 1872. *The Statistics of the Wealth and Industry of the United States, vol. 3.* Washington, DC: G.P.O.

U.S. Department of Labor, Bureau of Labor Statistics 1934. *History of Wages in* *the United States from Colonial Times to 1928, with Supplement, 1929–1933.* Bulletin No. 604. Washington, DC: U.S. Government Printing Office.

U.S. Immigration Commission 1911. *Abstracts of Reports of the Immigration Commission, vol. 1.* Washington, DC: U.S. Government Printing Office.

Vinyard, J. (1976). *The Irish on the Urban Frontier: Nineteenth Century Detroit.* New York: Arno Press.

Von Pirquet, C. 1909. "The Relation of Tuberculosis to Infant Mortality." Pp. 25–29 in Conference on the Prevention of Infant Mortality. *Prevention of Infant Mortality,* New Haven, CT, November 1–12, 1909, under the auspices of the American Academy of Medicine.

Wald, L. 1915. *The House on Henry Street.* New York: Henry Holt.

Waldman, M. D. 1913. "Preliminary Report of the Committee on Desertion." *Proceedings of the Seventh Biennial Session of the National Conference of Jewish Charities in the United States, Held in the City of Cleveland June 9 to 12, 1912,* pp. 51–57. Baltimore: Kohn and Pollock.

Walters, P. B., and P. J. O'Connell 1988. "The Family Economy, Work, and Educational Participation in the United States, 1890–1940." *American Journal of Sociology* 93(5):1116–1152.

Ward, D. 1971 [1925]. *Cities and Immigrants.* New York: Oxford University Press.

———. 1989. *Poverty, Ethnicity, and the American City, 1840–1925.* New York: Cambridge University Press.

Waters, M. C. 1990. *Ethnic Options: Choosing Identities in America.* Berkeley and Los Angeles: University of California Press.

Watkins, S. C. 1986. "Conclusions." In *The Decline of Fertility in Europe,* A. J. Coale and S. C. Watkins, eds., pp. 420–450. Princeton, NJ: Princeton University Press.

———. 1987. "The Fertility Transition: Europe and the Third World Compared." *Sociological Forum* 4:645–674.

———. 1991. *From Provinces into Nations: Demographic Integration in Western Europe, 1870–1960.* Princeton: Princeton University Press.

Watkins, S. C., and A. D. Danzi 1992 "Women's Gossip Networks: Information Exchange and Social Support Among Italian and Jewish Women in the United States, 1910–1940." Paper presented at the annual meeting of the Eastern Sociological Society, Washington, DC.

Watkins, S. C., and A. S. London 1991. "Personal Names and Cultural Change: A Study of Naming Patterns Among Italians and Jews in the United States in 1910." Paper presented at the annual meeting of the Eastern Sociological Society, Washington, DC.

Weber, A. F. 1899. *The Growth of Cities in the 19th Century: A Study in Statistics.* New York: Macmillan.

Weinberg, S. S. 1988. *The World of Our Mothers: The Lives of Jewish Immigrant Women.* Chapel Hill, NC: The University of North Carolina Press.

White, M. J. 1986. "Segregation and Diversity Measures in Population Distribution." *Population Index* 52:198–221.

———. 1988. *Neighborhoods and Residential Differentiation.* New York: Russell Sage Foundation.

——— 1989. *The Segregation and Residential Assimilation of Immigrants.* Washington, DC: The Urban Institute.

White, M. J., A. Biddlecom, and S. Guo 1993. "Immigration, Naturalization, and Residential Assimilation among Asian Americans." *Social Forces* 72 (September).

Wiebe, R. H. 1967. *The Search for Order.* New York: Hill & Wang.

Williams, P. H. 1938. *South Italian Folkways in Europe and America.* New Haven, CT: Yale University Press.

Wood, J. B. 1916. *The Negro in Chicago.* Chicago, IL: *Chicago Daily News.*

Woodbury, R. M. 1925. *Causal Factors in Infant Mortality.* Washington, DC: U.S. Government Printing Office.

Woods, R., and A. Kennedy 1911. *Handbook of Settlement.* New York: Charities Publications.

——— 1913. *The Zone of Emergence: Observations in the Lower, Middle, and Upper Working Class Communities in Boston, 1905–1914.* New York: Charities Publications.

Woodson, C. 1936. *The African Background Outlined.* Washington, DC: Association for the Study of Negro Life and History.

Wright, G. 1986. *Old South, New South: Revolutions in the Southern Economy Since the Civil War.* New York: Basic Books.

Yancey, W., E. Erikson, and K. Juliani 1976. "Emergent Ethnicity: A Review and Reformulation." *American Sociological Review* 2:391–403.

Yans-McLaughlin, V. 1977. *Family and Community: Italian Immigrants in Buffalo, 1880–1930.* Ithaca, NY, and London: Cornell University Press.

Zunser, C. 1924. *The National Desertion Bureau: Its Functions, New Problems and Relations with Local Agencies.* New York.

Zunz, O. 1982. *The Changing Face of Inequality: Urbanization, Industrial Development, and Immigrants in Detroit 1880–1920.* Chicago and London: The University of Chicago Press.

——— 1985. "American History and the Changing Meaning of Assimilation." *Journal of American Ethnic History* 4:53–73.

——— 1987. "Toward a Dialogue with Historical Sociology." *Social Science History* 1:31–42.

INDEX

Entries in **boldface** refer to figures, illustrations, and tables.

J